The Strange Case of Lord Pigot

The Strange Case of Lord Pigot

By

Sudip Bhattacharya

CAMBRIDGE
SCHOLARS
PUBLISHING

The Strange Case of Lord Pigot,
by Sudip Bhattacharya

This book first published 2013

Cambridge Scholars Publishing

12 Back Chapman Street, Newcastle upon Tyne, NE6 2XX, UK

British Library Cataloguing in Publication Data
A catalogue record for this book is available from the British Library

ISBN (10): 1-4438-4915-4, ISBN (13): 978-1-4438-4915-9

This book is dedicated to the girl who makes my life meaningful:
My daughter, Saranya

CONTENTS

ACKNOWLEDGEMENTS

Since few people helped me in writing this, my first book, my acknowledgements shall be brief.

I am grateful to Cambridge Scholars Publishing for bringing out this book. Mr Ranajoy Bose, Executive Member, Christian Burial Board, Kolkata, whose thankless and unrecognised task is to look after the South Park Street Cemetery, which he does very well, allowed me full access to that historic colonial burial site.

My family is my inspiration in this, as in all other matters: my father, Major-General Sujit R Bhattacharya, MD (Retd); my mother, Snigdha; my wife, Anindita; and my child, Saranya.

The Principal of the college where I teach, Swami Shastrajnananda, encouraged my research and, more importantly, granted me sufficient leave so I could write uninterruptedly.

FOREWORD

The urgency of our daily lives compels us to categorise everything we come across. When we cannot categorise, we theorise. So when we refer to Job Charnock or Francis Day as 'empire-builders', we are hurriedly engaged in casting them into roles they would not have recognised or comprehended. On the other hand, a postcolonialist standpoint would equally render unto them bewildering garbs and motives. My opinion, for what it is worth, rejects both categorisation and theorisation. Instead, I have learned to stroll through history, and to admire its innumerable great and small narratives, without bias. The reason for this is simple. I would not be here, living in this city, writing in this language, or even been alive, had it not been for a long series of events, both nationalist and colonialist. The acceptance of one and rejection of the other would be untruthful. Henry Louis Vivian Derozio was buried in South Park Street cemetery, where also lie Sir William Jones and many others who sought to understand our different cultures. On the other side of the road, in the Lower Circular Road cemetery, lie David Drummond, John Drinkwater Bethune, and Charles Freer Andrews. Across the road once more to the Scottish cemetery, and we come to the graves of the Revd Lal Behari Day, writer, and pastor, and Rai Bahadur Poran Chunder Bose of the Indian Political Department. Across the road again, back to the office of the Lower Circular Road cemetery, where one may meet the great-great-grandson of the Rai Bahadur, Ranajoy Bose, who is the Executive Member of the Christian Burial Board. Ranajoy Bose has done signal but sadly unrecognised service to the city in preserving its heritage. As Mr Bose sits talking on the phone on some complex matter of maintenance and administration, one may see through the window behind him the 100-acre burial ground whose existence and importance to the great confluence of nationalist and colonialist discourses is undeniable.

This aim of this book is to retell the curious tale of George, Lord Pigot, and not to analyse the politics of the Carnatic during last quarter of the eighteenth century. Since Lord Pigot's story is deeply connected to events in the Carnatic, we shall view its political history from the same perspective as his. Investors in the East India Company's shares kept as close a watch as they could, upon the effects of its political aspirations on its business. Herein lay the central paradox of the Company's character in

India: the relation between its role in local politics versus its mandate for trade. By the end of the eighteenth century, one would consider this paradox to have been resolved in favour of the former, purportedly as a guise for the latter. Other, severally interesting, motives were thereafter conjoined to mere territorial gain, such as good governance, and the local need for European education. Lord Pigot's case represents in this sense an episode, comparable to the recall of Warren Hastings, in a period of flux. The Directors of the Company were at that time required to report to their investors, as much as Whitehall had to take note of upheavals in its largest mercantile undertaking. What is one to think of a trading company with its own army and navy, and the right to execute treaties (as a sovereign body) with heads of states? No matter how many times one re-reads the tale of Lord Pigot, this unanswerable anomaly strikes one. Other significant differences with British society and culture in the nineteenth century may be found in the singularly charged atmosphere in Madras during 1777, echoed by violent disagreements in the Governor-General's Council at Calcutta. Such scenes would never again occur. Never again would a Governor-General duel with a Councillor, and never again would his dissenting Councillors imprison their Governor. By the second decade of the nineteenth century, when the time came for the renewal of the United Company's Charter, Whitehall had begun exerting still more its authority in the affairs of the Company, and in administering the Company's possessions in India.

For the sake of the congruency of this work with its sources, I have generally kept to the older, colonial spellings of peoples' and place-names.

PROLOGUE

Mr George Andrew Ram, 'the King's Coroner for Madras and its districts', received a letter from the Hon Edward Monckton on the afternoon of Sunday 11 May 1777. While this letter did not contain information likely to surprise Mr Ram in his personal capacity, on the professional level it would certainly have spoilt his Sunday afternoon. The letter read, 'The Right Hon Lord Pigot having died under confinement this morning at the Company's Garden-House at 11 o'clock, I am to request that you will be so good to hold an inquest upon the body before it is removed'. Even if he had wanted to, Ram could not have remained unaware of the turbulence and uncertainty in local government circles during the last 2 years, following the arrest and imprisonment of the Governor, George Lord Pigot, by order of the majority of the Council. The new council, reconstituted and headed by George Stratton as President without sanction from London, was governing Madras instead. Mr Ram realised the immense seriousness of Monckton's letter since the demand for an inquest contained in itself the allegation of unnatural death and, by extension, of murder.

The Coroner at once issued his summons, requesting the presence of 20 Englishmen for the selection of the Coroner's jury. Their names were George Smith, Andrew Ross, George Baker, Thomas Powney, Thomas Pelling, John De Fries, Robert Ewing, George Taswell, Alexander Cuthbert, Robert Farquhar, William Parsons, Quintin Crauford, John Turing, Andrew Majendie, George Savage, Edward John Holland, George Proctor, Hall Plumer, William Sedgley, William Ross, and Kenelm Digby.

The wording of his letter to them is significant: 'Gentlemen, I request your attendance to hold an Inquest on the body of George, Lord Pigot, deceased, under confinement at the Company's Garden-House; for which I beg the favour of you to meet me at the said Garden-House, at 3 o'clock in the Afternoon'. All knew Lord Pigot had been in confinement. Undoubtedly, Ram wanted it to be particularly noted, for purposes of record, in anticipation of a verdict antagonistic to the President and Council, even though they had no authority over the Coroner. Mr Ram sent a similar summons to the three doctors in Madras, Pasley, Anderson, and Mallet. Dr Gilbert Pasley had attended Lord Pigot during his illness, and his presence was vital.

The Coroner reached the Garden-House, situated about a mile away from Fort St George, a little before 3 pm, and found there the Hon Edward Monckton, who was Lord Pigot's son-in-law, having married his daughter Sophy, and Claud Russel and John Maxwell Stone, councillors who were supporters of Lord Pigot, and Dr Pasley. Those called for jury selection soon arrived, as did the other doctors. The Coroner then proceeded with his work, swearing in the first 12 persons on his list as jurors. George Smith, whose name was first on the list, was appointed Foreman of the jury. At half past 3 Ram swore in the doctors, and asked Dr Pasley whether he felt from his inspection of Lord Pigot's body that dissection would help the doctors understand 'to a certainty' the cause of his demise. Pasley replied that he understood the jury wished to know the cause of his Lordship's death but the disease due to which death had occurred, could not be made evident to them through post-mortem dissection. The Coroner put the same question to Anderson, the surgeon, and his reply was the same, with the additional information that, should the jury decide upon a post-mortem dissection, he had brought the necessary surgical instruments for an autopsy. The jury felt that if the majority of the medical men present thought that dissection of the corpse would yield no definite information about the disease that had caused death, there was no need for it.

Since Lord Pigot's family wanted his burial that evening, the Coroner gave permission for the body to be removed. The jury was ordered to meet at 9 am the following day at the home of the Foreman, George Smith.

One can imagine the pall of tension that descended on Madras that evening, and the rumours, which must have been doing the rounds, recounted in low voices by Europeans and locals: Monckton had refused a formal military funeral for Lord Pigot, offered by the president, George Stratton; Stratton had decided to override this refusal and issue necessary orders, but had later relented to the family's wishes. In any case, the governor, whose administration had been usurped, had died in confinement. There were loud whispers that he had been killed, since it was only a short while ago that William Randall, an English officer holding a commission in the Nawab of Arcot's army, and posted as aide-de-camp to the Nawab's younger son, Amir-ul-Umra, had created a sensation by swearing before John Turing, the Mayor of Madras, that he had been offered a huge bribe to help assassinate Lord Pigot. Writing from Trichinopoly as early as 1768, Christian Friedrich Schwartz, the missionary, had noted that the Nawab's younger son was 'inclined to cruelty'. Rumours flew about Madras, from the Nawab's palace at Chepauk, to Fort St George. Philip Dormer Stanhope wrote that these rumours had been 'industriously circulated' and 'obscure hints artfully thrown out' that the 'assassins' would soon be apprehended.

CHAPTER ONE

MADRASPATAM, 1640-1659

The oldest English settlement on the Coromandel Coast was at Masulipatam, set up during August – September 1611. Like the later settlements, it was called a 'factory' although it consisted of little more than some warehouses, and offices and residences, for the 'factors' and their attendants and guards. Masulipatam was the largest port in the region, but the English probably decided to move because they felt that a port further south would provide a more convenient staging point for onward connection to Bengal and Java, and also greater opportunity for inland trade. The climate was another aspect, since Masulipatam and its surrounding areas were (and are) prone to cyclonic storms. To this was added the turbulent politics of the kingdom of Golconda, which held Masulipatam, and whose ruler had permitted the English to trade from that port. The English had explored the feasibility of a change by shifting to Armagaum, but this had been very unsuccessful. Clearly, the answer was that they would have to find, establish, and operate from their 'own' port. To this end, the coast further south had been discreetly surveyed around 1630.

Francis Day, a member of the council at Masulipatam, and chief of the Armagaum factory, negotiated the purchase, from Damarla Aiyappa Naik of Poonamallee, of a piece of land 6 miles long and 1 mile broad, along the coast, about 3 miles from the Portuguese settlement of San Thome. J Talboys Wheeler, in *Madras in the Olden Time* (1861), tells us that this piece of land 'possessed one crowning advantage': there was a small island, separated from the mainland by a river. This was ideal for fortification. Eventually, this island, 400 yards long and 100 wide, became Fort St George, where only Europeans were allowed. The native or 'Black' town (the civilian European part was named Georgetown) was settled on the mainland. One does not know why the Portuguese did not object. However, they had been in India for over 150 years already, and probably did not mind another European settlement in the immediate vicinity. The yearly rent for Madraspatam agreed to by Day was £600 a year. After considerable discussions within and among the councils and committees at Masulipatam, Armagaum, Surat, and London, the dismantling of the settlement at Armagaum was ordered, and the move to Madraspatam sanctioned.

The English sailed from Armagaum in two ships, the *Eagle* and the *Unity*, reaching Madras on Monday, 20 February 1640, the same date on which, back in England, the Short Parliament was summoned. The first to land there were Andrew Cogan, and Francis Day, accompanied by one or two more factors, three or four Writers, a gunner, a surgeon, and a garrison of 25 British soldiers, commanded by a lieutenant and a sergeant, a certain number of English blacksmiths, carpenters, and coopers, and a small staff of English servants as attendants and kitchen staff. Political division in England was rapidly heading towards civil war, even as Madraspatam was being settled.

Andrew Cogan's own career, like those of most of his fellows, had its dark phases. His great-grandfather had been Mayor of Bristol, and his family was permitted to display the arms of an esquire. After joining the service of the East India Company in 1615, Cogan served in the factories at Bantam and Macassar, and made considerable money from private trade. The Company did not charge him for this because he then proceeded to marry the daughter of Sir Hugh Hammersley, a Director of the East India Company, and a former Lord Mayor of London. Instead, he was sent to Surat as a member of the council in 1638. From Surat, he was ordered to Masulipatam, where he became second in council. A letter to the Company, dated 5 September 1639, signed by Thomas Ivie (Agent), Andrew Cogan, Francis Day, Thomas Morris, and Thomas Winter, asking for permission to reconnoitre the coast for a possible settlement at Madraspatam, gives us the names of the English factors then present on the Coromandel Coast.

Fort St George was formally proclaimed on 23 April 1642. By 1672, Fort St George had 50 houses along 12 streets, with a large, three-storied, quarter for the Governor, which also housed some councillors as well as the Council's meeting room in an upper-storey. These houses were described around 1674 as 'fine mansions' of the same height as the fort's battlements. Their terraced walks, porticoes, and fine rows of trees were also noted, as was the cleanliness of the streets. However this may have been reported, the original fort, which lasted until 1714, does not seem to have been of very large dimension, since Charles Lockyer's report of 1711 informs us that the fort was 100 yards wide and 108 yards long. The council met every Monday and Tuesday at 8 am to transact business. The members included the Governor, the Book-keeper, the Warehouse-keeper, and the Customer (whose work was to collect customs and taxes, and whose responsibilities were later divided between the Land and Sea Customers). There was also a Secretary, whose work was to record all proceedings of the council in a diary, and to dispatch a copy of this, with a covering letter of summation, to London, each year. The usual Company hierarchy was followed. While the Governor was paid £300 a year, the Book-keeper got £100, the Warehouse-keeper £70, and the Land and Sea Customers £50. Next came 6 Senior Merchants, who got £40; 2 Junior Merchants, at £30 annually, followed by 5 Factors at £15 per annum, then some Writers, required to live on £10 a year and, finally, the Apprentices, very young men, mere adolescents, who were paid £5 a year. Two Chaplains looked after matters spiritual on a salary of £100 a year each, while the Schoolmaster imparted education on £50 annually to English children, and also to Portuguese and native ones, provided they received instruction in Christianity as well. The Surgeon got £36 annually. There were also two Essay-masters, who were paid £120 a year, while the Judge got only £100. There seems to have been a garrison of 250 European officers, non-commissioned officers, and soldiers, and 20 experienced gunners, in 1711.

Governance was very difficult. Nearly all major decisions had to be referred to the next higher body, the Governor and Council at Bantam or Surat. The arrival of a ship from home carrying clarifications relative to the same issues automatically meant the supersession of orders received from Bantam or Surat. This caused administrative confusion. Waiting for directives from London caused loss of time and money. While the Agent (later Governor) had the privilege of occupying the great three-storied residence to which he was entitled, he was also required to keep a liberal table at which Merchants, Factors, and Writers, would dine. On the other hand, he was an important personage, given to considerable pomp and ceremony later in the Company's history. For Andrew Cogan and Francis Day, it was an extremely trying period, because the civil war was about to begin in England, and insecurity clouded the minds of traders and shareholders alike. The Treasury did not meet the Company's liabilities, and in the meanwhile, civil war broke out in August 1642. Francis Day, at any rate, was not above suspicion. The minutes of the Court of Committees in London on 10 June 1640 record the receipt and reading of a letter from Andrew Coggan (*sic*) stating 'that Francis Day is accused of being a great private trader'.

Experienced Senior Merchants like Day, who had thus far survived, and could be expected to survive the rigours of further voyages, were rare. Hence, Francis Day underwrote by £500 the next major trading expedition, the First General Voyage, and when asked by the Committee in London what salary he expected for undertaking this voyage, for the round trip, he suggested £200 a year, and permission to carry out private trade to the value of an additional £100. The minutes say that Day was asked to withdraw, while the Committees discussed this regrettable practice among the factors of private trade. The Committees unanimously resolved that 'henceforth no factor shall be permitted any private trade either in the outward or homeward voyage or when in the Indies'. Realising that increased compensation for greater trading experience would remove corruption, the Committees offered Day unusually favourable terms. They would pay him a yearly salary of £400, if the voyage were to be concluded in 18 or 20 months. If it took longer than 2 years, they would pay him £200 a year from the expiration of 24 months, provided he indulged in no private trade. Should he be discovered doing this, he would forfeit his salary as well as the profits accruing to him from his investment of £500. This Day agreed to with alacrity.

The ship *Hopewell* was chosen for the voyage, and Andrew Trumball as her captain. She was to carry stock worth £15000 for quick trade. Moreover, Day took with him his son, also named Francis, as writer and accountant, on a salary of 20 shillings a month, again standing security that the junior Day would not engage in private trade. Trumball was placed under similar strictures against private trading, even though he had been allowed to carry goods worth £100 for this purpose by the Committees. *Hopewell* sailed on 31 December 1641. Glyn Barlow presents us with an imaginative description of Francis Day: 'His garb is that of a substantial merchant in the days of King Charles I … He wears a purple doublet and hose, a broad white collar edged with lace, and a gracefully short, black velvet, cloak. Curly hair falls beneath his broad-brimmed black hat…. He is in every way a fitting representative of the Honourable Company'. James Mill, in the first volume of his monumental work, *The History of British India* (1840), however, raises several pertinent questions as to who the members of these Committees might have been, unless they were directors of stock, and again, if they were, what means of representation did they exercise, and how? At any rate, the Committees obviously exercised great power. The success of this voyage was crucial to the Company, since it was deep in debt. The King had bought its entire stock of pepper, 607,522 pounds of it, for a total sum of just over £63,000. Charles I then sold this pepper in the market at a cost lower than the purchase price, and made £50,000 in ready money, which answered his immediate needs. Nevertheless, in doing this, the King contracted the Pepper Debt. To repay the Company, he had the Farmers of the Customs and Lord Cottington issue 4 bonds worth £14,000 each, and one worth £7,283. One bond was to be repaid every 6 months. The details of this deal were not made public, which in effect meant that those, who had invested in pepper, were cheated. In the event, only one bond was honoured, and the cash-strapped Company had issued a call for subscriptions to the Fourth Joint Stock. This realised only a small sum. Then the Company issued another subscription, this time for the First General Voyage. The tale of the Pepper Debt must end, at least so far as this book is concerned, with the Company's Petition to the House of Commons in 1642, under the head of 'Arrears of the Pepper Debt.' The following year Parliament wrote to the King suggesting he sell some of his houses and land to repay the debt. Civil war soon became unavoidable due to the King's Pepper Debt.

The bane of the Company had always been private trading. This would continue to ail until it culminated in emotions so strong as to lead to the overthrow of governors and, still later, to incarceration, and even allegations of homicide. Trumball in all probability was a disciplinarian, for a good ship's captain then had to be as fine a mariner as a martinet. It was his business to sail the ship to trading ports and bring back goods and money. Francis Day was a merchant, and his primary aim was to trade, chiefly for the Company and a little more on the side for himself and, secondarily, to survive to return home a rich man. Ideally, Trumball and Day should have been working in tandem, and thereby earning profits for their cash-starved Company. Trumball's 'Declaration of Some Passages and Observations', made to the Company on 18 September 1644, demonstrates why this never happened.

The *Hopewell*, having reached Madraspatam around 5 July 1642, anchored there for 15 days, and then sailed to Masulipatam. At Masulipatam, after some of the cargo had been dropped off, Day had a load of cloves taken on by way of private speculation. The ship then reached Balasore, where some more of the Company's cargo and the cloves, were unloaded. Trumball's intention, in keeping with his instructions, was to sail next to Bantam, and thence to Persia and home. Day disagreed, and the ship, having been at Balasore for 3 and a half months at the cost of £180 per month, sailed again for Masulipatam and Persia. This time there were passengers on board, taken against Trumball's consent. 16 passengers were for Masulipatam at 15 rupees per head, and 35 for Persia, at 40 rupees per head. The main issue lay elsewhere. Day overruled Trumball and took on private freight: 76 bales of cloth for 15 rupees per *maund* of 64 lb, 355 bales of sugar at 7 rupees per *maund* of 128 lb, and 42 bales of calico on the personal account of Day and some fellow merchants, at 15 rupees per *maund*. Moreover, Day so filled the hold with ‘hampers’ meant as ‘gifts’ for Persians that 60 bales of the Company’s cargo of cinnamon had to be left behind. Still further, the freight money amounted to 17,854 rupees, of which Day paid only 6,345 rupees into the Company’s account. To this must be added the fact that Day charged 1,400 rupees for provisioning the ship while she was at anchor at Balasore. Trumball adamantly stated in his Declaration that anyone who knew Balasore would realise that the ship could have been fully provisioned there at 60 rupees a month. The Company, according to Trumball’s version, benefited with only 700 bales of sugar and 34 of calico being carried on its account, in its own ship.

Masulipatam was reached on 8 December 1642, and along with 22 bales of cloth and 100 of sugar for the Company, the ship took on 76 bales of calico for Day, who now had 118 bales of calico for private trading. From Masulipatam the *Hopewell* sailed to Madraspatam, where 11 bales of cloth and 39 of cinnamon were loaded for the Company. Sailing resumed on 24 December 1642, the ship arriving at Gombroon (present-day Bandar-Abbas) in March 1643. Here Day handed over the Company’s cargo to the local agent, and at once hired a house where he sat all day dealing with brokers and selling his own bales of calico. To help him, Trumball complained, Day employed one of the ship’s mates, Thomas Clarke, the purser, and some seamen, so that the captain was left short-handed. The strangest incident recorded by Trumball is the murderous attack made upon him by Day because Trumball had insisted on checking the weight of the calico being carried out by the Persians in order to ensure that the Company was not cheated. Trumball says he was followed and set upon by Day, while out walking alone to a fort beyond the town, and he had only a rattan stick to defend himself with.

The *Hopewell* left Gombroon on 13 April 1643, made a brief stopover at Dabhol on 1 May, and then sailed on to Madraspatam. Day was miffed because Trumball had refused to stay longer at Dabhol. At any rate, they had taken freight and 95 passengers for Dabhol, and Day, as usual, per Trumball’s account, again short-charged the Company. Matters must have been coming to a head. Day received a tip that betel-nut was available at Tranquebar, and the ship would have been invaluable for some more private trading. Knowing that Trumball would have been absolutely right in refusing this voyage, since it had nothing to do with the Company, Day seems to have conspired to have Trumball removed from command following complaints made to the chief, Andrew Cogan, and his council, by officers and sailors from the *Hopewell*. These complaints addressed Trumball’s harshness and haste in handing out punishment. Cogan, probably preferring to disbelieve Trumball, ordered his removal. The ship's command was handed over to Francis Day, with permission to sail to Tranquebar and return within a month. Day sailed away in the *Hopewell*, and seems to have made the best of it. He returned with 30 bales of calico for the Company and 400 of betel-nut for himself, in addition to more loads of betel-nut privately conveyed aboard smaller vessels on his account as well. Trumball was then reinstated as captain, the ship having served its purpose. Trumball's 'Declaration' continues in this way, listing still more means of private trade, arriving lastly upon the issue of moral laxity. He names three Merchants, Henry Greenhill, Thomas Winter, and Thomas Penniston, who, in connivance with Francis Day, 'are all sworn brothers; and when they perceive they may benefit themselves in any project, they pass an oath one to another to prosecute their intendments and not dissent one from another until their ends be obtained'. They were the richest men around, with enough cash to invest in huge amounts of private trade, from which they derived profits of at least 50 per cent. When ships arrived to buy calico, Trumball narrates that these men told all weavers and brokers living within 16 miles of Madraspatam, not to sell below the price settled by the tetrarch, and in this way, they cheated both the Company and the locals. Finally, they were also moneylenders, using this as a means for obtaining property.

Andrew Cogan was not a member of this tetrarch, and he chose to leave Madraspatam at this point, handing over charge to Francis Day on 27 August 1643. He sailed to Bantam on the *Hopewell* in the company of Trumball. From there Cogan went to England, where he arrived towards the end of the same year. At home, Cogan faced the charge of having needlessly incurred costs on the establishment of the new fort and factory at Madraspatam. The first charge which Cogan addressed, in his written statement dated 13 January 1645, was 'To answer for the building of the Fort St George, the charge whereof hath cost from First March 1639 to the 30th June 1643 the sum of pagodas new 9250'. Following a long inquiry, both he and Francis Day were cleared of the charge. The committee conducting the inquiry concluded in its report dated 13 May 1645 that it had been a 'very indiscreet action to go about building such a Fort when the Company's stock was so small, yet if ever the Company have a plentiful stock, it may be very commodious and advantageous for them; … and if it should not prove so advantageous for the Company hereafter, it can be charged upon no man more justly than on Mr Day: and this Committee were jointly of opinion to clear Mr Cogan of this charge'. Having thus adroitly used his elevated connections, and passed on all financial liability for Fort St George to Francis Day, Andrew Cogan decided to try again for further gains from his trading experience. His offer for an investment of £3000 in stock was refused. Thereafter Cogan purchased an estate and planned to settle down to a well-deserved retirement. The times, however, being most troubled, he was soon drawn like all persons then living in England, into the great political maelstrom. Despite being fined by a Parliamentary Committee, Cogan continued to try living quietly upon his estate in Greenwich until 1648. In July 1648, Cogan joined the Royalist force under the command of the Earl of Norwich, which set out to occupy London. Comprehensively defeated by the Roundheads, the survivors of Norwich's command, including Cogan, crossed the English Channel. In June 1650, Andrew Cogan was named an enemy of Parliament, and his property was sequestered. Cogan's worth may be understood from his having lost a sum of more than £34,000 in the Royalist cause. Charles II raised him for his loyalty to a baronetcy while in exile. Sir Andrew Cogan returned home with the Restoration, but died within the year.

Cogan's resignation and departure thrust upon Day the responsibility of the Fort. Day realised that this would keep him from the kind of free-wheeling 'trade' he had been indulging in thus far, and so he too sent in his resignation on 30 August 1643, being relieved on 4 August 1644 by Thomas Ivie. He might have been afraid of being caught out. Governor Cartwright and his council, writing to the Company on 9 December 1643, note the existence of debts on the Coromandel Coast, for which there seem to be no explanations, the factors there being 'in obscurity, being destitute of a light to direct them, notwithstanding they have Day there all day long'. Immediately after this sideswipe, the letter seems to recant hastily, its writers clearly unwilling to be drawn into controversies, which would not bear scrutiny: 'And here we suppose it's not amiss to let your Worships understand that Mr Francis Day was the first projector and contriver of that fort or castle in Madraspatam.'

By 1643, the Company was in need of goods to sell in the home market, while being able to offer little in return, due to the uncertainties contingent upon the civil war then ensuing. The Coromandel Coast was particularly looked to for the supply of goods.

However, Thomas Ivie's Agency need not detain us, even though it passed through considerable travails including one of the worst famines of the time, and the conquest of the Carnatic by the Nawab of Golconda. Ivie wisely sided with the Nawab, with the obvious result that the change in rulers made no difference to the fort, factory, and its people. Ivie resigned, and handed over charge to Henry Greenhill on 23 September 1648. Greenhill's first administration ran for 4 years, until, in 1652, Fort St

George became the Company's centre in the region. Aaron Baker took over governance as President of the Council from 1 September 1652.

Aaron Baker's presidency was fraught with disagreements in council, which had as their source the same affliction as before, private trade. Considering the geographical distance between Britain and the furthest trading posts of her East India Company, one wonders that the system worked at all. One is also amazed at the way in which the hierarchy was sustained, orders given and taken, merchants appointed and dismissed, goods bought and sold. Given the scale of business, and the fact that private speculation was possible, provided no one reported it and most had shares in it, the Company, in trying to stop it, might have only been fighting its own shadow. Trumball, in his 'Declaration,' said that he had once at a moment of familiarity, asked Francis Day what he thought of private trade: 'he said to me at one time he would private trade so deep that he would neither value his wages nor his stock that he put in with the company ….' Francis Day was a man of uncommon ability; his purported reply to Trumball, however, sums up the general attitude of the East India trader, whose chief aim was to get rich, helping the Company along wherever possible, without overly compromising in that primary aim. Nonetheless, it would be wrong to accuse only the East India trader of the urge to accrue as much personal wealth as possible in the shortest time. The establishment of Madraspatnam also brought prosperity to local inhabitants. While the English, as traders, recognised and sustained the old administrative, legal, and functional systems as they had found them, such as the *Adhikari* or Headman. Even during the most serious stages of the Right-Hand Caste versus the Left-Hand Caste dissension at Madras in 1652, Baker had not interfered other than to identify localities to which these castes were to confine themselves against serious penalty for any violation. That this demarcation had not had the desired effect was not Baker's fault. The English did not have enough troops to defend their fort, which was still in need of completion. They would not be able to quell caste riots. In any case, European prosperity, whether through private or Company trade, was filtering down to the local population but some people were siphoning off more than others were, and this began another problem.

The Company employed locals in two capacities: as Company Merchants, who purchased and sold and otherwise interacted with their countrymen by contract on behalf of the Company, and the *Dubashes*, who performed similar tasks, but for the private trading carried on by most Europeans. The Company Merchants reported to a Chief Merchant, who was selected from among them. The Company Merchants and the *dubashes* essentially performed the same task, that of brokerage, the only difference being that the one was officially sanctioned, and the other not.

Sometime around 1647-48, Seshadri Nayak, who from the time of the establishment of the fort, had worked as Company Merchant, and his colleague, Koneri Chetty, were replaced by Venkatapathi, the Brahmin who had accompanied Walter Littleton on his journey to meet Nawab Mir Jumla of Golconda, then encamped at Gandikotta. Around the same time, Venkatapathi's brother, Kanappa, succeeded to the post of governor and magistrate of the town, in keeping with the ancient practice of hereditary succession. Seshadri and Koneri felt themselves fallen out of favour, as they indeed were. Thomas Ivie's departure and Greenhill's Agency changed nothing for them. Venkatapathi was a boastful man, and his power, combined with the magisterial office of his brother, worsened matters, wrote C S Srinivasachari, in his *History of the City of Madras* (1939). Greenhill did not assist Venkatapathi and Kanappa in driving away Seshadri and Koneri, and those Company Merchants who had sided with them. The ire of the disaffected Brahmin brothers was now directed at Greenhill, and upon Aaron Baker's arrival, they presented declarations claiming malfeasance on the part of Greenhill. He had, they said, compelled the Company Merchants to take up goods obtained through private trade rather than Company merchandise, at excessive prices, for sale. This was a very serious accusation. Baker took it up at once, but not much could be done until Greenhill, who had been away at another post, had returned. On being questioned, Greenhill accused Baker of having taken sides against him by recognising the accusations of Venkatapathi and Kanappa. A conflict resulted, with the councillors taking sides, until Baker preposterously concluded that he was about to be deposed. This led him to have his opponents, Agent Henry Greenhill, and the Merchant John Leigh, arrested and imprisoned in melodramatic fashion on 4 April 1654 for a conspiracy of which there was no evidence. They were taken after sunset, from the wedding festivities of a soldier of the garrison. However, as there was no proof against them, they were soon released.

This event, like that between Trumball and Day, shows once more the ugliness of blatant greed. There was easy money to be made at Madraspatam, and everyone wanted to, by the easiest way possible, that is, by cheating the Company. Greed is not unique, nor were these merchants and their adherents extraordinary in being greedy. Their pay was poor, and if they had families, so much the worse, since the Company's gratuity was nominal and limited. Seshadri and Koneri wanted money as much as Venkatapathi and Kanappa did. The sale at high prices of goods obtained through private trade by European merchants through their local contacts was usual. Trumball had written about the 'group of four' including Greenhill, who were engaged in this. Hence, there was enough mud to cover all concerned.

Another rather vile outcome of this mud-slinging was the accusation that because Seshadri and Koneri belonged to the Right-Hand and Left-Hand castes respectively, and their opponents were Brahmins, the aim of the brothers was to foment rioting. This was made murkier by Greenhill's implication of the Dutch and the Nawab in a complicated conspiracy theory centring on trade at Madraspatam that is hard to unravel even today. Add to this the suppressed mutual hatred between Puritans like Leigh and members of the council like John Chambers and Christopher Yardley, whom the former accused of cheating the Company. Leigh had particularly disliked Captain James Martin, of the garrison, whom he had accused since 1653 of being a Royalist. Martin died on 27 June 1654 at Madraspatam, following which Leigh's anger turned against Baker. While it is often claimed that the Company's administrators did not allow home politics to interfere with their judgment, one fails to see how this could have been implemented, even allowing for the fact that news was often very late in reaching these trading outposts. Sir Andrew Cogan was a Royalist, and lived abroad until the Restoration, and as will be seen later, in the case of Sir Edward Winter, political inclination often coloured reasoning completely. Sadly, John Leigh died by drowning on 24 July 1656 at Masulipatam, when the boat on which he was going out to board the ship *Mayflower* for England, suddenly capsized.

As one goes through the numerous letters couched in the spelling and syntax of an age long gone that these persons wrote to each other, one is astounded at their propensity for accusing each other, at implicating without basis third parties, and of moving from resentment to fawning within the space of a few paragraphs. Amidst all this, the Brahmin brothers submitted to Aaron Baker a list of 118 new accusations against Henry Greenhill. Baker passed on the list to Greenhill on 2 December 1654, and he, as amazingly, replied to each article on the list. For merchants and factors serving at trading posts abroad, the excessively closed society in which they lived was a problem. The end of council meetings did not mean dispersal to means to relax the mind. Instead they met again for meals, where the same official matters were again discussed, often more vigorously, with arguments and anger fuelled by alcohol. Sobriety brought with it repentance, and the swing from rage to penitence was common, but it took a toll on those who held positions of responsibility. Fortunately, for Aaron Baker, relief came soon and he sailed for England on 20 January 1655, having passed on command to Henry Greenhill. Baker sailed from

Madras, having suffered personal loss sadly typical of the time. He left his first wife, Elizabeth, buried in Bantam. Later Baker married Anne Cobham, and settled on an estate at Bowhay, Exminster. He died in 1683, aged 73.

Greenhill, enjoying his second administration, was not destined to be a President for long. The Company sent out its Commissioners to Madraspatam, with orders to reduce it from the status of a Presidency to an Agency, subordinated to Surat, with effect from December 1655. This reorganisation could have been the result of domestic financial problems, which had become serious in the final years of the Commonwealth. In a Petition to Cromwell in 1656, the Company argued desperately for exclusive trading rights. Free competition by 'licensed' traders had reduced the prices of Indian goods by 50 per cent, and reduced that of English merchandise by the same amount. However, the demotion of Madras could also have been the consequence of the Company's recognition that Madraspatam was riddled with corruption, and unsuited to the decorum of a Presidency. The other side of this was the weakening of the defences of Madras. The garrison had been reduced, and the Europeans had to depend on Portuguese and native troops. Nevertheless, the fort itself, with its bastions and artillery, proved its worth when the Nawab of Golconda blockaded Madras for 7 months in 1657. The following April there was an agreement, whereby the English regained the rights to their fort and town in lieu of an annual levy. In a sense the honours were even, since the previous year the Nawab's ship had been seized at Madras. In any case, all political dealings henceforth would be with the Nawab of the Carnatic, who drew his authenticity from the last great Mughal Emperor, Aurangzeb. However, Madras was no longer as it had been in Francis Day's or even Aaron Baker's time. The dire financial straits of the Company at home forced merchants to write to the Directors for permission to borrow money on the English market at 4 per cent interest rather than have to pay 8 or 9 per cent in India. Nonetheless, the Directors managed to send 5 ships with bullion to India, one of which carried £15,500 for Madras.

Agent Henry Greenhill died of illness on 4 January 1659 at Madras, his final days possibly hastened by the knowledge that the fiscal situation of the Company had worsened. His passing marked the end of the first era of the settlement, which had come a long way since 1640. Greenhill's problems with the Brahmin brothers remained unresolved at the time of his death. Thomas Chambers succeeded him.

In England, the political situation resolved itself within a year. The monarchy restored, and the Royalists were once more in favour. One would like to see this as a period of gaiety, of the abundance of colours and entertainment among the people, who were free of the strictures of Puritanism. The Company could look forward to healthy trading in cloth and spices, coffee and chocolate, now that social life had revived and relapsed into typical dissolution. J Talboys Wheeler writes that 'The reign of the Puritans – sad coloured gentlemen and pinched up sombre ladies – was gone at a bound'. The recovery of the Company's finances would take some time, since the Restoration did not fill the Treasury. James Mill writes that there is no account of the Company's equipments for 1659-60, and 1660-61. He inferred that their advances to India must have been small. However, things picked up to the extent that by January 1661 bullion had again been sent to Fort St George, which then proceeded to mint its own coins. The King, Charles II, would continue to tussle with Parliament for royal prerogatives. Dissidents would deliberately loose the spectre of a Catholic revival in England. This, in turn, would result in another upheaval before the century turned. The Company itself would undergo changes in its mandate at the same time. However, we anticipate. Chambers' Agency was poised on the brink of historic and tumultuous times in Britain and India: the Restoration, the long rule of Aurangzeb, and the rise of Maratha power under Shivaji.

CHAPTER TWO

THE CASE OF SIR EDWARD WINTER

Edward Winter, like his elder brother Thomas, was a merchant with long experience of service in India. Their younger brother, Francis, also became a factor. Thomas Winter died in Fulham in 1681, aged 66. The Winters were an ancient family who had distinguished themselves in the service of Elizabeth I. Thomas's father, Sir John, was a staunch Royalist, and his estate confiscated by order of Parliament in 1648. Thomas restored the family's fortune through his long service and private trading in the Company's employ, since he had been one of the infamous tetrarch named by Andrew Trumball.

The first reference about Edward occurs in 1644, when he is named as one of the Writers at Pettipoolee (Peddapalli, or Nizampatam), in a report dated 8 September of that year, by Thomas Ivie to London. Some time later, he moved to the small factory at Versashroone (Viravasaram). Winter remained in charge of this outpost until 1655, when the reduction of Madras from Presidency to Agency required him to take over Masulipatam. There trouble soon arose when the Nawab, Mir Jumla's, ship, which had been seized at Madras and subsequently released following the treaty, was once more taken, this time by Edward Winter. Despite being ordered to return the ship, he disobeyed, and was recalled to England in 1660 to explain his actions, for, like the others, he too seemed to have engaged in private trade. We come across a Court of Committees report dated 15 August 1660, accepting a bill of exchange from Fort St George, for £4,856, 'payable at two months' sight' to Edward Winter, on Thomas' undertaking that 'all the goods now returned for his said brother shall remain in the Company's custody until any difference that may arise shall be settled'.

For a politically minded person, this was the right time to be in England, and to declare one's fealty to the monarch. Edward Winter must have done so. It is also possible that Edward Winter had no desire to go back to India, as he had already put together enough money. We must note that with the ascent of Charles II, the Company presented its Charter for renewal. This was done on 3 April 1661. We may presume that Edward

Winter was then at the centre of matters. In any case, he was knighted in February 1662.

Thomas Chambers' Agency seems to have been coloured by an older style of functioning, which became increasingly redundant, whereby the Agent alone took all or most decisions. This soon caused serious problems, provoking a thundering rebuke from President Andrews and his Council at Surat on 15 December 1661: 'You say that you have given us timely notice. We ask where you had the Authority to give us timely notice to be obedient to your orders. You might learn better manners, but that a horse that never had oats could eat none'. 'We are very glad that Mr Chambers hath an Estate to pay for such Losses he puts upon the Company', Surat wrote, considering that Chambers was 'just like the Fish that leaps out of the frying-pan into the fire; for fearing, for his former unjustifiable Actions, the Company may seize upon his money that he may lend, he will send a ship empty home'. The intemperate tone of this letter is usual for those times. Administration and supervision over huge distances coupled with slow and unreliable communication, together with frequent illness, excessive eating and drinking, much quarrelling, and the ever-present spectre of imminent death, made for evil tempers. The democratic style of functioning of the Company's Agencies considerably neutralised these defects. Chambers' autocracy was an intolerable danger. Were he to be allowed to continue in this manner, others would soon follow, and the corporate structure of the Company, already beset by licensed privateers as well as competing agencies from other European nations, would collapse. By itself, such a collapse would not be a calamity. The President and Council in Surat had their own financial interests involved in the Company's continued survival, including private trade. This was the true cause of the anger directed at Chambers, and of the need to have him removed at once. The latest news at Surat must have summarised the financial crisis the Company was going through, during this period of transition from the Commonwealth back to the monarchy.

With the renewal of its Charter by Charles II, the Company felt emboldened to deal effectively with its internal problems, which it had been unable to do for the last 20 years. For the Company to survive, Chambers had to go, and so he was removed. William Blake replaced him with retrospective effect, as may be seen from the letter of dismissal dated 1 August 1662: 'Mr Thomas Chamber [*sic*], by virtue of the Honourable East India Company's Commission, given us, bearing date the seventh day of February, 1661, we discharge you, the said Mr Thomas Chamber [*sic*], of their service'. Chambers stayed on in Madras until 1665, when he left for England. He was knighted the following year, and survived until the last decade of the century. Similarly the Company dismissed Matthew Andrews from Surat, and John Trevisa from Bengal. Sir George Oxenden replaced Andrews with effect from 25 October 1661 and Sir Edward Winter from Chambers with effect from 11 December of the same year. William Blake was to move to Bengal and relieve Trevisa, and *en route*, Chambers.

Edward Winter's selection was not unanimous. The records of the Court of Committees for 6 December 1661 show that Edward Winter and Quarles Browne (a very experienced merchant who had been to Japan, later Agent at Bantam) had been named as candidates for the Coast Agency, but there was some objection against the former. The Court of Committees therefore ordered a special committee to look into these objections before anything was decided. The next meeting on this subject was on 11 December, and the clauses, which determined Edward Winter's appointment, show that he was quite willing to accept under any circumstance. The first clause fixed his salary at £100 and 'any further gratuity according to deserts [*sic*] and usual security given' but if Edward Winter became Agent, he would have to pay an additional security of £2000. The seriousness of this may be understood when one is told that the candidate chosen for the post of President at Surat had to provide a security of £5000. The demand for an additional security demonstrates that there must have been serious objections to Edward Winter's candidacy, backed by sufficient proof, for the Court to state this condition. Thomas Winter agreed to this additional payment and Edward, duly chosen, was called in, and informed of these conditions, which he accepted. On 30 December 1661, the Court, at Edward Winter's request, promised that he would remain Agent at Fort St George for a definite period of 3 years, and an additional 2 years if needed. This seems to have satisfied him.

Another significant change in policy was that the Company had decided to try once more to rid itself of private trading, which was a constant irritant, making serious inroads into its earnings. To this end, a Royal Warrant under the Privy Seal, dated 21 February 1662, was issued to Sir George and Sir Edward, permitting them to seize and deport to England all 'unlicensed' English subjects trading within the jurisdiction of their respective agencies. Both Sir George and Sir Edward were particularly instructed to report, dismiss from service, seize, and deport, all Company's servants engaged in private trade, under authority of the same Warrant, since such trade was also 'unlicensed.' Englishmen found sailing ships for local persons were also to be seized and deported. Sir Edward was to issue proclamations that all subjects of the King, who might have gone to India and settled in territories owned by local rulers, on whose behalf they might be trading as freemen, were to move to Madras, where they would be protected so long as they did not interfere with the Company's exclusive right to trade. This was an unprecedented move on the part of the Company. The new Agents had been given sweeping powers for improved administration and trading. Sir Edward Winter left England in February 1662 aboard the *Madras Merchant*. He had been permitted to sail only after the Court of Committees noted, on 18 February 1662, that Thomas Winter was accepted as surety for his brother's additional security of £2000, to be invested in the Company's stock. Neither Sir Edward, nor Thomas, seems to have paid this sum for another one and a half years. A Court Committee report for 19 August 1663, requested Thomas to 'perfect' Sir Edward's security. One wonders if the amount was finally paid up, for a subsequent Court Committees minute dated 2 October 1663 notes that no dividend was to be paid on any amount remaining in the Company's account as security, 'especially in the case of Sir Edward Winter', who was allowed a yearly interest of 4 per cent so long as the money remained with the Company after payment became due. As we have seen, William Blake had, in the meantime reached Madras, and relieved Chambers. Sir Edward landed at Madras on 22 September 1662.

No matter how fishy the conditions of Sir Edward's appointment, he came armed with a Royal Warrant, and the clear task of cleaning out Fort St George and its dependencies including Bengal, so that trade profits were maximised. The Company should have sent in someone other than an old East India hand, now elevated to knighthood, for this work. It called for a high degree of detachment and determination, which, given the Company's having sought a huge additional security from him, Sir Edward seemed to lack. For instance, a Court of Committees minute dated 30 September 1663, noted that calicoes and a 'suit of hangings' sent in by Sir Edward aboard the *Discovery* were to be delivered, and the fine charged to his account. J Talboys Wheeler, in the first volume of his history of Madras, writes that 'To us Sir Edward Winter appears to have been a brave and loyal subject of his Majesty; who had excited the enmity of his subordinates by his vigorous correction of abuses, and aroused their fears by his manly efforts to teach the natives that Englishmen were their equals and not their slaves; but who at last fell victim to a hot-headed zeal, which we may sincerely deplore, but which we cannot too hastily condemn'. One does not really know why Sir Edward's European subordinates would have been afraid of being considered the equals of natives.

We shall follow Talboys Wheeler's retelling of Sir Edward's case as we move along our own narrative. The fact is that Sir Edward was faced at once with several serious matters in need of immediate attention. The first was that he had only two factors at Madras, the rest having succumbed to the climate. The second problem was the intransigence of local rulers, who were frequently attacking Englishmen. At Masulipatam, whither Sir Edward went to consult with William Blake, he and Blake were twice attacked with the intention to murder. The third concern was Mir Jumla, who was harassing factors at Hooghly, Cossimbazar, and Balasore. The fourth hindrance, confided to the Governor of the East India Company, Sir Andrew Riccard, by Sir Edward in a letter written on 30 January 1663, was that some of the Englishmen were 'not so real and faithful to the Company … they mind more their own business than the Company's'. The fifth predicament was about the security of Fort St George, its garrison, and the sufficiency of their armaments. A letter sent to the Company on 10 January 1663, requested matchlocks to be sent as the muskets in the armoury were rusted, and swords. The sixth problem concerned the constantly troubled relations with the Dutch, which was increasingly affecting local trade. The intention of the Dutch was, as is normal in trade, to ensure that they dominated the Malabar and Coromandel Coasts, and to delay the English for as long as possible in procuring and dispatching goods, allowing thereby the Dutch to sell their merchandise in Europe first.

One immediate solution to all these problems was to consolidate the Company's holdings, and to staff them with such factors as were available, centring defence on Fort St George. This, we may recall, Sir Edward had already been told to do in his instructions from the Company. His confidential letter to Sir Andrew was also extraneous because it merely stated the reason why he had been given the Royal Warrant. The contentiousness of Mir Jumla dated back to Sir Edward's own seizure of his ship. The garrison at Fort St George had been reduced during Henry Greenhill's Agency, when Madras was made subservient to Surat. That too had been the consequence of consolidation but on other grounds. Mortality among Europeans in India was very high then, as it was, for nearly 2 centuries later. So losses among employees had to be made good, and the Company, not yet out of financial uncertainty, was perhaps unwilling to invest in sending factors out. In any case, there were not too many experienced factors around.

As is well known, the average period of survival for a European was popularly pegged at two monsoons. Every factor who had survived longer than that, and had made sufficient money on the side through private trade, wished to go home and buy an estate; unless he wished to continue and make still more money. Here the power of the Royal Warrant granted Sir Edward would answer. To do Sir Edward justice, he strove to surmount these crises. A letter from Fort St George to the Company, dated 6 January 1664, states that the general situation inside the fort was improved by the construction of a mansion for the Agent, where factors would also be quartered, and a chapel constructed, and lodgings, for the Chaplain. An interesting and unique aspect was the establishment of a Standing Library, made out of books purchased from a minister leaving for England. Besides, the inside of the Fort had been paved with stone. By 10 November 1664, Andrew Cogan's former residence had been rented for use as a hospital for soldiers and the following year, there arrived a 'Surgeon to the Fort.' Sir Edward also broached the possibility of the Company's provisioning Madras with what he called 'Double Stock.' This meant the sending of money and goods from Britain in sufficient quantity to allow purchase and trade not only for the current year, but also for the next year, so that local merchandise could be bought when cheapest, and kept ready for ships arriving from England. This was good thinking, since it would strike at the base of private trade. Private trade flourished because, as we saw in the case of Francis Day and the betel-nuts, merchandise was purchased when it was available locally at the lowest rates, and stored for later dispatch. Another measure that Sir Edward took was to directly challenge pilferage of, and levy of excess duty on, the Company's goods travelling downriver to Madras, by the local ruler's followers. He would prevent local ships from sailing by sea, he said, if this did not stop. Talboys Wheeler has recorded the local Nayak's imaginative answer: 'when the English horns and teeth grew, he would free them from the duties'. Sir Edward must have also been increasingly wary of the Dutch, who had established their complete dominance over the Malabar Coast. Indeed, war between Britain and the Netherlands was imminent.

In spite of all this, the basic underlying ailments remained and festered. The Company would not agree to defray the cost of all this refurbishing of the Fort unless they were sure that they would profit from it. The Company then was, with some exceptions, a harsh, cruel, inconsiderate, and exacting, taskmaster. In December 1663, the Court instructed Fort St George that merchandise from Bengal having sold well in England, one-fourth of all allotments was to be set aside for trade at Hooghly, and the factories at Patna, Cossimbazar, and Balasore, were to be dismantled. However, they had long realised the utility of Fort St George as a defensive position, harbour, and trade centre. Therefore, in December 1664 they dispatched artillery guns, muskets, and supplies of ball and powder. Along with this, they sent warning that hostility with the Dutch being inevitable, there was further need for consolidation, reinforcement, and preparation for a siege. Money was to be lent on interest to fill the coffer, and the purchase of merchandise reduced drastically.

Amidst the din and bluster of preparation for war, the Company, having received allegations of private trade against Sir Edward, sent Nicholas Buckeridge as Supervisor, to investigate matters on the Coast. Buckeridge seems to have lacked the objectivity necessary in a Supervisor. A Court of Committees minute records that on 3 October 1662, it had discussed the intention of the executor of Colonel Rainsford, who had died in India, to sue Nicholas Buckeridge for the recovery of money paid in Persia into the Company's cash by order of the President and Council, on goods consigned to Buckeridge by Rainsford. The Company did its best to save Buckeridge. Messrs Bathurst and Clarke were asked to stand bail for Nicholas Buckeridge in this case, where they were sure to be indemnified by the judge. The next important step in this matter is to be found the records of the Court of Committees meeting on 11 February 1663. Vide this, 'Messrs Willoughby and Canham are requested to be bound on the Company's behalf to stand to the order of Chancery to be made upon hearing after the return of the commission to examine witnesses in India in the matter depending between Mr Buckeridge and the administrators of Colonel Rainsford'. To have a commission sent all the way to India to examine witnesses, casts great seriousness upon the matter. Two days later, the Court notes that 'more money [was] likely to be spent by the Company in the business between Mr Buckeridge and Colonel Rainsford's administrators'. Therefore, the Court ordered all expenses to be charged to the account paid in by Buckeridge to the Company's cash. Still more interestingly, at the same Court discussion of 19 August 1663, at which Thomas Winter was requested to 'perfect' Sir Edward's security, Buckeridge was to be 'examined,' 'his account settled,' following which he would be asked to snitch on Matthew Andrews, which was 'likely to be of use to the Company', obviously in the Company's further dealings with Andrews. A single line, of enormous import, follows this: 'Colonel Rainsford's business to be settled'. This was partial payment to Buckeridge for snitching.

The other part comes a little later. The Court of Committees minutes for 25 September 1663 notes that 'Those appointed to examine Mr Buckeridge's business desire to know the Company's pleasure with regard to the increase of his salary in Persia from £50 to £125 per annum, the yearly gratuity of fifty tumans received from the King of Persia in return for what the Company presented him with (which is not mentioned in the account), and the expense of housekeeping in Persia beyond the Company's allowance'. The Court, unusually indulgent, and 'having a good opinion of Buckeridge', requested the committee to 'state his account, pass over his expense on housekeeping, for which there was some reason, and resolve to gratify his good services themselves as they see fit'. Nicholas Buckeridge suddenly seems to have established himself as chief informant for the Company. They needed good informers, and Buckeridge's value in this role, having turned with the Andrews episode, became indispensable, as made evident by the Court of Committees minute, dated 30 November 1663. The Court wanted to send some 'faithful and able' person to the Coast to ascertain its affairs there, and it 'esteemed' Nicholas Buckeridge as 'well qualified for this appointment'. Buckeridge's immediate consent is explained by the terms offered to him by the Court for snitching well. He would assume the rank of a Commissioner, standing next only to the Agent, Sir Edward, and superintend and examine all matters as instructed. He would therefore have unrestricted access to all matters at Fort St George and its dependencies. At the lesser factories, in the absence of the Agent, he would have the rank of Chief. His salary was £300, and £50 for the voyage, along with the 'liberty to trade in unprohibited commodities'. The Court seems to have fallen over itself in toadying up to Buckeridge, for they added that these terms were meant to 'encourage him to put forth his best endeavours faithfully and industriously in the Company's service'. The obsequiousness is taken to absurd and very suspicious heights, when we find the Court promising him new employment upon his return! This was not the end of it, either. On 4 December 1663, the Court was ridiculously smarmy when it declared that while the committee engaged in investigating the financial affairs of Nicholas Buckeridge had discovered that he owed the Company £323, 'he has acquitted himself so well and given such satisfaction in his late employment' (presumably in informing on Andrews) that the Court found it necessary to 'bestow upon him' this same sum as 'gratuity'. Moreover, it directed the Company to hand over to Buckeridge those of his goods that remained unsold, as well as the proceeds of those sold! One speculates that these 'goods' were private merchandise. A week later, on 11 December 1663, just before Buckeridge sailed, the Court decided that he would have to have someone stand surety for him to the amount of £2000. This they more than compensated by allowing him to take a youth along free of charge to attend him, and he was permitted to bring back, as private goods, 5 or 6 bales of 'Coromandel paintings' free of fine, and without prejudice to his bond or indenture! Buckeridge was being bribed with private trade in order that he would report properly on private trading. By 16 December 1663, Nicholas Cooke had agreed to guarantee the sum of £2000 for Buckeridge, and Mr John Craddon had deposited a security of £500 for his son to accompany Nicholas Buckeridge as attendant on his voyage to the Coromandel Coast. On 18 December, the Court, pulling out all stops in grovelling before Buckeridge, increased the number of bales of calico he was allowed to bring on his own account, from 5 to 10. Thus, this paragon of exemplary service to the Company sailed aboard the *Happy Entrance*, reaching Madras in mid-1664.

The evidence that Buckeridge placed against Sir Edward appears trivial to modern eyes. Buckeridge was bound to find Sir Edward lacking, and to report this to the Court, who of course would then have Sir Edward removed, for Buckeridge had been given the assassin's job and fee. Accordingly, he discovered that Sir Edward had admitted relatives into the Company's service; that he had not coerced Thomas Chambers (then still in Madras) to yield up the money he purportedly owed the Company; that he had exceeded the allowance for the general table (which Buckeridge himself had done while in Persia, and been forgiven by a kindly Court for it); that he had been irregular in attending chapel; and finally, that he had a decided leaning towards Roman Catholicism. Even though only 5 years had passed since Charles II had ascended the throne, it was public knowledge that he had been brought up in Roman Catholic surroundings. Already the Act of Uniformity of 1662 had made the Book of Common Prayer compulsory, and the Coventicle Act of 1664 had made the religious assembly of more than 5 people illegal unless such assembly took place under the auspices of the Church of England. Talboys Wheeler suggests that Sir Edward had drawn the ire of disaffected Company traders by his measures against private trade, by his bold steps to check pilferage, and his strategy of forcing native ships off the sea in order to neutralise the dictates of, and depredations by, local rulers. This might have been the case, for Buckeridge's accusations other than the religious ones, were very weak. This is not the place to examine the deeper implications of the religious charges brought against Sir Edward. In England, they would have provoked serious reactions. To be Royalist was not enough; one had to be Royalist and Anglican. Someone at either Fort St George or London appears to have written unfavourably about Sir Edward's religious views to a correspondent in 1663, which was communicated to the Court of Committees. These anonymous allegations also said that Sir Edward was guilty of over-spending; that he had spent this money for self-aggrandisement (he had had the three-storied Agent's manor built); and that he had employed the Company's servants in private trade for his own profit.

Sir Edward must have realised the implication of Buckeridge's arrival. He travelled with Buckeridge to Masulipatam, where he got into an argument with Jearsey, the chief of the factory, and left the meeting. This was a grievous mistake, for Buckeridge's instructions, as we have seen, allowed him, in the Agent's absence, to take over. However, all this uproar was soon rendered meaningless by the arrival from England of Mr George Foxcroft, with orders appointing him Agent at Fort St George. Why the Court had appointed and sent out Foxcroft before receiving Buckeridge's report, remains unexplained. Especially since they had gone to such lengths to ensure, Buckeridge's making huge personal profits from the execution of his commission. For one thing, we have already seen the manner in which Sir Edward's appointment had been sanctioned. He had not gone to Madras with the unanimous trust of the Court of Committees. Buckeridge, the Supervisor, along with Thomas Chambers, the former Agent, who had been lingering in Madras until *he* was cleared of the charges against him, left for England with a fleet of 5 ships, on 10 January 1665. The Company's usual toadying and duplicity was evident in their allowing Chambers, hitherto pariah, the temporary rank, and flag, of Admiral.

Sir Edward had written to the Company on 12 Jan 1665, urging them to relieve him if they had lost confidence in his administration, with the added plea that he be given a fair hearing in relation to whatever Nicholas Buckeridge might have to report. Without waiting for Buckeridge's statement, and probably acting upon further reports on Sir Edward's probity, the Company appointed George Foxcroft as Agent on 21 December 1664, and sent him to replace Sir Edward. The other members appointed to Foxcroft's council were William Blake, William Jearsey, Charles Proby, John Nicklaes, and Jeremy Sambrooke. This supersession was to take place as soon as Foxcroft landed at Madras. Foxcroft reached Fort St George on 22 June 1665, and assumed the Agency. Accompanying George Foxcroft as factors were his son, Nathaniel, and Joseph Farley. Foxcroft had been instructed to treat Sir Edward with due courtesy: 'Sir Edward to be next to you in Council, and to sit at your end of the table on the left hand of you our Agent'. A letter from the Court of Committees to Sir Edward asked him to relinquish command of the Agency to George Foxcroft, and offered him the second position in council. In order to compensate partly for the sense of slight that would assail Sir Edward, he was offered permission to bring home 2 or 3 tons of his own goods free of charge aboard the Company's ships when he returned. Pointedly, they acknowledged his desire to remit office at the end of the promised tenure of 3 years, which would terminate his services on 21 September 1665. Foxcroft had also been told to investigate the allegations against Sir Edward Winter. The Company was clearly playing the game of duplicity with excellence. In any case, it was undoubtedly better to be in Madras in June 1665 than in London, for there the plague was turning into a pandemic.

The charges against Sir Edward under scrutiny by George Foxcroft are very different from the ones listed by Buckeridge. As in the case of Seshadri and Venkatapathi, we now have Timmanna, and Verona (Kasi Viranna), two of the Company's Chief Merchants, the former having survived in this role for a quarter of a century. Sir Edward was alleged to have personally, in disobedience of Company's orders in bypassing the council, instructed Timmanna and Verona to purchase cotton cloth from weavers. They had sublet the contract to 16 lesser merchants, who had purchased the cloth directly from the weavers, for which the Company had been charged many times the amount that the weavers got. Moreover Timmanna and Verona dominated, as the Brahmin brothers had some years ago, all trade in Madras. They sold woollen cloth sent from England at prices many times higher than invoiced. It was also suspected that they cheated the Company of gold at the mint, in connivance with the native coiners and their officer. They made great earnings from the stranglehold that they had established, and allegedly shared their profit with Sir Edward, and when Sir Edward had them imprisoned, and a gibbet set up for their hanging, it was further said that they had offered him 30,000 pagodas to let them go. Probably their depredations had become so stark and widespread that Sir Edward had no option but to have them arrested and threatened. Foxcroft upheld the decision to have them in prison, and had them arrested once more. He further ruled that they would never again be allowed into the limits of Madras. If these were the allegations against Sir Edward that the reports to the Company carried to London, then it is quite possible for us to understand their haste in sending George Foxcroft down at the earliest. On the other hand it is equally strange to see the Company moving alternately between fawning upon those accused of cheating and corruption, and then, in Shakespearean idiom, engaging in sound and fury implying nothing. Many questions remain at this stage: for instance, one would like to know whether Buckeridge was aware of these suspected dealings between Timmanna, Verona, and Sir Edward. One would also like to know why the Company paid Buckeridge so much in cash and gratuity when it did not need his report. Perhaps the Company was hedging its bets.

Sir Edward obviously did not take kindly to being relegated from the post of Agent. He must also have resented having his monetary affairs investigated by Proby, on Foxcroft's orders. Daily proximity and the compulsions of appropriately courteous behaviour at dinner, added to the artificiality of submission, further strained Sir Edward's conduct. The psychological ill-effects of the small and closed English factory society made themselves felt through political differences. As Talboys Wheeler points out, Foxcroft was a Puritan burgher and Sir Edward Winter a Royalist. Even though nearly 5 years had passed since the Restoration, it was not enough to cool the impassionate. 'The single-minded and generous fidelity of the gentlemen of England, were the salvation of the Church, and but for the utter faithlessness of the reigning sovereign, might have been the salvation of their king', he writes. But in the ill-will of the civil war, the regicide, and the often vengeful and opportunistic Puritanism of the Parliament, 'the high chivalric code of the old Cavalier degenerated into a bitter hatred and contempt for the opposite party, and had led to a readiness to draw the sword upon hearing the slightest depreciation of the Lord's anointed'. Contrast this, said Talboys Wheeler, to George Foxcroft, 'evidently a plain business citizen from Leadenhall Street; and, like most of the commercial community of the day, who was probably a sober, God-fearing man, who may have been a regular attendant at his parish church, but who would not shut his eyes to the vulgar debaucheries that disgraced the Court of the Second Charles'. Frances Emily Penny notes that in the early correspondence from the Company's Agents, during 1613-1614, there is reference to one Adam Denton, who desired that certain packages sent on one of the ships be given to Mr George Foxcroft, Gent, living on Ironmonger Lane, London. Foxcroft, she writes, was 'a businessman to his backbone', 'accustomed to the desk and the counting house; and he took life with all the Puritanical seriousness of the day'.

There is a full memorial bust of Sir Edward Winter at St Mary's Church, Battersea. It shows a 'truculent and stolid-looking man,' of fleshy face, with a full-bottomed wig done in Cavalier ringlets, sporting a thick, well-trimmed moustache curving up slightly at the cheeks in what is today called the 'English' style, and a small beard below the lower lip, but above the chin, known these days as the 'soul patch', and, in those days, probably as an abbreviation of the Van Dyke. The presentation of Sir Edward is indeed that of the complete Cavalier. There seems to be no portrait of George Foxcroft. Given his purely mercantile and Puritan background, one supposes him to have adhered to the usual straight hair, worn shortened in length, clothes of modest cut and sombre colours, flat shoes, and the tall Puritan broad-brimmed hat with belt and buckle. To this, one must add differences in manner of speaking between the two men. The word 'Cavalier' came to denote an offhand or casually inconsiderate way of speech, while the Puritans pursued a scholarly and studied manner of conversation. The two must have taken an instant dislike to each other, Foxcroft probably less so, because of the Company's letter that gave him the Agency, and more in the case of Sir Edward, who saw in his substitute the continuation of a seemingly failed, despised, and defeated society and its culture. Here then was the cause for disagreements to commence.

George Foxcroft had hitherto been punctilious in allowing Sir Edward all the privileges he had been enjoying. This was due to especial kindness on Foxcroft's part. The quarter-guard was ordered to turn out whenever Sir Edward entered or left the inner fort. Similarly, Sir Edward was allowed the pomp and ceremony of his office, when on the road, being preceded by his band, escort, and flag. Probably Foxcroft was simply following the spirit of the Company's order, which asked that Sir Edward be treated with courtesy due to the second in council. While Foxcroft himself had been through the civil war, and in all probability supported Cromwell, his son was provoked by the Cavalier manners of Sir Edward. Jeremy Sambrooke, a member of council, wrote to his father on 11 July 1665, pointing out three obvious errors in the Company's policy. The first mistake, Jeremy writes, was to appoint Foxcroft, who had never been to India. The second derived from the first, in that if the Company had decided to heed accusations against Sir Edward, they should have had him recalled to England to face charges there instead of allowing him to remain in his former splendour at Madras. The third error had been to sanction Nathaniel to accompany his father. Nathaniel must have already come under Sir Edward's influence to a significant extent for Jeremy Sambrooke to write in his letter that no good would come to the Company of this association, since the son's sentiments would affect the father. These were prophetic words.

Before proceeding further, we need to become acquainted with Mr Simon Smythes, one of the Fort's chaplains. Smythes' appointment was announced by the Company (which always adopted a smarmy tone when referring to chaplains and surgeons going out to India, since these were necessary to the factories, and so had to be dispatched with flattery and low incomes) in a postscript to a letter dated 26 January 1664: 'Since writing and signing the preceding part we have entertained Mr. Simon Smythes, a Minister of God s Word, one that we hope will not only by his preaching and doctrine instruct and direct our people in their way to happiness, but also in his life and conversation be an example of holiness;

he proceeds on the Coronation; we have made his salary £50 per annum, and have also disbursed the sum of £20 in books, a list whereof we herewith send you, which books we do appoint shall remain in the Fort for the use of any succeeding Minister after the return or decease of the said Mr. Smythes'. To Smythes, the Company wrote: 'The good testimony we have received of your abilities for the work of the Ministry, and having a strong hope that your life and message will be such as becomes your calling, we have therefore entertained you to proceed on the ship Coronation for Fort St George, in which ship your accommodation (together with our factor Mr Jeremy Sambrooke) we have appointed the use of the great cabin .... In the town of Madras you will find several Priests and others of the Romish religion. And because we doubt not but you are a well grounded champion in our Protestant profession, we would have you, as opportunity may present, entertain a controversy or dispute with them in opposition to their Popish ceremonies and sacraments; although it may not so far prevail upon them as to a reformation, yet it may before the confirming of our own people to be constant in the Protestant profession according to the rules and directions in the Holy Scriptures'. Smythes eventually married one of Sir Edward's relatives, and so aligned himself with the Agent. He also appears to have taken greatly to alcohol, gambling, and other vices, within a year of his arrival in Madras.

The main events of the usurpation of power by Sir Edward at Madras began in the middle of August 1665, when, during the usual dinner at the Agent's table at the Fort, George Foxcroft prevented Simon Smythes from opposing and contradicting his son, Nathaniel. Nathaniel had asserted that his private interest preceded the King's, and that he was not bound to obey or serve the King, just as he could not protect him. Further, on another occasion in the same month, Nathaniel is believed to have asserted that the King, Charles II, had no right to his crown other than by conquest. His father purportedly supported his son, by telling Simon Smythes that no king in Christendom had any right to his crown other than by conquest. These were indeed treasonous statements, and particularly so in 1665. Even so, given both Nathaniel's youth, and his father's inexperience of an Agent's table in India, at which intemperate drinking led to drunken quarrels, these statements were probably excusable. However, time was running out for Sir Edward. He was to leave by the end of September and so probably had reason to cover up his misdemeanours by force if needed. There were other reasons at work at this time. The case of Timmanna and Verona, having been raised in council by Foxcroft, Sir Edward displayed violent anger, and declared he would never again attend council. Nevertheless, Sir Edward continued to occasionally attend dinners and join prayers. These occasions lessened and Sir Edward did not visit the inner fort for a while. In the meantime, it had become necessary for Foxcroft to meet Sir Edward for deciding on Mr Gurney's will, of which Foxcroft had probate. Mrs Gurney was then living in the European town in Madras, and the will had to be settled urgently. George Foxcroft sent word to Sir Edward through a common acquaintance, one Mr Read, suggesting that they meet on 14 September after prayers at Mrs Gurney's house, which of course was neutral ground.

On the morning of 14 September 1665, George Foxcroft was astounded to see Sir Edward enter the fort before prayers, bearing 6 charged pistols, sword, dagger, and buckler, accompanied by Joseph Farley with 4 pistols, sword, and buckler, Mr Smythes, the chaplain, similarly equipped, and followed by a retinue of armed servants. Foxcroft later asserted that he feared Sir Edward meant to incite the garrison to mutiny, engage the assistance of the natives, including the Nawab of Golconda, and take over the fort. Whether Sir Edward had such a grandiose plan in mind is not known. Sir Edward burst into Foxcroft's chamber and accused him and his son of treason. He demanded that Jeremy Sambrooke and William Dawes, who had also rushed to Foxcroft's chamber, assist him in arresting and confining the Foxcrofts. Sambrooke asked to be told the exact charges on which Foxcroft was to be deposed. Sir Edward and his associates refused to declare these unless Sambrooke and Dawes gave their word to support the usurpation. Sambrooke refused to be a party to arresting Foxcroft only because he was investigating Sir Edward's malfeasance. Sambrooke then advised Foxcroft to have Sir Edward arrested, upon which the latter challenged Sambrooke to do it himself by provocatively laying his hand upon his sword. Sambrooke replied that he would do so if ordered by the Agent. Sir Edward then made to leave the fort, whereupon Foxcroft, having recovered from his astonishment, ordered the gates shut and Sir Edward arrested, which was reluctantly done by Lieutenant Chuseman, the garrison commander. The story gets murkier at this point. Lieutenant Chuseman switched allegiance during the next 2 days. The reason for this was that Sir Edward had won over Chuseman's wife by his manners, gifts, and promises, including the raising of Chuseman's salary to that enjoyed by his predecessor, £500 to £600 a year. It reflects very poorly on the Company, that the garrison commander's low pay should lay him thus open to enticement. Sir Edward was disarmed in Proby's chamber, and confined there.

On 16 September 1665, hearing a commotion, Foxcroft, followed by his son Nathaniel, Sambrooke, and Dawes, rushed down from his chamber to the court to investigate,. At the foot of the stairs stood Lieutenant

Chuseman, armed with pistols and sword, along with some chosen men from the garrison, similarly prepared, whose belligerence was evident. On the Agent's demanding to know the reason for their presence in this manner, a volley of shots rang out, and swords struck, leaving Foxcroft and Sambrooke injured, and Dawes mortally shot through the belly. Nathaniel attacked the Lieutenant, and was set upon by the other soldiers, and seriously hurt. In a rather melodramatic gesture, Sir Edward then sprang out of Charles Proby's chamber, and leaped about in great joy with his sword and buckler in hand, shouting, 'It is done, it is done!' Indeed, it was done, and a terrible deed it was, no matter what the reason. Dawes lay dying painfully, the ball having exited through his back; George Foxcroft had two ribs cut bare, and all the clothes on the left part of his body burnt, and the left side of his face grazed by a shot intended to kill him; Sambrooke had been run in by swords on both sides, and then struck on the head by a halberd, and sat covered in blood.

Foxcroft and his party were taken to separate rooms and detained there, with sentries guarding them. Dawes having died, the other three were placed in close confinement, Sambrooke separately from the Foxcrofts, and not allowed paper, pen, and ink, for 10 days, during which time, Sir Edward had presumably written down his narrative, had it signed by his councillors, and dispatched it, interestingly, by the land route to England. Sambrooke later testified that the key of the Company's chamber, where the cash was kept, was forcibly taken from him by order of Sir Edward. Sambrooke soon contracted the 'spotted' fever, which kept him very ill for a long while, and the doctor was only sometimes allowed to see him. Rather, after he had recovered but remained weak, Sir Edward, or Lieutenant Chuseman, Charles Proby, or Joseph Farley, would visit him, and search him and his belongings for any letter he might have written,. This ensured that no direct intimation of the usurpation reached England until 1667. Meanwhile, Sir Edward and his council ran the government of Madras, while the Agent and his associates remained incarcerated until August 1668. Foxcroft, however, managed, with the assistance of the Capuchin monks, have his letters sent to William Jearsey at Masulipatam, and he forwarded them to England.

The general report by Sir Edward and his party to the Company dated 30 September 1665 presents the other side of this incident. Nathaniel Foxcroft had been guilty, in mid-August 1665, of uttering treasonous statements, and been abjured by Simon Smythes. Instead of similarly warning his son to better behaviour, George Foxcroft, the Company's commissioned Agent at Madras, had seen fit to berate and silence Smythes. Smythes reported the matter to Sir Edward, urging him not to allow, in the Company's interest, such treason to pass unchallenged. Sir Edward had the choice of either reporting the matter to England by tedious and uncertain communications, or to act immediately, charging the Foxcrofts with sedition. He chose the latter. Accosting George Foxcroft in his chamber, on Thursday, 14 September 1665, in the presence of several witnesses, Sir Edward accused him of treason. Foxcroft neither admitted his fault nor offered an explanation, but became abusive. Two councillors, Sambrooke and Dawes, sided with Foxcroft and refused to declare that he had made treasonable statements despite the fact that there were other witnesses to hand who were willing to do so. Sir Edward then went among the English soldiers at the main guard, and announced the impeachment to them, upon which Foxcroft had him arrested and imprisoned. The possibility of a bloodless takeover having been ruined, Sir Edward and Smythes drew up a charge the next day in the King's name, urging Charles Proby and Lieutenant Chuseman to depose and arrest the Foxcrofts. Chuseman chose to act on 16 September. He ordered a file of musketeers to accompany him in carrying out his task. The Foxcrofts, Sambrooke, and Dawes set upon them, and despite several warnings in the King's name to keep the peace, the opposite party opened fire on them, aiming their weapons at Chuseman. Dawes was killed, and the other connivers wounded. They were then arrested and confined. The report ends with the 'unanimous' selection of Sir Edward as the man most suited to conduct the affairs of the Company in Madras, by the officers and factors signatory to the report, until either the full council or the Company decided the matter. The report carried the names of Sir Edward, Charles Proby, Francis Chuseman, Stephen Charlton, Simon Smythes, Richard Clay, Francis Wainwright, Francis Hopkins, and Richard How. The points of contradiction are direct in the narrative attested to by Sir Edward and his party. In their view, Chuseman was fired upon, but remained unharmed, possibly because he had undertaken a just cause.

Charles I never accepted the legality of the Regicide Parliament, since he held that it did not have the authority to judge him. He derived his claim to rule from divine right, having been anointed king. As king, he was above all in the land. Cromwell, on the other hand, held that kingship was a post, and the individual who held it was answerable to his fellows, being their equal. Following this argument, Charles I asserted that he chose to be executed, while the Parliament voted to execute him. The same issue of the divine right to rule plagued the reign of his son. The initial period of the Restoration, with its accompanying gaiety, was soon overtaken by matters many times more serious, and often similar to those, which had caused Charles the First's tussle with Parliament. In far away

Madras, current developments in London would not colour views. Instead, the image of the brave, upright, and well-mannered Cavalier, leading his Royalist followers in the protection of the divine right of the King, was more relevant. Sir Edward decided to stake his reputation on this image. Sir Edward was subtle enough to know that this attitude would not impress the hard-headed Directors of the Company and his immediate care was to use this image to gain local approbation and support among the lesser European population, like the soldiery. His further dependence was on gaining popular attention in England. The popularity of his patriotic actions among the common stakeholders in the Company would induce the Court of Committees to shrewdly revaluate his actions. Popularity in England could be attained if Foxcroft's party were prevented from writing home; if his supporters were to send letters copiously, full of his praise; and if he were to ensure a local government free of complaining dissidents. Good governance meant that in subsequent letters to the Company, the subject had to be the securing of its interests and the highlighting of the dangers of local political turmoil, which was detrimental to trade. In effect, the Company would be forced to the conclusion that it would not be able to do without that stolid Cavalier, Sir Edward, in command at Madras. Therefore, Sir Edward embarked upon a dual strategy. His further reports would depict him as an Agent of initiative and efficiency, taken up with furthering the interests of the Company, in contrast to George Foxcroft, the Puritan with treasonable sentiments, who never having served in India, knew little of trade and how to make profits for the Company. The darker side of this plan called for threatening and removing all possible dissidents who might complain and reveal Sir Edward's wrongdoing.

George Foxcroft revealed in his letter to the Company dated 8 September 1666, this last part. Sir Edward had seized and imprisoned several local merchants who had dealt with the new Agent. Those he suspected of having exposed his misdeeds, he had branded, beaten, and turned out of town with their families in the most insulting manner possible, without any means of supporting themselves. Their town properties he seized by order, and disposed of in accordance with his wishes. He similarly dispossessed Mrs Dawes, the widow of the same William Dawes who was killed in the fort, and her family, of their home. Those English soldiers unwilling to support his claims were evicted from Madras. Mr Crandon, the secretary to the council, would not acknowledge the legitimacy of Sir Edward's usurpation, and so he was chained and fastened to a stake, to teach him deference. It may be questioned whether Sir Edward did all this out of spite. Sambrooke later attested to seeing merchants and others with burnt and mutilated faces long afterwards. Foxcroft's allegations do not read as preposterous. He was referring to a considerable number of persons who had been affected. Had such repression never happened, the hollowness of his accusations against Sir Edward would have been obvious.

News of what had occurred in Madras travelled the coast and reached Masulipatam and Balasore. The President at Surat, Sir George Oxenden and his council received information as well of the usurpation. Sir George issued a Declaration against it, noting that dissension between the English would give William Blake, Chief at Balasore and next in the chain of command to the Agent at Madras, an excuse to attempt to rescue Foxcroft. Jearsey protested the usurpation and wrote to Sir Edward on 18 January 1666, demanding that he yield Fort St George to him. Meanwhile Jearsey warned all ships leaving for England to avoid Madras. He even encouraged a futile attempt to reverse the coup. On 7 April 1666, a group of 16 Englishmen led by Benjamin Brond, purser on the *Greyhound*, set out to assist Foxcroft in escaping, urged to do so by letters from Foxcroft. On that day Sir Edward, Proby, and Chuseman, all went hunting. The Englishmen met at Greenhill's house. Brond had laid the plan. They were to wait until the guard had shut the gates of the fort, then display Sir George Oxenden's Declaration against Sir Edward. The guards on duty had become Brond's friends except the Sergeant, John Bossill. The only uncertainty in the plan was that Brond would need to have with him Hugh Dixon, the best gunner in Sir Edward's garrison, since they would need a good gunner to keep the pieces ready. Dixon agreed to the whole, crying off at the last moment, and since he was not accompanied by Dixon, all Brond's attempts to persuade the garrison to rise came to nothing. The following day, Brond and his companions were all imprisoned. Brond obtained his liberty after 24 days, after he had agreed to give a bond for £5,000. Brond reported to the Company on 14 October 1666 that his companions were still in prison.

On 26 March 1667, the council in Surat sent an official account to the Company, which carried still more fanciful information about Madras. The Company was informed that Sir Edward had entered into a treaty with the Dutch, in order to hand over Madras, and he was awaiting only the consent of the Dutch Governor at Ceylon. There was a ship supposedly standing ready at Madras for Sir Edward to flee in. Surat had no details about where Sir Edward intended to go. They had further been told that Agent Foxcroft was a prisoner, as were all factors and European soldiers. Sir Edward seemed to be governing through his native troops, and that the priest, who had brought about the mutiny, had since escaped, no one knew where.

This most garbled account stirred the Company into action not because they were worried about Foxcroft or Sir Edward. They had by this time received reports from both parties. They acted because they feared Sir Edward was about to hand over Madras to the Dutch. This would mean a serious body-blow to trade in India, and had to be prevented. The Company had invested much money in Madras, which could not be allowed to go to waste. The Dutch presented the greatest corporate threat to the Company, and this had to be tackled as soon as possible.

Contrast this to the letter sent on 8 June 1668 by Henry Gary, the new Governor of Bombay, to George Foxcroft, who was dismayed by Gary's proclamation of August 1667 against Foxcroft, which had been made public at Madras. Gary had been employed as a merchant with expertise in accounting and languages, being sent out to Surat in April 1644, to assist Edward Knipe. Two more factors, John Burnell, and Henry Hunt, were also to go to Surat with them. The ship assigned to carry them was the *John,* commanded by John Mucknell. The *John* was to sail to Mozambique, Madagascar, the Comoros, and then up the Malabar to Surat, which they expected to reach by 10 December 1644. At some time during the journey, Mucknell began to behave very badly, engaging in debauchery, and calling into his cabin similar souls from the ship. Remonstrance by the factors drew an apology, and on reaching Mozambique on 11 August, attempts were made at trading. On 29 August, while still in Mozambique, Mucknell invited the factors and his ship's officers, including the chaplain, ashore to a conciliatory dinner. After dinner, he slipped away and, leaving them ashore, sailed off on the *John*. Two of the quartermasters left the ship, returned in the jolly-boat, and reported to Knipe that Mucknell had addressed the ship's crew and told them that he was for the King, and that they were to sail for the Red Sea, and thence to England, where they would be welcomed, at Falmouth, Dartmouth, or Bristol. 18 sailors had disagreed with him, and were put into irons. Mucknell's subsequent career as a pirate need not detain us. After spending 8 days ashore, Knipe and his party were picked up by the *Thomas and John*, which had already met, and been robbed by, Mucknell, in the King's name. A report by Edward Knipe, John Burnell, and Henry Hunt written on board the *Valkenburg*, on 28 January 1645, noted that Henry Gary was accused by some of having encouraged Mucknell in his actions. Gary was subsequently acquainted with these accusations, and he answered them on 20 February 1645. He referred to differences between Knipe and himself; to Knipe's provocation of Mucknell; and after they had been picked up from Mozambique, to Knipe's further vilification and conspiracy against Gary. Knipe's reply of 11 March refers to Gary's passing confidential information collected from Knipe on the Company's matters to Mucknell, and of otherwise inciting him against Knipe. Gary was also presented as a man of loose morals (by Puritan standards), singing, dancing, and gambling, and of looser tongue, who disparaged London and insulted its women. Knipe was certain that Gary knew of Mucknell's plan, and had endorsed it. On 31 March 1645, the President and council at Surat wrote to the Company, informing them that Gary and the others against whom Knipe had brought charges, had been suspended, and would be sent home aboard the next available ship. Given the politics of the time, one may read between the lines here, and see that Mucknell and Gary had Royalist sympathies, while Knipe was for Cromwell and Parliament. This is borne out by the fact that Knipe had previously left the Company's service for Courteen's, but later returned. Cromwell believed in fair and open competition, and was doubtful about the Company's repeated pleas for exclusive trading rights. Gary has also been described as having been born to an English father and an Italian mother to which parentage was attributed his exceptional linguistic ability. He was fluent in Italian, Portuguese, Latin, Arabic, and in several Indian languages. John Fryer described Gary as 'a Person of a Mercurial Brain, a better merchant than soldier'. Gary was Governor of Bombay, while it was still a crown colony, by usurpation between May 1667 and September 1668 following the death of Sir Gervase Lucas. Like Sir Edward Winter, Henry Gary too held Bombay under his self-proclaimed governorship, in the King's name. Following the transfer of Bombay from the crown to the Company, Henry Gary, like Sir Edward, willingly and formally surrendered it on 23 September 1668 to the Company's commissioners.

Aware now of Gary's political leaning, we find his reply to Foxcroft's letter, which had been smuggled across the peninsula from Madras to Bombay, less amazing. Foxcroft's missive, Gary writes, 'surpasses immodestly the limits of a letter, and is extravagant in the licence of a libel … and, being acquainted with the principles and sentiments of your heart, out of the abundance whereof your foul mouth speaks, I wonder not at your sordid language and dirty dialect that is the true Shibboleth of a person of your party'. One presumes that Gary is referring to Foxcroft's Puritanism here. 'With how much effrontery,' asks Gary of Foxcroft regarding Sir Edward, 'do you brand a person of so much worth that his Majesty hath been pleased to signalise with the marks of Honour!' Gary is taking it for granted that as a former supporter of the Lord Protector, Foxcroft needs to learn that his treachery will find neither sympathy nor tolerance under the Restoration. However, Gary then unfortunately descends to using language unseemly to us, but not to the inhabitants of a nation so recently cloven and embittered by civil war and regicide: 'Can you deal so roughly with one of his Majesty's faithful Subjects placed in a far brighter Sphere than yourself, notwithstanding all that vanity of a painted tail of titles wherewithal, Peacock-like, you pride yourself, never humbling your thoughts in the meantime to and by the Contemplation of your black feet, coloured by the foul patches of your former practices?' The passage of 8 years, and popular disapproval of the court of Charles II, had not lessened the animosity of these men. For a businessman from Ironmonger Street (irrespective of whether he was the Company's commissioned Agent), to doubt a knight of the realm, dubbed by the King, was treasonous sacrilege. The reference to 'black feet' is particularly obvious, harking to the Puritans' preference for wearing black on formal occasions.

Meanwhile on 10 March 1665, the Company appointed Foxcroft Governor of the fort and town of Madras, to sit in Council, under seal of its Royal Charter. This gave Foxcroft and his council the right to pass judgment on all civil and criminal cases. Jearsey, at Masulipatam, was given a copy of this notification, the original having been dispatched to Madras. Jearsey wrote to Sir Edward, and was permitted to visit Fort St George on 28 March 1667. He met Foxcroft, gave him the letter appointing him Governor in the King's name, and a badly counterfeited warrant for his release, which was afterwards read out at the Fort's main guard. Sir Edward considered this warrant a forgery, and sent copies of it back to London. However, time was running out on Sir Edward's government by usurpation. News had reached England in January 1667, followed by Sir Edward's narrative (received 13 April), and George Foxcroft's letter (received 31 May). The Great Plague had just passed, having killed off a large part of London's populace. The Great Fire, between 2 and 5 September 1666, had followed this. This last event had caused an upsurge of conspiracy theories, attributing the source of the conflagration to French and Dutch agents, Catholics, and anti-monarchists. Charles II, forever unconfident of his throne, feared a rebellion against the monarchy. Into this atmosphere of uncertainty came news of Sir Edward's usurpation of the government of Madras. James Bruce points out in his *Annals*, that the first suspicion of the veracity of Sir Edward's accusations came from his having written first to the Governor of Bombay instead of Sir George Oxenden, then at Surat as the Company's President. Bruce says that this suspicion was strengthened by Sir Edward's having written directly to the King and to the Archbishop of Canterbury, rather than to and through the Company, whose employee he was. The epistle from Surat attributing to Sir Edward plans to hand over Madras to the Dutch prompted questions about the loyalty of the Company's servants to the crown. Contrary to Sir Edward's plan, his actions were interpreted in London as overtly seditious. Here one must keep in mind that London only had some distorted and questionable information about the events in Madras during 1665 – 1668. Their knowledge was based on correspondence and data prior to the arrival of George Foxcroft at Fort St George in June 1665. This data revealed Sir Edward as a dubious person with allegations against him, from as late as 1664, of private trading and Popish sympathy, which tallied with the exceptional circumstances under which he had been appointed in 1662, so much so that the Company had been at considerable expense to send a Supervisor to Madras to examine the accusations against him. In fact, to any interested researcher leafing through the Company's papers in 1667, in search of some clue as to what might really have taken place at Madras, Sir Edward would instantly appear as the pole of suspicion. Further, so intense and repeated the accusations against him had become, that the Company was compelled to send, without awaiting its Supervisor's report, a new and more reliable Agent to Madras. The situation becomes befogged only after the new Agent's arrival at Madras. Sir Edward's plan of evoking popular sentiment in England had failed. So oblivious had the Company been to these outrageous happenings that as late as 1666 they had sent out a letter appointing as Governor a man whose position had been usurped, and who was even then imprisoned, as he had been, for the past 3 years.

Given the weight of the evidence against Sir Edward, the Company formally petitioned the King in this matter, who placed it with the Lord Chancellor for investigation. After a considerable delay during which an attempt was made to understand the current situation in Madras as closely as possible and all its possible implications, a Royal commission was issued on 4 December 1667, to retake Fort St George and the restore the Agency of George Foxcroft. This commission was assigned to 15 persons: Captains Robert Price, John Brookhaven, Henry Risby, Thomas Harman, Richard Goodlad, William Wildey, and Messrs William Jearsey, John Nicklaes, Walter Clavell, Roger Broadnax, John Bridger, Richard Smithson, Joseph Hall, Matthew Mainwaring, and Thomas Moore. A fleet of 5 ships fitted for war and trade, and one frigate composed the fleet, which was placed under the admiralty of Robert Price. Before setting out, the commissioners were given carefully thought out instructions on 24 January 1668, meant to cover all possibilities. These ranged from offering a bounty to the garrison if Sir Edward should refuse to hand over the fort, to landing seamen and assaulting the fort with naval support, and in case the Dutch should have gained it, to parley with them, else to have San

Thome fortified and, failing everything, a spot nearby purchased from the Nawab and settled.

Two of the ships, the *Rainbow* and the *Loyal Merchant*, anchored in Madras Roads on 21 August 1668. Joseph Hall subsequently related by letter to the Company the events that followed. Charles Proby and Edward Locke came on board, and Proby, as Sir Edward's second in council, was shown the King's order, demanding the surrender of Fort St George to the King's commissioners, and the release of Governor Foxcroft. Proby relented at once, and wrote to Sir Edward recommending the King's orders. Sir Edward, on receiving the orders and Proby's letter, invited the commissioners ashore ostensibly to hand over the fort immediately. Accordingly, John Bridger, Matthew Mainwaring, and Joseph Hall, went ashore presumably around 7 in the evening. Sir Edward and Simon Smythes received them. The latter examined the King's Commission, and opined that such orders would never have come had the King been acquainted with Sir Edward's cause. The next excuse by Sir Edward and Smythes was that it was too late, and further discussions would take place in the morning. The three commissioners spent the night at Sir Edward's house, and in the morning again asked that the Fort be surrendered. This time the other party haggled first for Proby, who had been detained on the *Loyal Merchant*, to be returned to them. Then they bargained that after the surrender, their own liberty and the safety of their estates was to be guaranteed. They were assured that they were free to remain in Madras or to take a ship to Europe. Smythes pressed for an assurance about the safety of their estates, and for the release of Proby as a precondition. The commissioners withdrew, and seeing that none of the other ships had arrived, decided to give in to Smythes' conditions. The persons of the usurping councillors and their estates were to remain free. The commissioners were aware that they were in no position to bargain further, since they did not have the force to overwhelm the defenders.

To Sir Edward it was equally clear that resistance was useless. One does not know if he had planned to resist. Resistance would simply have brought out a larger fleet from England, and the terms agreed upon would be withdrawn. He would be proscribed as a traitor, and suffer trial and, possibly, execution. So on the night of 22 August 1668, the great drama ended. Sir Edward surrendered Fort St George to the King's commissioners, who turned all, including the guards, out of the fort, locked the gates, and set Governor Foxcroft free, handing over to him the keys.

Sir Edward remained in Madras for 4 years more. In allowing him to do so, the Company committed again the same error that Jeremy

Sambrooke had pointed out previously to his father. Sir Edward's presence was a painful source of suspicion to Foxcroft during the remaining period of his governorship. When Sir Edward floated the rumour that there would soon be another change in Madras, the council expelled him from his own house within the outer wall of the fort, where he had reportedly stocked arms for this alleged second coup. He was permitted to remain in his garden-house in Madras. Nonetheless his constant movement to and from the Dutch settlement at Pulicat was equally suspicious and unsettling to the authorities. Sir Edward Winter finally left India on 20 January 1672, taking passage to England from Madras on board the *Bombayn Merchant*. His first wife, who presumably was Indian, stayed back. Records show that she was living in Madras in 1681. On 20 December 1682, Sir Edward married Emma, daughter of Richmond Howe of Norfolk. Meanwhile, he engaged in lengthy litigation with the Company, because of which he was awarded £6,000. When he sought to return to India, a huge surety was demanded, and he forsook his intention. Sir Edward Winter finally settled at York House, Battersea, where he died on 2 March 1686, aged 64.

Sir Edward and his actions defy assessment. He was no Cavalier in the true sense of the term. Rather, his family's association with trade in the East Indies puts him into a special group of men: determined and adventurous traders of unusually hardy constitution and considerable luck. This seems to have been the difference between him and George Foxcroft. His Royalist leaning was incidental, and the Company appointed him because they wanted an old hand as Agent. They replaced him because they no longer wanted a hard-bitten trader canny in the ways of private trade at Fort St George. Foxcroft's Puritanism was equally incidental. He does not seem to have been malevolently treasonous. We might do better to see Foxcroft as a City trader with a job to do. To him rules and regulations were meant to be followed, and not bypassed for personal gain. His arrival burst Sir Edward's self-professed bubble of being a titled Cavalier favoured by the King, evidenced by the Royal Warrant he carried; it also made private trade difficult. This explains Sir Edward's discontent but it does not excuse his takeover. In particular, it does not explain the murderous attack made on Foxcroft and his party on 16 September 1665. One may speculate that had Foxcroft been shot dead, Sir Edward would have been able to explain his killing as incidental to the quelling of a seditious attempt to take over Fort St George. The intention, then, might have been to kill Foxcroft at that moment of confrontation. Killing him later would have alienated the rest of the English population. Therefore, Foxcroft, having once survived the shootout, should have realised in hindsight that no further attempts on his life would follow. The benefit of hindsight was not available to Foxcroft between the afternoon of 16 September 1665 and the night of 22 August 1668. Hence, his first actions on being reinstated were aimed at restoration of a different kind. Charles Proby was dismissed the service, and Smythes and Chuseman 'allowed' to return home. Other than the continued and unsettling presence of Sir Edward in Madras, and his frequent visits to the Dutch colony nearby, Foxcroft succeeded in ridding himself of the leaders of the coup. As far as Sir Edward is concerned, one doubts if it was ever his intention to hand over Fort St George to the Dutch.

George Foxcroft's first administration had barely survived 3 months. His second throve for 3 and half years. From 22 August 1668 until his departure on 18 January 1672, George Foxcroft was Governor and Agent at Fort St George. We may pass over his governorship since it holds nothing of immediate interest to our purpose other than the significantly impartial way in which he behaved with those involved directly and indirectly with his overthrow and imprisonment. Nevertheless, in England it was felt for some reason that while Sir Edward's actions were reprehensible, it might also be wise to have Foxcroft recalled. This might have been prompted by the need to ensure, with some subtlety, loyalty to the King. If someone accused of uttering treasonous words were to be allowed to go free while his accuser was punished, it might send the wrong message to other English subjects living in such far-flung posts as Bombay and Madras. In the same way, it would be unwise on the Company's part to disregard Sir Edward's usurpation, or even hint at supporting it. So under the guise of investigating the recent disturbance, Sir William Langhorne and 6 Commissioners were appointed by Royal sanction to Fort St George until all information to this end had been gathered, and Sir William Langhorne was told to take over the governorship from George Foxcroft. As an immediate measure, William Jearsey was removed from Masulipatam. Sir William Langhorne took over from him as Provisional Superior in 1671. William Jearsey seems to have become the scapegoat for the fracas between Sir Edward and Foxcroft, particularly due to his role in having tried to rescue Foxcroft by presenting a false warrant in the King's name to Sir Edward, which the latter had sent on to England. Sir William sat as second in council at Fort St George in his authority as Provisional Agent, until Foxcroft left. Jearsey settled in Madras, where he died in his own house in 1690, having seen the settlement pass through still more tribulations.

Jeremy Sambrooke was a member of the Committees of the East India Company during 1678-87; he also served as the Company's Deputy Governor during 1683-84, and 1695-98. He was knighted on board the

Earl of Berkeley's ship on 31 January 1681, and appointed by Royal Commission to be an Alderman of Cripplegate Ward on 1 July 1687. Sambrooke obtained his release from this post by paying a hefty fine of £520. A noted merchant, Sir Jeremy was one of 15 persons nominated to formulate the byelaws of the Bank of England in 1697. He was also one of the signatories to the Indenture Quinpartite, which was an important component in the formation of the United Company of Traders to the East Indies. He died suddenly while in the garden of his home at Edmonton, Middlesex, on 27 April 1705, and was buried at Edmonton Parish Church. Sir Jeremy had indeed come a very long way since those momentous adventures, desperate illness, and lingering imprisonment, at Madras.

Foxcroft was to have been accompanied by his son on his return journey but Nathaniel was dead. The inscription on his tombstone at St Mary's Church, Madras, reads, 'Here lyeth the body of Nathaniel Foxcroft, son of George Foxcroft, Agent and Governor in Fort St George. He was borne into this world the 6th of September 1635, and translated into a better to the Resurrection of the Just, the 26th October 1670, after he had finished his pilgrimage on the earth, of 35 years, having always exhibited all the honour, due from a dear and dutiful son to his parents, and by his universal obliging and ingenious conversation obtained a good report and left a good name with all men'. Thus assailed and overwhelmed by personal grief, George Foxcroft left India. His had been a strange tenure, full of pain, sorrow, and hardship. Of Foxcroft's past and future beyond Fort St George, little is known. He might have been one of the many wealthy London merchants who purchased stock in the Massachusetts Bay Company in 1628. George Foxcroft died at the, for those times, singularly advanced age of 91, on 25 January 1691. There was a memorial to him in the old Marylebone Parish Church, with a simple inscription, as behove a Puritan, about life being a mere bubble.

CHAPTER THREE

THE CASE OF CAPTAIN RICHARD KEIGWIN

The Company took no lesson from Sir Edward Winter's usurpation, since the usurpation itself held no monetary interest; neither did the suffering of those involved in it. In less than 20 years' time another rebellion in the King's name erupted, this time in Bombay, chiefly led by Captain Richard Keigwin. While our focus is on events in Madras, similar startling events at British trading establishments in other parts of India will also draw our attention. Keigwin's rebellion was the consequence of excessive provocation, the uprising was carried out meticulously, and the interim government was many times better than the Company's.

Keigwin was an ordinary European inhabitant in Bombay, having arrived there in 1676. He was a naval officer by profession, having been commissioned as lieutenant in 1665 on the *Santa Maria*. After accumulating considerable battle experience, he was appointed to the command of the *Assistance* in 1672. A fleet (including the *Assistance*) attacked St Helena under Commodore Munden in 1672, and Keigwin was appointed interim Governor in 1673. During his governorship, a mutiny took place, and he was deposed and imprisoned. Keigwin left the King's service after returning to England, and settled in Bombay as a freeman planter.

Following trouble with the Portuguese in March 1676, a troop of 40 cavalrymen was sanctioned at Bombay, with Keigwin as the captain. The troop soon proved its worth on land, when Keigwin heroically defended Bombay against the Maratha navy with only one English vessel under his command, the rest having fled on seeing the enemy. Meanwhile, John Child became Deputy Governor of Bombay and in February 1679, the Court of Committees ordered most impracticable measures. The troop was to be disbanded, all work at fortification stopped, and Keigwin discharged. This was clearly madness given the volatile position occupied by Bombay in local politics and geography. The Marathas under Shivaji wanted Bombay, as did the Portuguese in Goa, and the Mughals, who were not too far away either. The orders further embittered Company employees because they bore directives for drastic cuts in pay for all those posted at

Bombay. John Child's post as Deputy Governor was abolished, and he was reduced to Agent on a salary of £120 a year. This strange command first caused amazement, and then intense resentment, fuelled by suspicion of John Child's involvement, since his connection to Sir Josiah Child, then Governor of the Company, was popular knowledge. The Company had reasoned that the cost of defending Bombay was many times more than the profit it generated through trade. This was consistent with the Company's mercantile hope that investing in Bombay would help them to a greater share of the lucrative Malabar trade. The Company's illogicalness lay in thinking that this could be achieved without local political and military conflicts. The paring down of salaries in order to economise was further absurdity. Sir Josiah would propound the opposite view in respect of armaments within a few years but at Bombay John Child implemented the current orders. Keigwin, once more a freeman planter, returned to England early in 1680. There he appeared before the Court of Committees and made his case successfully, upon which he was reappointed captain of the garrison of Bombay in February 1681. He returned to Bombay in this capacity later that year with a salary of 6 shillings a day, a place in council, and an allowance for his 'diet'.

Meanwhile John Child's diligent execution of the Company's parsimony was worsening the situation at Bombay. Henry Gary, who in June 1668 had supported Sir Edward's usurpation, had settled in Bombay, and been elevated to the post of Judge. The Company sacked Gary because there were accusations against him of being Catholic and we have seen that he was Royalist. There were also doubts about his judgmental abilities, since he dispensed justice in a rough and rude manner. This provoked a unanimous reaction from the entire European population, who added their names to the letter of refutation dispatched to London. The morass of local politics became stickier with unchallenged forays by the Marathas, and the imposition of additional customs by the Mughals. John Child was recalled to Surat to become President in December 1681. At Surat, John Child sanctioned the Grand Enquiry into the Company's indictment of its employee, John Pettit, which recalled him from Persia, and after thorough examination, acquitted him in January 1682. Pettit asked that he be placed on the council in Surat, where he was appointed second, with George Bowcher as third. In August a letter from the Company, dated February 1682 was received, whereby Pettit and Bowcher were dismissed and ordered to return to England to face charges. Pettit and Bowcher, anticipating such a possibility, had already moved house from the factory to the town, and thereby left the Company's jurisdiction for the local governor's. This act terribly enraged the domineering and vindictive

John Child. He received some consolation from his mentor and namesake, Sir Josiah, who had instructed him to remove summarily, without going through the usual processes of inquiry, all disgruntled employees like Pettit. In London the tussle between the Interlopers, who had raised the old cry for free trade, and the Company, was at its height. John Child accused Pettit and Bowcher as agents for the Interlopers. Pettit and Bowcher carried on an insurrectionary war against Child's administration by bringing the Dutch and the French into the fray. Unable to seize them, Child took possession of their property and issued cautionary orders to women socialising with Mrs Bowcher, who was still living in the factory premises, and allegedly abusing the Company's merchants, especially John Child and his mentor, Sir Josiah, at her tea parties. Next John Child set about seeking the custody of the two rebellious traders. In this, he had already been thwarted by the combined efforts of the rebels and the Dutch chief, since the influence of the latter on the local government was clearly many times greater than Child's. Pettit's written protest sent in December 1682 to Child that he was no Interloper drew the ill-worded reply that Pettit's 'fig leaf Coat of pretences' would not cover him. Bowcher wrote in February 1683 to Michell, the English chief at Calicut, that his brother-in-law, John Child was 'the maddest President' that Surat had ever seen. Not only was socialising with Mrs Bowcher disallowed, the household servants had been seized, and local tradesmen ordered to keep away. Bowcher adds in his letter that he believed that if it were possible, John Child would forbid the entrance of those disobedient to him into heaven. Money was becoming scarce for Pettit and Bowcher, since Child had seized 40,000 rupees due to them from their own trade.

One interesting point of digression here is the fascination of the local nobility for the toy spaniel, made popular in England by Charles II. John Child reported to the Company in early 1683 that the local governor and his ministers wanted to be gifted water spaniels and toy spaniels, so he wished the Company would send out many 'neat little dogs, the less [smaller] the better'. With these and other bribes, John Child succeeded in moving the governor over to his side, because of which it became very hard for Pettit and Bowcher to remain confident of his protection. Child's perseverance in avenging himself on these two defiant traders is admirable. Afraid of being handed over to Child and transported, Pettit and Bowcher deliberately contracted debts from local merchants, who claimed they had not been repaid. The law being particularly strict in disallowing debtors to leave the Mughal Empire, it became impossible for the now pliable governor to permit their extradition. Pettit was imprisoned in the local jail in Surat around January 1683 as a debtor while Bowcher remained free to look after their common interests. Pettit had been a prisoner for 6 months, when he petitioned the Emperor Aurangzeb to be set free since the debts were because of his own trade, and would be repaid once the outbound ships from Europe arrived. To this unique and most peculiar series of events is added John Child's phenomenal doggedness. The tussle between him and the two rebels had become personal, and with Pettit in Mughal custody and Bowcher unable to leave the borders of Surat, Child offered to repay their debts by handing over the 40,000 rupees, which he had seized, for disbursal to the governor. The governor agreed but Aurangzeb, having received the petition, ordered that no further action be taken until he had considered all aspects of the case. Child was dismayed but recovered himself sufficiently to pay for representation of the Company's case at the Imperial court. He retaliated by seizing all incoming consignments addressed to Pettit and Bowcher, with Pettit sending up letters of protest to the ships' captains who handed them over. The Company, at Sir Josiah's orders, accommodated John Child's inexplicable animosity, and the outbound commodities for Pettit and Bowcher seized in Surat were paid for.

This strange story took another unexpected turn in August 1683 when Aurangzeb, having inquired into Pettit's petition, ordered his release. Child must have been flabbergasted at further Imperial orders, inviting Pettit and Bowcher to visit the Imperial court. They were to be granted permission to operate *their* own trading company. The provincial governor at once released Pettit, was kind to Bowcher, and permitted them to have their European shipments landed and not seized by Child, who was of course very much out of favour. Pettit and Bowcher, now triumphant, made elaborate preparations for their journey to the Imperial court. Having acquired fine accoutrements and put together a considerable convoy of carriages and animals, they set out from Surat later that month and camped outside its walls. The coin, however, flipped once more, and Child's representative at the Mughal court succeeded in getting new orders cancelling the former invitation to court. While the governor would not permit a procession to the Imperial court in view of these new orders, Pettit remained free and Bowcher took the chance to travel privately to the court. Meanwhile, the first of the Interlopers' ships, the *Society*, came to Surat in December 1683, and conducted business under Pettit's advice and the governor's benevolence, which must have been purchased at considerable expense. John Child, closely observing these proceedings with typical malevolence, hatched the wacky plan of capturing the *Society's* captain, purser, and Pettit, stowing them on board a Company ship, and sending them to England to face charges. The plan misfired, and all the intended captives fled. Surviving correspondence between the antagonists carries personal insults and challenges to duels. Pettit further aroused the governor against Child by revealing the methods by which the latter smuggled goods through customs.

On 5 January 1684 the Company's ship, *Rainbow*, suddenly returned to Surat with the shocking news that a rebellion had taken place in Bombay. Captain Keigwin had seized and imprisoned the Deputy Governor, Charles Ward, who was another brother-in-law to John Child. Ward was unpopular in Bombay because he continued the parsimonious policies demanded by Sir Josiah, despite being acutely aware of the unstable position he and his town occupied in local politics. Sambhaji was ably pursuing Shivaji's legacy. Ward was faced on one side by the Marathas and on the other by Imperial forces. Keigwin's command at Bombay consisted of two companies of European troops, and one of militia. The companies each had a commander, assisted by an ensign and two sergeants. The militia had only one ensign in command of 500 men. Around the end of 1682, Captain Niccolls, who commanded the senior company, was summarily discharged by the Court of Committees vide an order issued in January of that year. Keigwin was ordered to take over the company in addition to his duties as garrison commander. Since Keigwin was now a company commander, he was deprived by Child of his seat in the council and his extra allowance for food. Remonstrance on Keigwin's part drew no sympathy from the President at Surat, who referred the matter to London. 80 years later the issue of *batta* would cause discontent in the Company's army; in Bombay in 1683 the prime cause was another similar but strange military allowance. This was the 'dead muster'. Commissioned officers were allowed extra pay for the maintenance of their servants. While they actually employed locals, the officers drew allowances admissible for English soldiers. The locals were paid little and the officers pocketed the extra income. In order to make this swindling look correct on paper, fictitious English names were 'mustered'. John Child had made a detailed report on this practice to the Company while he was in Bombay, and was told to curtail it. In fact, the officers were ordered to refund the money they had been given through the 'dead musters'. Both John Child and the Company were quite correct in finding this practice reprehensible. As in the case of *batta* in Bengal 80 years later, the withdrawal of the 'dead musters' caused much anguish to the officers of the Bombay garrison in 1683. There were other contributory factors also. In May 1683, sailors from the Mughal admiral Siddi Kasim's fleet attacked two English soldiers in the bazaar at Bombay and killed one, leaving the other seriously injured. This caused enormous unrest among the troops, who demanded retribution and urged Ward to implement it. Ward demurred and mutiny was barely avoided. Another unpleasant brush with the Mughals took place in June, because of which the captain of an East Indiaman fired off his guns at the Mughal flagship anchored at Bombay. Henry Smith, a discontented, and probably unbalanced, merchant and councillor, had exchanged angry words with Ward while in council, and even drawn his sword. Child chided Ward and commanded that Smith be disallowed from wearing a sword for 4 months. Meanwhile Smith became involved in the events that led to the firing of the ship's guns on the Mughal admiral, which caused Child to face the anger of the Mughal governor of Surat, who was undoubtedly being egged on by Pettit. Child ordered the suspension of Henry Smith, who then left Bombay and shifted to Surat with his wife.

In the meantime, as Ward curtailed expenditure and devalued the Company's coin, inflation took hold of the market. Local politics was again taking toll on Bombay, which depended entirely on food imports. Keigwin's letter to Charles II accused Ward of 'buying cheap and selling dear' since basic foodstuff outside Bombay had not become costlier. Instead, Ward, so said Keigwin, ordered the export of corn, and the fixing of prices through the Clerk of the Market at values many times higher than 6 months before. 'Goa Arrack,' for instance, Keigwin said, the sole drink affordable by a soldier, was purchased by the administration at a cost 4 times lower than the sale price. Other than alcohol, one sees from Keigwin's list that ducks, pigs, goats, hens, and wood, were at least 2 or 3 times costlier. The fixing of prices has nowhere been free of personal interest. In this case too the same rule seems to have been applicable. Charles Ward was making money from inflated prices. Even as raised prices raised tempers, the officers' petition, in which they had requested that they be spared from refunding the amounts drawn by them under the 'dead musters' was considered seditious by the Courts of Committees, and a letter to this effect was received in Surat. The four officers, signatory to the petition, were to be dismissed and Child at once ordered this. At 7 am on 27 December 1683, the Bombay garrison mutinied. Deputy Governor Ward was taken from his chamber and cast into a cell. The troops, prompted by Thorburn, one of the dismissed officers now reinstated as a prominent leader of the mutiny, clamoured for Captain Keigwin to be appointed Governor, which was done in the King's name. One must remember that apologists have sought to clarify that the mutineers were not seditious towards their King or country but the Company, which had treated them scurvily. The parallel between the actions of Captain Richard Keigwin and his associates and that of Sir Edward Winter is obvious. It has been said that Keigwin had no particular personal interest to protect, which is open to argument. All who came to India came to make money. Richard Keigwin cannot have been any different. In any case, the ease with which the mutiny took place suggests that it was popular. Unlike the bloodshed in Madras, this occasion was peaceful despite the condition that all inhabitants of Bombay had to swear an oath of allegiance to the new government. All did, with four exceptions, and Keigwin did not force them. That Pettit and Bowcher were involved in the mutiny is evidenced by the importance they were given as commercial representatives of the 'freed' town and its government.

Every rebellion must have reasons that can be publicised, irrespective of whether true or false. The Bombay mutiny had several. While addressing the assembled troops before declaring the mutiny, Thorburn announced that Ward planned to sell Bombay to Sambhaji for 40,000 pagodas. This was the first indictment. Another is of corruption on Ward's part. To this is appended his use of witchcraft, calling for the use of human blood, to ascertain the whereabouts of hidden treasure. The others include the charge of allowing Siddi Kasim and his force open access to Bombay, the artificial inflation in prices, and the decision to disallow 'dead musters'. The basic reasons were of course Ward's weak governance and John Child's pathetic presidency.

With the arrival of news at Surat of the rebellion, Child and his council acted promptly. Three of the Company's 6 ships in port were dispatched to Bombay on 11 January 1684, ferrying the three councillors who had been appointed commissioners to parley with the rebels. The commissioners were Charles Zinzan, Francis Day (probably not related to the founder of Fort St George), and George Gosfright. Their attempts were in vain. Keigwin considered the demand for truce needless, as he was not at war against the King's subjects. He was, he wrote, the Governor of Bombay, holding it on behalf of the King, to whose possession it had returned from the Company's. On this matter there was to be no further discussion. The King's subjects, even though employed by the Company, were allowed ashore, but attempts to sabotage the King's government at Bombay were unacceptable. Consequently, the three commissioners went ashore and discussed matters amiably with Keigwin and his council. Nonetheless, it was obvious that all endeavours to reverse the rebellion through talks and the bribe of a 'provisional pardon' would be futile. Most of those concerned, including the commissioners, knew why Bombay had rebelled, and were sympathetic. Hence, John Child decided to sail to Bombay himself with the remaining ships. Arriving on 30 January, Child sent off a letter displaying characteristic feebleness to Keigwin: 'Come, one, two, or three of you, and look on your Governor; I am the same that lived amongst you not long ago'. Child urged Keigwin to allow such members of his council and garrison who wished it, to go aboard his ship and meet him. Keigwin's reply was polite and firm, which determined Child to try to starve out Bombay through blockading. Keigwin seized Zinzan and Day in reprisal, and Child was forced to lift the blockade. By February 1684, the hopelessness of the situation was evident, since Keigwin had repaired the fortifications, and ensured that Bombay was very strongly guarded. It was impossible for Child to take it by assault. Child's letters to the Company during February voice his helplessness. In contrast to the government of Sir George Oxenden, John Child's presidency had nothing to recommend it. In fact, all affected by its actions heartily disliked it. The only means left to Child was to induce and encourage division in the European population at Bombay. To this end, he sought Keigwin's permission to post a Company agent there, in order to protect the Company's interests given Keigwin's encouragement of free trade through the Interlopers, who now sailed regularly to Bombay. Keigwin ended this most unconvincing ruse by ominously warning Child that anyone caught undermining the King's government at Bombay would be severely punished. Besides, by the end of February, Child was beset by the fear of desertions to Bombay from his ships. So having finally accepted defeat, he sailed back to Surat on 3 March 1684. On returning there, he once again set about his old task of avenging himself upon Pettit and Bowcher. Later that month, he suborned Bowcher's cook to poison him, which the latter revealed to his master after having taken the bribe from Child.

Contrary to Sir Edward's rule by usurpation at Madras, Keigwin's was beneficial to English interests. He made Bombay secure by facing off the Mughal navy under Siddi Kasim, and by a treaty with Sambhaji. This latter pact permitted Fort St George to trade in south India, which was then under Maratha dominance. The inhabitants of Bombay were finally at peace with their neighbours and themselves. This rediscovered confidence is to be found in such insulting statements as these, in letters written to the Company from Bombay: 'Children that have crept under your Table now appear above board, and have out-reckoned you all in Arithmetic from Numeration to Multiplication only the Rule of Proportion is wanting to make them Complete Artists'. This gives way to overconfidence: 'They have outgrown the Stature of Men, though they retain a Childish name, and overtop you all … unless you borrow some additional height from them, that you may appear to be their Creatures.' That no further action on this front would occur until winter, was clear to both sides, and so this mutual animosity flourished, consisting of calumnies and protests on the part of John Child, and decisive action by Keigwin, enforced by popular firmness and courtesy. Keigwin's policy was exactly that which London, particularly Sir Josiah, now wanted the Company to pursue at all its factories. The factories were to ensure their own safety from incursions by local powers, which were often provoked and aided by traders from other European nations.

Keigwin's letter explaining his usurpation reached the Court in August 1684, by which time the Company had sent Sir Thomas Grantham and his ship, *Charles the Second*, with a company of soldiers, to recapture Bantam from the Dutch, make a show of force at Gombroon, and finally land the troops at Bombay in pursuance of the new policy at Leadenhall Street, which called for the proactive defence of trade. News from Surat about Keigwin's rebellion arrived at the same time, leading once more to the presentation of a set of conflicting reports. The link with the affair of Sir Edward Winter was established through the persona of Sir Jeremy Sambrooke, who was made one of the three members of the Secret Committee set up to investigate the matter and advise the King accordingly. The other members were Sir Benjamin Bathurst and Sir Josiah Child. To expect Jeremy Sambrooke to brook any usurpation is impossible. Sir Josiah Child was in correspondence with his namesake in Surat. Bathurst was an old Company hand, whom we have already come across, when he was asked to stand bail for Nicholas Buckeridge. The finding of the Secret Committee was as expected: the rebellion was treasonous, and since in previous cases (obviously Sir Edward's) there had been no effective punishment to serve as a deterrent, the ringleaders of this uprising were identified by name, and the King requested to allow them no pardon.

Unlike the case of Sir Edward and George Foxcroft, there was no dithering this time. John Child was rewarded with the pompous rank of 'Captain-General of All our Forces by Sea and Land in the North of India' and issued a Royal Commission allowing him to use all possible force to recover Bombay from the rebels. This was an enormous achievement for John Child. In addition, the King sent a letter bearing his signature to Keigwin, urging him to surrender Bombay within 24 hours of receipt of the letter. If this were done, the entire garrison except the four ringleaders, viz, Keigwin, Thorburn, Fletcher, and Adderton, would receive general pardon. Rewards ranging from 2000 to 8000 rupees were offered for the persons of the four leaders. Captain-General John Child was particularly urged to put the four rebel leaders on trial, and have them executed in Bombay. He was desired to set an example through the public execution of at least one of them. In a separate writ issued under privy seal, Pettit and Bowcher were to be seized and sent to England. Further, the headquarters of the Company were to move permanently from Surat to Bombay. To assist the Captain-General, the King also ordered a Royal Naval ship, HMS *Phoenix* to Bombay. These steps were harsh, and they reflect the obtuseness of the Company. The Company was not keen on sustaining Bombay for any reason other than to contain the Interlopers, who, by clever legal manoeuvring on the part of Sir Josiah, had become associated with Puritanism, dissatisfaction with the Restoration, and with attempts to assassinate the King. This is borne out by the fact that Captain John Tyrell of HMS *Phoenix* was ordered to seize the ships of Interlopers, and send them to the Court of Admiralty in India (John St John was sent as judge to this Court to be set up in Bombay, and he reached Surat on 15 September 1684). The demand for cautionary executions reflects the bitterness of Sir Jeremy's personal experience. The Company was as far removed from reality at its factories in 1684 as it had been in 1665. It is the figure of Sir Jeremy that dominates decision-making at the Company's headquarters, which is once more faced with conflicting reports that cannot be corroborated except over vast periods, and huge expanses of sea. To Sir Jeremy, primary report of a usurpation required immediate and exemplary action. This action would not be as tentative as it had been in 1668. Rather, usurpation would attract the use of an overwhelming force by way of response. In effect, the Company was being guided by the unpleasant experience of one man, in the absence of a proper process of inquiry. This was being encouraged by Sir Josiah in his desire to take over all European trade with India. The Interlopers were declared illegal and enemies of the state by the Chief Justice, Lord Jeffries, in 1685.

Meanwhile in an unfortunate series of events, John Pettit, who had so far successfully defended himself against Child, was seriously wounded and taken prisoner by local pirates, in whose town he died in April 1684, with only one fellow Englishman for company,. The Captain-General was delighted with the news of the passing of this 'naughty man'.

Sir Thomas Grantham reached Bombay on 3 November, having sailed from Surat on 30 October following various adventures in the pursuit of his orders. Sir Thomas met Keigwin and long consultations followed. On 10 November 1684, both sides agreed to terms. Keigwin was to be pardoned, and the resurrection 'buried in Oblivion'. Keigwin was further to be allowed to keep his estate and live quietly there, with the added liberty to choose to reside in India or to return to England aboard an East Indiaman at the Company's expense. The following day was chosen for the surrender of the fort. On 12 November, the entire garrison was summoned and addressed by Keigwin and Sir Thomas. However, some misunderstanding occurred regarding the general amnesty and possibly the future of the troops, especially in relation to their pay. Sir Thomas was heckled, and at one point, a pistol was pressed into his back, ready to be fired. Captain Fletcher of the garrison drew his sword and assisted Sir Thomas in fleeing. Grantham hid in the fort until evening, when he returned to his ship. The disturbance continued until 16 November, when Keigwin wrote to Grantham enclosing a list of 13 articles, which essentially re-stated the same terms although in much clearer and semi-legal language. This list being provisionally accepted, the final document of surrender was signed on 18 November and Sir Thomas on behalf of the Company took charge of Bombay the following day.

Charles Ward, freed from imprisonment, was not restored to his post. Instead, he was dispatched to Persia, and thence dismissed the service. Charles Zinzan was appointed Deputy Governor by John Child, who seemed to have finally overcome all his enemies. Zinzan reached Bombay and took over on 16 December 1684. However, he enraged the Captain-General by ratifying the provisional agreement accepted by Sir Thomas. This was the sensible thing to do, and John Child did his best to prove that Zinzan had overstepped his authority. Similarly, Richard Keigwin prudently chose to leave Bombay for England on board Sir Thomas's ship, *Charles the Second*. This sent John Child into a frenzied rage, complaining about how 'Keigwin that notorious naughty Rascal ... as Impudent as Hell, glorying in his roguery', was sailing off free. Zinzan too was paying no heed to the President's ravings about dismissing everyone associated with the mutiny from the service, to keep these persons from inciting a second rebellion. This possibility of a 'second rebellion' haunted John Child for the remainder of his days. Nonetheless, the Captain-General should have been a happy man otherwise, for he was made a baronet in 1685, and remained in charge in India until hostilities broke out between the Mughals and the Company, in pursuance of the previously mentioned policy of establishing factories capable of defending themselves. Sir John also contributed to this ill-will in his monomaniac determination to wipe out the Interlopers. He demanded that the Mughal governor seize and hand over to the Company, Interlopers' ships at Swally. These demands increased and in the end, he irritated the Mughals by having the Mughals' ships seized by East Indiamen. The Emperor Aurangzeb ordered attacks on the English. During this fighting the Mughal governor of Surat cast in chains all the English he could get hold of and made them walk through the town to gaol. Fortunately for Sir John, he was not present at Surat but in Bombay at that time. Bombay was invaded on 14 February 1689 by a huge force under Siddi Kasim, and besieged. When hostilities ended following the payment of a huge indemnity to the Mughal court,

Aurangzeb declared that the English would be restored to their former rights on condition that Sir John Child should be removed from India. Sir John, however, was also spared this since he died on 4 February 1690, before the Emperor's demand could be implemented. It was rumoured that Sir John left behind the enormous fortune of £100,000, at his death. Charles Zinzan fell out of favour due to his intransigence about being vengeful to the former mutineers. He was dismissed the service and died in Bombay.

Richard Keigwin sailed to England, and later thence on to the West Indies as captain of the ship he had commanded before, the *Assistance*. Keigwin was killed in a battle there in June 1690. George Bowcher, permitted by the Emperor to trade in his own right, throve in Surat at least until 1715, despite all futile attempts by Sir John Child to have him seized and transported to England, as demanded by the King's writ. Bowcher is listed by the padre Richard Cobbe, as one of the contributors in 1715 for the completion of St Thomas' Church in Bombay.

The Company of course again did nothing to improve management based on lessons drawn from this second curious usurpation in India. Low salaries and parsimonious policies were bound to create unhappiness among its employees. Disgruntled employees would occasionally rebel and some blood would be shed. So long as this did not interfere with the Company's trade and its exclusive rights, Leadenhall Street did not much care about manic Presidents spending more time pursuing personal vendettas, or weak factory chiefs allegedly willing to share fines accruing from the seizure of false dice with fellow councillors. What the Company had learned from its Bombay affair was that if its factories could defend themselves against local rulers and marauders, money and goods would be saved. This was what Keigwin had ably demonstrated. This was perhaps the only lesson worth the trouble.

Other changes had also taken place. The King himself was one of the Company's stockholders and therefore indebted to it. Sir Josiah Child held a third of the Company's capital, and the Company had 'jurisdiction civil and military, including martial law, the right of coining money in its settlements, and of employing troops and fleets against native princes and European Interlopers alike'. The Company, said Sir Josiah, was no longer an association of 'mere trading merchants'; it was 'a sovereign estate in India'. The Governor and the Directors of the Company were loath to part with their power and prerogatives. One haughty letter from the Company to a presumptive factory chief read: 'The great trouble we labour under is that you cannot get out of your cavilling way of writing or perverting or misconstruing, procrastinating or neglecting our plain and direct orders to you; as if you were not a subordinate but a coordinate power with us: which has and will (till you conform to our known minds and intentions) force us to make more changes in your council than anything else could have induced us to do'.

King Charles II died on 6 February 1685, aged 54. His brother James II succeeded him, and once more religion became the focus of intrigue and controversy.

CHAPTER FOUR

THE CASE OF ROBERT RAWORTH

As the trading activities of the Company from Fort St George grew, the ambition developed, to establish other factories for enhancing trade. To this end, Governor William Gyfford deputed Elihu Yale in 1681 to negotiate with the Maratha governor of Gingee Fort, Harji Raja, for permission to set up a factory in his territory. Consent was obtained and a factory set up in Cuddalore. The secret intention was the construction in close proximity to Madras of a fort armed with 30 or 40 guns. This would be an extension of, and a support to, Fort St George. Authorisation for this was not available at once. The political situation in the Carnatic was tense and fluid. Sambhaji, Shivaji's son and successor, was betrayed to, and seized by, Aurangzeb in February 1689. On Sambhaji's refusing to accept Mughal suzerainty, he was executed in August of that year. Aurangzeb also imprisoned Sambhaji's son, Shahuji, then aged 7. In these circumstances, the rule passed to Rajaram, who was crowned at Raigad in March 1689. The Mughals soon besieged Raigad, and Rajaram escaped to Gingee towards the end of the same year. The Marathas, struggling desperately against the Mughals, were in need of money. Elihu Yale began discussions with Rajaram for the purchase of Tevnapattam fort the following year. The minutes of a special meeting on 9 August 1690 at Fort St George give us the necessary details. The acquisition of the fort was in keeping with the Company's orders, and Tevnapattam came highly recommended, having a double wall, and being reasonably spacious, 500 feet long and 400 broad. The buildings within were in good condition, having reportedly cost its builder over 100,000 pagodas. The fort's situation was especially remarkable. It was placed in 'a plentiful Country for Cloth trade and provisions, near the Sea surrounded by a good river', which was capable of being negotiated by vessels of 100 tonnes. William Fraser, destined later to become governor, and to be embroiled in controversy, added a note of dissent to this minute, stating his complete disagreement with the reasons given in council by the governor for the acquisition of Tevnapattam. Fraser put in a similar note of dissent at a meeting on 14 August where a draft of the *firman* for the purchase of

Tevnapattam was discussed. In fact, this second note of dissent is more virulent, since it accused Elihu Yale of having negotiated through local intermediaries, including Sundara Ballal, Rajaram's adviser, and without any reference to the council. In effect, it accuses Yale of having taken an immense kickback from the deal. Nonetheless, the council sanctioned the deal on 19 August, and Thomas Yale, Elihu's younger brother, instructed to proceed in getting it confirmed. Rajaram sanctioned the sale on 2 September 1690, of the fort with all its guns, as well as all surrounding land within range of a cannonball fired from any point in the fort, for 33,000 pagodas.

On receiving confirmation from Thomas, Elihu Yale ordered the immediate dispatch (5 September 1690) of a council and garrison for the fort, under the command of William Hatsell, the most junior merchant on the council at Madras. The council was to comprise of some factors, and a garrison, comprising one lieutenant, 2 ensigns, and gunners and soldiers, with 30 cannon and sufficient firearms and ammunition. The notes of dissent make for interesting reading. Elihu Yale wanted his brother Thomas to be placed in command of Tevnapattam, already re-named Fort St David. Given the size of the council and garrison, the commander would be designated Deputy Governor, and Elihu wished this for Thomas. The council demurred, and Elihu reportedly used 'scurrilous language' before giving in to the appointment of William Hatsell. Another diversion may be found in the affidavit sworn in by one Captain Tuer in council the same day, repeating a message from Sir John Child at Bombay to Elihu Yale: 'I think the Devil is in those people of your side they are always writing one against the other, pray tell his honour that he had bad people about him which has writ very scandalous of him … the Author was a rascal, but he [Sir John] had a better opinion of Mr Yale than to credit it'. William Fraser, persistent as ever in his disagreement with Tevnapattam, put in another note of dissent on 9 September, stating that the locality of Tevnapattam was 'like to prove the Seat of War for some years' and was too close to Madras for any substantial increase in revenue from its acquisition. The argument intensified over the next 2 days, with Elihu Yale lamenting the lack of progress in taking over Fort St David at once.

Meanwhile, Aurangzeb, aware of Rajaram's escape from Raigad to Gingee, had sent his general, Zulfikar Ali Khan, in pursuit. On 22 September Zulfikar Ali Khan asked for munitions and soldiers from Fort St George. The English sent him 200 *maunds* of gunpowder. On 14 October a second demand followed, again for munitions, soldiers, and, additionally, cloth. This time he was again sent 200 *maunds* of gunpowder and 300 iron shot, but no troops were officially sent although several soldiers deserted to Mughal service, enticed by better pay and the prospect of loot. In return for assistance, Zulfikar Ali Khan granted the English permission to acquire the Tevnapattam fort. He additionally confirmed the English possession of Madras, Masulipatam, Madapollam, Vizagapatam, Cuddalore, and Porto Novo. 1690 was in general a good year for the Company. Job Charnock, who had been forced to withdraw from Bengal to Madras in 1689 with all his officials due to depredations by the Mughals, returned in July 1690 and established the factory, whose environs would become Calcutta. Despite the ready assistance given him by Madras, Zulfikar Ali Khan was aware of the possibility of the English helping out Rajaram by allowing him to secure passage on board a ship flying the flag of St George. He seems to have sought French assistance in preventing this. The territories of Gingee were in miserable condition, its inhabitants being harried and harassed by both Maratha and Mughal raiders. People fled to the protection of the English, the French, or Tanjore, an independent Maratha kingdom ruled by a branch family.

By the middle of 1691, the Maratha military position at Gingee had improved. Resorting to their usual guerrilla tactics, Maratha cavalry swooped down upon Mughal supply trains and prevented provisions from reaching the besieging army. The situation was turning against Zulfikar Ali Khan, when Aurangzeb dispatched Zulfikar's father, the Vizier Asad Khan, and Prince Kam Bakhsh, to Gingee in the winter of 1691. The Imperial Prince's presence was an irritant to Zulfikar, who probably took it more as an affront, intended to snatch credit from him. The stalemate continued, and the especially heavy monsoon of 1692 was a great nuisance to the besiegers encamped on the plains around Gingee. By December 1692, the Marathas definitely controlled the war. Ali Mardan Khan, the Mughal *faujdar* of Kanchipuram, had been taken prisoner. The Marathas demanded a ransom of 100,000 pagodas for him, which was conveyed to the governor of Fort St George by an Armenian merchant on 23 December 1692. The English were urged to receive the amount in jewels and currency, and then establish communication with Rajaram for ransoming Ali Mardan Khan. The English naturally declined to interfere but seem to have been compelled by the Armenians, who were of considerable help in their trade, to write to Rajaram, who released Ali Mardan Khan on receiving the ransom. Within a few weeks of this Dhanaji Jadav, who was probably Rajaram's greatest commander, attacked the besiegers at Gingee itself. Soon the besiegers were themselves besieged. This momentous recovery of the Marathas was singular. Food became scarce in the Mughal camp, which was worsened by internal squabbles, and raging epidemics. Moreover, Zulfikar Ali Khan's artillery was in poor condition, the cannon having burst due to excessive use. The Marathas spread rumours of Aurangzeb's demise, which could not be confirmed since communication with the Imperial Court had been disrupted. Kam Bakhsh became concerned with the succession and began writing to Rajaram. Zulfikar, already irritated by his presence, was quick to smell treachery. Kam Bakhsh, aware of the antagonism of both the Vizier and his son (who also had imperial aspirations), desired sanctuary with Rajaram in Gingee. He was placed under close surveillance, and his actions reported to the Emperor.

In the meantime, the situation at the Mughal camp became still more precarious, and retreat was the only answer. Rajaram allowed Asad Khan to move his troops to Wandiwash in the hope that the latter would intercede in a lasting agreement of peace with Aurangzeb. The siege at Gingee was abandoned, and the remnants of the Mughal army went into camp at Wandiwash between February and May 1693. The Emperor summoned Asad Khan and Kam Bakhsh, and with Zulfikar's withdrawal to Wandiwash, the war in the Carnatic seemed to have gained a very brief respite. Rajaram, exultant with this, demanded a loan from the English at Madras that year.

Zulfikar Ali Khan was on the march again in early 1694, moving close to Fort St David on the way to Tanjore. While gifts were rushed to him from Fort St David, and the English there gained a *firman* promising no incursions into their land, the devastation of adjoining areas once more seriously affected trade. The English were increasingly being drawn into areas that William Fraser 4 years ago had predicted would become 'the Seat of War'. Assisted by the Nayak of Trichinopoly, who had his own vengeance to pursue, Zulfikar Ali Khan reached Tanjore in March 1694. The Raja of Tanjore, Shahji II, capitulated under humiliating terms. He agreed to pay a huge indemnity, submit to Mughal suzerainty, and to surrender several strategically vital forts granted him by Rajaram in lieu of loans.

Zulfikar's own intentions were suspect, of which none who had achieved success in Imperial service was free. Moreover, Aurangzeb was old and frail, and though in complete command of his faculties, he was not expected to live much longer. All in touch with the affairs of the Imperial Court were aware of the wars of succession that would follow his demise. The more astute nobles, better informed by their spies at Court, also knew that Aurangzeb's successors did not share his exceptional ability for governance and military prowess. Zulfikar therefore might have been desirous of establishing his own kingdom in the Carnatic. For this, he would need Rajaram's help. It is impossible to find the truth of this.

Zulfikar might have been looking to his own preservation in the wars of succession that would follow the Emperor's death. Nonetheless, by 1695, the war resumed, and once more, the Marathas held against the Mughals. By 1696, William Hatsell, the Deputy Governor at Fort St David noted the dominant presence of Maratha cavalry in the vicinity, and wrote to Madras that it was more important to treat with Rajaram. Zulfikar Ali Khan, reduced to dire financial need, sought a huge loan from Madras in 1696, in return for rights to such land and villages as they wished. During these years of strife, the English played their cards well and obtained several villages around Madras.

The Marathas themselves soon succumbed to internal discord due to the same problem that plagued Zulfikar. The region had been thoroughly ravaged for over 6 years by contending armies and so it had nothing to offer for the further sustenance of either Mughal or Maratha. The treasuries of both sides had been considerably drained, and repeated incursions by the Mughals into small kingdoms like Tanjore had financially exhausted them as well. Like Zulfikar, who was in debt to his troops, having been unable to pay them for several months, Rajaram too was in great need of money. Rajaram therefore sought peace with Aurangzeb, who typically rejected the proposal and, conferring on Zulfikar the title of Nasrat Jung, urged him to press home the attack and capture Gingee. The Mughal treasury was able to bear the expense of prolonged warfare, Maratha raids nothwithstanding, and this was a huge advantage. Zulfikar commenced his second siege of Gingee in November 1697, and took the fort in January 1698. Rajaram escaped to Vellore, leaving his family, considerable treasure, and a number of his officers, behind. He remained a fugitive until March 1698, when he was escorted to Poona by a large contingent of Maratha cavalry.

Aurangzeb appointed Daud Khan the *faujdar* of the Carnatic, and appointed Gazanfar Khan the commander of Gingee fort. Gazanfar Khan's *jagir* included Cuddalore and Tevnapattam. Zulfikar Khan sent orders to Deputy Governor Hatsell at Fort St David to surrender Cuddalore and Tevnapattam to Gazanfar Khan. When Hatsell refused, his garrison was attacked on 17 February 1698 by Salim Khan, one of the commanders responsible for the capture of Gingee. The English garrison defended itself successfully. This is strange since the English had sent congratulatory gifts to Zulfikar Khan in order to secure his subsequent favour.

Fort St George tried in vain to arrive at terms through a payment that would confirm their possession of Tevnapattam and all surrounding land within range of a cannonball. Shrewd merchants made up the council at Fort St George. At their meeting on 20 February 1698, they noted that

Salim Khan's attacks would not be without Zulfikar Khan's 'order or privity'. They further surmised that they had always felt that the Nawab himself would probably not have acted without the Emperor's sanction. This bore ominous meaning for all English factories in India. The council considered that if Salim Khan had acted rashly on his own, and without the Nawab's foreknowledge, this would nonetheless give occasion to the Nawab to pick a quarrel with the English and seek a considerable sum as indemnity. Given these possibilities, the council advised the Company to 'prevent any further acts of Hostility if it can be done by fair means and for a reasonable expense'. The same day, even as the council was pondering these issues, Salim Khan attacked Cuddalore, this being his second attempt to wrest Gazanfar Khan's *jagir* from the English. A third attempt, with infantry, cavalry, assault ladders, and rockets, took place in the third week of March. These attacks were meant to unsettle the English, and even as the council was wondering why no word had been received since February from the Nawab's durbar, news came from their representative, Amirjeahn. One of the Company's letters describes Amirjeahn as an Armenian *vakil*.

At a council meeting on 28 March 1698, the Nawab's terms for settlement were discussed. The Nawab had demanded 10,000 pagodas for the settlement of the problem of Tevnapattam. This was the kickback, and the Company agreed to it, adding a further 'public' gift amounting to 500 pagodas. The merchants, wary as ever, worried over Amirjeahn's loyalty. At a meeting on 1 April, it was agreed that Amirjeahn was an 'able diligent solicitor' but 'the main question' was whether he could be trusted in 'single management', 'it being in the power of such *vakils* (and too common) to provide for an advantage to themselves'. Nonetheless, the Company's council at Madras would have to depend on Amirjeahn, especially since they had just received news that both Asad Khan and his son Zulfikar were very highly esteemed by the Emperor. The aim was to 'prevent trouble', given that the war against the Marathas was settled for the time being, and the Nawab's troops, with nothing else to engage them, would resort to such attacks as the one on Cuddalore. The Nawab himself was moving through the south Carnatic, extracting homage from the rulers of small kingdoms, including Tanjore. On 20 April, Amirjeahn's subsequent demand for 40,000 rupees as expense was considered and he was allowed 20,000. A letter from Amirjeahn followed this in nearly in May, reiterating the Nawab's demand for 8,000 pagodas for himself, and 2,000 for his officers. Even as this bargaining over bribes continued, Salim Khan was out pillaging once more. On 6 May, the council at Fort St George met to discuss Hatsell's letter from Fort St David, reporting the burning of villages by Salim Khan's forces, and urging Madras to 'speedy compliance' with the Nawab's demands for the procurement of his permission. The council therefore concluded that 'whether the Nawab go or stay, if it be necessary to get *parwanahs* for the prevention of such future trouble, they must be procured from him who is Conqueror of the Country, and if he goes away without giving his *parwanahs* his successors cannot grant them after they shall be by the Nawab brought into the King's books, and it will undoubtedly prove the occasion of a public quarrel between the Mughal and the Company one time or other'. To hasten the process, Amirjeahn was permitted to spend 1,000 pagodas more. The considerable scope of the Company's trade becomes clear when one realises how large these sums of money, being spent so easily, were. Salim Khan's feints were probably only meant to spur the Company into paying. Matters worsened as Salim Khan's ravages continued. At an extraordinary meeting of the council on 14 May, it was concluded that the situation was serious, and that Salim Khan 'doth what he do by the Nawab's order, and that either the Nawab gives such order to induce us to comply with his demands or that he is determined to take Fort St David and Towns from the Company … and deceives us with fair words that he might the better effect his design'. Salim Khan's feints continued unabated. On 24 May 100 horsemen and 200 infantry invaded Company territory at Fort St David, and retreated on the approach of English soldiers, leaving behind some houses afire. Amirjeahn continued his bargaining at the Nawab's durbar, and sent to Madras in June a draft *parwanah* that was unsatisfactory. For a *parwanah* in such form as the English wished, the Nawab now demanded 2,000 pagodas more. If the English were to refuse the first *parwanah* or the new demand, then they would have to prepare for war. Madras replied on 24 June 1698 that Amirjeahn was to try to get the Nawab to issue a *parwanah* in the form that the council wanted. Should this be impossible, he was to obtain the one sanctioned.

On 7 July 1698, Thomas Pitt, a former Interloper, landed at Fort St George and presented his commission as governor. Over the next few days, Pitt was familiarised with the current situation, especially that relating to Fort St David. Pitt dispatched a brief but succinct letter to Amirjeahn on 9 July, telling him to 'make an end of the business' and get as good a *parwanah* as he could. Decisive action soon became essential. A letter came from the council at Fort St David, sent on 1 July, bearing the information that local landowners and feudatories had been ordered by the Nawab to gather with troops at Chidambaram (close to Cuddalore, and around 150 miles south of Madras), where Salim Khan was already encamped with his force. Reports held that the force was intended to total

3,000. When this letter was received and its contents perused in council at Madras on 20 July, it was at once decided to send a ship with 20 soldiers, 10,000 pagodas, and sufficient stores, to Fort St David. A few days later, 16 cannon, suitable for Fort St David, were dispatched. The English having demonstrated their intention to defend themselves, Salim Khan withdrew, with the result that on 9 September Amirjeahn arrived at Madras bearing the *parwanah*, which was received with due pomp at the Company's Garden-house at 4 in the afternoon the next day, by the governor and his council. Daud Khan, Zulfikar's deputy in the Carnatic, visited Madras on 28 April 1699, to view the sea. He spent 2 days at a garden-house on the outskirts, provided by the council for his stay. In 1700, Daud Khan became the Nawab of the Carnatic, with Zulfikar being promoted to the command (*subah*) of the Deccan. Daud Khan revisited Madras twice, in 1701 and 1706, and apparently greatly favoured European 'Cordial Waters'. He was responsible for the blockade of Madras during February–March 1702, which was raised following the payment of 25,000 rupees by the English. Daud Khan moved the capital of the Carnatic from Gingee to Arcot, deeming the former unhealthy. He continued as the Nawab of the Carnatic until he became embroiled in the wars of succession following the demise of Aurangzeb in March 1707. In 1708, Daud Khan moved to the Deccan, leaving Mohammad Sayyid Saadatullah Khan to deputise for him in the Carnatic. Aurangzeb's passing left a vacuum. He had lived a very long life, and had survived many of his children. Aurangzeb was succeeded by his son Bahadur Shah I, who was 63 at the time of accession. Bahadur Shah I died in 1712, and was followed by Jahandar Shah, who reigned for one year only. Farrukhsiyar overthrew him in early 1713.

Changes also took place at Gingee. In 1700, Aurangzeb appointed Sarup Singh, a minor Bundela ruler and ally, the *quiladar* or commander of Gingee, with a *jagir* of 1,200,000 rupees. Saadatullah Khan was in complete charge of the Carnatic from 1708, and seems to have been confirmed as Nawab by Farrukhsiyar in 1713. Since Saadatullah endorsed Sarup Singh as the commander of Gingee fort, matters seem to have been all right between the two, until the turmoil following Aurangzeb's death and succession. Sarup Singh appears to have stopped paying the annual tribute soon after the Emperor's demise. By 1714, when, under Farrukhsiyar's rule, disorder at the Mughal court abated for a while, it was discovered that Sarup Singh had disregarded repeated warnings by Saadatullah Khan about the payment of dues and the arrears stood at 7,000,000 rupees. Even as instructions under imperial seal were sent out to

Saadatullah for the recovery of this huge sum, Sarup Singh died in January 1714.

Relations between the English at Fort St David and Sarup Singh were uncomplicated until 1710. The English indirectly fomented the trouble that ensued. The persons, to whom Sarup Singh had rented out land adjoining the English property at Tevnapattam, paid him no money, and escaped to English-controlled territory, where their presence was not only tolerated but also encouraged, since these absconders were engaged in trade with Fort St David. Sarup Singh demanded that the Deputy Governor of Fort St David, Gabriel Roberts, return the defaulters into his jurisdiction. To this end, he wrote to both Fort St David and Fort St George. His representations not being addressed, Sarup Singh proceeded to retaliate by seizing two officers, Lieutenant Hugonin and Ensign Reay, on 11 June 1711, and imprisoning them at Gingee. These two officers, along with a Company official, Mr Haughton, had been out on a hunting expedition from Fort St David beyond the bounds of the English territory. Mr Haughton escaped, perhaps having been allowed to do so, and bore the news to Cuddalore and the Fort. A small expeditionary force was sent out but in vain. Fort St George was in a quandary. It did not want to engage in battle with Sarup Singh, as this would draw upon limited military resources, particularly manpower. On the other hand, the capture of English officers called for an adequate response. Reports had come in of the captives being chained and forced to stand for long hours in the sun without water.

All through the remaining months of 1710, the English made repeated attempts in vain to ransom their officers. By early 1711, it was clear that money and gifts would not placate the angry Sarup Singh. In February of that year, a half-hearted attempt was made under the orders of the Deputy Governor of Fort St David to seize by way of retaliation some of Sarup Singh's prominent men, who were reported to be in the vicinity. Three of these men were killed in the encounter, and the English were still more worried, this being reinforced by reports that Sarup Singh had threatened to kill English emissaries to his court. In the meantime, the English were acutely aware of their rapidly falling status among the local population. Sarup Singh was unwilling to arrive at an understanding. Rather, he appeared to be deliberately provoking the English to act. English troops were dispatched, through April to July 1711, to lay waste areas crucial to Sarup Singh's revenue. Villages and standing crops were destroyed but Sarup Singh did not yield. Matters had reached the point where the English stood to lose their prestige if they could not act decisively and successfully. The council at Fort St George appointed Robert Raworth, who had hitherto been second in council as Sea Customer at Madras, to Fort St David in command of a fleet of 5 ships, with instructions to assume the Deputy Governorship at once and retrieve matters. Raworth reached Fort St David on 10 August 1711. There seems to have been fear of the daily-expected arrival of a French fleet at Pondicherry, which, it was rumoured, would be rushed to the aid of Sarup Singh. The consultation on Thursday, 12 July 1711, at which weighty decisions such as the selection of Raworth were discussed, also reveals panic about the hourly-expected arrival of French ships. This sense of alarm is underlined by the dispatch of an additional ship, the *Sherbourne*, commanded by Captain Henry Cornwall, to Fort St David.

Raworth's arrival was not particularly useful. The following day an English force under the command of Captain John Roach, was attacked and routed by Sarup Singh's men. Ensign Robert Somerville turned and ran on seeing the enemy approach, and seeing him scarper, the troops bolted as well. Captain William Coventry, the company commander, fought bravely, sustaining many wounds before he fell. This defeat was a comment on the bad morale of the officers and their troops.

One Jacob Vanbashayson, a Dutchman employed as 'Sentinel' in Captain Roach's command, attacked without provocation Sergeant Thomas Parsons and two others at Fort St David on 10 September 1711. Parsons was killed, and the others seriously wounded. Vanbashayson's excuse was that he was drunk, and he later urged that he be executed by being shot rather than be hanged for his crime.

A few days later two officers, Lieutenant Viver and Ensign Williams, were found drunk when on guard at Cuddalore. They were arrested and sent down to Fort St George for further proceedings.

On 22 January 1712, Captain Hercules Courtney, who had previously displayed ample leadership and bravery in engaging the enemy, quarrelled with Ensign Joseph Padle in the latter's room, then drew his sword and attacked and injured him. Courtney was disarmed, arrested, and placed in confinement by the guard. While in confinement, Courtney conspired with Ensign Brooks and Sergeant Peterson to get his company to write a petition to the Deputy Governor that would praise Courtney and state that he had been framed. Courtney himself wrote the petition, giving it the appearance of a 'voluntary act of the Soldiers', and passed it to Brooks, who copied it and gave his transcript to Peterson to be copied for the soldiers to sign, while Brooks burnt the original written by Courtney. This entire sordid matter was revealed under oath on 24 January by Henry Coghran, one of Courtney's men, who accompanied Peterson to get the company's soldiers to sign the petition, and so was aware of the complete train of events. 49 soldiers, including Coghran, had signed the petition. Courtney, Brooks, and Peterson, were sent down to Fort St George to face charges. Brought before the council on 29 January, Courtney confessed to all that had passed except that he had struck Padle before the latter had drawn his sword, and asked to be judged mercifully in consideration of his previous service. Courtney was charged under the Articles of War, and told that no forgiveness was admissible because military discipline and civil authority had to be preserved. He was cashiered and ordered to prison pending further decision about what was to be done with him, since it was likely that if set free he would defect to the 'Enemy'. One wonders if the French are included among the 'Enemy'. Brooks was similarly dismissed the service, and imprisoned. Peterson, a Dane, was only punished with confinement since the Deputy Governor and council had commended his bravery and exemplary conduct during the recent conflict.

The English were plagued by desertions. On 24 March 1712, 7 soldiers deserted. This was followed by another major incident, when Ensign Kirkbred, Sergeant John Lewis, Corporals Elisha Waters and Thomas Eves, and two local 'Sentinels', deserted to the enemy with their arms, from their post close to Fort St David on 8 September 1712.

Such erosion in military quality and morale shook the council. Among the reasons for this was the lack of a surgeon at Fort St David. There seems to have been none at Fort St George either, Dr Bulkley having given up his medical position in favour of the better pay and prospects of sitting fifth in council as Paymaster. In reporting Captain Roach's skirmish, Raworth and his council seem to have written to Fort St George for a surgeon. Unable to meet this request, the Governor and council replied, 'We will send you a case of Instruments by the very first opportunity in the meantime you must get what you can from Pondicherry, Mr Raworth knows we never have a Surgeon's Mate here that is good for anything … apply to the French and Danes to get one for the meantime'. The same letter deplored the defeat, and reminded Raworth of what was expected of him: 'We agree with you that you must treat sword in hand and now that your enemy is flushed with Success, we hope they will give you an opportunity to quit Scores, a Well-Dressed Ambuscado if your spies could be trusted would draw them into your power and if you part with them before you have revenged your Countrymen we shall think it high time to beg a peace'.

Then there was dissatisfaction over pay. In 1710, the Company had reduced the pay of officers, non-coms, and private soldiers. Following this order, Lieutenants received £4, Ensigns £3, Sergeants 30s, Corporals 24s, and Privates 21s, a month. This was very poor pay for military service in a foreign country and difficult climate. Appointment to Captaincy in the Company's service brought no extra money, the appointment being honorary, and limited to the exercise of command only. Most of the officers named above, including John Roach, William Coventry, and Robert Somerville, had signed a letter of protest against this reduction in pay, and this was endorsed by the council and forwarded to England.

The third reason was the abundant consumption of alcohol, which led to frequent and inexcusable acts of drunkenness among a force engaged in war. The fourth reason was the absence of a sound military tradition, good officering, regular drill, and suitably motivated soldiers. Overshadowing all this was the council at Fort St George, which had no military members, only traders to whom military action was mainly repugnant and intended for no more than defensive deployment. The Company, very far removed from the scene of action, had a negligible appreciation of ground reality. For them, the only purpose of the colony was trade that generated profit.

Following the case of Lieutenant Viver and Ensign Williams, Edward Harrison, Governor and President at Fort St George, told the council that 'the Military in this Presidency are by slack discipline for the past two years become so intolerably sottish and disorderly that 'tis high time a reformation should be made for the security of our Settlements and the Honourable Company's Estate committed to our charge'. The height of insolence had been reached, he said, when Mr Farmer, during his term as Deputy Governor, dared not go out of the fort for fear that the guard would shoot him as he passed the gate. If the officers themselves were found dead drunk on duty 'upon their posts in a time of service when surrounded by the Enemy what can be expected but ruin and destruction to the affairs of those that employ them'.

Even as these ineffectual military measures were being taken, Harrison wrote to Zulfikar Khan on 11 October 1711, seeking his intervention. The letter is forthright, and makes several points clear: 'we are a small handful of people and our business is trade, and therefore all quarrels with the government is [*sic*] extremely prejudicial to us'. If only Zulfikar Khan would obtain the Emperor's order restraining Sarup Singh 'to let us live in quiet and mind our trade', it was all the English wanted. Zulfikar Khan was urged to help look after English interests, such that 'upon any trouble, or molestation we meet with in our business, we may have leave to make our petition and seek for redress from you'. Zulfikar Khan never replied to this petition. He was too deeply engrossed in intrigues at the Imperial court and in defending the ascendancy of Jahandar Shah to the Mughal throne. Farrukhsiyar defeated Jahandar Shah 18 months later, and Zulfikar Khan was executed by order of the new Emperor.

On 29 October, the council at Fort St George was appalled to receive news hitherto unknown, from Robert Raworth that his predecessor, Deputy Governor Farmer, and his council, had sanctioned the retaliatory destruction of over 50,000 pagodas worth of grain and 52 towns and villages belonging to Sarup Singh, without clearance from Madras. Noting with dismay 'the unaccountable folly and ill management of these gentlemen', the Madras council wondered that Farmer had the audacity to add that this devastation made Sarup Singh's claims 'carry too much justice', which would require the Company to spend considerable money as recompense.

The war had now dragged on for nearly 18 months. On 3 November, Raworth sent to the council at Madras a proposal presumably from Sarup Singh, asking to be paid 16,600 pagodas for the cessation of hostilities. In return for this amount, the English would get three villages and full possession of those towns, which lay half within the limits of the territory controlled by Fort St David. At a meeting on the morning of 6 November 1711, the council at Fort St George determined that the Company was spending 4,000 pagodas a month 'for maintaining the war besides several stores and provisions' sent from Madras. No rent had been received from the villages in English possession at Fort St David due to warfare. This was 'an intolerable charge and no hopes of any ease' were visible to the councillors. The glum merchants concluded that the war was costing their masters 48,000 pagodas per annum. The sense of disconsolation deepened with the awareness that if the war continued, supplies of grain would have to be arranged for the Fort and its dependent villages, since 'most of their Inhabitants out of fear would desert them'. Worse, merchants who had already made large contracts would be unable to supply goods for export, while imported broadcloth would remain unsold when ships with merchandise arrived from England. The gloomy traders decided unanimously 'to continue the war never so long we can never hope to be reimbursed one farthing of our vast expenses, it would indeed have been well if all these things had been duly considered before'. They must have shaken their heads in dismay and further agreed, as they did, that 'it is never too late to repent of wrong measures', and they must now 'make the best of a bad market'. Hence, they considered it necessary to inform Raworth that they would never pay 'so unreasonable a sum of money' especially since the rent accruing from the three promised villages and the towns did not seem to be adequate recompense. The Deputy Governor was urged to bargain the amount being demanded, provided Sarup Singh and 'the rogues about him' would agree not to dispute English possession of the three villages and the promised towns. This letter was never sent to

Raworth since another letter from him was received the same evening and the morose merchants again sat down to discuss it.

This second letter bore news that the chief inhabitants of the towns and villages affected by the war had decided to leave if the tenuous line of hope held out through payment and peace, should break. If communication with Gingee broke down and the English were subsequently forced to apply for peace, the compensatory amount demanded by Sarup Singh would be doubled. The villages promised in return would yield a return rent of 3,000 pagodas. The council at Fort St George replied to Raworth that they would pay for peace. The terms were arrived at, and Raworth and his council communicated them to Madras on 24 November. These were the same as before, and Raworth was empowered to go ahead with the treaty.

However, on 28 November 1711, Sarup Singh's men suddenly fired upon persons living within the territory controlled by Fort St David. This revived the conflict, and the same night Raworth led an attack on the enemy camp, killing, so he reported in his letter dated the following day, an 'abundance of men and horse'. Their earlier concern with the expenses of the war notwithstanding, the council quickly concluded that this sudden resurgence of hostility showed that their 'willingness to have made an end of this troublesome affair did undoubtedly encourage the enemy to believe that we were so weary of the war as to submit to any terms and they really began to think we were afraid of their numbers', a misconception that they hoped was dispelled by Raworth's quick move. The council in their reply dated 3 December unanimously praised Raworth's action.

The list of the Company's servants at Fort St David, compiled in December 1711 gives us the names of the following persons: Robert Raworth, Deputy Governor, Richard Farmer, Second in Council, John Berlue, Third, Richard Harrison, Fourth, Philip Baker, Fifth, Matthew Weld, Sixth, Henry Cottrell, Seventh, and Thomas Gray, Joseph Houghton, George Wathup, and John Smith, Writers, and, finally, John Jolly, Surgeon.

On 19 January 1712, Raworth once more took the field, and carried out a successful daytime raid on an enemy camp reportedly holding 300 men, in which over a hundred of the enemy were slain. It was in this engagement that Captain Courtney had distinguished himself. At the same time, Fort St David was running out of grain, and the unavailability of ships to supply it worried Madras. Fort St David was also in need of money, which was remedied by the dispatch of 10,000 pagodas. The next battle took place on 23 February, a much bigger fray at which the enemy was again trounced under the generalship of Robert Raworth. This was followed by minor raids by the enemy all through March 1712, which were similarly beaten off. The English seemed to be flummoxed about the means of ending this conflict. They had already incurred an enormous expense in money and manpower. The enemy had now changed tactic from open battle to daily skirmishing using vegetation to cover sallies. This was low-cost warfare and it was intended to wear out the English. On 6 March, Madras received a letter from Fort St David reporting that every tree and bush within half a mile of the area most susceptible to attacks had been cut down and burnt.

A ray of hope appeared a few days after this. On 10 March 1712, the council at Madras was informed that Raworth and his council had received a letter on 6 March from the Chevalier Hebert, the French Governor of Pondicherry, saying that he had 'procured a power' from Sarup Singh 'to act as Mediator in a Treaty of Accommodation'. If the English were satisfied with this, Hebert proposed a 'Cessation of arms' while he brokered peace. This was not a chance to be lost. One imagines the councillors discussing this matter eagerly. The intervention of a third party in this matter was much needed, they said, because their previous attempt at treating with Sarup Singh had been in vain. However, that this third party should be the representative of a competing nation was a matter, which needed some consideration. M Hebert had offered his services, and 'interposed to procure the first advances to be made by the enemy towards a peace'. This offer could not be refused, since Hebert had it in his power to help Sarup Singh, 'which point indeed ought to have been well weighed and considered' before engaging in this war. This was a very significant observation that presaged the Carnatic Wars, barely 20 years in the future. Although wary of the increasing influence of the French, Madras agreed to accept M Hebert's mediation. Being circumspect about the French, the council urged that a 'proper person' be appointed to reside in Pondicherry to provide 'good information' about the forthcoming treaty, and to prevent 'misunderstandings' with M Hebert by communicating English 'sentiments' directly to him. It seems that hostilities ceased with effect from 14 March.

Bernard Benyon, Storekeeper and sixth in council at Fort St George, was appointed the English representative at Pondicherry, along with Kittee Narayan, a trusted *dubash*, and 'a very proper person to dive into the intentions of the Enemy and give Mr Benyon what passes amongst [them] in their own language'. Benyon was given his orders on 22 March. These orders advised Benyon to be cautious that M Hebert was a man of precision, who loved a great deal of 'respect'. Hebert was to be told that if the English were forced to pay a huge sum as indemnity, the French should be aware that friendship with the Gingee government might backfire and necessitate assistance. Further, Hebert was to know that the war would not have required mediation had Sarup Singh's men not violated the previous overtures for peace. Madras was suspicious of M Hebert's intentions. Benyon was informed of these reservations. Hebert had inexplicably asked for 'a full power to decide this affair as it were by Arbitration' but stated that he would do nothing without seeking consent from Madras. The council would not bind Benyon to any sum of money but wanted him to write to them, sending letters by peons, to which the council undertook to answer always in 3 days. Benyon's orders also carried instructions for Kittee Narayan. Narayan was 'well skilled in the Customs of the Country' and had earlier been used successfully in similar matters. He was to 'insinuate himself in the acquaintance and conversation' of Sarup Singh's representatives. Aided by suitable 'small presents', Narayan was to ingratiate himself with these, and push through the acceptance of the argument that prolonging the war would be detrimental to the interests their master, who had been misinformed that the English were weak. Narayan had 'a large field to employ his talent on this Subject', and it was hoped that his persuasiveness would bring success.

In the meantime, news was received of the death, in February 1712, of Bahadur Shah, Aurangzeb's son. The country was in a state of unrest. Madras noted that feudatory rulers who had long borne the Mughal yoke, were restive, and several important persons at Arcot and 'other neighbouring places inland' had sent in considerable sums of money to be stored securely 'against expected troubles' at Madras. Benyon had sent in information that peace would not be bought at a price lower than that previously sought. The council took stock of the situation very glumly on 7 April. The cost of the war had escalated, and even though an answer was expected from Zulfikar Khan, none was forthcoming. The death of the Emperor had worsened matters. Petty rulers were now at liberty to plunder at will. The shortage of grain at Fort St David continued because the enemy would allow no supplies by land. Trading contracts for supply of merchandise to and from Fort St David was similarly paralysed. The war had to be ended but no one knew at what price. The outlook was very grim.

Worse news followed on 17 April, when the governor of Madras, Edward Harrison, informed the council that Sarup Singh's representatives had left Pondicherry 'in disgust'. No treaty seemed to be on offer, and Benyon had asked for permission to return while M Hebert had written to Sarup Singh's *bakshi* or paymaster to know where matters finally stood.

This was followed by another letter on 19 April which mentioned how Sarup Singh's *bakshi*, probably Mahabat Khan, who held command of the fort at Valudavur, flew into a violent rage upon receiving Hebert's letter, and accused the French of having duped him. Benyon's personal assessment was that peace could not be bought for less than 50,000 pagodas. Resigned to letting the matter resolve itself as it would, the council sanctioned Benyon's return from Pondicherry. On 29 April, news was received by letter from M Hebert that he had arrived at a treaty with Sarup Singh. The articles included in this treaty were very different from those communicated by Benyon to Hebert. Consequently, Hebert was told that the amount demanded as indemnity, 12,000 pagodas, was agreeable but the articles of the treaty would have to be rewritten. Benyon sent welcome intelligence on 9 May from Pondicherry that the treaty was imminent, needing only the ratification by Gingee. Ten days later, the two officers who had been taken prisoner the year before, had been brought to Valudavur by the *bakshi* along with the ratified treaty, since M Hebert had expressed his irritation at the demand for payment prior to the handing over of the prisoners and the ratification of the treaty. Nonetheless, Lieutenant James Hugonin, who was more than 60 years of age, and Ensign Reay, as well as the treaty, signed by Sarup Singh, reached Pondicherry on 23 May 1712, thereby bringing down the curtains on the war with Gingee.

Robert Raworth had contributed greatly to the Company's successful conclusion of the war. However, he soon became involved in a rather sordid case in which he was implicated for malfeasance. His letter of 22 August 1712, to the governor and council at Madras, explains his side of the matter. Raworth was appointed Warehouse-keeper, and second in council on 1 December 1709. By August 1710, he was at Fort St David. In the meantime, he had been compelled to be dependent on one Tonnapa, the Warehouse Conicoply or registrar. On the eve of his departure for Fort St David, Tonnapa informed him that a 'parcel' of rupees and silver was 'wanting to balance'. Raworth, who had handed over full charge of the Warehouse to William Martin, authorised his friend Francis Cooke to look after this matter on his behalf and if needed make up the deficit pending reimbursement. While hostilities with Sarup Singh were on, the matter of the unbalanced account seems to have remained as it was, and after the war was over, Raworth was informed that he was indebted to the Company for over 130,000 rupees and 687 pounds of silver. Raworth accused Tonnapa of misappropriation of funds, and sought to repay the greater part of this sum, some time to collect the rest, and the assistance of the council for seizing Tonnapa's estate by way of reparation. At its next meeting, on 25 August, the council drew upon a precedent case, that of one Vicessimus Griffith, where the Company had stated that its covenanted servants were answerable for their conicoplies. This notwithstanding, the council extended its assistance to Raworth, and the governor, Edward Harrison, had it noted that Tonnapa and his accomplices were in confinement. Raworth must have been very wealthy, and the source of this wealth can only have been private trade since his salary, even if saved entirely, would not have added up to a fraction of the sum he readily agreed to pay up. The council further decided that given Raworth's position in the Company's hierarchy, and his contribution to the late war, they found no reason to proceed 'to the utmost severity' with him. There was another reason for this. Since Raworth's temporary departure from Fort St David for Madras, the European soldiers had committed two barbarous murders of locals, and the military clearly was in 'utmost disorder and confusion, for want of a severe hand and strict discipline'. Therefore, Raworth was at once ordered back to Fort St David.

In the meantime William Martin had written to the council the same day, stating that although he had shared charge of the Warehouse with Raworth, which was the usual practice so that if one Warehouse-keeper should fall ill, business would not stop, he would not pay part of the amount outstanding since he had been only nominally in charge, because Raworth had kept the keys to himself. Not only that, alleged Martin, 'he singly received all monies and delivered out everything'. Martin held that he was 'forcibly kept in the dark', and urged the council to clear him of the debt. This petition was dismissed at the next meeting and Martin ordered to pay 3,331 pagodas as his part of the debt. Martin wrote many times thereafter, and his letters were discussed, until the council directed him to pay the amount as security, and told him that they would not entertain any more papers from him on this subject. Martin continued to protest and the matter came to a head on 22 December when the council permitted him to resign the service and return to England to argue the case at the Company's offices provided he left behind enough money as surety in case the Company decided against him.

On 2 September, the council noted that Raworth had paid in cash 20,000 pagodas, and would pay the amount remaining in instalments through his attorneys. Raworth also mentioned his discovery of the means by which Tonnapa had removed 40,000 rupees in 1710. Consequently, the Mint workers were called in and questioned in the presence of Tonnapa. They listed the persons to whom Tonnapa delivered rupees under the pretended orders of the Warehouse-keeper, Raworth. Some of these persons to whom the money was given acknowledged it and put it to repayments of money owed them by Tonnapa. When asked, Tonnapa replied that he had acted under Raworth's orders. The council concluded that Tonnapa had indeed removed without permission 40,000 rupees between 29 March and 16 June 1710 from the Warehouse for his own use. Realising further that Tonnapa had been engaged in such defalcation since his employment at the Warehouse in 1706, the council ordered the seizure of all his property.

Raworth, at Fort St David, had found the Fort-house and the Garden-house in disrepair. He therefore spent 500 pagodas in rebuilding the latter, for which the council censured him on 1 December 1712, for not having sought their prior permission. In view of his 'frugal management', however, this cost was defrayed from the Company's account. These minor irritations alongside the larger and murkier affair of Tonnapa and the missing money, must have affected Robert Raworth considerably. However, the conduct of the Company's affairs on the Coromandel Coast seemed to be in proper shape and moving along as efficiently as possible, until a sudden and unexpected hiccup occurred.

On 5 October 1713, the governor announced to the council that the Deputy Governor at Fort St David had 'neglected and despised' the orders and principles of the Company in the governance of its garrisons and factories. A long list of accusations followed this statement, which astounds us but might not have been surprising to those immediately concerned. Raworth had 'assumed to himself a liberty of acting as if he was independent' of Madras. He had announced in a General Letter that the proceedings in council at Fort St George were prejudicial to the Company's interests. This was insubordination, and the governor and council decided to draw up charges against him in order to discourage others from similarly disputing and disobeying their orders. Ten articles were drawn up against Raworth, and the council discovered a precedent from 1708, authorising the governor and council to suspend any subordinate person for a just reason. Raworth's suspension was passed unanimously and Henry Davenport appointed provisional Deputy Governor and dispatched with a guard of 2 officers and 12 soldiers to take over Fort David. Raworth was to be recalled and formally presented with the charges against him. These included his allowing fictitious paymasters to pass fabricated accounts at irregular intervals, promoting officers on his own to the garrison, raising the salary of several persons, especially the table-money for the council, and treating the Company's Merchants shabbily. Raworth had disregarded orders from Madras, and rented out the Company's land without permission.

A formal letter was written to Raworth, informing him of these decisions. Davenport and his escort left Madras on the evening of 5 October 1713, for Fort St David. Davenport proceeded to the bounds of Fort St David, whence he sent a brief note on 9 October to Raworth along with the council's letter. Raworth soon replied that he would not allow Davenport 'any authority to rule' there by whatever commission he could receive from Madras, even though he was welcome to Fort St David as a private person and friend. Raworth did not recognise the authority of Madras to appoint Davenport his successor. He further stated that he could demonstrate that he had never disregarded any 'legal and practicable' order sent him. As Davenport progressed to Tevnapattam, he and his party could see warlike preparations afoot along the outworks. The Tevnapattam Gate of the fort was shut and Davenport disallowed entry. The officer in charge of the gate informed Davenport that he had been ordered not to let the latter in. Similarly, Ensign Hobbs, with a hundred men, guarded the garden. He too refused Davenport entry, telling him that if necessary he would fire upon the party from Madras. The council of Fort St David is reported as having gone to meet Davenport, with the exception of Richard Harrison. Perceiving the belligerence of the garrison, which amounted to 500 men, Davenport retired to Ninapas Choultry, 5 miles away, where he camped along with such gentlemen of the council from Fort St David as were willing to accompany him. Raworth's orders to the garrison commander, Lieutenant Patrick Johnston, were precise. Johnston was to escort any gentleman from Fort St George to the guardroom, showing him 'no more respect than ... to a private Merchant'. Johnston was particularly ordered not to receive any papers to be read from this person, or to allow him any occasion to speak to the troops. Should such a possibility present itself, Johnston was to order the troops to arms at once. In the meantime, two officers from the garrison, Ensigns Padle and Handlon had gone over to Davenport and reported that the troops were in a state of confusion as to whose orders they ought to obey especially as they had not been paid for 2 months. Raworth was reported as having been declaring through the previous year that he would avenge himself on Madras. In view of these developments, particularly the shakiness of the garrison, Davenport was ordered to stay put at Ninapas Choultry.

An additional force of 60 soldiers was sent off by sea via Pondicherry to Davenport's assistance on 13 October. A letter was conveyed to Pondicherry telling the French that this could happen to any European power, and Raworth's rebellion had set an especially bad example. The English therefore sought French assistance in both granting passage to troops from Madras and quelling Raworth. Davenport was given the power to issue pardons to such members of the garrison as would defect from Fort St David during the next 7 days. This order was bolstered by additional permission to Davenport to occupy such posts as were convenient if he deemed himself strong enough in numbers, to prevent opportunistic parties from Gingee or rebels from Fort St David from occupying them. By 15 October, a significant number of soldiers seem to have defected from Fort St David requiring Madras to tell Davenport not to come to blows but to peaceably draw the garrison out by issuing pardons and promising full payment of arrears. William Warre and the Revd George Lewis were ordered to go and speak to Raworth, warning him of his rashness. They left for Fort St David on the evening of 16 October 1713. Meanwhile the French allowed the English troops passage through Pondicherry and offered assistance.

Davenport, deeming his force strong enough, sallied out on 17 October, and entered the bounds of Fort St David unopposed. The Garden-house was still guarded by Ensign Hobbs, now with 50 men. Hobbs and his men absolutely refused to surrender, and Davenport would not or could not force them. While they were talking, a 24-pounder cannon was fired from the fort, the shot missing Davenport by 20 yards. Davenport then proceeded to occupy Cuddalore unimpeded. Madras ordered Davenport to make Cuddalore his headquarters while secret information about Raworth's intentions seem to have been received, which made the governor and council feel that he was 'determined to ruin all rather than surrender'. This was soon demonstrated. On 18 October, the rebels attacked with gunfire and grenades, a party of besieging soldiers. Three rounds of cannon fire supported the attackers. Fatalities occurred on both sides, and the attackers, who had come on horses, fled, leaving behind 5 mounts. Those of the besiegers, who were in occupation of Condapah Choultry, considered it wise to retire to Cuddalore for the night. Strangely, Raworth wrote to Madras about this action the same day, stating that his men had only gone to call upon some friends. Nonetheless, as in the case of Gingee, matters here too seemed to be getting out of hand. Nearly a month had passed, and the problem remained unresolved. Fort St David seemed jinxed. Again not only was trade affected, the prestige of the British was also plummeting once more. There was always the added danger of local powers, possibly with the assent and aid of competing European companies, taking this chance to weaken the English.

Warre and Lewis met Raworth on 20 October. He received them cordially, and heard them out. He seemed to be in 'very good temper', and asked for some time to consider. He would answer them in the evening as to his decision. Warre and Lewis went to Davenport at Cuddalore, and returned to the fort at 5 o'clock. Raworth tersely told them that he would surrender if the governor went in person to him, and provided those of his men who had stayed true were given higher recognition than those who had deserted. Warre and Lewis requested time to consult Madras, and Raworth agreed to a cessation of hostilities until they had a reply. Madras was uneasy. The governor would have to visit the Nawab, who was expected in San Thome in January. It was equally impossible for the council to consent to the other provision, since that would mean they were in the wrong, and all would follow Raworth's 'wicked and pernicious example' thereafter. One may visualise the flustered merchants groping about for a way out of this impasse. They decided to write to Warre and Lewis and tell them to offer Raworth everything that was in Madras's power to grant, provided he surrendered quietly and 'without any further trouble or mischief'. Warre was commissioned to receive the fort from Raworth 'to make all easy'. One wonders if one is to believe Davenport's report that Raworth's men were wreaking havoc in Tevnapattam, breaking open houses and godowns, and whipping and punishing ordinary people. Davenport further passed on the information that Raworth had invested over 9,000 pagodas in merchandise on board two ships, which were supposed to be in Bengal and about to return, since it was the time of year for ships from Bengal to arrive. Madras immediately issued letters to Bengal for the seizure of Raworth's goods. On 24 October, Warre and Lewis had been to see Raworth again, and he had repeated that he would surrender the fort only to the governor. Their letter was read in council on 28 October, along with a pessimistic one from Davenport, which said that Raworth would not surrender even to the governor, and the only way was to starve him out. Davenport was due to sail to Europe and he urged permission to withdraw. The weariness and defeatism of the council at Madras is palpable in their reply, in which they requested Davenport to stay 'some small time more', in hope that some means of accommodation would be found.

Nothing emerged over the next few days, and November arrived with discouraging news. On 1 November 1713, the council was informed that Raworth's people were almost starved, and that they were pulling down houses in Tevnapattam for firewood, and this was destroying the town. There had been no hostilities other than one occasion when at 11 at night on 24 October a cannonball had been fired at Cuddalore from the fort. Warre and Lewis were still convinced that the governor's presence would elicit Raworth's surrender. Left no choice, Edward Harrison agreed to go to Fort St David if it would put an end to present troubles before more mischief was done. Warre was ordered to stay back, while the Revd Lewis was permitted to return. Preparations were afoot for the governor's journey to Fort St David, and it was decided that Raworth, when apprehended would have to be imprisoned because of the seriousness of some of the imprecations he had cast on the governor and some others. On the evening of 4 November 1713, Edward Harrison, attended by several Englishmen, set out along the overland route to Fort St David. It was evident that the French were helping Raworth survive, since they sent in provisions, the want of which would otherwise have starved Raworth into submission. A meeting of the council on 6 November noted that hostilities were continuing, 6 shot having been fired on Cuddalore from the Fort. Edward Harrison reached Chemundulum Choultry on 8 November and at once sent a note to Raworth through Warre. No reply was received, and this confirmed the belief that Raworth was not going to surrender the fort. In fact, he had consolidated his defences by vacating the garden and gathering his remaining troops within the walls. Raworth sent the keys of the garden to the besiegers and they occupied it. The governor's presence was making its effect felt in terms of morale and general direction. The hitherto steadfast Ensign Hobbs deserted on 10 November, having been promised a pardon and his rank, setting an example that was followed, and more deserters trickled in. This must have angered Raworth, for the ceasefire agreement nothwithstanding, some of governor's retinue while out riding in the evening were fired on from the fort. Harrison decided to take the Tevnapattam Gate and the round battery on an outwork, which covered the town and garden, by force. Accordingly, 3 raiding parties were told off and briefed on their missions the same night. The attack commenced at 9 pm, and the detachment given the job of capturing the Tevnapattam Gate achieved its objective with no losses, capturing all of the guards except the sergeant, who escaped. The other task force failed in its objective. The officers leading it first called out to the garrison asking them in the governor's name to surrender, and offered pardon on his behalf. The rebels answered they would neither give nor take quarter, and began firing on the attackers. The assault was attempted twice but beaten off each time with loss to the attackers, which made them retreat. The third unit lay concealed near the gates of the fort, waiting for Lieutenant Johnston to come out with reserves to the assistance of his troops. This did not happen, and so the third unit withdrew before morning, having managed to bring away a gun from the gates and dismounting the other, so that it would be out of use for a while. The next morning the governor commanded Raworth and Johnston to assemble with 50 men in the garden. This elicited neither compliance nor reply.

Matters were looking up. Lieutenant Johnston, who had remained loyal to Raworth for such a long time, deserted on the evening of 17 November 1713. This was a serious setback for Raworth, who withdrew his remaining troops into the fort, quitting the round battery since he no longer had the forces to defend it. The governor's soldiers, who also took a post in Tevnapattam, close to the gate of the fort, so that none could enter unless permitted, immediately occupied the battery position. Looking through the accounts of Fort St David since 1712, the governor estimated that Raworth had with him 17,000 pagodas, which it was felt was the reason for his recalcitrance. Since the besiegers were now in strategic dominance, Raworth's provisions were very low. Deserters came in daily. The governor rode into Tevnapattam at night on 19 February to visit the troops there. His progress must have been sighted from the fort for his party came under heavy fire. The besiegers retaliated by firing from the round battery, and the shot was reported as having gone through Raworth's rooms.

The remaining members of the garrison were now reportedly nearly starving but Raworth showed no inclination to end the rebellion. Two and a half months had been spent and much money invested in reducing Fort St David and although the governor's generalship was effective, it seemed predictable. Davenport had been right. The only way to get Raworth was to starve him out; if the process had begun earlier, it might have been quicker. By the end of the month, another padre, the Revd Stevenson, who had gone out with Harrison, was meeting Raworth to negotiate peace. On 1 December, the Madras council discussed two letters, one from the governor and the other from Warre, wherein it was hinted that the accommodation finally arrived at, would allow Raworth asylum in Pondicherry. Once there, he would settle his accounts in 15 days, for which the French governor, Du Livier, stood surety. Henry Davenport, having spent several weeks in the neighbourhood of Fort St David, left for Madras to prepare for his journey to Europe.

The following day Edward Harrison entered Fort St David, where he was received by Robert Raworth 'in such manner as none but [he] could be capable of seeming no ways concerned for the many ill actions he has committed' and his garrison of 130 men, of whom 80 were European. Inconsistent with reports of a starving garrison, the governor discovered this 'rebellious crew' to be 'as stout men as any in the Company's service'. Harrison returned to Madras on 7 December, and placed his records of consultations at Fort St David before his own council for consideration. Raworth was no longer under English jurisdiction but with the French at Pondicherry. The French governor, Du Livier, had allowed

Raworth to bring along with him his chief *dubash* and others. On 15 December, Raworth, writing in from Pondicherry presented his accounts as per his calculations, from the records. He wrote that he was waiting for the first available ship to Europe in order to be able to present his side of the case to the Company. Harrison seems to have expected that Du Livier would deliver Raworth to Madras. Whatever the reason behind this hope, it was dashed by a letter from the French governor which stated that Raworth had publicly sought the protection from the King of France, and it was impossible to violate this request. Raworth knew that he would be incarcerated as soon as he was in English territory. Father Thomas of the Capuchins, who appears to have been another intermediary, appointed to influence the French governor and council at Pondicherry in this messy affair, reported that Raworth had been informed that Harrison and his council intended his assassination as soon as he was in their clutches. Raworth had reportedly seen a letter to this effect sent to a person at Fort St David from a councillor at Madras. Harrison and his colleagues swore that they had never entertained any such intention, forgetting their previous resolution of 2 November, of the necessity of imprisoning Raworth supposedly for his own good. Harrison protested that Raworth had often threatened him with similar consequences, for which proof was likewise available. Further, Raworth's settlement of accounts was deemed incorrect by Madras. The council sent Raworth a reply through Father Thomas, and his answer was presented at a meeting on 24 December 1713. This reply was 'full of notorious falsities and calumny, without any manner of ground or proof, and of a piece with all the rest of his behaviour' and the council realised that 'he will suffer or do anything rather than come to a fair account of what he has had under his charge'. The Pondicherry council stated that Du Livier had done as he had promised, in allowing Raworth asylum in Pondicherry in order to allow him to settle his accounts. Du Livier had agreed to urge him to submit to further orders from Madras, which he had also done. The English were miffed that this was not the sense in which they had agreed to Du Livier's mediation. The sense in which the English meant it must have been for Du Livier to seize Raworth and have him delivered as prisoner to Fort St George.

The new Deputy Governor and council sent representatives to Pondicherry with their accounts for Raworth's consideration on 4 January 1714. Raworth refused to receive their accounts. The council determined to pursue their case against Raworth. Letters written to Raworth and his *dubash* by Serapa, an inhabitant of Madras, were discovered in the *dubash's* house, which he had abandoned. These letters reportedly contained information that reflected badly on the members of the council. They also suggested that Tonnapa had concealed the money he had embezzled, in such a way that none other than himself would ever recover it. The council summoned Serapa and questioned him. His replies were deemed impudent, even when confronted with the so-called evidence of his letters, contending that they had been written without his knowledge. The council concluded that Serapa had contributed substantially to Raworth's rebellion through the latter's *dubash*, who had been Serapa's slave, and ordered Serapa into close confinement. Benyon and Warre, who had acted as Raworth's attorneys at Madras, had with them over 8,000 pagodas belonging to him. The council, acting for the Company, ordered them to pay this sum to the Company's account as part of Raworth's debt due. This debt was calculated to be a huge amount, 55,097 pagodas, the details of which were presented on 28 January 1714 to the governor and council by those appointed to audit the account. In March, Raworth's godown was searched and its contents audited as well. Little else other than 2 boxes of books was found there. These boxes were seized and delivered to the council's secretary. All else discovered there, including empty tar barrels and coils of rope, was auctioned, and the proceeds, amounting to 38 pagodas, paid into the Company's account. Witnesses were examined through the following months and in July, some of the 'Ring leaders in the late notorious Riot and Mutiny' were sent to England to be dealt with there.

Raworth left for Europe on board a French ship, and died in Paris while the Company was preparing to prosecute him in England. Henry Davenport had been permitted to resign the service and leave for England at the end of 20 years' service. He was allowed passage with his family and effects on the East Indiaman *Marlborough*, which sailed from Madras on 21 January 1714. Harrison was awarded a sword set with jewels by a grateful Company. Some of the military were rewarded with money and higher ranks. Ensign Peter Eckman, for instance, was moved to Fort St George the following year, and promoted to Lieutenant in 1723. He is noteworthy because he was the officer in command of the garrison at Madras when the French took it in 1746. Captain John Roach was awarded 500 pagodas for his service, and 3 years later, he was promoted Major, presented with a gold medal bearing the Company's arms, and appointed to the command of all the Company's forces on the Coromandel Coast and in Sumatra.

This curious, murky, and sad, series of events reads like a play, of which Raworth is the tragic protagonist. His deeply enigmatic persona raises unanswerable queries. He might have been the victim of circumstances, having been cheated by Tonnapa, just as he could have been Tonnapa's collaborator. Similarly, Raworth's actions at Fort St David during the war with Sarup Singh are not consistent with his subsequent rebellion. His reasons for seeking French protection could well have been either the wild imaginings of a diseased mind, or deep knowledge of deeper conspiracies involving the governor and his council. For the lay reader of records, coming across Edward Harrison's sudden announcement of Raworth's intractability in October 1713, is singularly surprising. One is just as amazed by Raworth's reaction to Davenport's arrival to take over governance. Unlike Keigwin's rebellion, there seem to have been no obvious causes for this uprising. Edward Harrison cannot be compared to Sir John Child. Another striking aspect of this issue is the enormous sum of money involved. One wonders how Tonnapa could have removed rupees from the Warehouse and this remain unaccounted for, no intelligence having been received about it by the council, despite the local minters having known it. Nonetheless, this was the third major rebellion in an English settlement in India, the first being Sir Edward's and the second, Keigwin's.

CHAPTER FIVE

THE CASE OF FRANCIS HASTINGS

If we were to turn our attention to matters at Fort St George, we would be amazed at how rapidly governance had deteriorated there since 1710. The Company noted with displeasure on 3 January 1710 that 'Files of Musketeers' had been 'Sent for to Keep the Peace at dinner time' at the Company's table where all factors and writers were expected to have their meals. 'For how can it be expected', the Company asked, 'that a due obedience should be paid to Government among all the People when it is affronted by such Youngsters?' This warning did not suffice, for the Company noted again 2 years later that 'Several Disorders' had been reported at the 'General Table', to prevent which 'persons in the service that are of a Superior Standing and might awe the young ones into better behaviour', were ordered to be present at mealtime. By 1717, provisions for the General Table had achieved gargantuan proportions, with over 5,000 pagodas being spent on European and Indian liquor. Feeding mainly on flesh, and consuming vast quantities of alcohol, the traders seem to have disregarded the dietary demands of the local climate, and gorged themselves to death. Joseph Collet had replaced Edward Harrison as governor in January 1717, and Collet declared in October 1719 his decision to discontinue due to his failing health. The Company had ruled the previous year that the Deputy Governor of Fort St David was to automatically succeed to the Governorship at Fort St George in case the incumbent there died or was otherwise absent. In accordance with this directive, Francis Hastings, who was in charge of Fort St David, took over from Collet when the latter sailed for England on 18 January 1720. Francis Hastings had 20 years' seniority in the Company's service. Nonetheless, he was soon plunged into sordid disagreements.

The first incident occurred on 19 February 1720. That night ox-drawn carts carrying bricks and straw belonging to the Company, were stopped at the *metto*, or toll station, near Egmore by the local ruler's *havildar* or military officer in charge of the garrison there, and the drivers beaten and imprisoned, most likely because they refused to be subjected to extortion. When Hastings was informed of this the following morning, he sent his chief *dubash* and some others to urge the release of the drivers and their goods, oxen, and carts, which, as the Company's property, were exempt from customs. To the *dubash's* 'mild persuasive arguments' the *havildar* returned 'a very saucy one', adding that he had no intention of allowing the Company's goods and people to pass. The *dubash's* arguments proved futile and he returned with his companions to Fort St George, and reported to the governor. Incensed, Hastings dispatched his Chief Peon with a party, to first try and persuade the *havildar*, and then, in case of further resistance, to force compliance. The Chief Peon was obviously meant to pursue the matter more harshly than the Chief *Dubash* had. The Chief Peon discovered that the *havildar* had in the meantime gathered a force of 50 men, who adopted 'a fighting posture' and accosted the former. Unfazed, the Chief Peon went up to the *havildar* to deliver the message from the governor. The *havildar* drew his scimitar and struck at the Chief Peon, who warded off the blow and, drawing his pistol, shot his assailant dead. Then the Chief Peon and his followers attacked the *havildar's* party and killed two of them, upon which the rest fled. The driver, oxen, carts, and goods, were recovered, and the governor praised the Chief Peon on his promptitude, which kept the matter from going out of control. At the same time, Hastings ordered the guards at the bounds of Madras to be alerted to surprise attacks. He also reported to the council that he had sent off an account of the matter to the English *vakil* at the Nawab's court in Arcot. He said this would ensure that the details of the matter were not misrepresented to the Nawab. Somehow Hastings' words in praising the Chief Peon remind one of similar language that would often be employed during and after 1857: 'if he had sat tamely down after this first insult, we should not have failed of receiving many more of a higher degree; and that our showing our resentment upon this occasion will have a good influence on all Metto people'. The *havildar* was undoubtedly in the wrong, and on 14 March 1720, the governor reported to the council that the Nawab had written to him in very friendly terms on the affair. The garrison of Madras was therefore asked to stand down from the state of high alert.

This matter was soon followed by a succession of events that became known as 'the Revolt of the Chetties'. Hastings' second in council was Nathaniel Elwick. Elwick was exceptional for the times in that he had been to the Merchant Taylor's School, and his older brothers, Thomas and John, were Directors of the Company. He therefore received the plum posting, in 1714, of being the Company's supercargo on a voyage to China, and was sent to Madras in 1719, in the senior position of third in council, which could not have endeared him to Hastings.

There were some disagreements between the two through February about the number of bales to be ordered under new contracts from England, Elwick contending that this was needless, as there were enough bales of broadcloth under the old contract to require only 2500 bales upon the new list. Hastings took this opposition personally and Elwick and those councillors who supported him claimed that their objections derived from their sincerity in serving the Company and not from any desire for opposition and contradiction. This does not seem to have conciliated Hastings, and the matter of the Chetties came up in council on 25 April 1720. A galliot had arrived some days ago from Goa, with a Portuguese man named Pereira, 'commonly called the one-eyed doctor', aboard it as supercargo. Hastings told the council that Pereira had subsequently been identified as an ambassador from the Romish Viceroy of Goa to the Chetties of Madras. The pilot of the vessel also had with him several presents, meant for prominent Chetties at Madras. This intelligence had allegedly been provided by a third Portuguese, who being well-disposed towards the English and suspicious of his fellow countrymen, realised that Pereira, who reportedly carried a letter from the Viceroy at Goa to the Chetties, was bent on conspiring against the English. Thus, Pereira publicly stood recorded as 'a Villain'. Hastings, on being informed of the matter by one of his councillors, Richard Horden, dispatched Lieutenant Fullerton and some men to arrest Pereira from his house in the Black Town. Pereira escaped while this detachment searched for his residence. However, they found his wife at home and she handed over to them several papers of Pereira's. In order to ensure that no evidence should be lost, the squad took possession of Pereira's escritoire. Several singularly incriminating documents had apparently been discovered in the escritoire, including 'authentic' *firmans* issued by the Nawab of Golconda in favour of the government of San Thome. It was suspected that Pereira's letters to the Chetties urged them to desert Madras and migrate to San Thome, which would in the meantime have become a Portuguese possession by dint of those *firmans*. The heads of the Chetties, being members of the Left-hand caste, and Company Merchants, were summoned and interrogated. They denied the allegations but their denials were rejected, and they were asked to provide security for their continued allegiance. The council's secretary was ordered to put up a notice at the sea gate saying that anyone concerned with this conspiracy would be pardoned and rewarded for turning informer.

Thereafter Hastings proposed the election of Joshua Draper to the council, which was objected to by Elwick and some others because of a standing Company order, which stated that 7 councillors constituted the necessary quorum, and the appointment of junior factors to the council was to be discouraged. The Company felt that this would make these less experienced persons think 'they had a Privilege to be Exempt from any Control and to leave our business to others under them, without taking the same pains about it as they used to be at before such promotion'. It was 'not good for Young men to come too nigh the Temptation, nor to be advanced too soon, lest their heads turned giddy, as seemed to be the case of Mr Raworth'. Hastings was compelled to agree to this and Joshua Draper continued as Secretary, 'a fatiguing Employment', which allowed him to attend the council's meetings but not as a councillor with a vote. Draper followed up this development by writing a long application to the council, pleading his case. His argument was that the Company's notification was being treated as an order, which it was not, and that he had been placed on the board by assent of the majority, with only 3 members, viz, Elwick, Richard Benyon, and John Emmerson, dissenting. Draper's lengthy letter is written with precision typical of a legal document. In voting for his election, the majority showed that they did not consider him 'a person desirous of being in Council for the sake of leaving [his] business to others ... or desirous of Power and Control, or that [he] was of Giddy unsettled Temper'. Of the three 'articles' set in the Company's notification, 'An Idle Lazy Disposition', 'An Imperious Mind', and 'The Want of Sense and Solidity', none described his character, Draper said. Draper then moved on to a consideration of whether the paragraph quoted by the dissenters had the quality of an order. An order, he said, was 'a Command expressed in a peremptory form of words', and it generally had a penalty accompanying it for the correction of disobedience. The notification was therefore in his view no more than an advice or opinion, and not binding upon the council.

Hastings brought off a coup when John Turton, the chief at Sumatra, died on 25 April 1720, and he offered the post to John Emmerson, one of the dissenters to Draper's election. Emmerson declined on grounds of health, and Hastings accepted Draper's hasty offer to go there as Deputy Governor *pro tempore*. This gave Draper the chance he needed to prove himself to the Company, for if he could ensure good trade and governance, they would have no objection to his promotion as councillor.

Meanwhile the 'revolt' of the Chetties had progressed no further. At a consultation on 30 May 1720, Hastings took up the issue again, citing a resolution by the council 3 years ago, whereby the heads of all castes were required to sign an undertaking that sanctioned the confiscation of their property in the event of desertion. The heads of the Chetties were called in and asked to sign the undertaking 'to clear up all suspicion of their intention to desert'. They refused. Enraged, Hastings resolved the dismissal of the two Chetties who were Company's Merchants. To this end, he drew up a list of allegations. The Chetties were in league with the Portuguese and had planned to desert to San Thome. They were thus to be regarded as enemies of the Company, and stood guilty of treachery and subversion. Their dismissal was sanctioned by the canon that 'they who conspire to subvert and betray a government are no longer to be trusted in places of Importance to the Government but are to be suspected as Traitors to it and treated accordingly'. Elwick was sensible of Hastings' undue haste in rushing to conclusions. He therefore offered to stand security for the two merchants to the amount of 10,000 pagodas each. Hastings at once turned upon him and inquired if he was willing to sign the same declaration that had been offered to the Chetties, under the same provision that his property would be confiscated if they should desert. Elwick must have felt very humiliated at being addressed in this manner by Hastings. The council meeting was probably overcharged with tension. Some of the other councillors sought to ease matters by telling Hastings that according to English law Elwick was only offering bail for the two merchants. Per English law, bail was not allowed to persons accused of treason. Nonetheless, the proposal to suspend them was voted upon with the result that Hastings, Draper, Horden, and Fowke, upheld the suspension while Elwick, Emmerson, Benyon, and Cooke disagreed because there was insufficient evidence for accusing them of treason and subversion of the government. One is therefore surprised to find that the view of the *majority* (due to Hastings' casting vote) was considered, and orders of suspension issued.

Hastings sought to consolidate his hold on the council by proposing on 7 June the appointment of Thomas Wright to the council in place of Joshua Draper, who was to go to as Deputy Governor to Sumatra. Elwick averred to this on 13 June, stating that Wright's promotion had resulted in the supersession of several meritorious factors senior to Wright. He again opposed Wright's election on 7 July when Nathaniel Turner, who had arrived from England aboard *The Duke of Cambridge* on 4 July, presented his commission as councillor and Land Customer. On 14 July, Elwick presented in writing his objections to the constitution of the board, and was supported by Richard Benyon, who added his dissent to Elwick's. Joshua Draper and Thomas Wright were reported in the consultations diary as having wondered why Elwick and Benyon 'should stickle so hard to get them excluded from the board', since their continuance at it 'could be no manner of disadvantage to the Company's affairs'. They sought, and were granted, permission to include a note of refutation. This note of refutation identified 'Pique and Prejudice' as the motives for dissent by Elwick and Wright.

Intolerance and bias notwithstanding, Elwick next proceeded, in his capacity as Warehouse-keeper, to urge the release of the two Chetty merchants, since their services were required for the sorting of goods. Hastings retaliated by convening the council on 19 July 'to reassume that affair, having received three Letters from Goa, whose Contents' would help the council decide finally on what to do. The Portuguese governor ('viceroy') at Goa had written the first letter to Hastings, and the second was by his Prime Minister, also to Hastings. The viceroy had written the third letter, presumably seized from Pereira, to one Monsignor St Hillair at San Thome. To Hastings' mistrustful eyes, the viceroy's letter appeared as though he was willing 'to conceal as much as possible the Chetties' and his own design'. The minister's letter similarly made it abundantly clear that he too had 'endeavoured to stifle the matter by writing in dark and obscure terms'. One may well imagine Hastings raving, as Sir John Child had half a century ago, that both letters seemed 'to have been contrived and drawn up together, for fear of contradicting each other in so nice an affair' endeavouring thereby to wipe out the Chetties' alleged 'treachery to this Government'. 'But we cannot at all think ourselves obliged to regard the purport of these two letters', Hastings craftily reasoned to himself, 'because it can't be supposed that the Viceroy of Goa and his Prime Minister, would be engaged in a Combination with the Inhabitants of this place to prosecute a design which might tend to the destruction of it, and then make an ingenuous confession of their whole proceeding'. Therefore, logic demanded that these letters from the viceroy and the Prime Minister be discarded, and the conspiracy revealed through a certain phrase in the third letter, 'For 'tis very reasonable to suppose that the Viceroy might communicate the real matter of Fact to his intimate Friend, and at the same time be cautious of making such a Confession to the Governor of a place whose Government he had endeavoured to subvert for fear of bringing himself in trouble and Disgrace'. The ludicrousness of this argument is unbelievable. If the Portuguese were really planning to overthrow the English at Madras, they would not be disturbed by the need of confessing their intentions to Francis Hastings; nor would they be bothered about getting into 'trouble and Disgrace' in this matter. Hastings however proceeded undaunted to further absurdities. The third letter, after 'being strictly examined into', yielded an incriminating sentence quoted by Hastings and recorded in the minutes. The Portuguese viceroy had written to Monsignor Hillair that the letter, which Pereira had brought him, 'with the procuration of the Chetties of Madras, as well as the Attestation of a religious Augustine (who without doubt has abundance of Merit) have brought me into a Labyrinth'. This sentence, Hastings said, was of singular importance, since this letter was to be depended on for reliability in revealing the plot. The Chetties were clearly guilty of treachery since they had sent 'a procuration or Letter of Attorney to the Viceroy of Goa in order to carry Criminal Correspondence with him'. His arguments having vindicated, at least in his own view, his previous decision to convict the Chetties of treachery, Hastings proceeded to put the matter of their imprisonment, and confiscation of their property, to vote. Elwick, Benyon, and Emmerson again dissented. Hastings was very angry at this. He told the council that Elwick had been 'very remiss in his business' as Warehouse-keeper, 'in not having given any account of the Contract ever since 'twas made'. Worse, 'out of a perverse, Obstinate Humour', Elwick had pressed Hastings once or twice 'while the Merchants were confined, for their releasement, in order to go to sorting'. Randall Fowke had dismissed Elwick's call for the release of the Chetties for sorting by recalling a previous imprisonment of one of them, which had not stopped work. Hastings chortled and crowed over this, and put on record that 'Mr Elwick, finding his plea for not sorting, proved to be nothing else, but an excuse for Idleness, began to be much enraged'. Elwick said the whole matter 'would draw very strange stories on the Stage, and that the consequence must take its course'. To this end, Elwick wanted the words to be recorded verbatim, and in his vicious magnanimity, Hastings agreed. Most interestingly, Elwick seems to have withdrawn from the meeting after this for his signature is not appended to the minutes, being the only one missing.

Although Elwick is recorded as having attended several subsequent meetings, his signature of affirmation is missing from all following consultations, including an especially fractious one on 4 August 1720, at which he registered protests in several matters. He objected to Hastings' decision to remove from service a factor, George Torriano; he wanted the governor's commission of inquiry against alleged cases of mismanagement to be publicly read at the Town Hall; and he urged that the part of the Company's letter granting immunity from customs to the inhabitants of Madras, be posted at the Sea Gate. Every proposal was dismissed, and once again, despite having taken a major role at this meeting, Elwick's signature is lacking. The relation between Elwick and Hastings was hurtling towards rupture, which finally took place on 8 August. This was 'a very extraordinary meeting', particularly convened by Hastings to discuss Elwick's refractory attitude and 'his Incapacity for the service of the Honourable Company'. Elwick withdrew at once and Francis Hastings proceeded with his declaration against him.

'You must … be sensible', he began, 'that nothing can contribute so much to the enabling us to think and to act … with Mildness, Calmness, and Moderation and in order to [do] this a decent modest behaviour and a becoming deference and respect to myself as President and to each other (which will always preserve Decorum) are of absolute necessity'. Rather than behave as behove him in his position as second in council, Elwick chose to be arrogant and insolent, until he had become insufferable. Hastings makes some interesting revelations. Elwick objected to Torriano's dismissal because he was Elwick's servant in some 'private Capacity'. Employment in 'private Capacity' meant that Torriano was Elwick's assistant in private trade. All the Company's traders engaged in private trade, since this was why they had entered the Company's service. Torriano's dismissal from the service meant that he would no longer be allowed to reside at Fort St George, even in any 'private Capacity'. Nonetheless, Torriano's dismissal having been resolved, Hastings said that as he was rising from the table after the meeting, Elwick went up to him and addressing him 'Saucily', asked when Hastings would proceed further in the matter of the Chetties, who, Elwick repeated several times, had been ill-used, having unjustly been in confinement for long, and 'denied the necessaries of Life'. In stating that the Chetties had been unjustly imprisoned, Elwick had cast a 'Scandalous, False, and Malicious Aspersion', which was also 'an Obloquy' as much upon Hastings, as the rest of the council, who had agreed that the Chetties be penalised for their 'Criminal Correspondences'. Allegations that are more serious followed. The councillors had to know, Hastings said, 'how Industrious' Elwick had been, 'in persuading the English and Native Inhabitants … into a Motion that the Company would appoint him to … Government' by displacing Hastings. Elwick had therefore encouraged 'Cabals, Irregular Assemblies, and Degrees of Conspiracy' against Hastings through the affront of his person and the dignity of his post. This they had done 'being prompted by a Notion that it was their private interest' to disrespect him. These were insinuations, the imaginary products of a sick mind that saw plots, schemes, and intrigues all about. Hastings, like John Child, was unaware of this, and moved on to the still more serious accusation against Elwick, that he was incapable. Three instances of his incapability followed. Elwick had not had the cloth sorted because the merchants were in prison, and this showed 'a weak and groundless pretence for Idleness' since there was no ostensible need for the Company Merchants to be present during sorting. Then, Elwick had not paid dues for the month of May, amounting to several thousand pagodas to other merchants. Lastly, Joshua Draper chipped in with a letter in which he informed the council that Elwick had not collected certain minor dues to the sum of 170 pagodas. Draper considered it his duty to draw the attention of the council to this final example of how remiss Elwick had been, despite the fact that the pointing out of these remissions fell beyond his 'own particular Employment'. Francis Hastings concluded his address to the council by declaring that he was informed by his conscience that Elwick was unfit to remain a councillor 'on account of his Insolent behaviour at it, and also on account of his Incapacity and Negligence'. In any case Hastings was 'fully resolved not to sit any Longer as President, if he is Continued a Member of it'. The council therefore resolved to suspend Elwick from the service, given that Hastings had done his best to disregard Elwick's insolence and had behaved with the members of the board with 'the Greatest Candour, Mildness, and Decency imaginable'. Nathaniel Elwick was thus declared suspended, *officio et beneficio*, until confirmation of the same was received from England. Turner and Benyon dissented to the resolution to suspend Elwick, saying that the Company's order 'did not allow sufficient Latitude for so doing'.

Elwick entered a formal protest against his suspension on 25 August 1720. This was a legal document claiming damages against the tarnishing of his reputation and the ruining of his finances.

For more than a year matters remained as they were. Then on 15 October 1721, two ships arrived from England, bearing the Company's letters. Francis Hastings was removed and Nathaniel Elwick made governor. The councillors named by the Company were William Jennings, Nathaniel Turner, Richard Benyon, Catesby Oadham, John Emmerson, Randall Fowke, James Hubbard, and George Drake. The same packet contained the dismissal of Joshua Draper, who had been serving in the meantime as the Mayor of Madras, from the Company's service.

The Company's letter was forthright in dealing with the decisions reached by Hastings and his council: 'When we told you our opinion some years ago why we would not have above Seven of Council if death or absence reduced it to that Number, This is to be interpreted only as an advice, not an order, and a Strange and never before heard of Doctrine advanced That the President and Council have an undoubted power to Increase that Number, nothwithstanding the Company's opinion Four years before, if the Majority see a just occasion'. This conclusion made the Company reconsider its position, which it stated in the most cutting way: 'Had this been only the hair [*sic*] brained Notions of a Giddy headed Youngster, We could have slighted and pitied it'. However 'when We find the Council in the General Letter Patronising it, and referring Us to justify their proceedings, It is time for Us to look about Us and crush this Cockatrice of Rebellion in the Egg'.

Moreover, the Company had attempted previously, on finding its affairs being mismanaged at Madras, to correct them in an 'Expostulatory mild manner'. 'But since Lenitives will not do and the Infectious Gangrene spreads so fast, We must, though with regret, apply the last remedy, lest the yet sound parts should be tainted and Our Affairs at Fort St George become incurable'. The Company also noted with dismay in the case of the Chetties that they were imprisoned and 'treated like the Vilest of Criminals being carried about the Town in the most disgraceful manner, then confined in the Cock House to a strait narrow hole of a Room, denied the Liberty of Common and the usual necessaries for Men of their Characters and Estates, which hath made the English Government to stink in the Nostrils of the neighbouring Country'.

Elwick at once ordered the sealing of the cash chest and the silver godown, and issued summons to Francis Hastings and Thomas Cooke to be present when the chest and godown were reopened the next morning. Cooke informed the council on 16 October that there was nothing at all in the silver godown, since he had sold the last 29 chests by order of Francis Hastings. When asked to pay in the amount received, Cooke said he was unable to do so, since he had not been paid for the silver sold. The council then held that he had carried out an unauthorised task, and asked him what security he could offer against subsequent payment. Cooke sought time until that afternoon, when he informed the council that he could offer no security that would satisfy them. Cooke was then asked to be available for further inquiries.

The same morning at 11, Hastings and Elwick met privately at the fort. At this meeting, Hastings admitted that the cash account was short but he would return the amount due in a week's time. Hastings also sought permission to live at the Company's Garden-house and later retire to the Mount-house, after it was ready to receive him, until there was a ship at the earliest to transport him to England. Cooke was again summoned and, once more, he gave the same answer, adding that the former governor was answerable for the sale of the 29 chests of silver, and hoped the council would accept a joint bond offered by Cooke and Hastings for the amount. Urged to make an immediate payment of part of the sum, Cooke replied he would be able to pay 10,000 or 12,000 pagodas in 5 or 6 days' time. The council next requested Elwick to go and discuss the shortfall in the cash account and the unauthorised sale of silver again with Hastings.

Elwick went to see Hastings and the latter assured him that the shortfall in the cash account would be made up in 2 days' time 'in money, Diamonds, or other sufficient security', and that the silver was sold on 20 days' trust, after which time the money would be paid. Hastings requested Elwick that 'no unkind expressions or entries be made, to Slur his reputation' in the new consultation book. Elwick reassured him that no member was inclined to do so. Richard Fowke was thereafter dispatched to secure from Hastings a letter admitting that the silver had been sold on trust and that he was answerable for it. Hastings continued to retain possession of the key to the cash chest, so that no one knew exactly how much the shortfall was.

The council sat until 6 pm on 18 October 1720, waiting for some answer from Hastings. None being received, Elwick sent a letter desiring a reply. However, Hastings was already seriously ill. At 8 at night, he replied that he was unwell, and unable to travel and make necessary arrangements, including the handing over of the key of the cash chest. He asked that the Company's fair cashbook, and minutes, until 15 October, be sent to him for settling the amount outstanding. In the meantime, Cooke was again summoned and ordered to give security for the silver. Cooke reiterated he had none to offer, upon which he was handed into the custody of the Commander of the Guard, Lieutenant Alexander Fullerton. Meanwhile the council agreed that Hastings' reply was 'evasive and frivolous' and ordered him to send the key through someone to open it before the board. Accordingly, Fowke went again to the Company's Garden-house and informed Hastings of the council's order. Fowke returned with the answer that Hastings would 'by and by send the key of the Cash Chest by Mr Walsh'. The matter was already grim because a perusal of the rough cashbook had revealed that Hastings owed over 72,000 pagodas to the Company. Hastings' reluctance made the council apprehensive, and their suspicions were confirmed when Walsh came with the key and opened the cash chest. There was money amounting to only one fanam (roughly one-fortieth of a pagoda) in it. The rest of the contents included *firmans*, commissions, and some other papers.

Shocked, the members of the council asked Walsh if he carried some other message from Hastings. He did not. By 11.30 pm, the council had agreed that Hastings' cash account would be drawn up and sent to him the following day, with orders to pay the balance immediately. In the meantime, Lieutenant Fullerton was commanded to place guards around the Company's Garden-house to ensure that Hastings could not escape before he had settled all outstanding debts.

Next morning the amount outstanding was once more confirmed at over 72,000 pagodas. Fowke and Emmerson went with the detailed accounts to see Hastings, who acknowledged it with his signature. Hastings said that he had sent Horden and Draper, both former councillors, to get the money together by that afternoon. The council ordered Joshua Draper, who had been Rental General and Scavenger, to put in his accounts in proper order to George Drake, his replacement. At 6 the same evening, Richard Horden paid 10,000 pagodas into the cash chest on behalf of Francis Hastings, for which Fowke was given a receipt to deliver to the latter. Fowke was also instructed to tell Hastings that the council awaited impatiently 'his further Offers'. Fowke returned with a letter from Hastings, wherein he said that the following day they would be sent security (a list of ships and stocks abroad) to double the amount outstanding, including the silver. Meanwhile the same notice that Hastings had disallowed to be displayed on the Sea Gate in accordance with Elwick's demand 14 months ago, was now put up. It promised impartial action in all cases of complaint against mismanagement at Fort St George. The notice was displayed in not only English but also Portuguese, and all the local languages. Other reversals of former policy followed. Portuguese priests petitioned that they be allowed to rebuild their church, which was granted.

Hastings' debts were getting worse. He gave a list to the council of his shares and stocks, in ships then at sea, on 21 October 1721, amounting to 26,000 pagodas. Discussion revealed that Hastings had already promised half of this amount to his main creditor, Captain Powney, and this had found no mention on the list. Captain Powney was called in and interrogated. He admitted to the truth of the matter but said he would relinquish his demands if the council accepted the list as security against Hastings' debt. The council rightly 'resolved to insist upon Some Security in Diamonds as he had hinted' to Elwick previously. This being intimated to Hastings, he agreed to deposit an additional security of 20,000 pagodas in diamonds with an accompanying request that he be allowed to redeem these diamonds as soon as he paid in the same sum in cash. The council, now probably somewhat relieved, relented, and agreed that Hastings' list of investments be accepted as security, making up thereby 56,000 pagodas, of which 10,000 had been paid in cash, 20,000 as security in diamonds, and the rest in his private trade investments. This matter having been temporarily settled, the council issued an Instrument of Assignment for Hastings to sign, and he typically prevaricated until told that the Instrument would not be changed to accommodate his demands. This, however, was a brief hiatus. On 26 October, some further errors were detected in the list of investments given by Hastings, and it was resolved to obtain more security from him. When visited by Catesby Oadham, Randall Fowke, and James Hubbard, Hastings said he had no more security to offer. The following day Hastings' pathetic condition revealed itself in his undertaking to repay his debt of 62,000 pagodas with an interest of 8 percent per annum, within one year, failing which the obligation would remain tied to himself, and in the case of his demise, to his executors, administrators, and heirs 'in full force and Virtue'. Hastings also acknowledged his debt of over 80,000 pagodas to Thomas Cooke, because of the silver sold from the godown on trust, also to be returned at 8 percent interest in one year's time. Cooke himself was indebted to the Company for over 73,000 pagodas. The following day the guards were withdrawn and Hastings allowed to move to a country house owned by Richard Horden, some miles from the fort.

On 12 December 1720, the council granted Francis Hastings' petition to be allowed to sail home aboard the *Marlborough*, taking into consideration the fact that he had provided sufficient security, and that he was so seriously ill that there was little possibility of his survival if he was to continue at Madras. The council also allowed his servant, Thomas Newton, to leave the military since he had completed his period of service, and accompany him. Francis Hastings never sailed home on the *Marlborough* since he died at 5 on the evening of 15 December. He was buried in the cemetery of St Mary's Church on 19 December 1720.

Of the other players in this tale, Randall Fowke, having sat in council for many years, and been in the Company's service for over 40 years, died on 2 March 1745, aged 72, and lies buried in the same cemetery, in company with Captain Alexander Fullerton, who passed on at the age of 40 in 1723. Catesby Oadham, who makes a brief appearance in this narrative, died aged 36, also in 1723. Captain Powney, one of the beneficiaries of his friend Hastings' will, also never left Madras. He died at the age of 58 in 1740. Others who lie forever exiled there include George Torriano (1741) whose dismissal Elwick disagreed with and later reinstated, and Joseph Walsh (1731), whose unpleasant task it had been to procure the key to the cash chest from Hastings.

Nathaniel Elwick married Diana Robson (or Robinson) in 1722, and their daughter, Elizabeth, was baptised in September 1724. Elwick left Madras with his family in January 1725, having handed over the administration to James Macrae, and never returned to India. He seems to have purchased an estate in Kent, as was common among nabobs who had survived and returned rich. Elizabeth married one Miles Barnes, later Member of Parliament, and predeceased her father. Nathaniel Elwick died on 25 October 1750, at the age of 76. His death is listed in Volume XX of *The Gentlemen's Magazine*, with the erroneous statement that he had been Governor of Bombay.

The case of Francis Hastings might have ended here, had it not been for a strange work, part play and part libellous pamphlet, which appeared in London in 1745, titled *An Essay upon Friendship, Delivered with a view to an Unhappy Gentleman deceased and a Monster just stripped of Power which he has abused, and is lately returned to England*. The author was anonymous, 'a Faithful Servant and Soldier of His Majesty's', later after revealed to be Joshua Draper, who joined the British army later on in another career. The materials drawn upon the writing of this work cannot have been accessible to anyone else, since he had served as secretary during Collet's governorship and councillor during Hastings'. Irrespective of bias, this account provides us with another perspective of the events.

Of great interest is Draper's description of the Consultation Room at Fort St George. It consisted of 'a large Table, spread with a Sea Green Cloth, in the form of a Parallelogram or Quadrilateral Figure; an Ebony Elbow Chair at the upper End of it; four common Ebony chairs on each Side, and a single one at the lower End, just opposite to the President's'. At each end of the table, there was a 'handsome Silver Standish'. Elwick's arrival in London in 1725 is described in the most outrageous terms, cast in the form of a handbill: 'This is to inform the Curious That there is arrived from the East Indies a most surprising Monster, above 17 Hands in height; he was taken on the Coast of Coromandel, near a place called Mad-ass-apatam, where he had lived in a Wood for some time and (in a Manner) reigned King of the Beasts .... Farther Particulars concerning the Brute may be had at the Jerusalem Coffee-House in Exchange Alley in London; and he is to be seen from Ten to Six every Day besides Sundays, at his Den at St Mary-Ax[e]'. Traders interested in England's flourishing mercantile shipping frequented the Jerusalem Coffee-House, later destroyed in a fire in 1748. The former medieval church of St Mary-Axe stood at the north end of Leadenhall Street, made famous by the East India House.

Draper melodramatically described how Hastings, aware of imminent death, tasked him with the recovery of his reputation in England: 'he raised at once his awful, venerable Head; ... reached forth that friendly Hand which he had exercised so frequently in Offices of Aid and Kindness; with it he grasped my own, pressed it, and charged me, in the most sad and solemn Tone of Voice (if Providence preserved my Life) to do him justice'. This Draper did by appending to his work a letter purportedly written by Hastings to the Company in November 1721, a month after his dismissal from governorship. Irrespective of authorship, its inclusion represents a spiteful racial bias that must have been common: 'The Fort is filled with Black Knaves of all Castes, and a Gentleman is ashamed to walk the streets; Shop-keepers, Shoe-makers and Tailors are bringing in their Bills, which they pretend were not duly paid some Years ago … and now Complaints and Informations are trumped up to ruin me in my Character and Fortune; of which you shall have a more plain Account if I live to return to my Country; but your ill Treatment and a long Sickness make that Life doubtful; yet I hope some friend will live to sue for Justice'.

Draper added to his essay an appeal dated 28 November 1721, and addressed by Hastings to his brother John and the executors of his will, Draper and the Rev Thomas Wendey, 'and all Mankind in general'. Hastings reportedly wrote that he had been 'entirely abandoned' by the Company, and 'thrown into the Hands and Power of Nathaniel Elwick'. Hastings had thereby been 'left destitute of all manner of protection and cast into the Hands of Catesby Oadham [Mayor of Madras in place of Joshua Draper]' and his Aldermen. These in turn had turned Hastings over to 'the lawless and merciless Power of the Natives to be arrested, thrown into Prison, impeached, arraigned, and treated in a most barbarous Manner by them'. Being then 'near the Approach of Death, occasioned by such Barbarous Usage,' Hastings urged his brother and the executors of his will, to vindicate his reputation, and clear his name of the several 'vile Aspersions' thrown upon him by wicked men. Another document that accompanied this appeal was a certificate signed by several Englishmen including three of Hastings' servants, attesting to the circumstances under which he was arrested.

This letter seemed to give Draper the authority to prosecute Elwick and his council as accessories to the death of Hastings. Later, Richard Horden and Thomas Wendey gave depositions that Hastings was very ill and not in his full senses when he signed this letter, which had apparently been given him by Draper to sign as one meant for his brother only. Draper narrates in his pamphlet that Thomas Wendey, his fellow executor, 'a Man in Sacerdotal Life, unskilled in Mercantile Affairs', recanted and refused to be involved in this matter even as Draper was about to board the *Marlborough* for England. Draper further alleged that his arrest had been planned and he had embarked almost by force. The matter does not appear to have proceeded much farther. In any case, the allegation that Hastings had been ill-treated by Elwick and his administration was false.

CHAPTER SIX

THE CARNATIC WARS I

Aurangzeb's demise in March 1707 heralded the end of the Mughal Empire. The Marathas under Venkoji Bhonsle, the younger half-brother of Shivaji, had overrun Tanjore around 1675. Venkoji had inherited his father, Shahji's, *jagir* or landholding, in Mysore, and was thus a feudatory of the Sultan of Bijapur. It was under the orders of the Sultan that Venkoji proceeded to invade Tanjore to restore the kingdom to its own Nayak dynasty, which had been overthrown by the Nayak of Madurai. Some say that Venkoji had a holy dream, which advised him not to vacate Tanjore. Others hold his personal ambition responsible for staying on at Tanjore. Venkoji was opposed to Shivaji's invasion of the Carnatic in 1677. In 1678, Venkoji attacked the garrisons left behind by Shivaji in control of the Carnatic but was repulsed. Shivaji disliked this needless bloodshed amongst Marathas, and wrote to Venkoji, because of which an accord was achieved whereby Venkoji was left in peace at Tanjore, while the *jagir* reverted to Shivaji. Just before his death in 1680, Shivaji gained the supremacy of the Carnatic from the Bijapur Sultanate, which created a deeper sense of alienation in Venkoji. Orme reports that Venkoji was recorded as ruling Tanjore in August 1687. In any case, Venkoji had established an independent Maratha lineage at Tanjore, and Maratha kings ruled Tanjore from 1675 on, until it passed into British control in 1855 following the infamous Doctrine of Lapse. The earliest European trading presence in Tanjore seems to have been a Danish factory, established during 1624-5. Tanjore was a beautiful and plentiful kingdom, with an eastern coastline covering 170 miles. To the north, the Kollidam River, which is the northern distributary of the Krishna as it flows into the Tanjore Delta, bound it. North of the Kollidam lay the territory of the Nawab of the Carnatic. To the south, the kingdoms of Sivaganga and Ramnad (Ramanathapuram) bordered Tanjore. Under Maratha dominance, Tanjore included the *zillahs* (districts) of south Arcot, Tanjore, and Trichinopoly. The town of Tanjore lies 320 kilometres to the south-west of Madras.

The primary enemy of the Marathas was Aurangzeb. Shivaji's exceptional military prowess had forced the Emperor to concentrate his forces in the Deccan, and embolden them with personal presence. A perusal of the history of the Marathas demonstrates the continual war they waged against the Mughals until Aurangzeb's death, and the military dominance they achieved through the eighteenth century as the Mughal Empire dissolved. This ultimately brought the Marathas into direct confrontation with the British, who were their most powerful opponents in the filling up of the vacuum that followed the collapse of the Mughal Empire. In 1692, Aurangzeb appointed as Nawab of the Carnatic his most successful commander in the Deccan, Zulfikar Ali Khan. This gave Zulfikar Ali Khan control of all Mughal-held territory south of the river Krishna. Additionally, the appointment of the Nawab gave Aurangzeb the opportunity of directly opposing the Marathas at Tanjore, limiting thereby the possibility of a concerted attack against his forces. The shifting of the capital of the Nawab of the Carnatic to Arcot took place many years later. As the Mughal Empire disintegrated following Aurangzeb's death, due to the ineptitude of his successors, who followed each other with brief and indecisive reigns, satraps like the Nawab of the Carnatic soon acknowledged no more than the nominal suzerainty of Delhi, and that too only for a few decades more. Internecine warfare took over, and Tanjore with its rivers, fertile plains, seacoast, and prosperous habitations, was an obvious target for forcible acquisition. The importance of Delhi declined with swiftness in the Carnatic, which was commensurate with the speed with which the influence of competing European nations rose there. By the middle of the eighteenth century, Nawabs of the Carnatic needed the support of either the English or the French to remain in power. Since our story from this point on shall be concerned mainly with matters related to the princely states of Tanjore and Arcot, one needs to know the irony that the line of the Nawabs of Arcot fell under the same infamous Doctrine of Lapse, and it too passed into British rule in the same year as Tanjore, viz, 1855.

The history of the Nawabdom of the Carnatic followed its own path through the upheavals that marked the death throes of the Mughal Empire. The main themes of its history include machinations for its own survival amidst the uncertainty and tumult of rapidly changing political alignments, and the securing of its continued preponderance over smaller kingdoms in its neighbourhood. These minor principalities, equally aware of the political volatility of the times, had already obtained from the powerless Mughal court the right to sustain their own armies, which had been previously disallowed.

Nadir Shah's invasion of 1738 revealed to all the hollowness of the Mughal Empire. In the Deccan, the Marathas took particular note of this, as did the English and the French on the Coromandel Coast. News of this invasion reached Madras in 1739, and was recorded. The Marathas invaded the Carnatic in 1740, under the pretext of avenging the plunder of Tanjore by Chanda Sahib, a son-in-law of Nawab Dost Ali Khan of Arcot. Dost Ali Khan along with one of his sons, was killed in battle on 9 May of the same year. Safdar Ali, the surviving son, declared himself Nawab and agreed to buy peace with a huge payment to the Marathas. Chanda Sahib, who had declared himself the Nawab of Trichinopoly, disagreed over this indemnity. In fact, Chanda Sahib had been an unwilling feudatory to Dost Ali. He had deliberately moved too slowly with his army to the aid to Dost Ali in the latter's final battle against the Marathas. Chanda Sahib subsequently refused to accept the vassalage of Safdar Ali. Hence, Safdar Ali wished Chanda Sahib away and so invited the Marathas once more into the Carnatic. This second invasion occurred in November 1740. Chanda Sahib, besieged in Trichinopoly, surrendered in March 1741. He was made prisoner and borne off to Satara.

The relations between Fort St George, Tanjore, and the Carnatic became pleasant during this period. Safdar Ali knew that his Nawabdom had not been confirmed by Delhi through his overlord, the Nizam of Hyderabad. He moved his family, consisting of his mother, his wife, and 4-year-old son, to Madras on 21 September 1741 for safety, where they were housed in the Black Town. The Nawab visited Madras formally the following day, and was received by the governor and council with appropriate respect, marked by the firing of gun-salutes by the fort and European ships in harbour. Safdar Ali himself moved to Vellore, where his cousin, Murtaza Ali was governor. During the year that followed, Safdar attempted to recoup his inheritance. He was in dire need of money not only to pay his troops and retainers but also to keep up the instalments promised to the Marathas. Additionally, he knew that the Nizam's favour could be obtained only by paying all arrears of tribute. Murtaza Ali was only the governor of the fort at Vellore, holding it for his elder brother, whose *jagir* it was. Murtaza hoped to win Safdar over to his side by hosting him in Vellore, and so he asked that the *jagir* be given to him. Safdar refused, and this enraged Murtaza, who retaliated by creating difficulties in collecting money. In any case, Murtaza did not intend to contribute to Safdar's treasury. In the meantime, Safdar Ali paid several more visits to his family at Madras, the last recorded visit being in August 1742. On 5 October 1742, Murtaza assassinated Safdar, and by placating Safdar's army with promise of payment, declared himself Nawab of Arcot in November. This favour of the army was short-lived since it demanded immediate payment of arrears, and with the Marathas declaring their opposition to Murtaza, he was compelled to escape from Arcot and return to Vellore. In the meantime, Safdar's minor son was proclaimed Nawab by the army, and he assumed the name of Muhammad Saeed (Muhammad Saadatullah Khan). This announcement was made ceremoniously at the Company's Garden-House in Madras on 22 December, and the new Nawab at once expressed his gratitude to the Company by granting it rights to 5 villages, the liberty to coin Arcot Rupees and Pagodas, and some other minor privileges like the lowering of duties.

The Nizam of Hyderabad, engrossed in matters of greater scope at Delhi, was compelled to look to the tumult in his own possession, and to take matters in hand. He moved with a huge army into the Carnatic, reaching Arcot in February 1743. He at once imprisoned the new Nawab, and placed in his stead his commander, Khwaja Abdullah Khan. The Nizam's point was plain: he wanted the Carnatic under his complete control. His experiences in Delhi had made him aware of the increasing power of the Marathas. Muhammad Saeed's Nawabdom would give the Marathas further access into the Carnatic; hence, he had to be removed. Those placed in charge of Muhammad Saeed were particularly instructed to treat him with respect. After a siege of 6 months, the Marathas gave up Trichinopoly, and Khwaja Abdullah was rewarded with the Nawabdom of Trichinopoly, in addition to Arcot. This makes the Nizam's intention clear: there were to be no further divisions of interest in the Carnatic, the whole of which would be ruled by the same person. The English attempted to make requisite presents to the Nizam, his son, and Khwaja Abdullah Khan, to secure consent to the awards announced by Muhammad Saeed in Madras. However, this was in vain since the Nizam chose to remain evasive.

Having settled the troubles in the Carnatic, the Nizam returned to Golconda in March 1744. The Nawab of Arcot had left his son, Nimatullah Khan, as his deputy and accompanied the Nizam. Khwaja Abdullah Khan unexpectedly died on the eve of his departure from Golconda for Arcot. Rumours of murder did their rounds, the culprit in these being Anwaruddin Khan, who was appointed his successor. Anwaruddin was a trusted agent of the Nizam, having been in his service since 1724, and, lately, in charge of Golconda (with its fabled diamond mines) while the Nizam had been away in the Carnatic. Muhammad Saeed was placed in Anwaruddin's care and sent to Arcot. The aim seems to have been that he should learn governance under Anwaruddin's guardianship until he came of age and took over his inheritance. Saeed appears to have been popular at Arcot, which might have been resented by Anwaruddin. Meanwhile Murtaza Ali had plotted to kill both Anwaruddin and Saeed. To do this he had hired 14 men, promising them a vast sum as payment. The Nawab, who was then aged 85, was indisposed, and so he escaped. Saeed was in the fort at Arcot on 23 June 1744, in attendance at a wedding, when he was set upon and killed, along with several other persons. The boy was only 7 years old. Few of the assassins survived. Those who did were put to death. The Nizam was at least outwardly much affected by Saeed's murder. Murtaza's implication in the plot along with his listing of Anwaruddin as the other victim seems to have mollified the Nizam. Saeed's presence was a thorn equally to the Nizam, Anwaruddin, and Murtaza. It is thus impossible to single out any one of these as the brain behind the murder. However that may be, to the English at Madras, Saeed's death was a serious blow. They had expected preferential treatment, had he lived to be Nawab. They now realised that the old ruling family of Dost Ali Khan no longer had any prospect of achieving kingship, having been wiped out in the space of 4 years. Anwaruddin was confirmed as Nawab of Arcot, and at once, he appointed his sons to various commands under him. Orme was of the opinion that Anwaruddin's confirmation disappointed the Carnatic.

The Carnatic Wars commenced in 1746 because of these machinations, into which the French entered deliberately, and the English reluctantly. In the meantime, the protagonist of our story, George Pigot, arrived at Madras on 26 July 1737. On 31 May 1741, Robert Clive reached Madras, that singular person who would be the catalyst of the transition of the East India Company from a trading corporation to a powerful political entity. Both Pigot and Clive were Writers, the former having come out at the age of 18, and the latter at 15. George's two older brothers, Robert and Hugh, stood surety for him, and Clive's father for his son. The stage was set for the train of events that would determine the strange case of George Pigot.

France and Britain had declared themselves as belligerents, aligning themselves with opposite camps in the Austrian Succession in 1739-40. Even though their respective trading companies were not eager to open hostilities between their settlements in India, this soon became irrelevant. Joseph Francois Dupleix, the Governor of Chandernagore, and Bertrand Francois de la Bourdonnais, Governor of Mauritius and Bourbon, foresaw imminent conflict with the English in India in the event of hostilities being declared in Europe. Bourdonnais was in France when war was declared and he used his considerable influence to gather a fleet of 5 of the French Company's ships. He sailed in command of this fleet, reaching India towards the end of 1741. Meanwhile Dupleix moved from the governorship of Chandernagore to that of Pondicherry, taking over on 14 January 1742. His predecessor, the Chevalier Benoit Dumas, had left in October 1741. The presence of a French fleet was useful in uncertain times, given that the French Company, like its British counterpart, was most averse to warlike preparations and engagements, even with the English, in India. Consequently, Dumas had not been able to carry out the necessary fortification and repairs of Pondicherry's defences. Deeming offence to be the best defence, De la Bourdonnais and Dupleix agreed to the capture of Madras through the intelligent surveys of that place by Paradis, a Swiss mercenary in French service and engineer by profession. De la Bourdonnais was not allowed to remain long on the Coromandel Coast by the French Company, to whom the expense of his fleet was not explained by its strategic relevance. He was ordered to return to Mauritius. The French Company hoped, as no doubt the English did, that trade routes and settlements would be spared. An uneasy yet mutually acceptable peace existed between the two nations, which were at war in Europe. In February 1744, Hinde, the new Deputy Governor of Fort St David, travelled from Madras to his post via Pondicherry, where Dupleix and his council accorded him full honours. The wariness is evidenced by the excitement caused on 29 September 1744 over the sighting of a ship flying a white ensign while approaching Pondicherry. Dupleix was convinced it was English, and ordered the gates of the fort shut, and the artillery manned. The ship turned out to be French, the *St Pierre*, from Mozambique. Locals, particularly trading agents and interpreters, were employed as spies by both sides. The proximity of the colonies allowed information to be passed very quickly.

The damage had however been done by De la Bourdonnais and his fleet, since the English, who had feared French naval dominance from the time of Raworth's rebellion, retaliated by sending a squadron commanded by Captain Barnet to India. Barnet's squadron reached the Coromandel Coast in July 1745. Dupleix, wary of the flotilla because he had received news in January of English ships preying upon French vessels on trade routes, wrote to Anwaruddin, asking the Nawab of the Carnatic to command the English fleet not to attack French possessions. Anwaruddin did this and at the same time informed the English that he would issue a similar restriction upon the French. The English protested that they would strive to maintain neutrality but the King of England had commanded Barnet to war, so they could not interfere with his actions. Anwaruddin replied that Barnet was equally under compulsion to heed the Nawab's orders, since it was his country. The Nawab added the ominous warning that Madras would have to answer for any infringement of his command to maintain neutrality. Fort St George took this warning very seriously and Barnet left the Coromandel Coast for the equally lucrative Balasore Roads, where French shipping to and from Chandernagore was easy prey. The news that 5 or 10 French ships were approaching Pondicherry reached both sides in February 1746. The English fleet had meanwhile been successful, having captured several French ships elsewhere. In all they were reported to have, so Ananda Ranga Pillai wrote, twenty-two sail, a huge force. Probably repeating what he had been told, Pillai added that a feint against Cuddalore would draw off some ships, while the English would be obliged to keep some in reserve, thereby halving the number of belligerent vessels available for action against the expected French fleet. Dupleix had in the meantime dispatched a force of 500 troops on the road towards Cuddalore. The English had reinforced their troops at Cuddalore and Fort St David, while villagers within the bounds of the land held by the English scattered to avoid devastation. Ananda Ranga Pillai noted the comparative weakness of the French at Pondicherry, hampered by the lack of funds, and placed his faith, as many must have done, in Dupleix.

War was imminent, and hostilities only needed a spark to break out. On 7 February 1746 the moment almost came when a Portuguese ship, the *St Louis*, sailed into Pondicherry, followed by 4 English vessels from Madras, which anchored in the roads beyond artillery range. Two more ships from Fort St David reinforced them. Once more Dupleix ordered his troops to their positions. In the meantime, the force sent out to Cuddalore deliberately provoked action by maltreating peons and other local persons in the employ of the English. When news of this was conveyed to the English ships, they unloaded a party of around 300 men, comprising Europeans and locals, in boats carrying about a hundred each. These boats tried to land the troops but found themselves covered by artillery, and so retired to their ships. Ananda Ranga Pillai brushed this incident off as a show of strength by the English as the French had done at Cuddalore. Dupleix however was playing a dangerous game in which he was outgunned and outmanned. The French feinting force returned to Pondicherry on the night of 9 February, and the English ships reciprocated by sailing off to the southward. Dupleix was aware of his colony's military weakness, and tried to remedy this partly by obtaining two brass cannon from Mahfuz Khan at Trichinopoly. He sent off a force of 50 soldiers and 2 officers to escort the cannon into Pondicherry past the bounds of Fort St David early in March 1746. On 18 March, Dupleix wrote to Nawab Anwaruddin Khan informing him that an English force was encamped on his land, close to the bounds of Pondicherry, waiting to attack. They had not heeded his warning and the French would have to retaliate by entering the Nawab's territory. The Nawab was informed that the French did not intend to violate the sanctity of the border, unless compelled by the English, and in defence.

Captain Barnet died on 10 May 1746 at Fort St David after a few days' illness. A few days later, the French dispatched a force of 150 men to ward off a rumoured treaty between the Raja of Tanjore and the English, by which the former was to attack the French by land and the latter by sea. Ananda Ranga Pillai's diaries reveal how troubled Dupleix was with the delay in the arrival of ships from France. He had expended money on reinforcing the fortifications at Pondicherry. Trade was suffering due to the attrition between the English and the French, and the opportunism of the Dutch. By the end of June 1746 Pillai reports that Dupleix had asked money of him: 'The mighty Governor has applied to me for money in terms almost those of a beggar, I would rather die than smile, show my teeth, and express my inability to meet his wishes'. Meanwhile a French fleet comprising 9 ships, under the admiralship of De la Bourdonnais, was met by an English squadron of 6 ships commanded by Captain Peyton off Nagapatam. The English had the advantage in gunnery, and the French in numbers. The English manoeuvred to gain a position from which to unleash their devastating firepower, while the French plan was to close in and board. The first engagement took place around 4 pm after much manoeuvring and ended with equal honours at nightfall. The English lost 35 men and, discovering that their largest ship had sprung leaks, made for Trincomalee. The French stayed where they had been, with De la Bourdonnais successfully bluffing the English despite running low on ammunition and victuals, and with one ship dismasted. With the English having left for harbour, the French proceeded to Pondicherry, where they arrived on the night of 8 July 1746, to the great delight of its populace. Ananda Ranga Pillai notes that the popular joy was due to the fact that for long trade had been depressed, with the English capturing all ships travelling eastwards, and no ships coming in from France: 'The tidings of the arrival of the ships have awakened inexpressible joy in the breasts of the citizens of Pondicherry … as though they had discovered a hidden hoard, or recovered a lost treasure; or as though their beloved dead had returned to life'.

Dupleix however soon viewed Bourdonnais's arrival and residence at Pondicherry ungraciously. The former having previously served as governor, and being then in command of the fleet by order of the King of France, considered himself of equal authority as Dupleix. He demanded that troops show him respect in accordance with this status. On the other hand, Dupleix regarded himself as the only one eligible for the ceremonials. In Dupleix's view, De la Bourdonnais became his subordinate while on shore, and hence was disallowed the same salutations. This strange clash of egos in the face of possible enemy action fortunately remained indirectly expressed, while the protagonists professed to great friendship publicly. Nonetheless, Dupleix confided to Ananda Ranga Pillai within a week of Bourdonnais's arrival that he 'was a strange man with an ungovernable temper', 'a babbler', and 'an impostor'. Amidst the tension of impending battle, the governors of Fort St David and Pondicherry sent each other polite secret notes through their *dubashes* inquiring after the well-being of their families and asking whether they were in need of red wine and other European liquors. Each governor presented his compliments to the other and replied that he had plenty. Plans were afoot about capturing Madras, since Ananda Ranga Pillai notes in his diary that he and some French councillors casually discussed this on 30 July 1746. They also discussed 'a cruise of the squadron commanded by M de la Bourdonnais to seek the English', and 'the prospect of the destruction of all the English ships of war'.

De la Bourdonnais sailed with his fleet at 11 am on 4 August to discover and defeat the English at sea. This was Bourdonnais's commission, and he determined to carry it out by adding firepower to his ships, removing thereby the imbalance in favour of the English. Bourdonnais soon came upon the English fleet, which had been repaired and refitted at Trincomalee. The two fleets remained in sight of each other, manoeuvring for advantage for 3 days, until the English reportedly disengaged and sailed away. Bourdonnais was ill, and his fleet returned to Pondicherry, anchoring in the roads on 24 August 1746. He seems to have been seriously afflicted with fever and diarrhoea, to need venesection. Nonetheless, the French proceeded with the planned assault on Madras. Intelligence had been received earlier about the panic at Fort St David due to the arrival of the French fleet. The robbing of mail from a peon in the English service showed that Madras was also preparing for an invading force. Land had been cleared of trees for some miles around the settlement, and fortification was being completed and repaired. While Bourdonnais was ill and abed, the French fleet had sailed into the roads at Madras, and tried to capture a ship there. This ship sailed into the cover of Fort St George's guns, and the French fleet withdrew after a fruitless gun duel. Several Englishmen were killed in this attack, and much panic was caused in Madras, led by the governor, Morse, who sent his wife off to Pulicat for safety. The English anticipated the landing of troops by the French. However, inexplicably, the fleet sailed away, to the amazement of the English and the chagrin of Dupleix. Later Bourdonnais prevaricated by saying that he would not allow his ships to be used for attacking Madras by sea, pleading that his commission ordered him to engage English ships at sea and said nothing about fighting on shore.

Dupleix, yet unaware of the chance that had just been lost, had put together a force, which was to have been commanded by Bourdonnais. Given Bourdonnais's illness, Dupleix put D'Auteuil in charge of the invasion. He allowed D'Auteuil an escort of 24 men. This appears to have been done by way of resuming the old game of one-upmanship against Bourdonnais, who had also provided himself with the same number as escort. Perusing Ananda Ranga Pillai's diary, one realises that Bourdonnais's illness was not as serious as it was a move to avenge himself upon Dupleix by pretending to be sick. Clearly, the assault on Madras had been Dupleix's plan, and Bourdonnais was going to have nothing to do with it unless he was in command. Moreover, there seem to have been arguments between Madame de la Bourdonnais and Madame D'Auteuil. There were also allegations about Bourdonnais's engaging in private trade by obtaining chintz and other kinds of cloth from Madras. 'Thus', wrote Pillai, 'it is clear that the projects of man will go astray, unless Providence favours them'. The expedition against Madras was being delayed by the clash of egos. Meanwhile, Dupleix had written to Nawab Anwaruddin Khan, informing him of the plan to move against Madras, and sought his approval. He also wanted to ensure Anwaruddin's involvement and consent, and so he applied for 3,000 soldiers to help attack Madras. The Nawab's reply came on 5 September 1746. Anwaruddin was not happy with the traders' fighting each other, probably because he stood to gain from both. He urged Dupleix to abstain from attacking Madras, which would be a serious provocation to the Nawab. Interestingly, Dupleix's response was to send him a brief evasive missive and 150 oranges. Anwaruddin was implacable. He dashed off another letter to Dupleix, warning him that because the French had proceeded with their plan to reduce Madras, he was marching to take Pondicherry. Dupleix's retort was dismissive; French warships were not bound to follow the orders of anyone other than the King of France. Dupleix was now bent on achieving his purpose. His reputation was at stake, as was his fortune. He therefore dispatched another letter, this one to the Nizam at Golconda, explaining that the English had provoked action by capturing a trading vessel bearing the Mughal Emperor's flag, and for this reason, the Emperor's representatives should help the French capture Madras. Anwaruddin's threats were mere blustering, since the English had not bribed him with an appropriate sum of money, and this parsimony, as Orme points out, was ill-judged.

On the morning of 11 September 1746, with all disagreements laid to rest at least for the time being, Bourdonnais assumed command of the operation against Madras, and sailed with sufficient troops, munitions, and supplies at 8 the following night. The French fleet, with Bourdonnais's 7 ships and a number of smaller vessels, was a considerable force. The necessity of a reliable *dubash* was removed by the appointment of Trivengadam, Ananda Ranga Pillai's brother, against Pillai's wish. The reason for Pillai's demurring was that Dupleix had given Trivengadam the authority to grant permits to merchants without reference to any of the French military or civil officers. Pillai reports that Dupleix asked him how much money they were likely to make through this arrangement. Pillai answered that if his brother did as he had advised, 'in all transactions with the Armenian merchants and others, and the English Governor and his Deputy' they stood to make 500,000 pagodas. As has ever been, the end of all wars is money. Nevertheless, the rest of India was watching the outcome of this conflict.

De la Bourdonnais hove into sight of Mount St Thomas on the dawn of 14 September 1746, and first anchored 4 leagues, or 14 miles, to the south of Madras. At this point 600 troops were offloaded, and these marched along the shore, keeping the fleet in sight. The fleet sailed on, reaching Chepauk, one mile south of Fort St George, where the rest of the troops disembarked and rendezvoused with the marching contingent. The entire French force comprised 1800 soldiers, including 1100 Europeans, and the rest African and Indian. In addition, 1800 European sailors manned the fleet. War was made in courteous fashion in those days. Bourdonnais determined to attack the White Town, which lay within the fort. On the north side of the White Town, the houses were built close to the wall, and attacking along this direction would result in civilian casualties. The eastern side could only be reduced from the sea, but to the south and the west there were plains that offered an assault route. Camps for the soldiers and ammunition and stores were established, and following a reconnaissance, a battery of 9 mortars was based to the west within 500 yards of the fort's walls. The fort's artillery fired upon the enemy camp in vain since it was out of range. Mrs Barnevall, a daughter of Madame Dupleix by a previous marriage, and at that time married to a free merchant of Irish-French descent, Francois Coyle de Barnevall, located in Madras, went that night to meet Bourdonnais. She requested him to allow European women to leave the fort before hostilities began. Bourdonnais ungallantly refused permission to all but Mrs Barnevall and Mrs Morse, the governor's wife.

The French mortars commenced firing on the morning of 17 or 18 September. The mortar batteries delivered barrages every half hour during the next 2 days, resulting in widespread panic. The locals, whether sepoys, house servants, or slaves, were typically reported by the English as having deserted soon after the bombardment began. The English, never before subjected to such massive continual salvoes, soon began to feel its terrible psychological effects. The French fired around 1200 rounds with such accuracy that few fell in the Black Town. By the end of the second day, most of the English artillery was out of action and the civilian inhabitants unnerved by the intense bombardment. Their daily activities had been rendered impossible, and they had had little or no sleep. Ananda Ranga Pillai refers to the governor, Morse, as having been unhinged by this incessant cannonade, and of his replacement by John Stratton, the chief of Vizagapatam. This is contentious, since Stratton was not next to Morse in the Company's hierarchy. Anwaruddin Khan sent Dupleix an urgent letter by 'camel express' on 19 September. This was a rather weak missive, in which the Nawab expressed astonishment that the French had attacked Madras despite his instructions to the contrary. He asked Dupleix to make certain that such incidents would not recur, and told him to ensure that Indian merchants were not harmed. In Madras by this time, the English were willing to make terms with Bourdonnais. They sent two representatives, William Monson, second in council, and John Hallyburton, chief of Madapollam, who was fluent in French, to parley at dawn on 20 September. Bourdonnais showed them the eighteen 24-pounder cannon he had prepared for breaching the fort and impressed upon them the pointlessness of resistance. Monson and Hallyburton wanted precise terms of ransom but Bourdonnais, troubled by the possible arrival of the English squadron, pressed for immediate surrender, and as soon as the deputies had returned to the fort, he recommenced bombardment to drive home the point that he would take Madras by assault if necessary, unless his terms were quickly accepted. More dillydallying followed in Madras, and Bourdonnais emphasised his purposefulness by continuing bombardment. Another representative, Francisco Pereira, was sent to request Bourdonnais to cease firing until the following morning. Bourdonnais refused, and subjected Madras to an intense bombardment through the night from ship and shore batteries. The following morning Monson and Hallyburton returned. Further negotiations followed, with Nicholas Morse pointing out that if the governor and his council were prisoners of war, it would invalidate the terms of ransom. Bourdonnais agreed to release them as soon as the terms were settled. Formal terms of capitulation do not seem to have been signed until 25

September. These terms were not acceptable to Dupleix and his council, and so the final terms were signed on 16 October, dictated as much by Dupleix's demands, as by Bourdonnais' realisation of how militarily weak the storm of 13 October, described later, had left him.

News of the victory reached Dupleix on 22 September 1746. He ordered the immediate firing of a 21-gun salute. A special thanksgiving mass at the Capuchins' church followed. Sweets were ordered to be distributed to every house, and Ananda Ranga Pillai was allotted the special task of having the town decorated and the houses illuminated. In 4 days, there came an ominous warning from Mahfuz Khan to De la Bourdonnais, telling him to depart from Madras with his ships, failing which he would march with an army to restore Madras to the English. Dupleix answered this missive along the usual line of argument, saying that the English had struck first; that Bourdonnais was following the orders of the French King; and a hooded warning inviting Mahfuz Khan to visit Madras and get to know the French better. In Madras, however, the prospect of loot had deepened the dissension between Bourdonnais and D'Espremenil and the other civilian officers, including Dulaurens and Barthelemy. In Bourdonnais's view, his commission from the King had freed him from civilian control. Unlike the civilians, who could make money by private trade and bribery, Bourdonnais would never have another chance like this at enriching himself rapidly. He had ransomed Fort St George to the English for the stupendous sum of 1,100,000 pagodas, to be paid over 2 years, even as he was filling his ships with merchandise with which he intended to sail right away to Mauritius. He alone would answer for his actions to the French Company, he wrote to Dupleix. Furious, Dupleix sent off a letter to D'Espremenil, authorising him to supreme governance at Madras, with the power to arrest De la Bourdonnais. Bourdonnais had acted under the instructions of the council at Pondicherry, and he could not disregard them. There were other reasons. Bourdonnais would sail away with his riches and his ships, leaving the French civilians to face the ridicule that would follow from all quarters. On receiving Dupleix's authorisation, D'Espremenil and the others met Bourdonnais on 2 October 1746 and acquainted him with the new orders. All the French officers present, military, and civilian, including the sailors, were called upon to draw their swords and swear loyalty to the King of France, and to obey D'Espremenil as the governor of Madras, appointed by authority of the Pondicherry council. Bourdonnais was next asked to swear fealty in a similar manner, failing which he would be arrested. Bourdonnais did this.

Civilian authority having been established for the time being, the English prisoners including the governor, Nicholas Morse, were called in to D'Espremenil's presence, and informed that the ransom of the fort as settled by Bourdonnais was cancelled, and that they were prisoners of war. However, Bourdonnais had the loyalty of his force, which also looked to shares from the loot in addition to whatever they could loot for themselves. Hence, Bourdonnais invited the French civilian authorities on board his ship on 4 October and having seized them, deprived them of their powers. He then proceeded with his previous plan of sailing away with the loot. Matters stood thus for the next 8 days, with Madras being guarded by Bourdonnais's men who were under orders not to let in any armed Frenchman from Pondicherry. Dupleix thought all was lost, especially since Bourdonnais had set D'Espremenil and the others free and they were on their way back along the overland route to Pondicherry. Suddenly on 12 October, Bourdonnais performed a volte-face. The English had hidden, he alleged, 200,000 pagodas under the flagstaff. They had not disclosed this, he said. Bourdonnais pretended to be angry about this breach of trust when he was about to let the English have their fort. He at once landed his troops again, and wrote to Pondicherry relating this incident and asking the civil officers to return. Bourdonnais held the centre stage because he had the troops. Within hours, he had changed his mind, and then again some hours later. Ananda Ranga Pillai wrote that Dupleix's jealousy was aroused when he asked Pillai how much Bourdonnais had made from Madras. Pillai's answer that he would have got at least 1,000,000 pagodas irritated Dupleix, since he knew Pillai was correct. The English, the French, the Danes, and the Portuguese, were all traders, and they were in India to shake the pagoda tree. If there was one common factor between them, it was that all their actions were determined by avarice. Pillai pretended to be baffled by Bourdonnais's behaviour: 'Knowing as we do that there is generally concord and good understanding among Europeans, and that they never disagree, we cannot see what he means by saying at one time that he has restored Madras, and at another that he has not, thereby disgracing others'. Retribution came upon Bourdonnais the next day, when a severe storm severely damaged the greater part of his considerable fleet, and forced him to write in a penitent manner to Dupleix, who remained unimpressed. Even though all his fleet lay in a shambles, the ships dismasted and their rudders broken, Bourdonnais's luck held, for the lading of the ships, which comprised his loot, was undamaged.

Bourdonnais now again handed over command to a civilian governor, under the same terms as before, and sailed back to Pondicherry. De la

Bourdonnais left Madras aboard the *Achille* on the morning of 23 October 1746.

The further exploits of Bourdonnais need not detain us any longer. He underwent several adventures, and caused his wife, children, and personal treasure to be conveyed to Lisbon but he was captured by the English, and imprisoned at Falmouth in 1747. He was repatriated to France, where he underwent imprisonment at the Bastille on charges of political subversion, corruption, and embezzlement. Subsequently released, De la Bourdonnais died in 1753.

Unknown to Ananda Ranga Pillai, Dupleix had striven to strengthen the French position by offering Anwaruddin Khan money if he did not interfere with the French invasion of Madras. Half of this was to be paid at once, and the rest after Madras fell. Dupleix had been calculating the amount he would make from the fall of Madras, which was why he had been infuriated by Pillai's reply that Bourdonnais had made 1,000,000 pagodas. To Bourdonnais Dupleix had misrepresented this by saying that he had obtained the Nawab's favour by offering him Madras itself. Madras probably did not yield much to Dupleix as Bourdonnais had already plundered it. Hence, when the time came to settle accounts with Anwaruddin Khan, Dupleix conveniently forgot the arrangement. Instead, he upheld the ransoming of Madras by the English, whereby the French would vacate Madras in January 1747. For this, the English would have to pay more than half the ransom amount to Pondicherry in 6 instalments by October 1749. The rest would be paid through bills presented to the East India Company in London. The French had taken on board their ships all of the English Company's merchandise and military stores, which added up to £130,000. They had also removed the Company's gold and silver, amounting to £31,000. The English, having no choice, signed the treaty on 21 October. Dupleix, however, was thinking otherwise. When Ananda Ranga Pillai asked a Frenchman about the treaty with the English, he was told that the arrangement would become void if the English failed to pay the first of the 6 instalments by the stipulated date. The English had no resources left in Madras. They would have to procure the money from home, and given the many uncertainties of sea-travel especially during hostilities, it seemed almost impossible that the English would be able to pay the ransom according to the schedule. Moreover, even though the English had given hostages to show their good faith, it remained doubtful whether bills drawn upon the Company in London would be honoured, since drafts tendered by prisoners of war were invalid. The French therefore were quite confident that Fort St George would remain in their possession.

Robert Clive, a lowly writer, was among the English prisoners in Madras in 1746. His future would soon be decided by one of the most of the decisive battles of the century, which would provide Clive with a salutary lesson about how a small, but exceptionally led and highly disciplined force could defeat huge local armies.

Anwaruddin Khan was smarting from the trickery of Dupleix. Realising that he would get no share of the loot, he sent his son, Muhammad Mahfuz Khan, at the head of an army of 10,000. The plan was to take Madras from the French. Three French emissaries, sent to confer with him on 1 November 1746, were confined. Summoned before Dupleix, Ananda Ranga Pillai was told that he had been chosen to go as emissary to Mahfuz Khan. Pillai was a man of extraordinary intelligence, a highly successful and influential survivor amidst corruption, chicanery, and uncertainty. He told Dupleix that his proximity to, and influence with, the governor was known to Mahfuz Khan, which would result in his imprisonment. Pillai was also a man of 'very high standing' in Pondicherry. He would find imprisonment intolerable and would accede to the Mahfuz Khan's terms. This veiled threat did not escape Dupleix, who had casually displayed his self-centredness and complete disregard of Pillai's safety by proposing that he go to Mahfuz Khan's camp. Pillai then gave some crucial advice to Dupleix, which demonstrated that even though he was not privy to Dupleix's duplicity with regard to Anwaruddin Khan, he had some inkling of it. If Dupleix sent representatives to Mahfuz Khan, the latter would think that the slightest rattling of the scabbard would scare the French into bribery. They would resort to this means oftener. Pillai thought that given the circumstances, 'it would be impolitic to treat with Mahfuz Khan'. Dupleix knew well that talks with Mahfuz Khan would be futile since Dupleix had reneged on his promises to Nawab Anwaruddin Khan. Pillai helped Dupleix draft letters to the Nawab and his son, Mahfuz Khan. Dupleix was bluffing as he had often done, in the hope that it would carry him through, for he wrote to the Nawab that the French were a valorous people, and if the Nawab chose to ignore this, they would first prove themselves and then proceed to raze Madras to the ground. This last threat was a direct one, for Anwaruddin had expected recompense from the capture of Madras. Razing it would yield nothing, other than the cutting down of the pagoda tree. The letter to Mahfuz was ominous. The French knew that he had 'gone forth with a view to interfere, against their interests, in the political affairs of Madras, and to restore the fort to the English'. He was being warned off matters that did not concern him directly. The Nawab and his son rightly suspected that the French had looted 150,000,000 to 200,000,000 pagodas from Madras, and they had not received a fanam.

The French did not react, D'Espremenil having been strictly warned by Dupleix not to initiate hostilities. Mahfuz Khan, misinterpreting this as fearfulness, proceeded to follow in De la Bourdonnais's steps for the reduction of Madras. However, Mahfuz Khan was unaware of the blessing in disguise, which the same storm that had destroyed Bourdonnais's fleet, had bestowed. Since several ships had been damaged or wrecked, the soldiers and sailors on them had been offloaded and formed into a disciplined force of 3,000 Europeans.

Mahfuz Khan pursued a well-planned strategy devised to reduce Madras fast. His troops would enter through the Black Town, with its low walls. At the same time, the White Town, seemingly protected by a mound of sand to its south where the shallow river entered the sea, would be attacked by cutting through the mound, which Mahfuz was told the English removed with ease when the rising waters of the river required it. To ensure victory, he seized the freshwater spring that supplied Madras. This was provocation enough for the French to commence firing on 2 November 1746 but with minimal effect since the spring was out of range. The cutting of the mound was stopped, and the Nawab's troops discouraged from escalading the walls of the Black Town, by French forces. It was important to secure the water supply, and the following day, 3 November, a force of 400 accompanied by two cannon marched from the fort to accost the enemy, who straddled the route from the town to the spring. The sentries giving the alarm, the enemy cavalry mounted and marched determinedly to meet the advancing Europeans. The standard European infantry tactic of the time was to advance in columns, deploy into lines to deliver volleys, and form squares to face cavalry charges. Successful evolutions depended completely on drilling, and the orderliness and rapidity of movement decided victory. Until 1746, the troops of Indian potentates had not faced these tactics because they had not had occasion to face European military in battle. The French troops used at Madras were not the best but even so, they knew the drill.

French cannon followed their infantry, and on perceiving the enemy, the latter formed a line. When the enemy cavalry approached, the line parted with a precision completely new to their opponents, and revealed the cannon. This was not really a surprise to Mahfuz Khan's cavalry. They had artillery too but here again, European drill added a new and insurmountable factor. The French could reload and discharge their four-pounder cannon every 5 minutes, providing a rate of fire of 12 rounds an hour. Indian cannon were heavier and 4 rounds an hour was considered satisfactory. The French infantry did not have to get into action; their guns' accurate and rapid cannonading killed several of the enemy and the rest fled. The infantry then moved into the enemy's camp and, having ransacked it, returned to the fort. They had achieved their objective without a single casualty on their side. Mahfuz Khan withdrew to San Thome, and set up camp on the strip of land between the river Adyar, which ran into the sea a little to the south of the town, and the town itself, with his artillery facing across the river.

On 4 November 1746 a French column from Pondicherry commanded by M Paradis arrived on the other bank of the river and found Mahfuz Khan ready for them. It had been planned that a column of 400 troops from Madras under De la Tour should attack Mahfuz Khan from the north, while the Pondicherry detachment struck from the south. The former force however was late and Paradis's detachment determinedly crossed the river, which was fordable, and fired a volley on gaining the shore. Without waiting to reload, they carried out a bayonet charge on the Nawab's troops who were composed of massed infantry and cavalry. The enemy fled in disorder to shelter in the southern fringes of the town where they had constructed some palisades. Again subjected to volleys by the French, they retreated pell-mell through the town, led by Mahfuz Khan on his elephant. There was great confusion as enemy infantry and cavalry competed to escape through the narrow streets. Resistance was the last thing on their minds even though they were subjected, while trying to flee, to continual fire from the French. Many were therefore killed while trying to run away. So hasty was this retreat to the west, in the direction of Arcot that they missed the force from Madras, which was proceeding to San Thome. Both the Pondicherry and Madras columns then devoted their attention to looting the enemy camp. Mahfuz Khan withdrew to Arcot with his terrified army. His defeat had suddenly opened up a whole new world to the European traders, who had hitherto assiduously avoided all disagreements with local rulers, fearing escalation and battle, for which they presumed they had neither their respective Companies' mandate, nor training, nor enough men. In fact, both the English and the French had preferred to bribe local rulers to ensure their neutrality.

Paradis had, by his victory, returned to Dupleix the prestige he felt he had lost through acrimony, bungling, and avarice, in his dealings with la Bourdonnais. Dupleix thus appointed Paradis Governor of Madras. Dupleix knew, as Ananda Ranga Pillai did, that Bourdonnais's plundering was the act of a privateer. The terms of the ransom were impracticable. The only feasible answer was the permanent French occupation of Madras, which would ensure complete French dominance of the Coromandel

Coast. This, in turn, would yield higher returns over the long term. Dupleix was not worried about Fort St David, for it would not survive without Madras. In fact, by taking Madras the French had removed the lynchpin of English trade in the Bay of Bengal. Ransoming Fort St George back to the English would undo the entire exercise. Dupleix therefore determined against this.

Paradis, having been appointed governor of Madras, ordered its inhabitants to assemble, and with the guard drawn up, the directives of the council at Pondicherry were read out. The treaty between De la Bourdonnais and the English for the ransom of Madras was declared annulled. The French were to continue in possession of the magazine and all of the English Company's property including merchandise. The English inhabitants were given the choice of swearing fealty to the King of France, which would allow them to remain in Madras as they had been living, in their former condition as Englishmen. Those electing not to take the oath, were given 4 days to move out of the bounds of Madras with their families and all moveable property, including cloth and jewels. They would not be allowed to stay at any of the country houses formerly belonging to Englishmen outside the bounds of Madras. Finally, irrespective of status, all Englishmen would have to give parole not to act against France until they were repatriated. Ananda Ranga Pillai was told that this was customary in Europe, and that the English who were paroled, were required to attend to their conquerors whenever required to do so. Those unwilling to give parole would be arrested and sent to Pondicherry.

This directive was implemented immediately and it ruined all the traders. The local merchants, more uncertain about their future than the Europeans, who could at least expect repatriation and compensation, quitted Madras in large numbers. This Dupleix did not want since their continued presence in Madras, was essential for trade. His primary aim was the dominance of commerce on the Coromandel Coast. With Madras in his possession, he was in a position to neutralise Calcutta by using Chandernagore as the business centre for Bengal. The English factories in Masulipatam and Bantam would also lose their importance, and the English would only be left their trade on the Malabar Coast. It was grandiose scheme, for with Mauritius in its control, the French would be in complete strategic control of the trade routes as well. He therefore told Ananda Ranga Pillai on 14 November that the local merchants in Madras had dispersed, and that Pillai should write to them, inviting them to settle in Pondicherry. If they settled in Pondicherry, Dupleix offered to return them their property in Madras. Pillai was to tell them that there was no possibility of the English regaining Madras but the merchants would recover their fortunes if they sided with the French.

On 17 November 1746 Ananda Ranga Pillai informed Dupleix that Fort St David had somewhat recovered from thc shock of the fall of Madras. The Deputy Governor, Mr Hinde, had instructed merchants to deliver goods for trade there, and a force of 100 Europeans and 400 sepoys had been dispatched towards Gingee to protect and provide safe passage to some of the English who had fled from Madras. Among these were English military officers and Company's officials who considered themselves free of the parole they had given to Bourdonnais, since the treaty with him was annulled. John Hallyburton and Robert Clive were among these escapees. Clive and his friend Edmund Maskelyne disguised themselves as *dubashes*, and escaping the town by night, took to the country. Clive reached Fort St David the same month. Hallyburton was killed in action in 1748. George Pigot, senior in the service by 4 years to Clive, chose to remain in Madras, where he was Junior Merchant and Clerk of the Peace. Later Pigot elected to leave for England, where he remained until 1750.

Nicholas Morse, accompanied by his family, William Monson, and some other English people, including the Barnevalls, reached Pondicherry on 24 November 1746, in the company of some French officials and soldiers. They were ceremonially received by Dupleix, who made it all look like a victory parade, which Ananda Ranga Pillai noted. Morse's grimness reflected his deep sense of shame. All Pondicherry seemed to have turned out to see these Englishmen and women cross the town to Dupleix's house.

The political implications of this headlong retreat having become equally obvious to the Nawab and Mahfuz Khan, they planned to re-establish their prestige. Similarly, it was obvious to Dupleix that reducing Madras was meaningless until Fort St David too was taken. He therefore focused his attention on this latter task. Ananda Ranga Pillai records how Dupleix exclaimed on 1 December that unless Fort St David soon fell, trade would never flourish in Pondicherry. Dupleix ordered Pillai to arrange for 150 bullocks to bring in as much rice as possible from the environs of Fort St David, the intention being to create a shortage of grain there, and to build up stocks at Pondicherry. Pillai informed Dupleix that Fort St David was readying for an assault by the French, and passed on other vital local intelligence to him including the number of troops garrisoning Cuddalore and Fort St David, and the supplies of food and munitions available there. There were, Pillai told Dupleix, 300 to 400

English soldiers and 200 Indian troops, in Fort St David. Orme wrote that the garrison consisted of 200 English and 100 sepoys.

In order to take Fort St David Dupleix recalled Paradis from Madras and put him in charge of a force that marched in the first week of December 1746 for Fort St David. Although harassed by Mahfuz Khan's cavalry en route, Paradis reached Sadras, a Dutch settlement, with his command largely intact. He had a singularly large command comprising 900 Europeans, 600 sepoys, 100 Africans, 6 field-pieces, and 6 mortars. There soon arose problems over Paradis's right to command. Dupleix wanted Paradis but this meant the supersession of several senior officers, who objected, as did several junior officers, and so the command of the force passed to the senior-most officer, General de Bury on 14 December 1746. Paradis's antecedents were questioned 4 months later, when Dupleix planned another assault on Fort St David. Rumour held that he had only been an engineer's assistant in Mauritius and had become engineer because he had married the commandant's widow, and obtained her wealth, which he had used to purchase influence. He was not an officer commissioned by the French Company, and so the issue of the legitimacy of his position recurred in March 1747.

Meanwhile, the Nawab's forces under his other son, Muhammad Ali Khan, had moved to oppose the French advance, less to rescue the English and more to recover their own esteem. Muhammad Ali Khan's forces amounted to over 1500 horse, 1000 infantry, many elephants, and several cannon. Mahfuz Khan joined him.

The change in command having been effected, the French force moved to Ariyankuppam during the night of 19 December, crossing the river Pennar the following morning. Dismissing brief skirmishes with local troops, who fired and fled, the French moved into the Deputy Governor's garden-house and settled in to rest after having marched 12 miles. De Bury posted no sentries, and the entire force gave in to relaxation without, strangely, bothering to establish any pickets. While they were readying their meal, the Nawab's cavalry attacked. The French retreated headlong to the river, which they crossed in relative safety thanks to their artillery commander, who moved his cannon over first and held the enemy off. Nonetheless, considerable damage had been done to the French cause. Ananda Ranga Pillai noted that the stores left behind in the French camp included 250 muskets and 50 kegs of powder. The English now came out from their posts and accompanied the Nawab's troops in pursuing the French. Soon the pursuers found that the French had recovered and were drawn up in proper order to fight the enemy, and did not attack. The French thereafter retreated to Ariyankuppam, from where they had marched the day before, having lost 12 men. The French made further attempts at attacking the English, even as Dupleix undertook diplomatic manoeuvres to break the alliance between the English and the Nawab. On 30 December 1746, a force of 100 French troops embarked on boats to take Cuddalore, a strategy that Pillai says he recommended to Paradis and Dupleix. However, given the roughness of the sea, the boats leaked and the invasion force had to turn back. Dupleix also ordered the laying waste of villages around Arcot, offering deliberate provocation to the Nawab for his complicity with the English. Soon there arrived at Pondicherry, in the third week of January 1747, 4 French ships, under Captain Dordelin. This was a major coup for Dupleix, for when news of this reached Anwaruddin Khan, he ordered his sons to cease hostilities and come to terms with the French. To demonstrate his goodwill, he had the two French emissaries who had been seized and imprisoned at Arcot the previous November, released. Anwaruddin, already hard-pressed on one side by the Nizam to pay revenues due, and on the other by the rising power of the Marathas in the Carnatic, was eager for peace with the Europeans, who had much to offer by way of trade. Fights between them, originating in political disputes involving their distant home countries, were not his business. Anwaruddin was 87, and he had been sick through the latter part of 1746. His sons however did not heed his orders. Mahfuz Khan, in particular, continued to stay encamped in the neighbourhood of Ariyankuppam. Despite negotiations being then in progress between Dupleix and his father, his troops continued to make incursions into French territory. Dupleix, in order to reciprocate the release of the Frenchmen, had withdrawn the main force from Ariyankuppam, and left a garrison of 50 Europeans and 50 sepoys.

By 15 February 1747, the talks had come to a standstill, with Arcot demanding a payment of 500,000 pagodas, and Dupleix willing to pay only 30,000 following the logic that, since the Nawab's sons and his forces had begun the war, the French were not bound to pay any indemnity. Dupleix's boldness paid off. The Nawab's representative in Pondicherry, Muhammad Tavakkal, went to talk to the two brothers, Muhammad Ali Khan and Mahfuz Khan. Ananda Ranga Pillai records the latter in his diary as having displayed great belligerence to Tavakkal. Dupleix then invited Mahfuz Khan to Pondicherry for discussions, since even Dupleix was bluffing. He could not afford to fight both the English and the Nawab. The pillaging by the Nawab's forces and the French in the area had already created a crisis in the supply of grain, for Pondicherry was supplied only by grain allowed to come in through territory controlled by the Nawab. Mahfuz Khan accepted Dupleix's invitation, and he visited

Pondicherry two days later. Soon an accord was reached, extravagant gifts bestowed, lavish entertainments arranged and viewed, and peace contrived. The two brothers broke camp and marched away on 25 February 1747, thus withdrawing, at least for the time being, from the first Carnatic War. Dupleix and Ananda Ranga Pillai had played their cards very creditably, and had overcome nearly insurmountable odds within a short time. Pillai now became the subject of Madame Dupleix's suspicions. She was always concerned about money, 'Such being the greed that filled her soul, it appeared to her that it was not advantageous to remain inactive in these troublous times', he complained. She engaged in slandering Pillai, in the hope that she would thereby be able to remove Dupleix from his influence and place as advisers her puppets.

With Mahfuz Khan gone, Dupleix planned the next attack on Fort St David, led by Paradis. Paradis's qualifications for command having been protested by De Bury, De la Tour, and others, Dupleix was compelled to put De la Tour in command, with Paradis as his adviser. A day before the operation was to take off, Dupleix informed Pillai that he had received news that the Wars of Succession were over, and the next ship from France would order the cessation of hostilities but before that Fort St David had to be captured. Dupleix was looking far into the future, and trying to secure for the French not a couple of trading stations more but a kingdom. The expedition began its assault on the night of 11 March 1747. It began well enough and would have carried through, had the squadron commanded by Admiral Griffin, having sailed from Bengal, not appeared at the most crucial moment off Fort St David. The French officers, De la Tour, Paradis, St Jacques, St Martin, Vincens, and Soliminac, conferred and decided to return to Pondicherry, which they believed had become vulnerable to attack by this squadron due to their absence. The ships brought in additional forces from Bengal for Fort St David. Their sailors augmented the garrison, and slowly more reinforcements arrived, from Bombay, Tellicherry, and, later, Europe.

Matters were changing in the English camp at Fort St David also. The fort was well placed for defence. Properly garrisoned and armed after the fall of Madras, it presented a serious obstacle to the French, irrespective of the fact that from the French perspective it looked easy to take. With the arrival of Griffin's squadron, the balance tilted suddenly in the favour of the English. News of the fall of Madras had reached England quite fast for the times, by the end of April 1747. Rumours from France that had seeped in even earlier and been dismissed, now shook Leadenhall Street. The Company dispatched one of its most momentous letters in July. 'We have Judged it proper' they wrote, 'upon such a Surprising Revolution in our

Affairs as the loss of Madras, to Constitute Fort St David our Head Settlement'. John Hinde was appointed the President and Governor, and his council included Major Stringer Lawrence, who was en route with orders to take over military command of the Company's affairs. 'Astonishing Reports' had been received 'of the Capitulation and Ransom of Madras', and Hinde was forbidden to 'Enter into any Treaty with the Country Government or any other Power relating to the Payment of any Sum of Money for the Ransom or the Re-Delivery of that Place'. The General Court of the Company had decided this. The despatch also stated that the Company's servants at Madras 'Ceased to be so on the Loss of the Place' but 'such of them as, from their Behaviour' might seem proper, were to be reemployed at Fort St David. The others were to be allowed a 'Reasonable Subsistence' if they applied for it.

In 1747, Clive sought escape from the duties of a writer by seeking an ensigncy, which was granted. This was propitious for the English and for him, since these were trying times, and superior strategic thinking would win for the victor an empire. Stringer Lawrence reached Fort St David in January 1748. He was a seasoned officer, then aged over 50 and with 20 years' experience of campaigning in Europe. While canonical English historians of this train of events tend to dismiss French intrepidity as coincidental, the fact is that the French and the English were quite evenly matched, both at sea and on shore. Lawrence's induction infused fresh martial fervour, which was coincidental with the arrival and stationing of Admiral Boscawen's fleet in July 1748. Boscawen superseded Griffin, who retired to Trincomalee, and commenced offensive action against Pondicherry immediately on arrival. A naval encounter between a French fleet under Admiral Bouvet and the English under Griffin, had already taken place early in June. Bouvet pretended to be readying for an attack on Fort St David roads but withdrew during the night and, having accomplished his primary task by landing troops and treasure in Madras, sailed for Mauritius. Griffin, stationed off Pondicherry, sailed to engage Bouvet but found him neither off Fort St David nor off Madras. Griffin was later court-martialled for having failed to fight Bouvet and found guilty.

With Griffin and his fleet sailing away on 10 June, Dupleix at once planned another attack on Cuddalore. This took place on 27 June. Around 2000 French troops including 900 Europeans set off to take Cuddalore by surprise the following night. The French were betrayed by 'the son-in-law of Kuttan', who, Ananda Ranga Pillai writes, was a double agent. He pretended to show the French the way to Cuddalore, then slipped away. Stringer Lawrence had the Cuddalore garrison and artillery removed to

Fort St David to convince the French that the English had fled. As soon as darkness fell, Lawrence moved these back so that the French were taken completely by surprise when they launched their attack at midnight. The French, finding themselves under intense cannon and musket fire, took immediate flight. Conflicting reports were received in Pondicherry until the troops, who had not even halted at their camp, returned to the bounds.

Meanwhile with Admiral Boscawen's arrival, the English fleet comprised more than 30 ships, and 13 of them were ships-of-the-line. The English had achieved absolute mastery of the sea on the Coromandel Coast. A counterattack was planned to wrest Pondicherry, and to this end a huge force of 3720 Europeans and 2000 sepoys accompanied by 80 artillerymen and their guns, set out. They were to be helped by Boscawen's fleet. The ships anchored off Pondicherry, out of range of the guns, on 11 August. The force marched on 19 August and operations commenced. Panic set in at Pondicherry, and Dupleix was desperately looking about for a means of countering the English, who he knew were descending upon him in incontestable numbers. He asked Pillai to ensure the availability of paddy in the town, and readied for defence even as he corresponded and once more tried to bluff his way with local potentates. He knew the latter would be convinced by the size of the English force, the like of which he could never expect from his mother country. He should not have troubled himself since the English botched the attack on Ariyankuppam, which they had to subdue first, in the same manner in which the French had wasted their efforts on Cuddalore. The English had done no reconnaissance, and did not know how Ariyankuppam was defended. Based on information from a deserter, they went into attack by daylight, and were subjected to well-directed fire. 150 of the attackers including a King's officer, Major Goodere, were killed.

Ariyankuppam was besieged and captured, and artillery duels followed, accompanied by unproductive raids by the English. On 30 August, a body of 60 French cavalry attacked an English battery and the latter fled. Stringer Lawrence tried to rally them but was captured. On the French side, Paradis, Dupleix's ablest officer, was ambushed in an attack and killed on 11 September 1748. By 17 October, the rains had set in and it was no longer tenable for Boscawen to keep his ships anchored. Therefore, the great English force struck camp and retired, leaving a third of its number dead due to illness or enemy action. The following month news of the Treaty of Aix-la-Chapelle was received, preliminaries to which had been signed in April 1748. Hostilities ended between the English and the French for the time being. Madras was ordered to be returned to the English by a clause of the final Treaty, signed in October 1748.

Madras was returned to the English on Monday, 1 September 1749. Ananda Ranga Pillai calculated that had been in French possession for 2 years, 11 months, and 10 days, 'And in spite of people flocking back there,' he wrote, it would 'take twenty or thirty years for Madras to become the Golden City, for it is no easy affair for a city 121 years old to recover its prosperity after it has been once dashed to pieces'.

CHAPTER SEVEN

THE CARNATIC WAR II

Peace came uneasily to the Carnatic, for there had been armies marching across it for the two previous years. Crops had been laid waste, and trade had suffered but it would not be allowed the time it needed to recover. The Mughal Emperor, Muhammad Shah, who had purged his empire of the Sayyid brothers, died in April 1748. His reign had been marked by constant struggle with the Marathas, whose power was growing. In 1739, Nadir Shah of Persia had humbled Muhammad Shah, by looting Delhi of its riches, including the Kohinoor diamond and the Peacock Throne. In 1748 also died the Nizam, who had the viceroyalty of the Deccan. While his son Ahmad Shah Bahadur succeeded Muhammad Shah, the Nizam's death resulted in a war of succession between his son Nasir Jung and his grandson, and Nasir's nephew, Muzaffar Jung. The English supported the former, and the French the latter. The division found echo in the Carnatic, where the English supported the continuance of the very aged Nawab, Anwaruddin, while the French under Dupleix supported the claims of the sole surviving representative of the family of Dost Ali Khan, Chanda Sahib. Chanda Sahib extended his support to Muzaffar Jung, driving the discord deeper into imperial politics. Dupleix had been forced to treat with Anwaruddin Khan and his sons, in particular Mahfuz Khan. This humiliation he would not forget. Dupleix therefore ransomed Chanda Sahib from the Marathas, whose prisoner he had been since 1741, for the huge sum of 700,000 rupees. The Europeans might have superficially been at peace with each other but each side actively aided its candidate in hopes of extensive concessions and much trade. The second Carnatic War thus began due to increasing political instability. Chanda Sahib's family had been living in Pondicherry and Dupleix assured him 2000 French troops including 400 Europeans. In return, Chanda Sahib, as Nawab of the Carnatic, would grant the French the settlement of Villiyanallur, in partial recompense for Madras. This train of events forced Anwaruddin, although 90 years old, to take the field, along with his sons Mahfuz Khan and Muhammad Ali, in order to protect his realm.

The opponents met at the Battle of Ambur. The details of the battle will not detain us long, being beyond the scope of this work. The climate of Ambur is dry and hot in summer, with temperatures reaching 43 degrees Celsius, and 10 degrees in winter. D'Auteuil, assisted by De Bussy, commanded the French force. Anwaruddin's army comprised 12,000 cavalry and 8,000 infantry. Orme noted that the English were blind to their interests and so did not assist Anwaruddin. The latter, Orme said, 'from the parsimony of his disposition', did not ask for help from the English. Chanda Sahib and Muzaffar Jung seem to have rendezvoused with the French at Pallikonda, approximately halfway between Ambur and Arcot, and moved southwards to meet the Nawab's troops, encamped under the cover of the fort at Ambur. Chanda Sahib had at his command 40,000 troops. The fort was situated at a height, and the Nawab's artillery, manned by Europeans, probably deserters or mercenaries, was lined along an entrenchment that stretched from the fort to a lake. Water from the lake was diverted to flood the land in front of the entrenchment. The battle commenced on the morning of 3 August 1749. Loot goaded the French to lead several assaults that initially failed, since the Nawab's artillery was well handled. D'Auteuil was wounded but the French troops were well led by De Bussy. A final assault carried them over the entrenchment, which the Nawab's troops promptly deserted. The French then formed into line and advanced towards the Nawab's main force, where Anwaruddin, astride an elephant, was urging his cavalry to stand firm. Chanda Sahib's soldiers had hitherto remained spectators to French prowess. Now they too surged forward. Orme wrote that Anwaruddin was misinformed that his son Mahfuz Khan had been slain by a cannon shot, and on seeing the elephant bearing Chanda Sahib, he urged his mahout to move up against Chanda Sahib's mount. At this crucial moment, a ball from a French musket killed Anwaruddin. On his death, his army fled. Many were killed while fleeing. Dupleix's archenemy, Mahfuz Khan, was taken prisoner, while Muhammad Ali escaped to Trichinopoly. The enemy camp yielded much loot. Chanda Sahib rewarded the French with money. Muzaffar Jung returned to Arcot, proclaimed himself Nizam, and confirmed Chanda Sahib as the Nawab of the Carnatic.

Muhammad Ali sought refuge in Trichinopoly, where his father's treasure and his mother were. He knew that in order to survive he had to obtain help from the English at once. This he did, pointing out that Nasir Jung was the rightful Nizam, as he was the true Nawab of the Carnatic. The English were in a quandary for they had just indulged in an expensive and largely needless expedition against the Raja of Tanjore, to wrest from him the village of Devikottah. Besides, Admiral Boscawen, with his huge force, departed the coast on 1 November 1749, leaving behind a squadron of 5 ships under Commodore Lisle. For the English it seemed too expensive and uncertain an investment to engage in military forays when their attention should be directed to the rebuilding of their trade. Muhammad Ali's references to the Mughal Emperor were no surety for the English, since Delhi was far away and had long ceased to be a factor in local politics. Dupleix on the other hand was playing for stakes he knew could only enhance his prestige, and, thereby, the importance of Pondicherry, which, unlike Madras, had not yet suffered occupation. He urged Muzaffar Jung and Chanda Sahib to reduce Trichinopoly. Nonetheless, various circumstances protracted their march through Tanjore, which they failed to capture despite French assistance. The Raja of Tanjore paid a huge indemnity and Muzaffar Jung and Chanda Sahib were diverted by the warlike preparations of Nasir Jung, who had in the meantime occupied Golconda and declared himself the Nizam (December 1749).

Dupleix, ruthless in his pursuit of the absolute control of the Carnatic, paid Muzaffar Jung the enormous sum of £50,000, and bolstered him with a French force 2,000 strong, accompanied by artillery. These forces camped at Villiyanallur in March 1750. Nasir Jung's encampment was at Valudavur, a few miles from Pondicherry, and there he was joined by Muhammad Ali, whom he declared the Nawab of Arcot, and by a force of 600 Europeans under Major Stringer Lawrence. The officers of the French force were unhappy with their shares of loot from Tanjore and, under various pretexts, 15 of them resigned their commissions and returned to Pondicherry on the morning of 4 April 1750. Their actions disheartened their troops and by evening, these too decided to withdraw. The alliance was broken. Chanda Sahib promptly decided to seek safety in Pondicherry, while Muzaffar Jung, who had been receiving messengers from Nasir Jung, was told by his ministers that as Nasir Jung had offered him amnesty, he should surrender.

Dupleix had by now lost his best officers, all prey to his ambitions. Paradis had fallen in the defence of Pondicherry, and Duquesne had died at Tanjore. Goupil, the next in ability, was ill, and command devolved on D'Auteuil. Muzaffar Jung went to meet his uncle Nasir Jung and was imprisoned. D'Auteuil marched back through the night, keeping his troops in close order until dawn found them near the prickly-pear hedge that marked the bounds of Pondicherry, which they reached only after warding off repeated and determined attacks by Maratha cavalry, who had discovered the retreat of the French and given pursuit. The French lost several Europeans in this unfortunate encounter. Dupleix was most upset with his allies and his countrymen. He had the mutinous officers arrested, and D'Auteuil court-martialled, for retreating without orders. The soldiers were not allowed to enter Pondicherry but halted outside. Dupleix went to address them and infuse them with courage. At the same time, he amazingly opened negotiations with Nasir Jung's camp. Du Bausset and De Larche were dispatched to Nasir Jung's court as Dupleix's ambassadors on 19 April 1750. Dupleix also carried on secret talks with three of Nasir Jung's feudatories, the rulers of Cuddapah, Kurnool, and Savanur, who were disaffected. The French ambassadors argued that the French had meant all along to desert Muzaffar Jung, being convinced that Nasir Jung was the true Nizam. They had provided Muzaffar's mother, Nasir Jung's sister, shelter in Pondicherry and wished that Muzaffar's estates would not be seized but given to his son. Chanda Sahib they wanted appointed Nawab of the Carnatic. Lawrence meanwhile had written on 12 April to Dupleix, offering to broker peace. This proposal was rejected. By 22 April, it was clear that nothing was to be achieved through further discussions with Nasir Jung. The following day the French envoys returned to Pondicherry.

Even as secret talks continued, Dupleix determined to demonstrate his army's prowess to Nasir Jung as well as to instil courage in his troops. In fact, he had been advised to commence warlike moves by the three unhappy feudal lords of Nasir Jung. Hence, on the night of 27 April 1750 French troops attacked Nasir Jung's camp with considerable success. Nasir Jung struck camp on 30 April and moved into Arcot with the intention of settling the Carnatic from that strongpoint. To avenge himself on the French he had their factory at Masulipatam seized. Dupleix took advantage of the arrival in mid-July, of two ships sailing from France to Bengal, the *Fleury* and the *d'Argenson*, to embark a force of 200 Europeans and 300 sepoys whose mission was to take Masulipatam. With the element of surprise on their side, they did this very effectively, without any bloodshed. Simultaneously he sent off D'Auteuil (now restored to grace, having successfully convinced Dupleix that retreat from Villiyanallur was the only option left him) with a force of 500 to capture the bastion at Tiruvedi, across the Pennar. This was a brilliant strategic move since this position dominated Muhammad Ali's army, encamped nearby. Its occupation by the French also made the English uneasy since they did not want a French fortification in the proximity of Fort St David. D'Auteuil took the citadel, garrisoned it, and then set up a fortified camp some miles downriver. Muhammad Ali was as nonplussed by this swift action, as his overlord, Nasir Jung, was, with the precipitate recapture of Masulipatam.

Aware of Muhammad Ali's timorousness, the English sent reinforcements on 11 July, a column of 400 Europeans and 1500 sepoys under Captain Cope, to shore him up. D'Auteuil was outnumbered but determined. On 30 July 1750, the first battle began. Muhammad Ali feinted to attack Tiruvedi hoping to draw out the French garrison, which failed. He then attempted to overrun the French camp, which also failed. The French artillery fired with devastating accuracy and rapidity, causing great loss to the attackers. Muhammad Ali would heed no further counsels by Captain Cope, and the English column withdrew to Fort St David. Muhammad Ali stayed where he was, and sought advice from Nasir Jung at Arcot. Dupleix, now determined to force matters, ordered D'Auteuil to attack Muhammad Ali. D'Auteuil was to rendezvous with De la Touche, who had command of 1300 Europeans, 2500 sepoys, and 1000 cavalry provided by Chanda Sahib. The second Battle of Tiruvedi took place on 1 September 1750. Muhammad Ali had 20,000 troops and his camp was situated between two villages with its back to the river. The French carried Muhammad Ali's camp without losing a soldier. Large numbers of the enemy were slaughtered while the rest fled across the Pennar like their commander. Muhammad Ali escaped with a few attendants to seek refuge in Arcot, leaving the French army to focus on other targets. Dupleix wanted D'Auteuil to proceed to Arcot by way of Villupuram and Gingee, in order to alarm Nasir Jung into agreeing to his terms. Nasir Jung, immersed in the opulence of his position, provided no solace or support to his underling, Muhammad Ali. The English too found themselves deprived of any reason to engage the French, since the two nations were then at peace in Europe. Major Lawrence was scheduled to sail for England soon, and he left India knowing that the indefatigable Dupleix had once more bested him. Chanda Sahib's cavalry had played an important role in these two battles and his prestige was thereby re-established in the Carnatic.

Matters had not been going well with the English. Due perhaps to the supersession of trade by warlike activities, gaming and duelling had become endemic among them. The Company's letter of 12 January 1750 to Fort St David, brought by the East Indiaman *Lynn*, commanded by Captain William Egerton, makes for interesting reading in this regard. From the fall of Madras, through its rendition, and until April 1752, Fort St George was subservient to Fort St David. The governor at Fort St David, Charles Floyer, was dismissed the service because he and several other 'Superior Servants' of the Company had 'Connived at and practised' the 'Spirit of Gaming'. This had engrossed all their attention and resulted in 'Extravagant Expenses' and 'general neglect and want of Order'. The 'pernicious Vice of Gaming' had 'spread like a Contagion' among 'all the

Ranks and Degrees' of the Company's servants. The Company was therefore 'determined to put a Stop to it by making Example of Every Person infected with it'. Convinced of the need to restructure the council, the Company appointed in Floyer's place Thomas Saunders, followed by Richard Prince, then Deputy Governor at Fort St George, Stringer Lawrence as Third, and others, including George Pigot, who had been sent out on the same ship to rejoin the service as tenth in council at Fort St David. The new governor was to look closely into the vast sums spent during Floyer's tenure, and 'Reprimand Suspend and even dismiss from … Service' depending on 'the Degree of their Guilt' any Company servant, civilian or military, found gaming. While Pigot had returned from England to sit in council, Clive had fought with great valour at the reduction of Devikottah. At the conclusion of this military task, he reverted to the civil service in 1749 and resumed work at Madras. His health soon failed and he went to Bengal to recuperate. There he passed the winter. Following his return, Stringer Lawrence, aware of Clive's keenness for the military profession, appointed him commissary for the army.

Raja Sarup Singh, the *quiladar* of Gingee, who had featured so prominently in the train of events leading up to Raworth's Rebellion, was dead by January 1714. His son, Desing, who succeeded him, scorned the advice of the secretary or *vaknavis* of Gingee, Payya Ramakrishna, to apply with adequate presents to Saadatullah Khan, the Nawab of the Carnatic, for the confirmation of his accession. This was only a formality since Saadatullah Khan would recommend Desing to the Emperor, who would merely endorse the appointment. Saadatullah Khan also seems to have been accommodating, for in the face of Desing's deliberate offensiveness, he persisted in trying to get the young Bundela chief, aged 22, to see reason. Saadatullah Khan was forced to draw up his army and march to Gingee since Desing remained adamant. Desing on the other hand moved towards Arcot with a small force in order to coerce the Nawab to battle. At Varahanadi Desing and his troops were briefly held up by the river but they crossed it and accosted the Nawab's army at Kadalimalai, about 4 miles from Gingee. Saadatullah Khan's strict order was that Desing should not be harmed. This order was followed until sufficient provocation obliged the Nawab's soldiers to shoot Desing dead. Nawab Saadatullah Khan occupied Gingee on 3 October 1714. It has been said that the Nawab had used Desing's refractoriness as an excuse to take Gingee, as ordered by the Emperor, Farrukhsiyar, following Sarup Singh's refusal to pay his dues to the Imperial court. In any case, Saadatullah Khan made Gingee his residence for the next 4 years, until its unhealthy climate made him return to Arcot, leaving his relative, Sadat Tiyar Khan, as *quiladar*. During the following decades, Gingee lost its greatness. In 1721, the Nizam visited Saadatullah Khan to elicit details of revenue collections and generally settle the administration of the Carnatic. Saadatullah Khan died in 1733 and Sadat Tiyar Khan in 1747. The next *quiladar* was Ghaziuddin Khan, who ruled until 1752.

De Bussy reached Villupuram on 5 September 1750, and D'Auteuil, with the consent of his officers including De Bussy and De la Touche, sought Dupleix's permission to take Gingee. Accordingly, De Bussy reached Gingee on 11 September with a small force of 250 Europeans, 1200 sepoys, and 4 field-guns. Muhammad Ali, aware of the ignominy of his previous defeat and that he would have to look to his own interests, also reached Gingee with a far larger army. He now commanded 8000 cavalry, 2000 infantry, and 8 field-guns operated by Europeans, who, as has been mentioned earlier, were deserters or mercenaries. More importantly, Muhammad Ali additionally had 1000 sepoys trained by the English. Muhammad Ali's army was drawn up along the glacis and, emboldened by the European-operated artillery and heartened by their sheer superiority of numbers, attacked De Bussy, who waited until the enemy was at pistol-shot range, and then opened fire with his artillery, doing great damage to the cavalry. Meanwhile, D'Auteuil was rushing up to De Bussy's assistance with the rest of the force. On seeing the reinforcements arrive, Muhammad Ali's troops retreated rapidly towards Gingee, their disorderly withdrawal being covered by the fort's cannon but they seem to have initially been denied permission by the *quiladar* from seeking refuge within. They had deserted their field-guns and the gunners. The former were captured, and the latter mostly slaughtered, by the French. Untroubled by the fort's cannon, De Bussy followed several of the enemy to the gate and, blowing it up, entered the town. He then personally led his men to the temporary buttressing of their position and the placement of mortars. By now, it was night. The fort of Gingee enclosed 7 square kilometres ringed by 3 natural mountainous redoubts, and each peak was protected by a series of fortifications leading up to a citadel, and this site had made Gingee virtually impregnable. The enemy, occupying higher ground, fired continually upon the French until the moon set, to which the French replied by mortaring. As soon as the moon had set, De Bussy's troops took the advantage of darkness to assault the enemy entrenchments, engaging in desperate hand-to-hand fighting. By daybreak, they were in possession of Gingee, having lost 20 Europeans. The prestige of the French soared due to De Bussy's astounding feat.

Muhammad Ali hurried back to Arcot to seek Nasir Jung's assistance. The latter hitherto immersed in the pleasures of his position rather than attending to its onerous responsibilities, now understood the unpleasant consequences of having Gingee in the hands of the French. Resorting to the usual contemporary strategy, he sent emissaries to Dupleix to seek terms. Dupleix demanded the restoration of Muzaffar Jung and Chanda Sahib and that the French should keep Gingee. These were terms calculated to offend and Nasir Jung decided to fight. He gathered a huge army, comprising 60,000 infantry, 45,000 cavalry, 700 elephants, and 360 cannon, and marched from Arcot in mid-November 1750. He camped at Vellimedupettai, about 18 miles from Villupuram, and was planning a concerted assault on Gingee, when Himmat Bahadur Khan, the Nawab of Kurnool, betrayed him. De la Touche had been in touch with Himmat Bahadur Khan, who told him to attack Nasir Jung's camp on the night of 15 December 1750. This De la Touche did with a force of 800 Europeans, 3000 sepoys, and 10 field-guns. Nasir Jung mounted his elephant to take on the enemy before dawn on 16 December. He moved eastwards and up the right side of his camp to the place where Himmat Bahadur Khan, along with his fellow conspirators, the Nawabs of Cuddapah and Savanur, waited on their elephants, with their troops in marching order. Nasir Jung greeted Himmat Bahadur Khan, who shot him dead and, then, having cut off his head, held it aloft on a spear for all to see as the day dawned. This resulted in chaos, with the French taking Nasir Jung's camp, and the various feudatories either retreating or staying, depending on their relations with the French and the English. Much loot was obtained, and Muzaffar Jung proclaimed the Nizam. This was the highest point in Dupleix's career, and probably the most tenuous period for the English. Muhammad Ali, ever wary of such coups, fled yet again, this time to Trichinopoly.

News of the victory was first received in Pondicherry by that other prominent persona in the Carnatic, Chanda Sahib, who, Orme says, rushed at once from his house to Dupleix's mansion, and dismissing all ceremony, told him. The two embraced in their mutual delight, and Dupleix once more ordered celebrations. Muzaffar Jung was aware of having been made Nizam only due to the promises he had made to the disaffected Nawabs and the machinations of Dupleix. Unable to trust the Nawabs, he decided to move at once to Pondicherry under the pretext of consultations with Dupleix, there to seek advice on how to deal with the former, promises to whom he would be unable to fulfil. Fobbing the Nawabs off until then, Muzaffar Jung proceeded to Pondicherry, reaching there on 26 December 1750. Here he was received with unprecedented ceremony, and 'invested' by Dupleix with his powers. By his strategic brilliance, Dupleix seemed to have abrogated unto himself imperial prerogatives. Similarly, Muzaffar Jung went out of his way to heap gifts upon Dupleix. He awarded Dupleix a *mansab* of 7000 horse, and appointed him imperial governor of all territory south of the river Krishna. Further, he gave to Dupleix as a personal mark of favour, the fort of Valudavur, and its dependent villages, along with a separate *jagir* with revenue of 100,000 rupees. A sum of 500,000 rupees was given to Dupleix for distribution among his soldiers. In all, the French East India Company was granted territories that yielded annual revenue of £38,000, while its coffers were filled with the payment of £50,000. Chanda Sahib was confirmed as the Nawab of Arcot with Dupleix as his superior. Dupleix had in the meantime settled the issues of the disgruntled Nawabs by bringing them to discussion and impressing upon them the need to reduce their claims in proportion to the limitations of Muzaffar Jung. Nasir Jung's treasure was valued at £2,000,000 and half of this, minus the jewels, which would go to Muzaffar Jung, would be given to the three traitorous Nawabs. Their territories would be expanded by the addition of revenue-yielding districts. Such dealings between a European trading company's representative and local princes had never been seen before. Malleson writes of Dupleix that he 'emerged from that tent' where the ceremony was held 'the virtual superior of the lord of Southern India'. He was rumoured to have made a personal fortune of £200,000 from these deals.

The three Nawabs had merely pretended to consent to Dupleix's recommendations. Additionally, Muhammad Ali was still ensconced at Trichinopoly, and the English were yet to be brought to heel. The year had barely turned, when a sudden unpleasant turn in fortune took place. Muzaffar Jung, at the end of the long festivities following his elevation, decided to proceed to Golconda and put his kingdom in order. Dupleix was agreeable to his suggestion that a small French contingent accompany him. Accordingly, De Bussy, with a force of 300 Europeans, 2000 sepoys, and 10 field-guns, joined Muzaffar Jung, and the march commenced on 15 January 1751. By the end of January, the Nizam's army reached Cuddapah, whose Nawab had been one of the three conspirators against Nasir Jung. Some of the Nizam's rearguard got into an altercation with some villagers, and indulged in looting and burning. The Nawab of Cuddapah used this opportune moment to direct a skirmish, whose target was Muzaffar Jung's *zenana*, which had an army escort. This was a predetermined move and it stopped the march. Muzaffar Jung turned to accost the refractory Nawab. De Bussy was rather nonplussed and he sought to mediate. However, information soon came that all three conspirators had once more gathered with their forces and they had occupied a defensive position along a pass, well enfiladed by cannon. Muzaffar Jung at once moved with a part of his army to meet the challenge. De Bussy followed as well, considering it his duty to protect the Nizam. Muzaffar Jung might have done better to keep pace with De Bussy. This however he disdained and moved ahead. Muzaffar Jung fought his enemies well enough. The Nawab of Savanur was killed, and Cuddapah fled. The Nawab of Kurnool found himself cornered and turned to fight to the last. Muzaffar Jung, like Nasir, heeded no warning but headed off to personally defeat his enemy. Muzaffar Jung was then around 28 years old, and brave. He ordered his elephant brought up to the Nawab's. This done, he raised his sword to kill but was killed instead by a spear thrust by the Nawab of Kurnool. The Nawab and his few followers were at once despatched by Muzaffar Jung's troops. Nonetheless, the harm had been done. Muzaffar Jung was dead and so, apparently, was Dupleix's future. De Bussy's battalion received the news and its commander at once grasped the gravity of the situation. De Bussy withdrew to the camp, where chaos was looming. Showing exceptional presence of mind, he attempted to save the fortunes of the French by calling the feudatories together to decide on the succession. The candidates included Muzaffar Jung's infant son and the three brothers of Nasir Jung, who had been imprisoned by Nasir to keep them from rebelling in his absence. As Orme writes, no one wanted a minor since this would carry the need for a regent. Instead, De Bussy and the others decided to name Salabat Jung, the eldest of the three brothers, Nizam. On his elevation, Salabat Jung agreed not only to honour all the promises made to the French by Muzaffar but also offered additional concessions. When these developments were communicated to Dupleix, he at once recognised Salabat Jung as Nizam. The army then resumed its march to Golconda under its new commander. En route they paused only to reduce Kurnool (18 March) and reached Hyderabad on 21 April 1751. On 29 June 1751, Salabat Jung entered Aurangabad, where he was confirmed in his office by imperial edict. Meanwhile, Muhammad Ali, acutely aware of the ascendancy of Dupleix, agreed to treat with the Nizam. With the exception of the English, Dupleix was in complete control of India southwards from the Deccan.

Now it was the turn of the English to be intensely aware of the precariousness of their settlements. Benjamin Robins had been sent out from England to fulfil the need for a military engineer in August 1749, reaching Madras with 6 assistants on 14 July 1750. He had been sent as replacement for Captain Alexander Delavaux, who had taken charge less than 2 years before, but following the death of a fellow Englishman in an accident, and allegations of malfeasance, had deserted to Pondicherry in May 1749. The English were very lucky that Robins had agreed to come out to India, for he was an exceptional mathematician, having become a Fellow of the Royal Society when aged only 20. Later he specialised in civil engineering and advocated the use of rifled guns. He became still more famous with his book of 1742, *New Principles of Gunnery*, which remained the standard textbook in Europe on the subject until the turn of the century. In 1749, the Company appointed him under covenant to be 'Engineer General, as likewise Commander in Chief of the Artillery'. His instructions were to visit Fort St David, Fort St George, Fort William, Bombay, and St Helena, survey fortifications and artillery, and send drawings and recommendations to Leadenhall Street. His proposals were indeed were of great benefit to the Company. At the end of December 1750, Muzaffar Jung moved Nasir Jung's enormous treasure from Gingee to Pondicherry under guard of a detachment of his own troops and 300 French soldiers. This guard was insufficient in number and slack in discipline. Intelligence of this must have reached Fort St David, for Robins suggested to Thomas Saunders the need to attack it with 800 Europeans and take the treasure. Saunders agreed but his officers did not and in this, they were correct for he had no business provoking the French and the Nizam while Fort St George was in need of fortification, and still recovering from the recent French occupation. Their respective nations were at peace in Europe and Saunders would be unable to answer Leadenhall Street in case of fatalities and prolonged and expensive hostilities. Hence, Orme's criticism that such an action if undertaken precipitately would have succeeded, and Nasir Jung's treasure carried to Fort St David instead of Pondicherry, is untenable. Robins, who might later have played a far more important role in the affairs of the English, died of fever, probably malaria, on 29 July 1751. His last letter to the Company was written on 25 July, and in it, he urged the Company to ensure that Calcutta 'be well secured, for it is a Place of Infinite Consequence'. Long before any of his contemporaries, Robins alone foresaw the weakness of Fort William and its susceptibility to an invading force, either from Chandernagore or from up north, where the Nawab, Alivardi Khan, ruled at Murshidabad. 5 years later the truth of his opinion was confirmed. The Fort St David council deeply regretted his passing, writing home of Robins' 'Judgement, Assiduity and Disinterestedness in the Management of Affairs under his Direction'. They wanted as his replacement someone 'as capable and agreeable a Man as Mr Robins'.

The English sensed that Salabat Jung's ascendancy had nearly tilted Muhammad Ali's anxiety and indecisiveness towards accommodation with the Nizam. Once Muhammad Ali submitted to Salabat Jung, Dupleix would bring his considerable faculties to bear on removing the English from the Coromandel Coast. They realised that he was very close to achieving this. Muhammad Ali had been looking to them for help but with Stringer Lawrence away, they were unconfident. Nonetheless, they sent 280 Europeans and 300 sepoys commanded by Captain Cope to Trichinopoly in February 1751, mainly to boost Muhammad Ali's confidence. Muhammad Ali thereupon declared that he would never surrender Trichinopoly, nor would he accept Salabat Jung's ascendancy.

Muhammad Ali was Chanda Sahib's challenger to the control of Arcot. Chanda Sahib probably knew this was his last chance at vanquishing his adversary. Once more, the Carnatic became the focal point of the struggle for mastery between the English and the French. Chanda Sahib marched in March to Arcot, to formally occupy his capital. His army comprised 8000 troops and a French detachment under D'Auteuil of 400 Europeans, some Africans, and a few field-guns. Chanda Sahib's suzerainty was recognised by most of his feudatories. This was galling for Muhammad Ali, who attempted to coerce some rulers whose territories fell within his jurisdiction, to recant. Among these was Madurai, a daunting fort, commanded by Alam Khan, who had sworn fealty to Chanda Sahib. Muhammad Ali sent a force with a small English column in March 1751, to take Madurai and so teach other similarly obstinate governors a lesson. Alam Khan and his troops proved too hardy and several of Muhammad Ali's troops, who had in any case been cavilling about arrears in pay, deserted. The English too retreated. Soon news was received of Chanda Sahib's having marched from Arcot to take Trichinopoly.

The English, aware of the importance of the outcome at Trichinopoly for their survival, sent an additional force in mid-April from Fort St David, of 500 Europeans, 100 Africans, 1000 sepoys, and 8 field-guns, commanded by Captain Rudolf Gingens, to assist Captain Cope. Robert Clive was Gingens' commissariat officer. A detachment from Muhammad Ali joined this force 6 weeks later, which gave Gingens the necessary excuse to commence operations, since European forces could not fight each other directly while their nations were notionally at peace. Gingens proceeded to take Verdachelam, which was a strong bastion overlooking the main road between Fort St David and Trichinopoly, commanded by a *quiladar* loyal to Chanda Sahib. Thereafter Gingens moved to Volkondah, having been joined en route by 100 Englishmen, and 2000 cavalry and 2000 infantry from Muhammad Ali.

Volkondah was an impressive stronghold, comprising a rock 200 feet high and a mile in circumference, enclosed by three walls cut out of stone, the whole surmounted by a fort. Its importance lay in that it dominated the road from Arcot to Trichinopoly. Gingens got to Volkondah first and camped in a grove to the southwest, while Chanda Sahib's troops established themselves on the north-eastern side. Guards of the two camps were in sight of each other. The *quiladar*, who had previously declared for Chanda Sahib, now seemed to be awaiting the outcome of the battle. For two weeks, prolonged discussions took place between the *quiladar* and the two warring parties for the surrender of Volkondah. Finally, Gingens, his temper probably exacerbated by the hot and humid weather, gave way to impatience and ordered an assault on the night of 19 July 1751. This assault proved ineffective since the English were thwarted by the fort. The *quiladar* at once sought Chanda Sahib's help, and the following day the French battalion marched up to the fort. Meanwhile Chanda Sahib had received reinforcements. Gingens dithered about what to do next, and his vacillation, compounded by the defeat of the previous night, affected the morale of the English troops. Nonetheless, they were drew up and advanced towards the French, who had formed up at the foot of the great rock. The French, brought under ill-directed cannon fire, fled, led by D'Auteuil, into the fort. There they re-formed, and brought the English under heavy fire. This caused the English, already wavering, to flee in haste, brushing aside their officers' – Gingens, Kilpatrick, and Clive – attempts to stop the rout. It was left to the Africans and Muhammad Ali's troops to move back in order, collecting the dead and wounded as they retreated. The English left behind 6 field-guns, many muskets, and considerable stores of ammunition.

The French lost their greatest chance until that date, 20 July 1751, of destroying English military presence in the Carnatic, when D'Auteuil, a most unenterprising officer, gave no chase. 'Never before,' Malleson writes, 'had such an opportunity been given them; never had such an opportunity been neglected'. Gingens' English soldiers constituted the only sizeable body of troops the Company had on the Coromandel Coast. Captain Cope at Trichinopoly had only 150, and a few had been left in garrison at Forts St David and St George. The comprehensive defeat and dispersal of Gingens' troops would have forced Cope to rush back to the defence of the settlements, and caused Muhammad Ali to surrender. However, D'Auteuil was ill and could depend on none of his officers to accomplish this. Hence, Gingens was able to regroup his battalion and march out under cover of darkness towards Trichinopoly.

The following morning D'Auteuil and Chanda Sahib's troops set off in pursuit. Several skirmishes took place wherever the English and Muhammad Ali's men made their stands. At Utatur, for instance,

Lieutenant Maskelyne was taken prisoner but later released on parole by Chanda Sahib. The two forces, thus skirmishing, reached Trichinopoly by the end of July 1751, where it became obvious that it was merely a matter of time before the fort fell to the overwhelming superiority of numbers of the French and Chanda Sahib's army. In addition, a younger commander of proven ability, Jacques Law, replaced D'Auteuil, now wholly incapacitated, on 18 September.

Clive left the English force after the debacle at Volkondah, and returned to Fort St David. Thomas Saunders, who had decided that the English interest lay in the victory of Muhammad Ali, was informed of the need to rid Verdachelam of a ramshackle 'army' belonging to a local landowner loyal to the French. Verdachelam was the only fortress other than Trichinopoly that had declared for Muhammad Ali, and its allegiance kept the road to Trichinopoly open to the English. Verdachelam's fall would have disastrous strategic consequences. To hand was Clive but he was not senior enough, and so Saunders requested George Pigot, whom Orme calls 'a man of resolution', to take command of a force of 80 Europeans, some recently arrived from Europe, and 300 sepoys and considerable stores. Verdachelam was close to Cuddalore, and the distance from Verdachelam to Trichinopoly is 75 miles. Pigot was to take Verdachelam, and move on to Trichinopoly and there deliver the stores and the troops as reinforcements. Clive volunteered to accompany Pigot on this mission. They set out, surprised the enemy at Verdachelam on the night of 3 June 1751, and scattered them. Then they proceeded through land belonging to the Raja of Tanjore, to Trichinopoly. Having accomplished their task, Clive and Pigot, escorted by 12 sepoys and several retainers, were returning via Verdachelam to Fort St David when they were ambushed by some elements of the 'army' they had earlier dispersed. These were armed with matchlocks and their ambush was effective. Pigot, Clive, and their escort and servants were pinned down. 7 sepoys and several servants were killed. Soon the English party ran out of ammunition and Pigot ordered the sepoys and servants to scatter and make their own way back to Fort St David. He and Clive got on their horses, and were saved by the speed of their mounts, from a detachment of enemy cavalry that gave good chase.

On 22 July 1751, Clive was made brevet Captain and he returned along the same route a few days later, leading another batch of reinforcements to Trichinopoly. Captain Clarke joined him with a similar detachment from Devikottah. Clarke took command of the force, which amounted to 100 Europeans, 50 sepoys, and one field-gun. While passing through the territory of Tanjore, this force skirmished with a French detachment from

Koilady over the possession of the village of Kadavur, through which the high road passed. The French officer was injured and 10 French Europeans killed, because of which the rest of the force fled. To preserve their scanty manpower from further similar incidents, the English took a circuitous route to Trichinopoly. Nonetheless, despite all efforts, the English garrison at Trichinopoly remained inferior in numbers to the besieging French, while Muhammad Ali's forces were badly outnumbered by Chanda Sahib's. Clive is credited with diverting Chanda Sahib's attention from Trichinopoly, by attacking Arcot. Returning from Trichinopoly with the report of a demoralised garrison and a patient enemy awaiting imminent surrender of the fort, Clive convinced Saunders of the need to draw away the besiegers. On 19 August 1751, the council at Fort St David concluded that 'a Diversion in the Arcot Country' was imperative. Captain Clive was thus to be provided with all the Europeans and sepoys from both Forts St David and St George, who could be spared. With this force, he would attack Arcot. Saunders took an important decision in agreeing to Clive's plan, which depended entirely upon Clive's abilities. The garrisons at both English forts would be reduced to less than the minimum required, and would be vulnerable as never before if the French attacked.

Clive sailed to Fort St George, received reinforcements, and took the road to Arcot on 6 September 1751 at the head of a column of 200 Europeans, 300 sepoys, and 3 field-guns. He had with him 8 officers, most of whom were his fellows in the mercantile service. On 9 September, Clive stopped at Kanchipuram, wrote back for some additional artillery, and then proceeded. On 11 September, he approached Arcot through a fierce thunderstorm. A garrison of 1000 defended Arcot, with considerable artillery, helped by French gunners. The garrison fled without exchanging a shot with the invaders. A force that could march through a squall apparently overawed them. Clive took command of Arcot on 12 September but this did not at once relieve pressure on Trichinopoly, for Chanda Sahib made no immediate haste to recover his capital. Instead, Clive found himself outnumbered, and besieged in Arcot. This did not dismay Dupleix, the master strategist. Dupleix at once realised that the English were again cornered. It took him a moment to turn the situation around. Raza Sahib, Chanda Sahib's son, was sent to hold Clive in Arcot while Trichinopoly was reduced.

At this point one must pause to take account of the doings of these trading companies. They were obviously spending many times more on their armies than on trade, and the small profit they were earning was insufficient to offset the loss accruing from war. Individuals like Dupleix were making a lot of money very fast due to the instability of the country and the war. De Bussy, Kerjean, Vincens, all were reported to have earned huge fortunes, based on which they later retired to estates in France. Ananda Ranga Pillai reported on 21 June 1751 that Salabat Jung had decided to gift De Larche 100,000 rupees, which Dupleix said he did not deserve, and the money was given to Madame Dupleix instead. Clive was later to face similar accusations. The aim then, as previously and later, was to get rich as quickly as possible. In this context, one finds relevance in Dupleix's anger at English interference in what he considered was French turf, during the tussle for the Carnatic. He might have assisted the Raja of Tanjore in holding back the English at Devikottah but he did not do so since it was not European policy to poach once peace had been declared in Europe. The English resisted Dupleix due to similar reasons; they were being elbowed out, and by losing political influence, losing profits. Between June 1748 and April 1754, Dupleix had at Pondicherry bullions worth 6,300,000 rupees. During the same period, he had received merchandise, from Europe and elsewhere, worth around 4,200,000 rupees. He had sent back to France goods worth 6,200,000 rupees. He had therefore retained the enormous sum of 4,200,000 rupees at Pondicherry, from which he paid the expenditure of the first Carnatic War, 700,000 rupees. During 5 years Dupleix used up 3,000,000 rupees of the French Company's money, in addition to its annual revenue of 500,000. For each year between 1748 and 1753, he therefore spent 700,000 rupees on the wars. Similarly, the English spent 1,100,000 rupees a year on waging war. One is astounded by these stupendous sums. It was impossible, for either the revenues of the Carnatic or the private incomes of its princes, to meet more than a fraction of these sums. Local income or treasures, then, did not fund the Carnatic Wars. One is equally amazed to read of governors being recalled to Europe to answer charges of malfeasance. Their brazenness in spending these enormous sums must have had at least the secret acquiescence of their superiors in Europe.

On 25 September 1751, Clive sallied out and launched a surprise attack on the enemy camp. They scattered, and later re-assembled. This kind of fighting continued for some days. Meanwhile, Chanda Sahib had sent a force of 4000 led by Raza Sahib, and accompanied by 150 Europeans, to recover Arcot. Dupleix knew that Arcot was a diversion, and the issue of the Carnatic would be decided at Trichinopoly. He therefore pressed Chanda Sahib harder to focus on taking Trichinopoly at once. Raza Sahib proceeded to Arcot, gathering more troops en route, taking his force up to 10,000. He got there on 4 October and occupied the town. By 19 October, the battering train and two 18-pounders were obtained from Pondicherry. Clive's garrison was soon reduced to 120 Europeans and 200 sepoys.

Although offered honourable terms on 10 November by Raza Sahib if he capitulated and death otherwise, Clive chose to remain. There was another reason for his dismissal of the offer. 6000 Maratha horsemen led by Murari Rao, who was a nominal ally of Muhammad Ali, were encamped a few miles away. Rao had been unsure about supporting Muhammad Ali so far, but the defence of Arcot fort by Clive decided him. He would help Clive. Alarmed by these intelligences, Raza Sahib determined to take the fort by assault. This was attempted on 25 November 1751, and Clive's leadership saved the day. By the time the enemy realised that their assault had failed, it was 2 in the afternoon. By the following morning, Raza Sahib had retreated to Vellore. In conceding defeat, Raza Sahib lost most of his allies, who returned to their homes, unwilling to engage in these battles any further since that would lessen the chances of alliances with the victors. Clive had not only taken Arcot, he defended it with unequal valour during a siege of 50 days, and finally forced the enemy to retreat.

Relieved by a detachment under Captain Kilpatrick, Clive marched off in pursuit of Raza Sahib. Battles took place at Arni (3 December), and Kanchipuram (16-18 December), which was garrisoned by the French. Raza Sahib fled from the former, but his treasure chest, containing 100,000 rupees, was seized. Kanchipuram was taken by assault, and Clive returned singularly victorious to Madras and thence to Fort St David, having tilted the scales single-handedly against the French in the Carnatic. On 10 March 1752, Clive was again victorious at Kaveripak, in spite of having been ambushed and outnumbered. Enemy survivors sought, and were given, sanctuary in Kaveripak fort, while Clive marched on to Arcot, having decided that he would move from there to Vellore, which was commanded by Murtaza Ali, who had declared for Chanda Sahib. En route to Vellore, Clive was redirected, on 25 March 1752, to the defence of Trichinopoly.

Jacques Law, although an effective councillor, seems to have been an indifferent commander. He had a large army in his charge. It consisted of 900 Europeans, 2000 sepoys, and an artillery park of 50 guns. 30,000 cavalry under Chanda Sahib bolstered this legion. Dupleix had been forwarding to him every detachment of troops that was landed at Pondicherry by ships coming in from France. He had also written to Law numerous letters, urging him exasperatedly to employ the force to take Trichinopoly immediately. Like Gingens, who was content to be besieged, Jacques Law was happy to be a besieger. Even though Clive had undone much of Dupleix's work in other parts of the Carnatic, there remained the chance of recovering all by taking Muhammad Ali. However, Dupleix failed to get his commander to make the least movement to this end.

Stringer Lawrence returned to Madras on 26 March, and was immediately put in command of the army for the defence of Trichinopoly. He marched two days later, with Clive as his deputy. They led a column of 400 Europeans, 1100 sepoys, and 8 field-guns. Once more Dupleix wrote to Law, commanding him to sally out from his camp and resoundingly defeat the English as they marched 150 miles, across 8 rivers, from Fort St David to Trichinopoly. The English had no reserves, and if this column were dispersed, Trichinopoly, already very short on supplies, would fall at once. Law sent a weak detachment of 350 Europeans and 400 sepoys to intercept and defeat Lawrence. Brushing past these, Lawrence soon reached within 10 miles of Trichinopoly. There the English and the French, aided by their local allies, clashed on 9 April 1752. The English were able to take advantage of the promptness of its commander and the initiative of its officers, especially Clive. The French lacked both and suffered accordingly. The heat of the day, which took a toll on both European forces, forced hostilities to end by midday. By 12 April, Law had convinced himself of the tenuousness of his position. Therefore, he chose to retreat to Srirangam, a long strip of land between the rivers Cauvery and Coleroon. Deaf to all advice, including that of Chanda Sahib about deserting a strong position that encircled Trichinopoly, Law insisted on withdrawing. A French force was left isolated on a rocky fortress called Elmiseram, which surrendered almost as soon as the main army had moved off.

Dupleix had no officer to replace Law, since De Bussy was in Aurangabad with Salabat Jung. Nonetheless, he sent D'Auteuil on 10 April 1752, with 120 Europeans, 400 sepoys, and 4 field-guns, in the forlorn hope of replacing Law and somehow turning the tables on the English. Much desperate fighting followed, with the result that on 7 May 1752 Lawrence took Koilady from the French. He moved against D'Auteuil on 20 May, forcing the latter to retreat to Volkondah. Law was left to fend for himself. Clive followed D'Auteuil and captured him at Volkondah on 8 June 1752. Law was now completely isolated, as the direct road to Pondicherry had also been cut off. Nevertheless, Jacques Law still had at his command 800 Europeans and 2000 sepoys, along with around 5000 of Chanda Sahib's adherents. With this substantial force, he could have fought his way out, and even turned matters around. Law, however, pondered on surrender and Chanda Sahib was unable to move him from this position. Both Law and Chanda Sahib knew that capitulation meant death for Chanda Sahib. Muhammad Ali was now the victor after having suffered much tribulation. He would not allow his rival to survive and revive. Law therefore interceded on his behalf with Manoji, the general of Tanjore's army, which was allied to Muhammad Ali, and negotiated an escape. Money was paid, and Law sought a hostage for Chanda Sahib, which was refused even as oaths were sworn to give him safe conduct to the French territory of Karikal. On the night of 11 June 1752, Chanda Sahib climbed into a palanquin for the presumed journey, being handed over by the French into the charge of an escort provided by Manoji.

At Manoji's camp, Chanda Sahib was seized and fettered, and his fate discussed over the next two days. The first meeting included Major Stringer Lawrence, who was asked by Manoji to take Chanda Sahib into custody. Lawrence refused, and the others, including the representatives of Murari Rao and Muhammad Ali, were offended, since they all claimed possession of Chanda Sahib. On 13 June, after protracted negotiations, Jacques Law capitulated. 35 French commissioned officers, 785 Europeans, and 2000 sepoys surrendered, as did Chanda Sahib's cavalry, who were allowed to leave with their mounts and weapons. None of these had received any pay for over 3 months, and the officers were deeply resentful of their commander. The English captured all the French artillery, ammunition, and stores. Meanwhile, Manoji found himself in an unenviable position with regard to Chanda Sahib's person. The only solution was Chanda Sahib's death, and so he was executed, and his head sent to Muhammad Ali. The English and the French were mercenaries for the contenders for the Carnatic, and the English had no reason to see to Chanda Sahib's survival since he was a creature of Dupleix. Lawrence therefore washed his hands of Chanda Sahib and focused on disarming the French. Dupleix had apparently been thwarted for the remaining part of the year. Salabat Jung was unable to help because he was indigent, aware of his political precariousness, and dependent on Dupleix. The treasury was nearly empty, and no revenues had obviously come in from the Carnatic or indeed other parts of the Deccan due to the war, the rising power of the Marathas, and the generally unsettled condition. The Mughal Emperor's powers were already nominal.

400 French prisoners of war were taken to Fort St David, and the rest housed at Trichinopoly, where the artillery and stores were also kept. Muhammad Ali had already promised Trichinopoly to the Raja of Mysore in return for his alliance and service, which the latter now demanded. Protracted negotiations with Captain Dalton as the English representative, and Murari Rao as the mediator, took place. Murari Rao wanted a 'neutral' Maratha force present in Trichinopoly. Muhammad Ali did not want to give the fort to Mysore, or to have Marathas stationed in it. He sought some time from Mysore, saying that he would have to stay at Trichinopoly

until Arcot had been made fit to receive him and his family, while the English garrisoned Trichinopoly. Accordingly, Captain Dalton took command of a garrison of 200 Europeans and 1500 sepoys. Lawrence and Clive had both retired to Fort St David for recuperation. On 9 July 1752, Nawab Muhammad Ali set out for Arcot escorted by 500 Europeans and 2500 sepoys. He had only 2000 horse of his own, since his allies had all dispersed to their homelands. Dupleix had in the meantime received confirmatory letters from Salabat Jung appointing him to the governorship of all Mughal territories south of the Krishna, as had been promised by Muzaffar Jung. Around the same time, Dupleix was raised to a marquisate by pleasure of the King of France. Ananda Ranga Pillai noted how Dupleix showed off an enamelled watch set with brilliant stones gifted him by Madame Pompadour. Dupleix told all that the watch cost 60,000 rupees but Pillai was sceptical and wrote 'it was really worth only 1000 pagodas, because he formerly sent that sum as a bribe to the king's concubine and she has sent these two things [the other a finely-worked golden case for scissors, etc] in return'.

Dupleix, however, was not to be thwarted and for him the war had not ended. He secretly negotiated with the Raja of Mysore and the Marathas to allow them the freedom of Trichinopoly, if it fell, and they in turn agreed to allow him freedom of dealing with Muhammad Ali and the English. Another battle took place between Stringer Lawrence and the French under Kerjean on 6 September 1752, to the loss of the French. However, this changed little since both Mysore and the Marathas moved their allegiance from the English to the French. Dupleix however was dogged by ill luck. A ship from Mauritius to Pondicherry, carrying 700 European troops, commanded by the redoubtable De la Touche, caught fire at sea with the loss of all on board. Dupleix attempted to fill Chanda Sahib's place with Murtaza Ali, the *quiladar* of Vellore, and descendant of Dost Ali Khan. Murtaza, having whiled away in the safety of his fort a decade of the greatest political turmoil in areas surrounding his *jagir*, was a willing candidate for Arcot. Continued losses among European troops had weakened Dupleix's military reserves. Even though he had a substantial force of 500 Europeans and 5000 sepoys under De Bussy with Salabat Jung at Aurangabad and Golconda, Malleson writes that at the beginning of 1753 he only had 360 Europeans in the Carnatic, 2000 sepoys, and 4000 Maratha horse under that old turncoat, Murari Rao. The common feeling of surprise on seeing Murari Rao aligned with his former enemies might be answered by De Bussy's comprehensive defeat of the Marathas, and his having marched with Salabat Jung almost all the way from Aurangabad to a few miles short of Poona in the previous year. Once more armies were on the march across the Carnatic albeit with realigned allegiances. Clive had left for England the previous year, and the English depended on Lawrence. Dupleix's intention was again the capture of Trichinopoly. He was certain that the fall of Trichinopoly would destroy English influence and remove Muhammad Ali from the centre of affairs.

There is a dreary repetitiveness in the war, which makes for boring reading. Detachments of Europeans and locals are constantly skirmishing for tactical advantage, and Dupleix is obsessed like a monomaniac with the taking of Trichinopoly. There were nevertheless certain variations. Lawrence, having stayed close to Tiruvedi for 5 months, engaged the French under Astruc at Trichinopoly on 21 May 1753. Dupleix, unfathomable as usual, at once revealed that Trichinopoly was a feint, and Tiruvedi the aim. Maissin, commanding 160 Europeans and 1500 sepoys aided by Maratha horse, launched assaults that led to the fall of Tiruvedi. Murtaza Ali in the meantime sallied forth with his own troops and defeated several opposing forces. The focus of the fighting shifted once more to Trichinopoly where another long-drawn and vital battle was fought on 7 July 1753. There was no outcome, with Lawrence being able to retake the Golden Rocks from Astruc but retreating for want of men to hold the position, harried all the way by Maratha horsemen. Astruc resigned his commission, and Brennier replaced him. The next battle took place on 18 August 1753. Lawrence went to see the Raja of Tanjore, and obtained troops from him. Brennier was as unimaginative a general as Law had been. He allowed Lawrence to outmanoeuvre and drive him from the field despite his having the stronger force. Brennier retreated to Waikonda, and when pursued there by Lawrence, moved back across the Cauvery to keep the lines of communication open. Brennier was reinforced by Astruc, who had been restored, at the head of 400 Europeans, 2000 sepoys, 3000 Marathas, and 6 field-guns. Brennier was replaced by Astruc but his previous defeat had made the latter over-cautious. Lawrence once more read the French strategy perfectly and made them play right into his hand. As soon as he was reinforced on 27 September 1753, Lawrence attacked. Once more, the French were soundly defeated, and Astruc, along with several fellow officers as well as European soldiers, captured. Dupleix would still not be dissuaded from his aim. He dispatched another force of 600 Europeans under De Mainville, which was somewhat more successful, having got inside Trichinopoly by climbing over the outworks at 3am on 9 December 1753. Nonetheless, due to their inability to keep silence, they were detected, and their ladders being thrown away, were unable to retreat. 364 attackers, including all officers except one who had been killed, were captured. 200 jumped down the walls, several injuring themselves very seriously, while 40 men were killed in action. Meanwhile, Dupleix, aware of the help being given by the Raja of Tanjore in sustaining the English at Trichinopoly, had several times threatened to let the Marathas loose into Tanjore. The final defeat of the French at Trichinopoly made Dupleix apply for terms to Thomas Saunders.

The two parties met at Sadras, a Dutch settlement about 6 hours from Madras and 12 from Pondicherry. The English representatives were Robert Palk and Henry Vansittart, and the French, De Kerjean, and Bausset, and Father Lavaur of the Jesuits. The discussions, held between 23 January and 4 February 1754, led to no consensus, and the following day the English commissaries left, followed three days later by the French. The English declared that no discussion could begin without the French acknowledging Muhammad Ali as the Nawab of the Carnatic. The French tried to evade the issue by suggesting that he be given a suitable governorship, thereby signifying that Dupleix be considered the legitimate successor to Chanda Sahib vide the letters-patent issued by Salabat Jung. These were examined by the English commissaries, and declared doubtful on the bases that the letter bore no seal engraved with his name and titles, and was stamped in ink, and that the imperial seal on the cover of the letter belonged to an Emperor who ruled 33 years ago. The French might have similarly queried and examined Muhammad Ali's letters-patent. The discussions could also have continued if the French had asked the English to recognise Salabat Jung if they acknowledged Muhammad Ali. Saunders was willing to have his emissaries concede that the English and French be put into possession of lands in different parts of the province whereby their commercial interests would mutually flourish without conflict but the entire issue pivoted upon Dupleix's recognition of Muhammad Ali as the Nawab. Dupleix was not interested in resuming the negotiations. De Bussy had already obtained for him from Salabat Jung the territories of Rajahmundry, Eluru, Srikakulam, and Mustafanagar. In addition to the previous grants of Masulipatam and Kondavid, the French now controlled nearly 600 miles of uninterrupted coastline on the Coromandel.

Rather than rest upon his laurels at having obtained so much for himself and his Company, Dupleix decided to continue hostilities at Trichinopoly. De Mainville sallied out on occasional raids upon English supply trains and by May 1754, had occupied Koilady. He proceeded to divert the Cauvery into the Coleroon to deprive Tanjore of water. Murari Rao meanwhile defeated the army of the Raja of Tanjore. Dupleix had directed his efforts at eroding the supply base of the English. Having seen to the diversion of the river, De Mainville returned to his position outside Trichinopoly to impede provisioning.

Dupleix's term as governor was about to end. 1752-53 had been disastrous for the French. The French Company had already invested much money and the dividend was unsatisfactory. Dupleix had promised high returns once the war, which he had predicted would not last long, was done. At this point, he should have stopped and sent off news of the provinces he now held, thereby drawing the attention of investors. However, the investors, who included many wealthy and influential people, were unhappy. In 1752, M Duvalaer, a director of the French Company, and his brother, the Comte de Lude, went to London to discuss the cessation of hostilities in India with Lord Holderness (1718-1778), the Secretary of State for the Southern Department. Since both Companies were concerned about trade and making money from their investments, they agreed completely on the needlessness of both warfare and interference in local governments and their methods of governance. Duvalaer strove to defend Dupleix's actions against Saunders' complaints. In any case, both sides agreed to order their governors back home, and appoint commissaries who would examine the matter and establish peace. While the English did not remove Saunders but authorised him to act as commissary, the French appointed Charles Robert Godeheu, a director of the French Company, to replace Dupleix. Godeheu had long been a close friend of Dupleix's but at the same time had conspired unceasingly for his removal. He professed friendship on a personal level, compelled only by orders to be distant. Godeheu arrived at Pondicherry on 1 August 1754, having written to Dupleix from Mauritius only that he had been appointed Commissary of the King and Company in India. When his ship anchored in Pondicherry roads, Godeheu refused to disembark, until suitable accommodation was found for him. He then let his old friend, Dupleix, have the King's order of dismissal. The following day Godeheu landed, was received with the usual ceremony, and made his way to the council chamber, where he read out his commission. Godeheu was aware that given Dupleix's fame and popularity, he could easily refuse to hand over governance in the way many Englishmen had. He therefore told Dupleix that 2000 soldiers were expected soon on ships that were following him, and that Dupleix should arrange to leave for Europe at the earliest. Dupleix did not complain, or fuss about handing over charge. In fact, after Godeheu had finished reading his commission, Dupleix was the one to give the loyal hurrah, *Vive le Roi!*

At three on the morning of 15 October 1754, Dupleix and his family sailed for France. Dupleix died on 10 November 1764 in abject poverty, having spent the intervening years trying to get his dues from the French Company, which, already embarrassed by the treaty signed by Godeheu and reverses in the Seven Years' War, it refused to acknowledge. Three days before he died, Dupleix wrote in his memoirs, 'I have sacrificed my youth, my fortune, my life, to enrich my nation in Asia … My services are treated as fables; my demand is denounced as ridiculous; I am treated as the vilest of mankind'. Godeheu had deliberately suppressed Dupleix's considerable dues from the French Company. Ironically, the Controller of Finances, De Machault, had speedily sent after Godeheu a letter addressed to Dupleix, replacing the latter as Governor and the former as Commissary only. This letter sadly reached Pondicherry two weeks after Dupleix's departure.

Dupleix's plans for the French Company found no sympathy in Godeheu. Dupleix's replacement had shaken De Bussy, who desired to leave as well but was dissuaded by his former superior. Similarly, Moracin, then in charge of the districts ceded to the French by Salabat Jung, too felt uncertain. Godeheu eagerly desired to treat with the English at any cost, and make peace with the local rulers in order to resume trade. His inexplicable urge to avenge himself upon Dupleix blinded him to the powerful political position in which his predecessor had left him. The English were happy that Dupleix had been removed. Even though the French now had 2000 Europeans recently landed, the English had nothing to fear, for Dupleix was gone. Godeheu made the usual overtures for peace to Saunders, released prisoners to restore goodwill, and alienated De Bussy, Moracin, and De Mainville by not providing them with instructions, troops, or money.

While the English exulted, the local rulers who had hitherto depended on Dupleix, and had trusted him implicitly, were now in a quandary. Godeheu informed Salabat Jung that he had been ordered not to interfere in the governance of local kingdoms, so the Nawab would have to look to his own interests rather than seeking guidance from Pondicherry. The situation of Mainville's army investing Trichinopoly, supported by Murari Rao and his Marathas, was piteous. Deprived suddenly of orders, provisions, reinforcements, and money, they realised that they were doomed. In commenting on this policy of Godeheu, Malleson writes it is certain that 'had Governor Saunders himself been appointed successor to Dupleix, he could not have more effectually injured French interests than did this nominee … of the French Crown'. Godeheu removed De Mainville from command on 16 August 1754, and replaced him with Maissin, who was ordered not to interfere with English supply trains to Trichinopoly. Hence, Trichinopoly was reinforced and Lawrence had the freedom to rove about the country, with Maissin fleeing, as ordered, from him.

Godeheu told Bussy to stay with the Nawab, a role suddenly rendered meaningless since Moracin had been informed that holding the 4 provinces was not to French interest. Contrary to French policy, the English had grasped through their debacles and lucky victories, the strategic importance of the Carnatic. Admiral Watson led a fleet to Madras roads and landed for the first time in India a battalion of the regular army, His Majesty's 49th Regiment of Foot. All hostilities between the French and the English ceased from 22 October 1754, and by December, a treaty was drawn up, whereby all of Dupleix's achievements were squandered by Godeheu. The French ceded all their territories along the Coromandel, and thus forced their allies, the Marathas, the Raja of Mysore, and Salabat Jung, to accept English supremacy. Further, they allowed Muhammad Ali to become Nawab of Arcot by keeping silent on Dupleix's claim. Within 3 months of Dupleix's departure, the political picture of the Carnatic had changed dramatically. The French had receded to their bounds, and the English were all-powerful, thanks to the Raja of Tanjore and Muhammad Ali, the Nawab of the Carnatic. Godeheu signed the treaty on 11 January 1755, and it was sent to Europe for ratification. In effect, the French lost annual revenue of £855,000. Thomas Saunders sailed for England on 14 January 1755, and was succeeded by George Pigot. Pigot had spent the intervening years as chief at Vizagapatam, and had been sent down as Deputy Governor of Fort St David in 1754. Godeheu left on 16 February 1755, and Charles Duval de Leyrit, who reached Pondicherry on 25 March, took his place.

Robert Clive had sailed for England in February 1753, soon after his wedding to Margaret Maskelyne, the sister of his fellow escapee from Madras, Edmund. In England, he was received with much approbation and the Court of Directors, praising his services, wished to gift him a diamond-hilted sword worth £500. Clive refused to accept this unless the same gift was also given to Stringer Lawrence, who had in the meantime been given a King's commission as Lieutenant-Colonel. Colonel Lawrence had however been superseded as commander of the English forces in Madras because the commanding officer of HM 49th Foot was senior in service. In the usual manner of the time, Clive spent his wealth repaying his father's debts and restoring his family's fortunes. He also lived in the extravagant manner expected of a nabob who had returned with fame and fortune from India. In any case, Clive might not have returned to India, had his election from St Michael's, in Cornwall, not been declared unlawful in mid-1754. He sought the Company's service once more and they were eager to have him. He was appointed to the Deputy Governorship of Fort St David. *En route* to his command, Clive was temporarily diverted to Bombay, where he was expected to command an expedition in alliance with the Peshwa, Balaji Baji Rao, against the French in the Deccan. However, the council at Bombay decided to abide by the treaty signed by Godeheu and Saunders, and decided against hostilities. Instead, Clive, with Admiral Watson and his fleet, attacked and reduced the fortress of Gheria, the stronghold of Tulaji Angria, the Maratha sea-lord whose depredations on shipping had become a serious cause of concern to Bombay. Gheria was simultaneously attacked on land by the Peshwa's troops, and it surrendered to the English on 13 April 1756. Clive thereafter sailed with Watson to Madras, and took up his position at Fort St David on 16 May 1756. This date is doubly interesting since the Seven Years' War commenced on 17 May 1756 in Europe.

CHAPTER EIGHT

THE CARNATIC WAR III

News of the formal declaration of hostilities in Europe reached Pondicherry by the end of 1756, and De Leyrit was prepared. He had maintained Bussy at Salabat Jung's court, and he had enough troops to try once more to take Trichinopoly. On the other hand, the English were embroiled in battles elsewhere in India. Alivardi Khan, the Nawab of Bengal, died on 9 April 1756, and in accordance with his wishes, his favourite grandson, Siraj-ud-Daulah, succeeded him. It is far beyond the scope of this book to discuss the affairs of Bengal. Siraj-ud-Daulah moved against the English, taking Cossimbazar on 4 June. He then marched to Calcutta, which was ill defended by the English. Additionally, the governor, Roger Drake, accompanied by Captain Minchin, the garrison commander, and several others, embarked on ships and deserted Fort William as soon as Siraj's troops moved up close, having pillaged through the Black Town, on Sunday, 20 June. From Sunday through Monday afternoon, those defending Fort William sought help from the ships to embark Europeans, but these stood away. At 6 pm, Monday, 21 June 1756, Fort William fell to Siraj-ud-Daulah. The infamous and controversial tragedy of the Black Hole occurred the same night. News of the fall of Calcutta reached Fort St George on 16 August. Letters from England indicated a formal renewal of war with France. They also contained information that the French were determined to regain control of the Deccan, and that a huge fleet of 19 ships carrying 3000 regular soldiers, was ready to sail from Brest to Pondicherry. The issue immediately before the council at Fort St George was how to retake Calcutta. Pigot had sent for Clive to join the council at Fort St George. Admiral Watson's fleet would be of use. It would sail troops to Bengal, help take Calcutta, and return to Madras by April, during which time it would not be possible for the French fleet whose arrival was rumoured, to arrive and land troops with safety, given the rigours of the southwest monsoon.

Pigot was willing to be the military commander and Company's plenipotentiary but he had no campaign experience; neither was the council of Madras authorised to grant Pigot these powers. Colonel

Adlercron, commanding HM 49th, was considered next, and his candidacy had the advantage that he was the senior-most army officer. However, he had little experience of warfare in India. Colonel Stringer Lawrence would have been the best candidate but he was afflicted with asthma, which rendered him unfit for the field. The only person, and ideal choice, was Colonel Clive, who satisfied all the conditions including the fact that as Deputy Governor of Fort St David, he would enjoy the Company's confidence in conducting its affairs in Bengal. The council decided to invest Clive with military powers and funds independent of Roger Drake and his council. The latter were nonetheless to continue to enjoy their commercial and civil authority despite the inherent contradictions in their statements regarding the capture of Calcutta. Deliberations along these lines continued through 2 months, and Watson's fleet having been readied, Clive sailed on 27 October 1756, with 900 Europeans and 1500 sepoys. Colonel Adlercron, enraged by his supersession, had refused to allow any soldier of his regiment to serve in Bengal. Adlercron does not really seem to have intended to go to Bengal. He was of the opinion that he had been considered for the command so that the Company could get his field-guns. However, 250 men led by Captain Eyre Coote volunteered to serve as marines, to which Adlercron did not object. Much time had also been spent deciding on the division of property, since looting was a fast and easy way of getting rich. There had already been a disagreement over shares at Gheria between Clive's officers and Watson's. The army officers felt that Clive should have received the same amount as Watson's deputy, Rear-Admiral Pocock. The naval opinion was that Clive, given his King's commission as Lieutenant-Colonel, deserved no more than a post-Captain did. Watson had tried to solve this problem by accepting the naval view but giving Clive £1000, the same amount as was due to Pocock, making up the difference from his own share. Clive refused the entire amount, saying that he had no wish to enrich himself at the Admiral's cost. Nevertheless, this shows why rights to the sharing of the loot were so hotly debated.

Matters had also soured for the French in the Deccan. In January 1756, Salabat Jung had marched against Savanur, which had rejected allegiance to him. Now, reinforced by Murari Rao, the Nawab of Savanur had openly defied the Nizam. Balaji Baji Rao had also marched from Poona, and allied himself to Salabat Jung in order to bring Murari Rao to obedience. At Salabat Jung's court the usual intrigues against De Bussy gained momentum amidst these alarms. Murari Rao, on seeing the united forces against him, decided to seek De Bussy's help for peace. He offered De Bussy the surrender of his monetary claims on the French for his military services at Trichinopoly and elsewhere. De Bussy conducted peace between the Nawab of Savanur, Murari Rao, Balaji Baji Rao, and Salabat Jung, vide which the Nawab and Murari Rao would submit to their superiors. The intriguers, busy with discrediting De Bussy, filled Salabat Jung's ears with rumours about how the French, even though in possession of the governorship of the Carnatic, had failed to pay him any money while Muhammad Ali, who was also an aspirant to the same position, was ready to gift 1,200,000 rupees, and ensure annual revenue of 3,200,000 rupees. Salabat Jung was a weak ruler, and this weakness had worsened with the departure of Dupleix, the inexplicable policies of Godeheu, the waning power of the French, and the increasing willingness of his feudatories to ally with the English. The conspirators had even attempted in vain to draw Balaji Baji Rao into their group. Soon the Diwan, Shah Nawaz Khan, ordered De Bussy in the name of his master, Salabat Jung, to leave the territories of the Deccan. De Bussy at once complied, and proceeded towards Masulipatam, having written to Pondicherry to send him as many troops as could be spared. Shah Nawaz Khan meanwhile appealed to the English in Salabat Jung's name for assistance in removing the French from the Deccan. However, it was a long march for De Bussy and his men. On 25 June 1756, De Bussy camped at Hyderabad, unable to move further without first dealing with his pursuers, skirmishing cavalry sent by his enemies at Salabat Jung's court. On 5 July, he moved his troops into the gardens at Charmahal. The first of the reports of events in Bengal reached Madras around the same time. English assistance would not be immediately forthcoming for Shah Nawaz Khan and his fellow intriguers. French support, though, began pouring in, even as De Bussy defended himself most ably at Charmahal against heavy odds. His sepoys, enticed by promises of better pay and other rewards, deserted in large numbers with their firearms. On 10 August 1756, a substantial body of French troops including 480 Europeans, 1100 sepoys, and 11 field-guns, arrived within 50 miles of Hyderabad. By 20 August, peace had been contrived between Salabat Jung and De Bussy, with the reinstatement of the latter with all honour in the Deccan. Having spent the interceding period in Hyderabad reinforcing his position at the court, De Bussy moved out on 16 November 1756 leading a column of 500 Europeans and 4000 sepoys, in order to enforce allegiance in the 4 ceded districts. He had overcome almost alone one of the worst times for the French in India.

Calcutta was recaptured on 2 January 1757, and it was seen that the warehouses had remained untouched, while the Europeans' houses, mainly grand dwellings, had been emptied and often destroyed by fire. Admiral Watson had disembarked Captain King, RN, to take Fort William in the

King's name, and appointed Captain Coote the governor. On approaching Fort William, Clive was told that none of the Company, or its army, could enter. He wrote to his friend George Pigot that he did so unopposed, the guards allowing him to pass. Within the fort, Clive met Coote, who showed him with the commission signed by Watson, which appointed Coote governor. Clive, whose lieutenant-colonelcy superseded Coote's captaincy, opposed this. Clive suspected that 'this dirty underhand contrivance was carried on in the most secret manner, under a pretence that I intended the same thing, which, I declare, never entered my thoughts'. Matters deteriorated to the extent that Clive threatened to have Coote arrested, while Watson threatened to open fire on the fort if his orders were disobeyed, upon which Clive informed him that if fired upon by the English fleet, he would not answer for the consequences. In the end, Clive handed over charge of the fort to Watson, who passed it back to Roger Drake. This incident has been dismissed as hotheadedness in a hot country, fuelled by a high sense of duty. Clive also informed Pigot that a few days earlier he and his men had been disembarked 16 miles to the north of Budge-Budge by Watson, the men 'suffering hardships not to be described', while Coote was landed at Budge-Budge with the King's troops. 'The mortifications I have received', Clive confided to Pigot, 'from Mr Watson and the gentlemen of the squadron, in point of prerogative, are such that nothing but the good of the Service could induce me to submit to them'. To someone used to hard, indeed desperate, campaigning in the Carnatic, pitted against a strategist like Dupleix, this insistence upon protocol seemed ludicrous, when there were innumerable critical issues to be resolved urgently. To add salt to injury, the Bengal men considered him an interloper since he was a 'Madras Man'. The Madras council, aware of its susceptibility to an attack by the French at any time after April, wanted Clive to return. Drake and his councillors were concerned about their private trade, and not about either the Company or the prestige of the English in the region. Now that Calcutta had been retaken, they would not be diverted into considerations of strategy. All of this smacks of the same kind of obsession with private trade and personal gain that had been at the root of factory politics and rebellions thus far. The Bengal councillors therefore ganged up against Clive and strove to prejudice Watson against him. 'I am sorry to say', Clive penned to Pigot, his fellow 'Madras Man', 'that the loss of private property, and the means of recovering it, seem to be the only objects which take up the attention of the Bengal gentlemen'. 'Believe me', he continued, 'they are bad subjects and rotten at heart, and will stick at nothing to prejudice you and the gentlemen of the committee'. Having reached Calcutta, and having got an idea about what had actually happened there, he wrote, 'I shall only add, their conduct at Calcutta finds no excuse, even among themselves'.

Around the second week of January, news reached the English came that war had been declared in Europe between Britain and France. Chandernagore, which had hitherto played, in the English view, a dubious role in Bengal, having allegedly supplied Siraj-ud-Daulah with gunpowder, now became a dangerous place. However, when Siraj-ud-Daulah marched for the second time against the English at Calcutta in February 1757 to retake Calcutta, the French, instead of helping him suggested to the English that the two European nations should maintain peace in Bengal irrespective of matters in Europe. This change in attitude might have been due to their having been threatened and coerced by Siraj-ud-Daulah into paying an indemnity of 150,000 rupees. In February 1757, several clashes between the English and the Nawab's troops took place. None of these were notable, with lives being lost needlessly on both sides, the English especially less able to sustain the drain on their manpower. On the other hand, Siraj-ud-Daulah, aware that this English force was unlikely to be overcome easily as the previous one, wished for peace. On 9 February 1757, he sought negotiations, and confirmed the English in the same rights they had previously enjoyed plus permission to fortify Calcutta. The Nawab moved his camp two days later further to the north and sent presents to Watson and Clive. These were accepted, and the treaty ratified. Clive now turned his attention to Chandernagore despite the French having provided no support to the Nawab during his second march to Calcutta. Orme wrote that the Nawab was unhappy with the decision of the English to reduce Chandernagore. Nonetheless, anxious to prevent further engagements with the English, he acquiesced, washed his hands of the matter, and turned towards his capital, Murshidabad.

The English army crossed the river at Howrah, captured the town of Hooghly on 8 February 1757, and readied to attack Chandernagore. The French pleaded with the Nawab to intercede, which he did, writing a peremptory letter to Clive, ordering him to desist. Further machinations including the bribing of the governor of Hooghly, Nanda Kumar, by the English, took place. Siraj-ud-Daulah was adamant that the French should not be harmed. He dispatched 100,000 rupees to the French and sent a column under Mir Jafar to their assistance. Clive was compelled to give a written assurance to the Nawab that he would not attack Chandernagore without the latter's permission. More plans were devised, and a month spent through attempts to coerce the Nawab to allow the capture of Chandernagore. Admiral Watson was opposed to a treaty with the French while Clive, intensely aware that precious time was being lost while the

Carnatic fended for itself against large French armies, urged him to choose whether to treat or assault. Watson was also unwilling to assault Chandernagore without the Nawab's explicit permission. He wrote a letter to Siraj-ud-Daulah, in which he pointed out the danger of the situation: 'You are too reasonable not to see that it is impossible for me to conclude a treaty with people who have no power to do it [the French council at Chandernagore]; and which, besides, while it ties my hands, leaves those of my enemies to do me what mischief they can'. He asked uncomfortable questions of Siraj-ud-Daulah: 'They have also a long time reported that Monsieur Bussy is coming here with a great army. Is it to attack you? Is it to attack us?' The Nawab's evasive reply angered the irascible Admiral, and he ordered the assault on Chandernagore. Watson also received official confirmation of the declaration of war in Europe in the first week of March 1757. Hence, on 7 March Watson wrote to the Nawab, 'I will kindle such a flame in your country as all the water of the Ganges shall not be able to extinguish'. The peremptoriness of this letter marks the effective conclusion of discussions to save Chandernagore. Some further unproductive correspondence between Clive, the Calcutta council, and Watts, the Resident at Murshidabad, continued right up to 14 March, when the attack on Chandernagore commenced. Chandernagore was vulnerable from the river, and subjected to heavy cannonade from the English ships, which had managed to negotiate a way through the channels thanks to Terraneau, the French artillery officer who deserted to the English. Clive and his force had only the role of holding the French at the bounds, which soon became contentious because Chandernagore was not taken by assault on land. Chandernagore fell due to the vulnerability of its riverfront. Renault de St Germain, the governor, surrendered Chandernagore on 23 March 1757. Writing to Pigot on 29 March, Clive stated 'It was with great reluctance Mr Watson consented that I should sign the articles of capitulation, though drawn out in his name, notwithstanding it was impossible the fort could ever have been taken without our assistance'. He would return in September to Madras, he said, for he was convinced that due to the fall of Chandernagore 'the Islands [The Isles of France, Mauritius] must starve, and Pondicherry suffer greatly', for it had been a 'most magnificent and rich colony'. Madras needed his services but there was no one to replace him in Bengal. Siraj-ud-Daulah had allegedly written to De Leyrit and De Bussy, seeking their assistance. Writing again to Pigot on 30 April 1757, Clive noted that they would soon have to take arms against the Nawab, for 'he is a compound of everything that is bad, keeps company with none but his menial servants, and is universally hated and despised by the great men'.

Irrespective of the moral and political issues, the fall of Chandernagore yielded £100,000. This was fine compensation. The defeat of the Nawab would yield still more. Mir Jafar was disaffected and willing to be the instrument of the English in overthrowing Siraj-ud-Daulah. After considerable deliberations, the cost of restitution communicated to Mir Jafar included the following sums: 10,000,000 rupees to the Company as indemnity; 5,000,000 rupees to the Europeans; 2,000,000 for the Indians; 700,000 for the Armenians; and donations of 2,500,000 to the Army and the Navy each. Additionally Mir Jafar agreed to grant the English 600 yards of land beyond the Maratha ditch, and all land south of Calcutta up to Kulpi. On 4 June 1757, Mir Jafar ratified the treaty and thereby sealed his Nawab's fate. The historic Battle of Plassey was fought on 23 June 1757, and Siraj-ud-Daulah replaced by Mir Jafar. The main issue of the money was settled at a conference with local businessmen on 30 June 1757 at which Clive and Mir Jafar were present. The amount outstanding was a staggering £2,750,000. In addition, there were, Orme says, 'other donations ... promised, which have since been the foundations of several fortunes, though not then publicly avowed'. Since it was impossible for the Nawab's treasury to fund this amount entirely, it was agreed that half would be paid, in coins, jewels, plates and other effects; the remainder in equal instalments over the next 3 years. Siraj-ud-Daulah was captured on 2 July and hastily transported to Murshidabad, where he was killed in the early hours of the following morning. He died aged 24, having been Nawab for only 15 months.

Clive received a gift of 1,600,000 rupees from Mir Jafar. More than the victory at Plassey, the money promised as restitution galvanised the European population at Calcutta. By 30 August, 10,765,737 rupees had been paid in coin, gold, and jewels. Further payments were not forthcoming because it was impossible for the Nawab's treasury to meet the amount due. English officers and soldiers squabbled in unseemly fashion over the division of the money. The army was unwilling to share prize money with the navy, and wanted immediate distribution. Clive overruled this. Yet the officers who were pressing for payment delivered him a letter of protest at Murshidabad. Clive replied to them on 5 July, complaining that they had treated him 'with the greatest disrespect and ingratitude'. 'You have stormed no town and found the money there', he told them, and 'neither did you find in the plains of Plassey after the defeat of the Nabob'. 'In short', he said, 'what you are to receive is entirely owing to the care I took of your interest'. The officers later apologised to Clive and he returned to Calcutta on 14 September 1757. However, he soon had to return, for he had to settle payment of the money due. This was done through the end of December, when arrangements were made for the disbursement of the remaining 230,000 rupees.

News of the fall of Chandernagore reached Madras on 28 April 1757 but without any troops being returned. Madras was in dire need of the troops who were then being readied for action against Siraj-ud-Daulah. Pondicherry, informed by spies of how matters stood in the English territory, at once put together as huge a force as possible, with D'Auteuil in command. On 14 May 1757 D'Auteuil invested Trichinopoly with 1150 Europeans, 3000 sepoys, and 10 field-guns. He cannonaded the fort until 20 May, when he sent a missive in vain asking the garrison to surrender. Meanwhile he got news that English reinforcements were en route to Trichinopoly. D'Auteuil covered all feasible approaches but Captain Caillaud, who was leading the small English reinforcement column, outwitted him. Caillaud marched 9 miles through rice-fields, which were under water, to circumvent the French. D'Auteuil was so disheartened by this that he at once retreated to Pondicherry without pausing to attempt an assault, despite the fact that his force vastly outnumbered the English garrison, including Caillaud's reinforcement. De Leyrit, astounded by D'Auteuil's inexplicable retreat, nonetheless ordered Moracin and De Bussy to move against English factories in the ceded districts. The English garrison at Vizagapatam surrendered, as had Madapollam, Bandarulanka, and Ingeram, and even though Chandernagore had fallen, the French continued to control huge territories along the Coromandel Coast.

Attention next moves to Wandiwash, where the garrison had declared for France. Colonel Adlercron marched against it, getting there on 5 June. His troops strove to take the town but were unable to carry the fort, whose fire enfiladed the main streets of the town. De Leyrit removed D'Auteuil from command, and replaced him with Saubinet, with instructions to proceed at once to Wandiwash. Saubinet reached Wandiwash on 11 June, and was surprised to see the English moving back towards Madras, to which they had been recalled. The English at Madras were precariously placed. Their resources had been strained by the need to send assistance to Bengal. They had been further straitened by the expense of keeping substantial forces in the field. With the fall of the factories in the Godavari basin, they could expect no income. In addition, they were required to keep a lookout for French reinforcements that might arrive any day and try to force the issue again at Madras. Adlercron set fire to the town of Wandiwash as he withdrew, bringing a new viciousness into the campaign. Saubinet followed him to Kanchipuram, where the English used the temple, whose sanctity had hitherto been strictly respected by both sides, to fire upon the enemy. The French, unwilling to storm the temple, set fire to the town and retired. This contrary practice embittered the war further. These were very uncertain times, and the war had been continuing without resolution in the Carnatic for over a decade. War is unpleasant and prolonged war destroys morality. To the credit of the French, it must be said that despite their numerical superiority, they did not begin these violations in the Carnatic.

The French, having returned to Wandiwash, entrenched themselves. The English under Adlercron, now with Colonel Lawrence as a volunteer, returned to the same place, and both sides despite receiving substantial reinforcements, remained inactive in their positions for 40 days. On 26 July 1757, the English broke camp and returned to their bases, having left a garrison in Kanchipuram. Saubinet remained at Wandiwash until September. On 9 September 1757, 12 French naval ships, including 4 ships-of-the-line of 60 guns each, reached Pondicherry, and landed a huge force, the Regiment de Lorraine, the first arrivals of the army dispatched from France in December 1756. Major-General Marquis de Soupire commanded this force. Only 3 years had passed since Dupleix had left. With such an army at his command, one wonders what grand stratagems he would have devised and achieved! The Commodore of the fleet, Bouvet, having received information sent erroneously to him by the English at Fort St David that Admiral Watson was shortly expected, decided to leave at once for Mauritius. He would not stay even to unload the artillery and heavy ammunition. The English in the meanwhile, aware of the arrival of this Regiment, had withdrawn all forces in the field to Madras and Fort St David, certain that assaults would follow. They were pleasantly surprised by the precipitate departure of the French fleet, and cautiously resumed their positions. Soupire, who assumed supreme military command of French troops in India, was unwilling to move against Trichinopoly until the rest of the army, scheduled to land soon, reinforced him. The army commander was Thomas Arthur, Count De Lally and Baron Tollendal. He was of Irish parentage, his father, Sir Gerard O'Lally, having migrated to France in 1691 after the capture of Limerick. Thomas was born in 1700, and his youth had been spent in the French armies. Thomas had fought in 1745 with great distinction at Fontenoy, where Marshal Maurice de Saxe recognised his bravery in the field. Thomas had even worked for a month with Voltaire, who had found in him 'a stubborn fierceness of soul, accompanied by great gentleness of manners'. His contemporaries treated him with great respect and he was widely seen as the only man who could continue with the same vigour and determination the expansionist policies of Dupleix. To send out Dupleix might have been better for De Lally was a quick-tempered man. Maybe

Voltaire had misread him, for he was haughty and dismissive of Franco-Indians, and lacked the diplomacy, humility, and tact of Dupleix. De Lally was a soldier, and a commander. Dupleix had used his charisma to establish close relations with local rulers, and had made great achievements using only a fraction of the number of troops now available. As both diplomatist and strategist, he had outwitted the English, never allowing a defeat to hold him back but strengthening his resolve to succeed. Worse, while Dupleix had been careful about observing local customs and civilities, his wife's religious bias notwithstanding, De Lally was haughty and dismissive of Indians.

Soupire, aware of De Lally's imperiousness, and the toll that the long voyage had taken on the health of his troops, knew that an attack right then on Trichinopoly would fail again. Instead, he agreed to cooperate with Saubinet in reducing the forts of the Carnatic that owed allegiance to Muhammad Ali. The first to fall was Chittapet, invested on 25 September 1757 with a besieging force that included a detachment from the Regiment de Lorraine, and much artillery. The fort was breached and taken by assault on 13 October. The French appeared before Trinomalee on 18 October and took it. Other forts in the Carnatic that fell to the French include Thiyagadurgam, which was occupied on 4 November. In all, before being recalled to Pondicherry, Saubinet had managed to reduce 8 forts in the region of Chittapet, Trinomalee, and Gingee.

On 28 April 1758, the Comte de Lally reached Pondicherry, announced his commission, and began preparations to send a force overland to besiege Fort St David. 1000 Europeans and 1000 sepoys soon marched off for this purpose under the command of Count D'Estaing, who had come with De Lally. De Lally indeed held a formidable commission, as commander-in-chief and Commissary of the King. As such, he was to be implicitly obeyed by every French subject in India. He had been dispatched with other extraordinary powers. The French government had told him to look into corruption, in both military and civil administrations. They had also ordered him to examine the treaties with local rulers and to see if these were designed for the enrichment of private individuals – as appeared to be the case with Dupleix – and detriment of the French Company. His main task was of course to fight the English and drive them from India. When asked for his opinion in Paris in 1756, he had offered a choice from three strategies to the French ministry: to invade England, to invade Canada and take it from the English, or to drive the English out of India. The importance of the last had been realised after a year of dithering and losses. Unfortunately, the nature of his briefing about corrupt administration coloured his opinion overmuch, and he tended to be dismissive of officials with long service in India. Of all the serving French, only De Bussy had been recommended to his attention. De Lally therefore came to India with unusual powers but was handicapped partly by his own personality and partly by the information he had been given in Paris. De Leyrit, who was unable to brief him satisfactorily either about Fort St David or the English forces on the Coromandel, confirmed his impression of the incapability of French officials in India.

The column that had marched to Fort St David forced the capitulation of Cuddalore on 4 May 1758. De Lally found himself without any logistical support on the part of De Leyrit and his council. Nonetheless, De Lally continued with his assault on Fort St David, where matters deteriorated even as the garrison awaited the arrival of the English fleet under Admiral Pocock. This naval officer had already had a brush with the French the previous month, and De Lally managed to convince the French Admiral, D'Ache, to hold off the English fleet, by meeting the sailors' demand for arrears of 2 months' pay from his (De Lally's) own funds. On 2 June 1758 Fort St David, which Dupleix had attempted to take only a few years previously with far fewer resources, surrendered to De Lally. D'Ache then proceeded with his fleet to anchor close to Sri Lanka to recuperate, while De Lally had the fortifications of Fort St David destroyed. He had at his command 2500 Europeans and 2500 sepoys. Following the fall of Cuddalore and Fort St David, he sent D'Estaing to Devikottah, whose English garrison fled to Trichinopoly. Devikottah thus fell on 4 June. De Leyrit did not have the money to furnish De Lally's army with the logistical support for an assault on Madras, which was the next obvious target. De Lally also realised probably for the first time the inherent superiority, gained over the centuries, by English sailors. With a better naval commander supporting him, De Lally could have achieved more. Both the French council, and Father Lavaur of the Jesuits, misled De Lally, telling him to invest Tanjore on behalf of Sahuji, who had been deposed in 1739. The main intention was not to place Sahuji on the throne but to extract from the Raja of Tanjore 5,600,000 rupees for which he had given Pondicherry a bond when his fort was besieged by Muzaffar Jung and Chanda Sahib. Without money to arrange provisions, and perhaps intending to live off the country, De Lally marched with his troops to Tanjore and invested it. He was about to successfully assault the fort when news came that D'Ache had been defeated by an English fleet and Pondicherry was about to be besieged by a large army from Madras. De Lally decided to retreat, which was worse because not only had he expended men and money on this futile venture, he also had no provisions on the way back and, moreover, was harassed by Tanjore cavalry all the way to Karikal. De Lally reached Karikal on 18 August and Pondicherry on 28 August. No entreaty could deter D'Ache from his intention to retreat to the safety of Mauritius. The only good to emerge from D'Ache's otherwise vain blustering, was his seizure of a Dutch ship carrying 300,000 rupees, which answered De Lally's purpose of preparing an assault on Madras. D'Ache sailed with his fleet on 3 September 1758, leaving behind 500 sailors to bolster the army. The English fleet stayed for 3 weeks more and then sailed for Bombay.

On 13 June, De Lally had written to De Bussy, asking him to meet up with Moracin and march with all troops who could be spared, to Arcot. As Watson had threatened Siraj-ud-Daulah in his letter to set such a fire that all the water of the Ganges would not be able to put out, De Lally wrote to De Bussy of his ultimate aim to get to the Ganges by land or sea, thereby putting into practice his policy, 'no more English in India'. This letter reached De Bussy on 15 July 1758, and he followed orders despite remonstrance from Salabat Jung, whom De Bussy had hitherto protected from his enemies with unusual devotion. De Bussy handed over command at Masulipatam to the Marquis de Conflans in August 1758 and left the Deccan with 250 Europeans and 500 sepoys for the Carnatic. Arcot fell to the French on 4 October, and by 10 November, De Lally was prepared to march on Madras. De Bussy did not impress De Lally despite what he had been told in Paris about the former. The dislike was mutual. De Bussy wished to be back in the Deccan, as did Moracin. De Lally clearly wanted nothing more than to destroy the English and thereby consider his task done, for he had no plans, unlike Dupleix, then languishing in France, of creating a French empire in India.

Money was still scarce and De Lally's attitude was not calculated to conjure it. De Leyrit adamantly held to having none in the public treasury for funding a war. Moracin had brought 100,000 rupees and this, along with contributions from the private purses of the senior officers, all of whom belonged to the aristocracy, helped put together a sum to furnish the army. We should remember that Dupleix's stratagems had cost over 6,000,000 rupees with far fewer troops, at a time when French prestige was at its height. De Bussy and Moracin held military commissions from the French Company, while De Lally and his officers held King's commissions. Moreover, De Bussy held the local rank of Lieutenant-Colonel. Nonetheless, at the outset of the expedition against Madras, D'Estaing and 5 other officers petitioned De Lally that De Bussy be placed above them in view of his far greater experience. De Lally suggested later in his memoirs that De Bussy contrived this by giving or lending these officers huge sums. In his memoirs, De Lally also accused De Bussy of having offered him 460,000 livres. De Lally nevertheless appointed De Bussy Brigadier. De Bussy thus became the third in the chain of command, following De Lally and De Soupire. The army, comprising 2000 Europeans, 300 cavalry, and 5000 sepoys, was divided into 4 brigades, commanded by De Soupire, D'Estaing, Crillon, and Saubinet. De Bussy held no particular post in the chain of command. The French army took Kanchipuram on 27 November and on 12 December 1758 invested Madras. The governor of Madras was George Pigot.

George Pigot was born on 4 March 1719. He joined the East India Company as a Writer in 1736, and, as we have already seen, he reached Madras on 26 July 1737. His brother, Robert Pigot (1720 – 1796), was commissioned into the army, and commanded HM 38th Regiment of Foot at the Battle of Bunker Hill (1775). Promoted Major-General, Sir Robert commanded the British forces at the Battle of Rhode Island (1778). He became Lieutenant-General in 1782 and, having inherited his brother's baronetcy of Patshull in 1777, resigned the service and died in 1796 at Strafford. Hugh Pigot (1722 – 1792), George Pigot's other brother, joined the Royal Navy as an able-bodied seaman in 1734. Clearly possessing officer-like qualities, Hugh was commissioned Lieutenant in 1742, Commander in 1745, and Captain in 1746. He served in the West Indies, and eventually turned to politics, which was usual for the times. Hugh became MP for Penryn in 1768 and later (1778) for Bridgnorth, which had been occupied by his brother George. In 1775, he was promoted to Rear-Admiral, rising to Vice-Admiral later in the same year. In 1782, he became one of the Lords of Admiralty. Appointed to the West Indies command, he returned after peace was declared but lost his parliamentary seat in the elections of 1784.

At the time Madras fell to De la Bourdonnais, George Pigot was a Junior Merchant and Clerk of the Peace. Captured, he chose to return to England, where he stayed until peace was concluded and Madras returned. Returning to the Coromandel in 1750, Pigot was appointed tenth in council at Fort St David, to which all administrative powers previously enjoyed by the council of Fort St George had been transferred. We have seen how Pigot, though not a military officer was requested to take a relief column, via Verdachelam to Trichinopoly, with Clive as a volunteer, which was ambushed on the way back, with Pigot and Clive barely managing to save themselves due to the speed of their horses.

Pigot left the military arrangements to Colonel Stinger Lawrence, who was one of the officers of the garrison at Madras. Lawrence was well-served since he had under him officers particularly experienced in fighting in the Carnatic, including Major Caillaud. On the morning of 13

December, the French captured and pillaged the Black Town. It yielded loot estimated at £600,000 but only the paltry sum of £3700 made it to the war chest. The following morning the English sallied out and since the French mistook their scarlet uniforms for Bourbon colours, they succeeded in capturing D'Estaing and scattering a French detachment. The French retaliated, and would have gained access into the fort, had De Bussy not refused Crillon permission to cut off the English retreat by holding a bridge. A long and depressing siege followed. De Lally's army was badly officered and poorly soldiered. Discipline was lax, looting rife, and desertion common. By February 1759, De Lally had lost most of his engineers and artillery officers. The troops had had no pay for 2 months, ammunition was running out, and to crown it all, even though a practicable breach had been made, De Lally could not get the officers or soldiers to assault the fort. Additionally the English were using their allies in harrying the French right up to the gates of Pondicherry. On 16 February Admiral Pocock's squadron sailed up from Bombay, and with Pondicherry now threatened, De Lally left his wounded behind under the care of a surgeon with a letter to the governor, George Pigot, and retreated to Pondicherry the following day. Similarly, in the Deccan, Conflans was defeated close to Rajahmundry on 8 December 1758 by Colonel Forde, sent by Clive from Bengal for this purpose. Conflans retreated into Masulipatam, where Forde besieged him, and took the place by assault even as the fate of Madras remained uncertain and Salabat Jung was marching with a huge army to save Conflans. Conflans and his soldiers surrendered to Forde. Masulipatam again passed to the English. Salabat Jung soon made peace with the English, and the huge territories that Dupleix and De Bussy had obtained and held for France passed to the English as well. Official displeasure was rife in Pondicherry, for De Lally, in carrying out his orders to put a stop to corruption, had confronted rampant malfeasance. The councillors used to pay in treasury bills, which, since the treasury was in straitened circumstances, meant that a treasury bill was worth 20% of its value in cash. The owner of the bills later collected the dues, when money became available, with a clear profit of 80%. The councillors who were engaged in this practice resented De Lally's presence. Hence, De Lally was hindered at Pondicherry even as the enemy harassed him in the field. The French Company's officers, for example, like De Bussy, contributed little, if anything, to the conduct of the siege of Madras. They seem to have been sympathetic towards their civilian counterparts. De Lally's forces were depleted, his own regiment having lost a substantial percentage of its soldiers to disease, action, and desertion. Following a prolonged period of action during the siege, De Lally himself fell seriously ill at Pondicherry. Meanwhile, money was not forthcoming and in August 1759, his own regiment mutinied. The soldiers did not want to go on fighting in a strange land on irregular pay any more. Two hundred former prisoners of war, exchanged with the English, had been coerced to join the regiment. These were the most disaffected, since they were no longer inclined to the hard military life. The officers rushed after their troops, who had marched out with the intention of joining the English, and brought most of them back with promises to pay their arrears. On 10 September, D'Ache arrived from Mauritius, with diamonds and other jewels worth around 400,000 rupees. The English fleet too reached Fort St David at the same time and a battle ensued. The honours were equal but D'Ache was wounded and he chose to leave again for Mauritius. Despite being repeatedly begged to change his decision, he sailed away on 30 September and never returned to India. De Bussy too had been ill following great exertions during the siege of Madras. Nonetheless, he suggested to De Lally that Basalat Jung, the brother of Salabat, who had now gone over to the English, be encouraged by making him the Nawab of Arcot. De Lally, distressed by want of money, agreed but the event never came about, for on 17 October the French garrison at Wandiwash, comprised of the Regiment of Lorraine, mutinied because 10 months' pay was due to them. They chose to go over to the English but were prevented from doing so by various enticements, including the dispatch of Crillon carrying 6 months' pay raised through contributions at Pondicherry in the teeth of De Leyrit's opposition, and promises to pay the remainder by 10 November.

All these narratives reach their nadir for the French on the night of 21-22 January 1760, at the Battle of Wandiwash. Wandiwash had fallen to the English in December 1759. De Lally was in tremendous difficulty now. Common military sense suggested that he spend the next few months allowing his troops to recover, until further funds came in from France. He also needed to keep them active by directing ambushes and depredations on the English lines of communication. Meanwhile he should have consulted with his senior officers on strategy and tactics for the next campaign. To such patient and long-term thinking, he seems to have been temperamentally unsuited. Moreover his soldiers were seriously disaffected both by the arrears of pay due to them as well as by their inability to acquire loot through successful battles. They had been losing their battles for quite some time. In any case, the inhabitants of the Carnatic, having now suffered nearly 20 years of warfare, did not have much loot to offer. Many had hidden or spirited away their wealth. Trade was almost at a standstill. De Lally realised that waiting would not do. He had to act soon. Hence, he decided to divide his meagre force into two divisions. One he led on a feint on Kanchipuram to draw Colonel Eyre Coote there, while he marched across to recapture Wandiwash. This worked to an extent. De Lally reached Wandiwash on 12 January 1760 but failed to take it by night attack. The town fell the following day. Coote, having caught on, followed him to Wandiwash. De Lally's engineer officer, Durré, took nearly a week to install a battery to use for the reduction of the fort, by which time the English were close. The other division of De Lally, under De Bussy, joined him on the evening of 20 January, and on being informed of the proximity of the English, readied for battle outside Wandiwash. The battle was desperately fought. The opponents probably had the prescience to know that the outcome would decide which European nation would dominate the Carnatic henceforth. De Bussy had his horse shot from under him as he led a bayonet charge, and was taken prisoner. Several French officers were killed. The French cavalry, who had performed with extreme distinction throughout, now fought a rearguard action that allowed their infantry to withdraw, reassemble, and retreat in reasonably good order. With De Lally's defeat at Wandiwash, all possibilities of French domination of the Carnatic and the Deccan ended forever. The rest of De Lally's story in India is worse.

De Lally retreated to Pondicherry via Gingee and Valdore, saved from being cut off only because the English, themselves badly mauled at Wandiwash and in want of reinforcements and supplies, moved slowly, reducing the forts that that been occupied by the French. On 5 February Karikal, the other French port, was surrendered, ironically by the same Renault de St Germain, who had delivered Chandernagore to the English 3 years earlier. By 15 February 1760, De Lally was in Pondicherry. This was hardly the place for him to find shelter in, for it was clamorous with accusations of how he had frittered away French India. De Lally continued to strive for the defence of Pondicherry, which was soon besieged, by offering an alliance to Haider Ali of Mysore. In addition, he attacked the besiegers on 4 September with vigour and precipitation but in vain. By 16 September 1760, the French had to withdraw within the walls of Pondicherry. Time was running out for the French. Food supplies were low, and hopes pinned on the arrival of D'Ache. He never came, and on 16 January 1761, Pondicherry surrendered to the English. Even as De Lally, who had been sick and abed for nearly 3 weeks, was being carried from the city into captivity in Madras, 80 Europeans including two members of council attacked his palanquin. They insulted him, and probably meant to kill him but were prevented by De Lally's English escort. Ananda Ranga Pillai, who, with Dupleix, had contributed to the rise of French power to its highest point, was probably fortunate in dying on 12 January 1761, four days before the surrender.

De Lally was taken to England, leaving Madras aboard the *Onslow* on 6 March 1761. From England, he travelled on parole to France, where he was arrested and put on trial. His intention was to reveal the true cause of the French defeat in India, which meant the implication of all the French Company officials who had personally garnered huge personal treasures through corrupt practices detrimental to their Company and country. Here of course he faced vituperative opposition from nearly every Frenchman associated with the Company: De Bussy, Moracin, Father Lavaur, D'Ache, and the councillors at Pondicherry led by De Leyrit. Confronted with such opposition it was suggested to De Lally that he fly but this he would not do, and was heard in a travesty of a trial, denied legal assistance by his judges because he stood accused of high treason. After he had spent three long years in prison, the French parliament sentenced De Lally to death, and King Louis XV confirmed the sentence. Even a request from the army for a pardon was rejected. On the afternoon of 9 May 1766, De Lally was gagged and carted to the Place de Grève, where he was beheaded; this too was not an easy death, for the executioner had to hack due to either inexperience or a blunt weapon. He died at the age of 65. The French East India Company wound up in 1769. De Lally's execution was judicial murder, and after the Revolution, his reputation was restored. Pondicherry, with its defences demolished, was restored to the French following the Peace of 1783. It was recaptured in 1793, and restored by the Peace of Amiens (1802). Retaken again following the resumption of hostilities in Europe the following year, Pondicherry finally returned to French possession in 1815.

Considering that all this fighting between the English and the French for two decades had been for the sake of money, one is hardly surprised to find that between August 1755 and January 1759 Clive had remitted to England £280,000, of which £210,000 accrued from the enthroning of Mir Jafar, and the remainder from prize money. With the subsequent grant of a *jagir*, Clive's annual income was pegged at £40,000. Corruption did not begin in Bengal. It began in the Carnatic with the princes vying for the use of European troops, offering additional payment and loot as enticement. Nonetheless, as we have seen, the wars had rendered the Carnatic poor because they continued for 20 years. The pattern of corruption, however, that became well known later, was established in Bengal.

CHAPTER NINE

THE GOVERNORSHIP OF GEORGE PIGOT, 1755-1763

George Pigot is unique in that he was governor of Fort St George during one the most crucial periods of English dominance in India, for it was during Pigot's administration that the English East India Company ceased to be a trading corporation only. Instead, it succeeded to the governance of huge territories, to protect which, its employees, emboldened by the presence of the Company's troops, negotiated with local princes on equal terms. Pigot was also unique in that he was governor of Madras for 8 years, thereby serving longer than all his predecessors had. As has been seen, he succeeded Thomas Saunders on 14 January 1755. On 26 October 1755 Robert Orme, then Warehouse-keeper at Madras, wrote a long letter to John Payne, who became Chairman of the Company's Board of Directors in 1757. Towards the end of this gossipy letter, Orme refers to Pigot's 'Indolence of Disposition', which made him wish that Mr Pigot 'could bring himself to a more continued Application of Affairs, or that he had greater Vivacity in the Dispatch of them'. 'His Understanding', Orme wrote, 'though not quick, is sure: His Disinterestedness such that Twice the Term of any of his Predecessors in the Government' would not 'give him any half of their Fortunes'. Not just Pigot, Orme also slandered Lawrence, disparaging his military talents: 'his Military Command must have everything dependent on his own Will, or that Will which, infused into him by others, he is taught to think his own'. Lawrence, Orme told Payne, was 'sadly accessible, from the Side of his Vanity, which indulges itself in frequent and honourable Commemoration of his Exploits'.

Pigot soon realised that Orme was secretly corresponding with their superiors at the Company's offices in England and passing along personal information as well. On 11 March 1758, Orme reported to Payne that Pigot's manner towards him had undergone a distinct change. Pigot had stopped visiting his home, and this made Orme certain that he knew Orme had been writing to Payne about Pigot's attachment to a married woman in

Madras, whose husband was away in the Company's service. The fact is that Robert Orme considered himself sufficiently well connected to be able to supersede several persons senior to him on the council and become governor, if he managed to malign Pigot's character successfully. That Pigot should have been singled out for Orme's ire, is sufficient testimony to the abilities of the former.

Orme almost succeeded to the governorship, despite the fact that he was shunned by nearly all at Fort St George, to the extent that he decided to resign and return home under the pretext of ill health. Orme indeed had commendable qualities but his sniping was unacceptable. He therefore rose through the council, until the letter that he had been working so assiduously for, finally arrived. Dated 8 March 1758, the letter appointed him second in council, to succeed Pigot as governor. In his cleverness, Orme had miscalculated, as the clever often do, his rival's astuteness. On 25 September, soon after this letter was received, Pigot, having gathered enough evidence, brought charges against Robert Orme.

Fort St David had fallen to the French and De Lally's troops had overrun the Carnatic. Madras was in danger of being besieged at any time. 'At this crisis, I say, Gentlemen,' Pigot told his council, 'Mr Orme thought it not unbecoming his Station to dispose of his Effects and Concerns, to remit his Fortune home in Dutch Bills, and publicly to avow his fears in taking Passage for Europe in the *Grantham*'. This was 'an Example so Unmanly and dishonourable', and Pigot was deliberately unsubtle in emphasising the enormity of this desertion, referring to 'the Natural Propensity of Mankind to Censure'.

This was not all. Within the last few days, other occurrences had intervened, 'of such a Nature as ought not to be concealed'. Pigot had visited the Nawab, Muhammad Ali, alone after the ceremonies of reception were over. During this meeting, he had been told that Orme had often ordered the Nawab's *vakil* to call on him. Orme had spoken vainly to the *vakil* about his own power and services to the Nawab, hinting that he had not been adequately recompensed. Pigot's previous suspicions that Orme was up to no good came from information about a letter that Orme had written to the Nawab soon after the Company's ship, the *Pitt* had reached Madras from England and 'some Circumstances of a Visit' that followed, both of which the Nawab wanted Pigot to know about. When Orme got news of his appointment as second in council from the packet that came aboard the *Pitt*, he wrote to the Nawab that he had been made the Deputy Governor, and that Pigot had been ordered home, and Clive to Bengal. Clearly, Orme was arm-twisting the Nawab into secret payments. The Nawab told Pigot that Orme 'expected to be largely rewarded', or be allowed to 'put the Management of the greatest part of the Nabob's Dominions into hands that would amply gratify him'. The Nawab was thus being told that he would henceforth have to rely on Orme's goodwill, which would need compensation. Even though he knew what Orme had previously said to his *vakil*, the Nawab replied that he would congratulate Orme when they met. Orme soon proceeded to meet the Nawab. At the meeting Orme was profuse, relating to the Nawab the many services he had done, 'Not in the least doubting but that the Nabob would make him a Suitable Acknowledgement'. The Nawab, 'in his usual polite manner', agreed to make Orme 'proper Acknowledgements'. However, 'that kind of Eastern Compliment' did not answer Orme's purpose. 'He very frankly came to the Point himself', Pigot said, 'and acquainted the Nabob that he thought he well merited a present of Twenty Thousand Pagodas'. The Nawab told Orme that his treasury was dwindling and he would not be able to pay this sum for a couple of years. Orme, venting his extreme irritation at this, rose 'in a very abrupt Manner', and 'declared that, if the Sum he had mentioned was not immediately paid down, He should take the necessary Measures' to put portions of the Nawab's territories into the management of others.

This was a terrible insult to the Nawab. In the hearing of his durbar, and his sentries, he had been spoken to in a rude and offhand manner, as if he were no prince. He considered that if this was the kind of treatment he could expect from the English when Orme succeeded to the governorship, he 'Thought it even better to forgo the Protection of the English and leave himself to Fortune than to be subject to such Affrontive Treatment in the Face of his Durbar'. He therefore told Orme that the visit had lasted long enough, and he could do as he wished about the management of the territories.

Then Pigot drove home the point, linking Orme's precipitately planned journey to England on board the *Grantham* to his unacceptable behaviour, driven by crude greed, with a princely ally. He established that Orme had single-handedly done his best to undermine English efforts at a time when the Carnatic was in turmoil, and the English needed their ally, Nawab Muhammad Ali Khan, to survive. Pigot implied but did not state that Orme's actions had been treasonous. 'It will give me pleasure', Pigot concluded, 'if the Gentleman whose Reputation is so nearly touched should be able to Vindicate himself to the Satisfaction of the World .... And that he may have full opportunity of doing so before the departure of the *Grantham*'.

Speaking in his defence, Orme fumbled. The reasons for his departure from the Coromandel did not arise 'from that want of Resolution which is called Personal, or from the want of that other kind of Resolution … which is called Steadiness'. 'Infirmities both of body and Mind' had made him feel 'incapable of rendering any material Services in the present involved Circumstances of the Company's Affairs'. The truth of the matter, which all the councillors must have been aware of, then came out. One can imagine Pigot listening intently, waiting for Orme to entangle himself inextricably in the web of his own careful making. Orme admitted that he 'had long thought the assurances which were given him by the Principal Members of the Court of Directors on his leaving England were so long Postponed that he could not but esteem himself no longer in their favour'. Orme seems to have been rather disconcerted by his own admission, and he lamely repeated that 'a very ailing Constitution and particular Habits in his way of life had for a long term rendered his stay in this Country very irksome'. He had put together his 'small Affairs' and was ready to leave for England, having submitted to Pigot's censure, though he did not feel that his actions merited 'so harsh an Epithet as the President ha[d] Characterised it with of being dishonourable'. He rejected the letter as a forgery, and all allegations about seeking payments from the Nawab in return for favours as falsehoods: 'such is the Misfortune of Mr Orme's Defence that he is able only to oppose a single Negative to perhaps the Voice of Multitudes', the secretary had recorded in the consultation book. Consequently, Orme felt 'too sensibly affected with the degradation attending such Imputations to have even the Capacity left of filling any Station in this part of the World'. He thus begged permission once more to resign the service.

Pigot was not going to let Orme off so easily. It was resolved to make an inquiry into the letter, which Orme denied having written to the Nawab. On 28 September 1758, the council met the Nawab and his *vakil*, Antaji Pantulu, at the Company's Garden-House. The Nawab confirmed everything that Pigot had alleged about Orme's demands. He also confirmed the receipt of the letter, which was given him by Orme's *dubash*. The missive was produced, and its contents too were confirmed to be the same as stated at the council meeting. The next day the *dubash* was questioned alone, and he said he knew nothing about the letter. When faced with the *vakil*, he changed his statement and confessed that he had written and delivered the note without Orme's knowledge. This of course was deemed another lie.

On 29 September, the findings of the inquiry were laid before the council. Orme's actions in selling his property, remitting the money home, and readying to leave, at a time when it was necessary for the Company's servants to stay on in order to display their confidence to the locals, 'was an ill-timed Step, and unbecoming of the Station he bore in the Company's Service'. While the council would not charge Orme with bribery given the lack of evidence, his role in the affair struck them as 'extraordinary and unaccountable'. Finally, in the matter of Orme's meetings with the Nawab and his *vakil*, the council held him guilty, 'The Testimony of the Nabob and his Vakil appearing strong and clear, and no Circumstance or reason being even suggested as an inducement to the Nabob to make such a Complaint … undeservedly'. Since Robert Orme had resigned the service with effect from 25 September, the council only referred the matter to the Company for further action. Pigot had won. However, fate intervened. The French captured the *Grantham*, which carried both Orme as well as the letters incriminating him, near the Cape of Good Hope on 4 January 1759. Orme eventually made his way to England but the letters were lost. The Company, acting upon later information, wrote to Madras on this matter, noting that Orme's travelling to Mauritius aboard a French ship rather than landing at the Cape and awaiting an English ship laid 'his views and designs' open to doubt. In any case, the Company was satisfied that Orme was 'a very unfit Person to continue in India'. Were he to reappear anywhere in its jurisdiction, Fort St George was urged to deport him immediately. From 1761 to 1769, Orme was out of the Company's favour, despite the appearance of and acclaim for the first volume of his *History* in 1763. In 1769, Orme was appointed Historiographer to the Company, on £400 a year. The second volume of his work appeared in two parts in 1778. Robert Orme died at Great Ealing, Middlesex, in 1801 aged 73. There is a memorial plaque to him on the north wall of the tower of St Mary's Church, Ealing. To Orme's credit, he did not allow his animosity for Pigot to appear in his *History*.

Following De Lally's raising the siege at Madras and his retreat to Pondicherry on 17 February 1759, Orme wrote that Pigot at once surrendered all special powers that he had exercised during the crisis. Orme noted that Pigot 'had visited the works every day, encouraging the garrison by his presence, and rewarding those exposed to severer services with money'. Under his particular supervision, 'Provisions of all kinds and of the best condition, had been laid up, and as well as all the military stores, were distributed from the different magazines, under the direction of the members of the council, assisted by the inferior servants of the company, whose habits of business established and continually preserved these details free of all let and confusion'. Madras had given hard battle to De Lally. Orme says that the fort had fired 26,544 rounds from its guns, and there remained over 30,000 rounds, enough for another siege. 7,502 shells had been lobbed by the mortars, while 1990 grenades had been used.

200,000 cartridges had been fired in musketry by the defenders. Madras was thankful to its governor. Orme displayed no ill will towards Pigot when he mentioned that on the fourth day following the surrender of Pondicherry, Pigot demanded its delivery to the presidency of Madras, as property of the Company, following the King's Patent of 14 January 1758, which determined the Company's shares of, and rights to, captures. A council, comprising Rear-Admiral of the Red, Watson, Rear-Admiral of the White, Pocock, 4 post-Captains, Colonel Coote, and 3 Majors in the King's regiment, sat down to consider this demand. They decided that the Patent did not apply to the capture of Pondicherry, which was to be held by the King's representatives on his behalf, and not by the Company. Pigot at once declared that that being the case, he would furnish no more money for the King's troops and the French prisoners. Stumped by this, since neither the senior admiral, nor the army commander, was authorised to draw bills on the home government for these expenses, the council submitted to Pigot's claim with an appended note of dissent against the means used and 'the insult it conveyed against the King's prerogative, and declared the Presidency responsible for the consequences'. Having taken charge of Pondicherry, Pigot ordered the destruction of its fortifications, to the extent that, as Orme writes, by the middle of 1761, 'not a roof was left standing in this once fair and flourishing city'.

Pigot had contributed significantly in other ways to the war effort. When Adlercron's regiment went home in 1757, several of the officers and 350 soldiers opted for the Company's service, with many getting an additional promotion in rank. Adlercron's 49th Foot was replaced by Colonel William Draper's (1721-1787) 79th Regiment of Foot, which reached Madras in September 1758. William Draper was unusual for the times in that he had been educated at Eton and had obtained an MA from King's College Cambridge, before he joined the army in 1744. Another officer who rose to prominence was Eyre Coote, who had served in the 49th and returned home with it. Promoted to the command of the 84th Regiment of Foot in 1759, he came out to India with his unit in October of the same year. The sepoys, who served in companies until 1759, were given uniforms from 1756 by order of Pigot, passed in council. These uniforms were made of European broadcloth, of which there was excess stock, and Pigot felt that this would give the sepoys the necessary military appearance.

By 1757 the Company, smarting from the capture of Calcutta, was convinced of the need to fortify Madras, and in its letter of 25 March, gave Fort St George full clearance to achieve this, telling the council, 'You cannot but be the most competent judges of the Facts'. Because the fortifications had been in disrepair since the rendition of Madras, it was left to two military engineers, John Brohier and John Call (Brohier was sent to Bengal in June 1757 to design the new Fort William and Call, who had been at Fort St David, replaced him) to carry out extensive reconstruction during the following year so that Madras was quite prepared to defend itself against De Lally, whose siege commenced in December 1758. In his letter to the council on 15 January 1758, Call suggested names for the newly constructed areas of the fort, 'yet undistinguished by any Particular Names'. These 'Particular Names' would help avoid 'Circumlocutive Descriptions' currently necessary, and allow proper garrisoning and rapid deployment. The names suggested included 'The Bastion lately built at the North West Corner of the Town to be called *The Royal Bastion*', 'The Bastion at the South West Corner *The Nabob's Bastion*', 'The Earthen Bastion to the Northward of the Nabob's Bastion *Lawrence's Bastion*', and 'The Earthen Bastion to the Southward of the Royal Bastion *Pigot's Bastion*'. Other measures followed, including the razing of some buildings and the repair of the boundary hedge 'with Caldera Bushes and such Prickly Shrubs as can be Collected nearest at Hand, erecting between each Brick Out Guard a Redoubt of Palmeira Trees stuck vertically in the Ground, between the Intervals of which Troops may fire under good Cover'.

The movements of De Lally's army having made clear its intention to take Madras, the council 'unanimously Agreed' on 12 December 1758, 'to Leave the Conduct of the Defence to the Governor, who, with Colonel Lawrence, is Desired to take the Assistance of the other Field Officers and the Engineer as often as may be Requisite, and Immediately to Issue the necessary Orders'. Some further idea of Pigot's abilities may be obtained from his reply to De Lally's complaint on 31 December that his headquarters had been fired upon. 'In War mutual Civilities and mutual Severities may be expected', Pigot wrote in a letter sent under the white flag, 'Upon your entrance into the Black Town, I gave Orders to the Commandant of Artillery that no fire should be directed at the Church of the Capuchin Friars, where I heard you intended to reside, although it is nearly within Point Blank Shot of the Cannon of the Fort, a distance very Unusual for a General's Head Quarters'. Having thereafter come to know that De Lally had moved from the Capuchin Church, which had then been occupied by French troops, Pigot had ordered the artillery to cannonade it. Pigot concluded his letter to De Lally by telling him that if he would inform Pigot 'at what Pagoda' he next intended to set his headquarters, Pigot would endeavour to respect that location. As Orme noted, Pigot had been at the forefront during the siege, often visiting the defences and encouraging the troops. This was dangerous business, for on 2 February 1759, Pigot went to the 'South East' or St Thomas' Bastion at 5 in the evening, and ordered a 24-pounder gun to be laid to fire upon a French position. This was done but the gun burst at the trunnions and seriously injured 6 men while Pigot escaped with a slight wound to his leg.

Great relief followed the withdrawal of the French and a thanksgiving was declared on 23 March 1759 at Madras. At the end of all the fighting, Pigot thought he deserved a higher salary, for costs had risen. The Company replied that they entertained 'very favourable Sentiments of Mr Pigot's Abilities and good intentions'. They acknowledged 'his great Merit in the Masterly Conduct and very gallant behaviour in the siege of Madras'. Therefore, choosing to 'handle this Subject in a tender manner', they raised his annual salary including expenses for 'Diet, Cattle, Servants, Palankeen, Wax, Damar [resin for torches] and Oil' from £300 to £3000. The Company nonetheless considered his claim 'an astonishing, an alarming Asservation'. They asked 'Can the Company bear the weight of such immense Expenses?' The answer was an admonition to Pigot: 'it would draw Shame and Censure upon us, when the Company's distresses have forced us to reduce their dividend one quarter part, that our President's Table Expenses should infinitely exceed those of any of His Majesty's Governors in the British Dominions'. It was only in recognition of his services in preserving the trade in the Carnatic that Pigot's demand was being met, and 'if there are other Charges, they must be Comprehended'. There remained the perquisites of office, which actually paid much more. The Company allowed the governor his 2.5% on the net produce of all farms, a percentage on the coinage of silver and gold, and upon coral imported from Europe. While he could accept no gratuity from the Nawab, he was allowed another 2.5% on the revenues of the lands mortgaged to the Company. By the time he left, Pigot's income from the Company's *jagir*, which he had induced the Nawab to cede, must have been considerable, for its annual revenue was assessed at 2,000,000 rupees. No matter how much moderation at dining the Company exhorted its employees to, the French councillors and other 'Principal Officers' who had been taken at Pondicherry were allowed a table 'to be kept for them at their direction without limitation of Expense'. However the prisoners repaid 'Politeness with reproaches, and seemed to have intended Revenge by Profusion', for the amount spent on feeding them stood at over 6000 pagodas.

Other, more ominous, changes took place. The Company decided to form its own permanent army of 2600 Europeans and 4000 sepoys, with adequate artillery and cavalry. Stringer Lawrence was the first commander-in-chief, from which post he retired in 1766. He died in London in 1775. Pigot resigned his governorship and sailed on the *Plassey* on 14 November 1763. Robert Palk (1717 – 1798) succeeded him. Sir William Draper had been involved in the capture of Manila and although discussion of this is beyond the scope of this book, it had the effect of making the Company clarify the powers of its governors. In an order dated 19 February 1766, the Company notified that the 'Governor for the time being shall be considered, by virtue of the Commission he bears from Us (and derived from the Company's Charter) as Commander in Chief of Our Forces, the Superior Military Officer, and in consequence thereof invested with a Power of Commanding all others, of putting such in Arrest who shall disobey his Orders, and in general with every other power belonging to a Superior or Commanding Officer'. This direction would later have tremendous implications in the strange case of Lord Pigot.

Another person who soon appeared in Madras was Paul Benfield, appointed Civil Architect and Assistant Engineer, with the rank of Lieutenant. He came, the Company wrote on 30 December 1763, 'exceedingly well recommended to Us as having been regularly bred as an Architect, Surveyor, and draughtsman, and for his knowledge, in fortification and other Branches of the Mathematics'. Benfield served under John Call, and was involved in the restructuring of the defences of Madras. Benfield must have worked his way into the Nawab's favour, for on 21 March 1766 Muhammad Ali wrote to Robert Palk reminding him that the Nawab had been granted permission to build a palace within the walls of Fort St George. The Nawab had engaged, with the assent of Palk, John Call to build his house. However, Call was often falling ill, and having come to know that he intended to return to England soon, the Nawab asked that Paul Benfield be allowed to take over, 'he being a person that drew out the plan of the house and presented it to me before, and likewise [as] he has a good skill in beginning and finishing the works of buildings'. The Nawab asked that Benfield not be reassigned to some other work until the palace had been constructed. While Palk was forthcoming, the Company was unsure about allowing the Nawab to reside within the fort, and so the matter was dropped. John Call sought permission to resign as Engineer of Fort St George on 17 January 1768. He wrote that he had been continually afflicted 'with a Bilious complaint' during the last 6 months. While he was willing to continue as the Company's Chief Engineer on the Coromandel Coast, he recommended the appointment of Paul Benfield in his place at Fort St George. Call knew of 'no person so capable' as Benfield, 'being well persuaded of his Capacity and application to business'. Meanwhile the Nawab found a suitable spot for his palace at Chepauk, a few miles south of the fort. There the palace was built in 1768. Eventually the Nawab acquired more adjoining land and built a wall, enclosing 117 acres within his grounds. Unlike Benfield, Warren Hastings stayed briefly at Madras. He had joined the Company in 1750, and was imprisoned at Murshidabad after the fall of Cossimbazar. Following the recapture of Calcutta, Hastings had joined George Vansittart's council in 1761. In 1764, he left for England, returning in September 1769, as Third in council at Madras. On 31 January 1770 Du Pre, then second in council, became governor, and Hastings took his place. As second in council, Hastings was Export Warehouse-keeper, and Commissary-General and Agent for Army supplies. Hastings remained in Madras until February 1772, when he was appointed governor of Bengal and, a year later, Governor-General.

George Pigot had been made a baronet on 5 December 1764. Between 1765 and 1768, he was MP for Wallingford, which used to send up two members. On 19 January 1766, he was raised to the Irish peerage as Baron Pigot. The previous year Pigot had purchased Patshull Hall in Staffordshire, about 10 miles from Bridgnorth, which had been built around 1730 by James Gibbs for Sir John Astley (1687–1772). From 1768 until his death, Pigot was MP for Bridgnorth. In 1769 Pigot was created an honorary LL.D by the University of Cambridge (Clive had been made an honorary DCL of the University of Oxford in 1760). He had accumulated great riches while in India, for these honours would have cost him much, as reportedly did Patshull, for which he paid £100,000. In fact, it was estimated that Pigot had accumulated £400,000, mainly by lending money on interest to the Nawab and others. He wielded considerable political influence in tandem with his brothers, who were also MPs, since they collectively had three votes to offer. George Pigot passed Wallingford to his brother Robert in 1768, while Hugh Pigot was elected from Penryn. Pigot also brought with him to England the diamond that bore his name. The Pigot Diamond must have originated at Golconda, like the Pitt. The diamond has its own story, which has been well documented and is beyond the scope of this book. Pigot, like many Englishmen of the times including Clive, returned home with several other rare jewels. As Clive said in his speech of 1772 to Parliament, there were only two channels available to an employee of the Company to send his money home - by paying it into the Company's treasury, or through diamonds. Since it was necessary for him to remit home his income from the *jagir* given him by Mir Jafar, Clive 'sent an agent into a distant and independent Country to make purchase of Diamonds'. These he then registered and paid duty on, and sent to England. Such particularity was rare. Smuggling diamonds out was easier than drawing pay orders on the Company. In November 2012, the 76 carat Archduke Joseph diamond, mined at Golconda, fetched € 16,900,000.

Colonel John Call left India in February 1770, having amassed, like nearly everyone else, a huge fortune, earned mainly through usury. He settled in Cornwall and tried to become governor of Madras a decade later. His candidacy was not successful, and he went on to become MP for Callington in 1784. He became a Fellow of the Royal Society on 9 November 1775, and died in March 1801, aged 69.

CHAPTER TEN

PIGOT'S SECOND GOVERNORSHIP, 1775-1777

The Nawab of Arcot, Muhammad Ali Khan, had been awarded the title of Wallajah by the Mughal Emperor, Akbar Shah II, in 1765 in recognition of his influence. Moreover, his enemies having all been removed either by the victories of the English or by the passage of time, it was natural for him to seek two apparently contradictory ends simultaneously. He wished to maintain good terms with the English and he wanted to be independent, a ruler in his own right. The former was necessary for his own safety, since the English had become supremely powerful with the removal of French influence. He also wanted a sanctuary, which Madras afforded. Hence, in addition to his palace at Chepauk, the Nawab had also purchased by 1771, around 8 houses in the White Town, several in the Black Town and in San Thome, in addition to 'Three Capital Houses' in the fort by persons in his employ including two English surgeons. This great acquisition of property alarmed the council. Its Select Committee, which included Du Pre, the governor, Warren Hastings, and Samuel Ardley, communicated its fears to the Company's Secret Committee on 25 March 1771: 'If it be the Nabob's inclination to increase the Number, no doubt he may, in a very short time, become possessed of most of the principal Houses in the Place, since Houses are frequently, in consequence of the Death or departure of the Incumbents, offered to sale, and the Nabob can always afford to give more for them than any one else, as a few thousand pagodas are to him of no consequence'. The reasons for apprehension lay elsewhere. Three years before the Nawab had tried to end the contradiction between his urge to be independent, and at the same time seek English help whenever needed, by appointing one John Macpherson (1744 – 1821), to his service. Macpherson came out to India as purser on board his uncle's ship. He was then 18, having been born at Sleat, in the Isle of Skye, in 1745. His father, also John Macpherson (1710-1765), was a minister, having been to King's College, Aberdeen, and thence to the University of Edinburgh. John Macpherson met Muhammad Ali, and was sent to London argue the Nawab's case at St James's court, in order to reduce his debt to the Company, remove him from the Company's power, and to provide him access to the English government as an independent ally.

The Nawab had been made unpleasantly aware of the rise of Haider Ali in Mysore when the latter invaded the Carnatic in 1767 with the connivance of the Nizam. Colonel Joseph Smith took a force to tackle Haider Ali and achieved some success at Trinomalee on 26 September 1767. Even though the enemy's cavalry under the command of Tipu, Haider Ali's son, made a very successful raid on Madras, entering the bounds and moving up to the Mount by 29 September, Haider Ali withdrew for a while. The Nizam sought peace with the English, and in 1769, Haider Ali struck again. This time he drew Colonel Smith away southwards from Cuddalore, and with a force of 6000 troops made a forced march to Madras. He reached the Mount on 29 March, throwing the defenders into confusion. While defensive troop placements were being hurriedly carried out, Haider Ali sent a letter to the governor, James Bourchier, and another for the second in the council, Josias Du Pre. Haider Ali wrote that he only sought a lasting peace between their governments. Accordingly, Du Pre went to see Haider Ali the next morning, and discussed terms. The council deliberated, and drew up the treaty on 2 April 1769. Haider Ali ratified it the following day. The treaty forced the English to agree to the alliance and the mutual restitution of conquered lands. The English were glad that Haider Ali had not attacked, since they were unprepared. He could have inflicted great and lasting damage to Madras and its adjoining lands. Nonetheless, Haider Ali's strategic move was an embarrassment to the English, and they could foresee that this alliance would lead them into other conflicts.

By 1769, the Nawab's debt to the Company stood at 2,200,000 pagodas. He had moreover borrowed sums from various individuals. A list of his debtors included Charles Bourchier (66,000 pagodas), James Bourchier (29,150 pagodas) John Call (58,950 pagodas), Josias Du Pre (15,100 pagodas), George Mackay (51,250 pagodas), and George Stratton (34,100 pagodas). Given this colossal debt, a Select Committee of the council decided that individual creditors should transfer their dues to the Company allowing it thereby full leeway in recovering the consolidated amount. The creditors thus placed themselves under the Company's protection for the recovery and proper distribution of the money accruing to them. The Nawab was aware of his huge liability, and it was with the intention of forcing the Company, through government influence, to either postpone or write off repayment that he sent John Macpherson to England. Macpherson met the Prime Minister, the Duke of Grafton, in 1768. His advocacy of the Nawab's cause was successful, and the government appointed Commodore Sir John Lindsay (1737-1788) naval commander of the East Indies station with the powers of a Minister Plenipotentiary to the durbar of Nawab Muhammad Ali Khan Wallajah. Despite being disliked and regarded with suspicion by the Company's officials in Madras, Macpherson nonetheless achieved popularity at Leadenhall Street, for he too returned to Madras in 1770 as a Writer. The council had written to the Company on 6 April 1770, warning it of the Nawab's attempts to subvert its dominance: 'We can truly assert that he does not appear the Man he did'. 'A Change of Circumstances' they noted (his huge debt to the Company), had produced 'a Change of Character'.

Sir John Lindsay's appointment as ambassador to the Nawab's Durbar was viewed with incredulity at Madras. Du Pre refused to allow him access to papers relating to the Nawab, and did not accompany him to the Nawab's palace at Chepauk whither Sir John went to present his credentials. The council countenanced no communication with Sir John in any matter concerning the Nawab and his affairs. They were further incensed by Sir John's insistence, on behalf of the Nawab, that the Company's forces engage Haider Ali, with whom an alliance had just been signed. Urgent letters were dispatched to London protesting Sir John's presence and actions. One wonders how the Directors of the Company could have remained uninformed about Sir John Lindsay's appointment until they were alerted to it by Madras. However, they took up the matter with the government with the result that Sir John Lindsay was recalled. The most peculiar thing was that the government replaced Sir John Lindsay with Rear-Admiral Sir Robert Harland (1715-1784) both as naval commander and as ambassador at the Nawab's durbar, investing him with the same powers as had been given to his predecessor. Sir Robert reached Madras in September 1772. In exercising his ministerial duties at the Durbar, he soon faced the same problems as Sir John. This resulted in his sailing from Madras to Bombay with his squadron in October 1772, at the beginning of the monsoon, without paying either the governor, Du Pre, the usual complimentary visit before leaving, or informing the council of his intention to leave. Sir Robert remained in India until 1775, when he was promoted Vice-Admiral of the Blue, and recalled. His replacement as naval commander was Commodore Sir Edward Hughes (1720-1794), who served until 1777, and was later engaged in naval warfare in Indian waters against the French Admiral Suffren.

Two army officers were assigned to the Company's service in India during this period. Major-General Eyre Coote (1726-1783), appointed Commander-in-Chief of the Company's forces in the East Indies, reached Madras in July 1779. He lived in Madras for some time before proceeding to Calcutta to serve in his military capacity on the Governor-General's council. The other officer was a controversial figure, Colonel Sir Robert Fletcher.

When Lord Clive resumed the governorship of Bengal in 1765, he reorganised the army. The first brigade, commanded by Lieutenant-Colonel Sir Robert Fletcher, was sent to Monghyr, 300 miles from Calcutta; the second brigade, under Colonel Smith, went to Allahabad; and the third brigade, under Colonel Sir Robert Barker, was stationed at Bankipore, near Patna, 100 miles beyond Monghyr. Sir Robert Fletcher had begun his career in very humble circumstances. On 24 May 1757, he had been appointed assistant to the Military Storekeeper at Fort St George, in the capacity of a 'Monthly Writer'. This was a local, not Company's, appointment. In September 1757, given the military exigency of the time, he transferred to the army as an ensign. The desperate need for officers and the high casualty rate raised him to a captaincy in 1760. That this was entirely due to the paucity of officers, is evidenced by the fact that Fletcher had been accused of insolence when a lieutenant and recommended for dismissal but was saved by the intervention of Eyre Coote. Sir William Draper appointed Fletcher Brigade-Major during his expedition to Manila in October 1762, where he distinguished himself in action because of which he was knighted. He became Major in 1764, and came out to India, where he was promoted to Lieutenant-Colonel and commander of the first brigade in lieu of Brigadier-General Carnac, who had been recalled to Calcutta to sit on the council.

In keeping with the Company's instructions to curtail military expenditure during peacetime, Clive ordered that 'double *batta*' [double field service pay] be abolished for the first and third brigades with effect from 1 January 1766. The second brigade was permitted this allowance in the field since it was posted a long way from Calcutta, where provisions cost more, as did European goods sent out from Calcutta. In cantonment, the second brigade would be allowed the original 'single *batta*' for the same reasons. The first and third brigades would only be permitted to draw half 'single *batta*', even in cantonment. Detachments on garrison duty in Calcutta and the subordinate factories would get no *batta* at all. This rule was made applicable to all ranks. Angry about the cessation of this allowance, officers of the three brigades held secret meetings and corresponded from December 1765 about the means of forcing the council to change its position.

The dissatisfaction began at the Monghyr brigade. At each brigade a secret committee of correspondence was formed, whose decisions were held supreme on the formation concerned. Over 200 captains and subalterns handed over their commissions to these committees, which would pass them on to the brigade commanders on 1 June 1766 as a mass resignation by way of protest. All these arrangements were made in the greatest secrecy, such that senior officers had no inkling of what was about to occur. The mutiny was so well planned that every officer involved in it not only signed a bond of £500 not to accept his commission again unless the 'double *batta*' was restored, but also paid a sum proportionate to his rank into a general fund that would support those who would be cashiered. The fund would provide for their return to Europe and the purchase of commissions in the King's regiments. On 24 April 1766, a peculiar incident took place at Bankipore, when Ensign Davis refused to hand over his commission to Captain Duff, and so had had his quarters set on fire. Colonel Sir Robert Barker, amazed at this incident, whose details came out during the court-martial that followed, wrote to his fellow commander, Sir Robert Fletcher, about it. Clive received a letter on 28 April from Sir Robert, dispatched 3 days previously, stating that the officers of the first brigade were unhappy with the withdrawal of the 'double *batta*' and would attempt to recover this allowance by handing over their commissions to him on 1 May. They had decided to accept no pay for the month of May but would continue in their duties, until the final decision of the governor and council was made known to them. The discovery by Sir Robert Barker at Bankipore had forced the conspirators to advance the date for the mass resignation from 1 June to 1 May 1766.

Clive at once set in process means of thwarting the mutiny. Letters were sent to Fort St George for the dispatch of all officers who could be spared. The brigade commanders of the two worst affected formations, the first and third brigades, were informed of these measures. While Colonel Sir Robert Barker of the third brigade corresponded regularly with Clive about the steps he was taking to scotch the plot, Sir Robert Fletcher's silence made Clive suspicious about where that officer's sympathies lay. That Fletcher was biased towards his officers was confirmed by a packet dated 1 May 1766 from him, which Clive received on 4 May. It contained 42 commissions that had been deposited with Fletcher, and a covering letter from that officer informing Clive that the officers who had tendered their resignations would serve until 15 May by which time they expected an answer from the governor.

Barker had gathered his officers and harangued them about the seriousness of their actions. Although he was held in great respect, the officers stuck to their decision. Barker provided Clive with the further information that the mutiny had received additional funding of £16,000 from some gentlemen in Calcutta. While Barker had refused to accept his officers' resignations, which the officers had then sent direct to Calcutta, Fletcher had accepted and forwarded them. Fully aware now of the depth and spread of the disaffection, Clive moved fast. He decided to go to Monghyr and left Murshidabad on 6 May. Stopped briefly by a river in flood, Clive reached Monghyr on 15 May 1766, by which time an abortive mutiny by European troops and officers had already occurred. Sepoys led by one Captain Smith had subdued this. Fletcher's involvement in the conspiracy from the beginning was disclosed in the letter he sent on the evening of 14 May, after the mutiny had been quelled. In the letter, Fletcher admitted having known of the conspiracy since January. At Bankipore and Allahabad, thanks to the firmness of Colonels Barker and Smith, the conspiracy was broken. By the end of May, officers had arrived from the Coromandel Coast and they were commissioned into the Bengal army in the same ranks they had held before. Many of the conspirators now recanted, and were re-commissioned. Two of the ringleaders, Duffield and Robertson, were ordered to be embarked from Calcutta on the *Lord Camden* for England. Robertson declared that he too ill to travel but was subjected to medical examination and declared fit. Thereupon he and Duffield locked themselves up in their houses and refused to be embarked. Sentries were posted to see that they did not escape and no provisions reached them. They had stocked enough food within and had wagered that the council would not be able to delay the sailing of the *Lord Camden* long. It sailed, and as soon as they received news of this, they came out of their houses and were arrested. Thereafter they were put on board a sloop, the *Ann*, taken to Madras, and thence to Bombay, and England.

Meanwhile evidence of Sir Robert Fletcher's encouragement of the mutiny reached Clive on 19 June 1766 in a letter written by a surgeon in the first brigade. This letter set out in detail how Fletcher, seeing that mere exhortations to resign were ineffective, said at mess that his brigade-major and aide-de-camp would set the example. Fletcher also maligned Clive, accusing him of insulting the army, of beggaring it, and of showing it ingratitude. Having somehow learned of this letter, Fletcher wrote to Clive on 23 June, saying that he was being defamed by his enemies, and made a scapegoat for their ill conduct. Clive did not answer this letter for he had summoned all senior officers to Patna where the general courts-martial would be held. He did not want to rouse the suspicions of Fletcher, whose implication was being corroborated by the confessions of other ringleaders. Sir Robert Fletcher reached Patna on 3 July 1766 and was promptly arrested. A grimmer note was added to the proceedings through a letter sent to Clive from the council on 24 June, and received after

Fletcher's arrest, which said that one Captain Stainforth had plotted to kill Clive.

Fletcher wrote to Clive on 3 July, asking to be tried by the governor and council in Calcutta. Clive replied that since Fletcher had been arrested for a military misdemeanour, he would have to face general court-martial and the governor and council would confirm the sentence. Accordingly Sir Robert Fletcher, Captain Stainforth, Captain Parker, and Ensign North, were tried for mutiny. Sir Robert Fletcher was found guilty of mutiny and sentenced to be cashiered. The council upheld the sentence. Fletcher then sailed to England to get the sentence quashed. Like most Company men, he first attempted to get into politics. Having lost at Malmesbury, he stood for election at Cricklade, and was returned, having allegedly paid £4000. Now an MP, he turned back to his primary aim of getting the sentence at Bengal overturned. Defeated by the opposition of Clive's friends in the Company's general court, Fletcher requested Clive through a common acquaintance to desist. Clive agreed, and Fletcher was reinstated. On 15 December 1769, Fletcher was appointed Colonel in the Company's service in Madras. However, he left England in mid-1771, and reached Madras early in 1772. He soon came into conflict with the governor, Josias Du Pre, who removed him from council and posted him to Trichinopoly. Fletcher now claimed his rights as an MP and sailed for England in March 1773. Fletcher reached England in 1774 and at once attended Parliament. In April 1774, he was promoted Brigadier-General and reappointed to Madras. The general elections were due and he soon realised that Cricklade would not return him. Conceding the day before the polls, Fletcher soon sailed for India, reaching Madras in June 1775, where he became commander-in-chief and third in council on the resignation of Major-General Joseph Smith in October of the same year. Colonel James Stuart was posted on 25 November 1775 to Madras as 'Colonel of Infantry in the Fort St George Establishment, to take Rank next to and immediately after Colonel [*sic*] Sir Robert Fletcher'. Stuart reached Madras on 1 May 1776. Stuart was an experienced officer of long service, having previously held the King's Commission for 29 years.

The Nawab's debt had in the meantime been growing and he had been borrowing from the Company's servants, in their personal capacities, at outrageous rates. As Edmund Burke pointed out in his speech in the House of Commons in February 1785, 'If we fix the commencement of this extraction of money from the Carnatic at a period no earlier than the year 1760, and close it in the year 1780, it probably will not amount to a great deal less than twenty millions of money'. As more and more of the Company's employees returned from Madras with vast fortunes, the Court of Directors began assessing the amounts due from the Nawab. Following Burke, this devolved into four parts. The first was constituted of his private loans, which added up to an astounding £888,000, mainly owed to Englishmen living in Madras. This was consolidated, as has been related, by the Select Committee and the repayment settled at £88,000 annually, on an interest of 10%. The Nawab's debts to the Company were also merged under the Consolidation of 1767. There was a second Consolidation of 1777, in which additional debts of £2,400,000 were rated at 12% annual interest. Burke added to this the 'Cavalry Debt', amounting to £160,000. These four debts, from 1767 to 1777, accrued to £4,444,000, and their annual yield was calculated at £623,000. 'Of this interest', Burke said, £383,200 a year 'stood chargeable on the public revenues of the Carnatic'.

Resentment had been brewing in England over the 'nabobs' who were returning home with immense fortunes. 'During the deep, silent flow of this steady stream of wealth ... happening at some periods to meet rifts of rocks that checked its course, it grew more noisy and attracted more notice', Burke declaimed. That the Company had taken no notice of this was beyond belief, 'when all England, Scotland, and Ireland had for years been witness to the immense sums laid out by the servants of the Company in stocks of all denominations, in the purchase of lands, in the buying and building of houses, in the securing quiet seats in Parliament or in the tumultuous riot of contested elections, in wandering throughout the whole range of those variegated modes of inventive prodigality which sometimes have excited our wonder, sometimes roused our indignation, that, after all, India was four millions still in debt to *them*?' Burke then proceeded to review the debts, of which only the first, the Consolidation of 1767, shall be of interest to us now. This sum, Burke stated on the basis of the Company's letter dated 23 March 1770, was owed to John Pybus, John Call, and James Bourchier. In repayment of the loan, they were assigned the revenues from 15 districts, which in peacetime yielded annually 800,000 pagodas, or £320,000. Additionally, they were granted the annual tribute of Tanjore, of 400,000 rupees, or £40,000.

By the time Josias Du Pre left India, the Nawab was not only very deeply indebted to various individuals but also to the Company. New means of income were not forthcoming. Annual revenues from large territories had already been signed away in repayment. It remained for the Nawab to invade Tanjore and annex it in order to borrow more and cede more. As Burke pointed out, this was a vicious cycle, 'between him and them, combining and confederating'. 'Refusing one shilling from his hoards for the satisfaction of any demand', said Burke, 'the Nabob of Arcot is always ready, nay, he earnestly, and with eagerness and passion, contends for delivering up to these pretended creditors his territory and his subjects'. He was not really at fault for this attitude. The Nawab had been so advised by those who should have known better. John Macpherson had a role in this, as did everyone else. 'The great fortunes made in India, in the beginnings of conquest, naturally excited an emulation in all the parts and through the whole succession of the Company's service', Burke said, referring certainly to Clive. Over time, two contradictory problems arose. The absence of war, which was discouraged by the Company in the fear that 'the fortune of war might take away what the fortune of war had given', left very limited scope for making quick money, something to which Europeans had become used during the Carnatic Wars. So the Company's servants were prohibited from receiving presents in order to prevent them from being bribed to engage in warfare. This was a useless measure, for 'The Company's servants were not only stimulated, but better instructed by the prohibition', Burke said, since 'Instead of receiving presents, they made loans'.

One could make considerable money by lending money to Indian potentates, who were always in need of ready money given their lavish lifestyles, large armies, and numerous dependents. Since their income came from annual land revenue, this was generated slowly, and fell far short of actual need. Almost every European, who came to India to shake the pagoda tree all through the eighteenth century, made his fortune from usury and that too without actually lending a rupee of his own. Edmund Burke revealed the manner of doing this in his speech of 28 February 1785 on the Nawab's debts to Europeans. Burke refers to an unnamed correspondent, from Madras, of Lieutenant-General Sir John Clavering, who wrote, describing in detail how this was done. The Nawab was always indebted to the Company. The governor, who was the Cashkeeper for the presidency, would press the Nawab for repayment of a particular sum. The Nawab would go to a banker, or any person with whom the governor had arranged matters, and ask for a loan, which would be given as promissory notes against an interest of 2 to 3% per annum. The governor would keep these notes in his cashbook, and ensure that it never became necessary to call in the money. In the meantime, the revenues ceded by the Nawab for the repayment of the principal demanded by the governor would mature, and the cash would be made up. Sir John Clavering's correspondent did not mention that the governor then probably destroyed the promissory notes but he did write that the amount derived from the interest charged by the banker was divided between all involved in this transaction. 'Here, Mr Speaker', proclaimed Burke, 'you have the whole art and mystery, the true free-mason secret, of the profession of *soucaring* ... by which a few inexperienced young Englishmen ... without property upon which anyone would lend themselves a single shilling, are enabled at once to take provinces in mortgage, to make princes their debtors, and become creditors for millions'.

Alexander Wynch was a nephew of the Rev Robert Wynch, who had been appointed the Company's chaplain in 1730 at the then high salary of £50. Robert Wynch was a son of George Wynch, then serving in Bengal. He reached Madras in July 1731 and was the sole chaplain there for a year. In August 1732, on the arrival of the Rev Eden Howard at Madras, Robert was sent to Fort St David. In 1735, Robert was permitted at his own request to return to England. He soon applied to be reinstated, and was allowed to do so as Senior Chaplain. Howard and Wynch served together in Madras between July 1736 and September 1742, when Howard went home. In the meantime, Robert successfully applied for transfer to Bengal. He went to Calcutta in August 1743, and died there in 1748. Robert's brother, William, who lived in England, was Alexander's father. Alexander came out to India at the age of 13, and became an unpaid assistant in the Secretary's Office in Madras. In 1738, he was made 'Monthly Writer' and obtained a regular post as Writer in 1740. He was sent to Fort St David in 1743, and made sixth in council and Sea and Land Customer in 1744. He remained there until appointed a commissioner along with Stringer Lawrence and William Holt, to receive Madras from the French in 1749. In 1754, he became ninth in council and Storekeeper at Fort St George. Appointed officiating Deputy Governor of Fort St David during Clive's absence since 1756, he surrendered to De Lally in 1758. As a prisoner of war, he chose to resign and return to England. In 1768, he resumed the Company's service and became the chief at Masulipatam in 1770. From this post, he was promoted to the governorship of Madras on the resignation of Josias Du Pre, on 1 February 1773. In spite of having joined the Company's service early, and having considerable seniority and experience, Alexander Wynch does not seem to have made as much progress as could have been expected. He spent a decade in obscurity in England, trying to erase the blemish of capitulation. Even though he achieved the governorship, he was soon unseated because he allowed himself to be convinced by the Nawab to overrun Tanjore and cede it to him.

Nawab Muhammad Ali Khan and Raja Pratap Singh of Tanjore had signed a treaty in 1762. This agreement recognised the willingness of the Nawab and the Raja to establish peace in the Carnatic following the defeat of the French. It also took cognizance of the fact that the Raja had been unable to make his *peshkash* to the Mughal emperor, his ultimate suzerain, due to the wars. This *peshkash*, or tribute, was made through the emperor's representative, in this case, the Nawab of the Carnatic. The treaty also noted that the wars had financially burdened the Raja, and his expenses needed just settlement. The Raja agreed to pay 2,200,000 rupees, or the equivalent amount in Star pagodas, coined at the Company's mint at Fort St George, as *peshkash*, at the rate of 350 rupees for 100 pagodas. In accordance with the payment schedule, the Raja paid 300,000 rupees on the day of the signing of the agreement, with two instalments of 500,000 rupees due in April and November 1763, one of 500,000 rupees due in April 1764, and the last instalment of 400,000 rupees in August 1764. The final amount would clear all dues up to 1762 from the Raja. The Raja also undertook to pay 200,000 rupees annually every July as tribute. Tradition demanded that the annual tribute be accompanied by suitable presents for the Nawab and his courtiers. Raja Pratap Singh promised to pay an additional 200,000 rupees in lieu of these gifts.

The Nawab showed his goodwill by ordering the return to the Raja of a bond for 700,000 rupees, given to Nawab Anwaruddin Khan by Pratap Singh, treating this payment as cancelled. The Raja insisted that the greater part of the sum had been paid, despite the fact that the bond bore no marks of receipt or endorsement. The Nawab declined to press the point out of politeness. Muhammad Ali ceded to the Raja the districts of Koilady and Elengad. A thorny issue was the recalcitrance of the *quiladar* of Arni, Thirumala Rao, who had refused to help the Nawab. Arni had been taken by assault, and Thirumala Rao and his family imprisoned, and the *jagir* of Arni sequestered by the Nawab as an example to others. Since Arni was feudatory to Tanjore, the Nawab assured the Raja that with the signing of the treaty and payment of the first instalment of the tribute, he would set Thirumala Rao and his family free and return his *jagir* into his possession except the fort. The Nawab asked the Raja to give surety for Thirumala Rao's good behaviour in the future, which would be evidenced by the Rao's adherence to certain conditions. He would not be allowed to build any fortress or stronghold in his territory; he was also prohibited from constructing a wall, exceeding 8 feet in height and 2 feet in thickness, around his home; and he would have to pay a tribute of 10,000 rupees annually to the Nawab and his successors. The Raja agreed to do this, since he put his seal to the treaty.

The treaty, which was signed on 12 October 1762, was pompously attested by George Pigot, 'We, George Pigot, Governor of Fort St George, and all the forts, factories, and places subordinate thereto, President of the Council for all the affairs of the English East India Company on the coast of Coromandel, and also the said Council whose names are hereunto signed, having greatly at heart the peace and tranquillity of the country where the Company hold possession, and to which they trade, see with great satisfaction the conclusion of the Treaty of friendship ... and accordingly we do hereby promise, as far as in us lies, that in case either party shall fail in the performance of the Article he hath thereby undertaken to perform, or any other part thereof, we will to the utmost of our power assist the other party to compel him who shall fail to fulfil his agreement and to render due satisfaction for his failure therein'.

The Company had sided with the Nawab after 1767, when the danger posed by Haider Ali had passed, and Thuljaji, the new Raja of Tanjore, had stopped paying tribute, in spite of repeated notices. Thuljaji, born the eldest son of Pratap Singh in 1738, had acceded to the throne on his father's death in 1763.

In his letter to the Court of Directors, published later by Thomas Cadell in 1777 along with several 'Original Papers', Muhammad Ali referred them to their own letter dated 17 March 1769 to Fort St George. In this letter, the Company had sided with the Nawab, taking umbrage that 'the Raja of Tanjore should hold possession of the most fruitful part of the country, which can alone supply our armies with subsistence, and not contribute to the defence of the Carnatic'. That three previous princes of the Carnatic had received sums of up to 10,000,000 rupees from the Raja of Tanjore, seemed 'notorious' to the Company. 'How just then does it appear', they asked from London, 'that he should be made to pay some part of the expense of these measures, to which he owes his security, and the peace of this country?' The conclusion was foregone. The Company instructed Madras 'to give the Nabob such support in his pretensions on the Raja of Tanjore as may be effectual; and if the Raja refuses to contribute a just proportion to the expense of the war, you are then to pursue such measures as the Nabob may think consistent with the justice and dignity of his government'. The Company did not wonder why Thuljaji was to be forced to impoverish his kingdom to pay for Pratap Singh's treaties, or the injustice of arm-twisting the owner of the most fertile land in the region into paying for protection he did not need or seek. There had been correspondence between Thuljaji and Haider Ali, which made it clear that the Raja had gifted to Haider Ali 400,000 rupees and 4 elephants. Haider Ali acknowledged this gift, and replied that his one aim was the destruction of their 'mutual enemy', the English. This letter is appended in translation to Cadell's publication of Muhammad Ali's letter of 1777. On 25 September 1771, Josias Du Pre replied to the Nawab's anxious and urgent missive of 18 September seeking English assistance in reducing Tanjore. The Nawab complained that Thuljaji was instigating the

Marathas to invade the Carnatic, while corresponding with the Nizam and the French with the same end in mind. The Nawab had proposed to pay to the Company 1,000,000 pagodas in return for their help.

Du Pre began by being prim: 'We have no orders from the Court of Directors to receive any money from you, but what they have disbursed, and may disburse in your service'. Nonetheless, his orders from the Court of Directors told him to support the Nawab in his government at all times, to maintain peace in his and the Company's possessions, and in particular, to help him against the Raja of Tanjore in any manner that the Nawab thought proper. To this end, Du Pre wrote, 'I have undertaken this business in the best manner I can, and sent many guns, with a large quantity of warlike stores to Trichinopoly, and a well appointed army, who are now assembled under the command of General Smith; and I leave to yourself the settling of affairs with the said Raja, in whatever manner you think proper; and have given full power to General Smith, concerning the same, and to take the fort and country of Tanjore'. At the end of the letter, Du Pre wrote, 'If, of your generosity and friendship for the Company, you may think proper to make any present to them, and pay it into my hand, I will receive it with great pleasure, and inform the Company thereof'.

The unfinished invasion of Tanjore in 1771, resulted in a new treaty, signed on 20 October 1771. Here the Raja, Thuljaji, agreed to a tribute of 800,000 rupees, presumably under the same conditions as before, in rupees coined at the Company's mint, or paid in pagodas at an agreed rate of exchange. For the army's expense, including the English force, he would pay 3,250,000 rupees. The Raja would restore all land and goods he had seized from neighbouring landowners. The worst was the fifth article, which made the Raja say, 'Should the merchants and people belonging to the Company in the Tanjore country have been plundered of paddy, I am to answer it'. We shall soon see how the crop and the claims laid to it by both the Nawab and Paul Benfield created such bad blood that Pigot was deposed and confined, only to die. The Raja further assented that 'If the Company's trade in the whole Tanjore country shall be continued, I am to use their weavers well'. Koilady and Elengad were accepted as part of Tanjore but the Raja had to cede Arni to the Nawab, in addition to some other villages. To pay for the army, the Raja, Thuljaji, ceded the district of Mayavaram and parts of Kumbakonam in a separate agreement dated 26 October 1771, which would pay 1,625,000 rupees annually to the Nawab for two years. At the end of this period, these districts and their revenues would revert to the Raja of Tanjore. In the third treaty, to which Thuljaji also affixed his seal the same day, he agreed to send his troops, horse, sepoys, and peons, to the service to the Nawab whenever called to do so without deducting the amounts for their upkeep and *batta* from the annual tribute. This treaty, which superseded that of 1762, was most humiliating. Moreover, the English broke their promise to move against the side in violation and support the injured party.

The pamphlet, *An Enquiry into the Policy of Making Conquests for the Mahometans in India By the British Arms; In Answer to a Pamphlet Entitled 'Considerations on the Conquest of Tanjore'* published in London in 1779, possibly authored by William Burke (1729–1798), who had obtained a similar appointment from the Raja of Tanjore, noted that since 1769 the Nawab had employed a number of persons in Europe to argue his cause in Europe 'in a great variety of ways'. 'These gentlemen', the author wrote, 'have endeavoured to recommend themselves to their employer by their extraordinary zeal and activity in his service'. They had 'filled the world with many new topics of argument, and new narratives of fact'. 'They have even been', he wrote, 'at the pains of correcting and amending history', all this to help Muhammad Ali Khan achieve his ambitions by using English troops. William Burke's own career will not bear scrutiny, for he too went to India twice with the sole objective of making money from his appointments. Nonetheless, these advocates of the two princes carried the battle to England.

The Nawab was unhappy with the settlement of 1771, for it did not give him that which he was most in need of then, specie. Josias Du Pre would, at least, not allow Muhammad Ali to put further pressure on Thuljaji in the matter. Hence, Alexander Wynch's governorship brought about a timely change for the Nawab. On 18 June 1773, Muhammad Ali Khan wrote to Alexander Wynch at Madras that while the previous invasion of Tanjore had been intended to chastise the Raja for his 'bad conduct', the latter had persisted in his attempts to disturb the peace in the Carnatic. As evidence, the Nawab presented Wynch with a copy of a letter purportedly from Poona, which said that Thuljaji had invited the Marathas to raid the Carnatic. More ominously, the Nawab had intelligence that the Raja had granted some *taluks* or subdivisions to the Dutch and the Danish under the pretext of repaying loans. This, the Nawab pointed out to Wynch, 'is not proper either for your advantage, or mine'. Madras had previously suggested that the Nawab maintain 3 battalions of the Company's sepoys, which he had been unable to do because he had not the money. In order to maintain these troops the Nawab would not only have to meet all charges for their provisions and other expenses but also *batta* or field pay. Now the Nawab was agreeable to this, if Tanjore was taken and put into his possession with English military help. He was also willing to pay for 7 more battalions, provided they were called 'the Nabob's

Battalions'. The English were cautioned that if Tanjore did not fall, the Nawab would not be able 'to keep those three battalions'. Muhammad Ali Khan had not paid the Company the 1,000,000 pagodas he had promised Du Pre in 1771. This he now offered to meet, despite the fact that taking Tanjore would cause him great expenditure: 'yet I will cheerfully pay it to give all security to the Company's possessions, and peace and tranquillity to my country'. The Nawab, if nothing else, was honest in admitting that he could not pay the amount promised in 1771. The Company had not demanded it of him either, yet he knew that 'such a sum of money will be very acceptable to them in these days'. In case Wynch should prove reluctant to move once again to take Tanjore, the Nawab added that the delay would allow the Marathas, or Haider Ali, or the French, to take it. He knew well how badly English trade had been hurt not only during the Carnatic Wars but also in Bengal. This war with Tanjore would cost the Company little, earn them much, and keep the Carnatic free for commerce.

Alexander Wynch was effusive in his reply to the Nawab's letter. Wynch wrote on 7 July 1773. He considered 'the present object' of the Nawab, 'the total reduction of Tanjore on the present footing of affairs ... essentially necessary for the safety and tranquillity of the Carnatic'. The governor and his council had also received intelligence of Thuljaji's correspondence with the Marathas and Haider Ali. Thomas Mostyn, the English Resident at the Peshwa's durbar in Poona had reported on 14 May 1773 the arrival there of Tanjore's *vakil* who had sought 10,000 cavalrymen for his master's service, to be used against Muhammad Ali Khan. Therefore, Major-General Joseph Smith was again ordered to Trichinopoly, where a considerable army would assemble. This army would march to Tanjore, take the fort, and put it into the possession of the Nawab's son, or any person nominated in his place. All ammunition and stores recovered from the fort would become the Nawab's property only if Tanjore capitulated. If taken by assault, these would qualify as loot for the captors. The coolness of this discussion is rather unnerving. The devastation of a principality is being debated only in terms of the division of the spoils, and not the suffering of its people. In a similar vein, Wynch moved first to the topic of the 3 battalions, whose expense until 30 June 1773 would have to be paid into the Company's account as a present by the Nawab. The 10 battalions would thereafter be fully carried on the Nawab's account and the expenses discharged monthly. The payment of 1,000,000 pagodas was the last item to be considered. Wynch, like Du Pre, was coy about this, saying he would willingly receive whatever the Nawab gave him by way of presents to the Company. The governor and council knew what havoc would be wreaked on Tanjore, and the only thing to their credit is that Wynch told Muhammad Ali Khan clearly that no harm was to befall the Raja and his family, who were to be accorded treatment in keeping with their 'quality and character'. This eventually proved to be the thorn in what would otherwise have been a straightforward annexation. The Raja's survival allowed his restoration. His death would have simplified matters infinitely for all concerned. In the event, it was Pigot, whose death and alleged homicide took the question to England, the General Court, and Westminster.

Major-General Joseph Smith took the field in early August 1773. Tanjore offered token resistance, and surrendered on 17 September, the English taking advantage of a practicable breach in the wall. The Nawab's dues on this expedition amounted to £3,303,936. Of this stupendous amount, interest (at 30% simple interest payable to English individuals) alone accounted for £1,120,000. Against this, the annual revenue of Tanjore was pegged at 3,000,000 rupees for 1774, and 5,000,000 for 1775 and 1776. The Nawab had agreed to pay the interest on his borrowings over periods varying between 3 to 5 years, ending in 1776. The 5-year loans had been carried over from the 1771 war, while the 3-year loans applied to the 1773 annexation.

Wynch and his council did not inform the Directors of the invasion and capture of Tanjore until 23 September 1773. Other letters, including one by the Select Committee, dated 26 and 29 October, followed. The council's decision had been unanimous on the point of assisting the Nawab, given the information provided by him that the Raja had been plotting against the Company. The Raja's actions posed possible danger to peace in the Carnatic, and in this regard, the Company's orders of 1769 were clear. The Nawab was, in all such cases of evident belligerence by other princes in the region, to be assisted by the English in re-establishing peace. Besides, there was the precedent set by Du Pre, of two years earlier, that guided Wynch in responding to the Nawab's solicitation. In the great national furore over Lord Pigot's overthrow and death, Josias Du Pre too brought out a book in 1778 arguing his side of the first and incomplete invasion of Tanjore, titled *A Vindication of the Government of Fort St George, relative to the Expedition against Tanjore, in the year 1771.* There he mentioned that the Court of Directors had thanked him in August 1773 for his role in that incident. Wynch is not to blame, for even George III had written on the matter to the Nawab on 7 April 1772, and sent the letter through Sir Robert Harland, the King's 'Commander-in-Chief and Plenipotentiary', who had been dispatched with an additional naval force for the security and confidence of the Nawab and the Company. The royal letter said, 'It gave us satisfaction to hear that the Governor and Council at

Madras had sent the Company's troops with yours to reduce your tributary, the Rajah of Tanjore, to obedience, in which we hope, by the blessing of God, they will be successful'. Given such sanction, obedience to the wishes of the Nawab seemed to be in keeping with the express wishes of both Leadenhall Street and Westminster. In any case, the winds were favourable, and all the letters sent by Wynch and his council reached London on 26 March 1774. These were not treated as extraordinary happenings, and inexplicably, it was not until 12 April 1775, after more than a year had passed, that the Court of Directors suddenly awoke to the subject of Tanjore. This date, interestingly, coincided with that on which the Court of Proprietors met to elect the new Directors of the Company.

The letter of the Select Committee at Fort St George, dated 28 September 1772, was a straightforward complaint against the muddled policy of the Court of Directors, whose ineptitude in diplomacy was obvious. The Select Committee felt that following the Treaty of 1762, 'this Government, as guarantees, ought to have marched a force to maintain peace between the contending parties, to have required deputies from both, to state the demands of each respectively, and, upon a fair discussion, to have decided between them, and to have enforced the decision, whether in favour of the Nabob or in favour of the Rajah'. The Company's instructions to the Select Committee, vide their letter of 17 March 1769, were clear, for they represented the Directors' view that 'the Rajah stood in a degree of favour with this government, which you did not approve'. Into this confusion stepped the King's ambassador, Admiral Sir John Lindsay. Sir John, 'ranging himself on the side of the Nabob, received all his complaints against the Rajah as gospel, attacked us openly, but with flagrant injustice, and accused us of withholding that assistance from the Nabob which our trust required'. The conclusion to this was inevitable: 'The Rajah, so early as September 1770, represented to the President his apprehensions of the Nabob's designs and representations to the King's Minister, but finding no tendency to redress, and seeing the weakness of this Government, and its inability to protect him, too hastily and indiscreetly stood forth in open opposition; most probably expecting support either from the French or the Marathas'. The Select Committee, since it had to answer directly to the parties concerned, for the Company's incompetence, did not hold back words: 'A steady regard for the public welfare obliges us to say, we are amazed that we have got thus far so well; and if your Honours will consider every embarrassment in which we have been entangled by the Nabob, his chicanery in respect to money and provisions, his views to compel us into a Maratha alliance, his wishes to possess Tanjore, his fears of the Company if it were subdued, his hope of support against the Company from the Crown, and his jealousy of the future effects even of that support, we think your Honours will see cause to rejoice, that we are at no worse state at present'. The Company had two choices: 'either to take Tanjore openly and avowedly under your protection, and give him proofs of your impartial justice, which we think even now, notwithstanding what has passed, will bind him firmly to your interest, or to conquer and subdue him totally'. This had been Josias Du Pre's opinion, firmly and clearly stated. However, Du Pre left India in February 1773. Alexander Wynch was malleable and willing to follow the Nawab's argument.

Philip Dormer Stanhope, formerly of the 1st Dragoon Guards, had come out to India in hopes of a career that would make him wealthy quickly. His letters to England, which provide us with a perspective from the Nawab's court, were collected and published in 1784 as the *Genuine Memoirs of Asiaticus*. He travelled to Calcutta via Madras, and there fell ill with 'an affliction of the liver' and Warren Hastings' promise to appoint him to a commission in the service of the Nawab of Awadh was negated by the arrival of Sir John Clavering, Richard Barwell, and Philip Francis, as councillors. Stanhope then travelled to Madras with an introductory letter from Hastings to the governor, Alexander Wynch. He reached Madras on 30 May 1775. He was already acquainted with Wynch since he had spent some time at Madras on his way to Calcutta in the previous year. Wynch offered him an ensigncy in the Company's army, which Stanhope accepted. He had no option, though the ensigncy paid only 5 shillings a day, 'an income not only insufficient to procure the luxuries of life, but even greatly inadequate to the common necessities'. Major-General Joseph Smith advised Stanhope to apply for secondment to the Nawab's army, in which there were a number of European officers, whose salaries and emoluments were considerable. The only problem was Stanhope's possible qualm about serving a local prince. However, in this matter his views were clear: 'nor did I hesitate to prefer the service of an Indian monarch to the honour, however great it may be deemed, of carrying arms in the employment of a trading company'. Smith gave Stanhope the necessary introduction and soon the latter was an officer in the Nawab's cavalry. Until commanded to move to the place where his corps was stationed, on the bank of the Coleroon 200 miles south of Madras, Stanhope spent his time in agreeable idleness, and regular visits to the durbar, to which he had free access by courtesy of the Nawab.

The Nawab had two sons, Umdat-ul-Umra and Amir-ul-Umra. By April 1775, Wynch and his council had become suspicious of the ambitions of the younger son, Amir, who had been placed in command of the Nawab's army. At a consultation on 25 April 1775, Wynch informed the council of his reservations about Amir: 'That he is known to be … enterprising and artful, a master in Intrigue, and that in the execution of his designs he is indefatigable and would spare no expense to accomplish them'. More importantly, Amir was opposed to dependence on the English, and he wanted to be put in charge of Tanjore. Stanhope's report on Amir is similar, and he was probably Wynch's source at the durbar. Amir, Stanhope wrote, was the Nawab's favourite, and it was to him that the English chiefly paid court. 'He is enterprising, deceitful, and unprincipled, and would long ago have imbued his hands in the blood of his family', wrote Stanhope, 'had not his father, rendered wise by experience, removed his court from Arcot, and resided under the immediate protection of the governor and council at Madras'. The complexity of this matter becomes clear when one reads the long note of dissent that Joseph Smith wrote on 1 July 1775 to the council's decision that no European should attend durbar other than the governor. In keeping with his soldierly character, Smith noted that Amir-ul-Umra, as army commander, had an English staff, among whom was Alexander Wynch's son. Like Stanhope, these Europeans were gentlemen who had left England in search of fortune, and their employment was no military danger to Madras. They would not take up arms against their own people. The Nawab's army was notable for its cavalry, whose upkeep was very expensive. The Nawab's cavalry, officered by Englishmen, thus served a dual purpose: it kept ready an allied force for rapid deployment, and it saved the Company the cost of maintaining this force.

The council remained unconvinced, and on 4 July 1775, warned London that the Nawab's attitude towards the English was changing. He wished to be free of their influence. Over the last decade, the Nawab had used the Company's forces in accordance with the treaty that permitted him to do so in the interest of keeping peace in the Carnatic. He had thus occupied several minor kingdoms, the last being Tanjore. This had made him supremely powerful in the Carnatic and he had conveniently forgotten that this had been accomplished with abundant English help. The Court of Directors was asked to note particularly the rise of Amir-ul-Umra. In addition to his propensity for intrigue, Amir was resolute in his actions. He had improved the Nawab's army from a rabble into a substantial and disciplined force of 7 corps, constituted of infantry, cavalry, and artillery. He paid them regularly, and they returned his concern for their welfare with unwavering personal loyalty. Aware of his father's weaknesses, Amir had exploited his popularity with, and command of, the army, by asserting great influence over his father. The Nawab was then nearly 60 years old, and the council was concerned about a war of succession. As events turned out, Muhammad Ali Khan ruled for another 20 years. However, the Company's instructions to Madras, written in November 1775, were clear: 'a Just and Lineal succession' was to be secured for the Nawab's children, which meant that the English could march against Amir-ul-Umra if necessary. Stanhope, meanwhile, prepared to leave Madras for his station, in joyous anticipation of being 'mounted on an Arabian charger at the head of my whiskered troopers, whose courage I hope will fully correspond with their ferocious looks'.

A duel between two English officers in Stanhope's regiment had made him write to Amir-ul-Umra, who was at Tanjore, since he had been given its governance. Encouraged by Amir-ul-Umra's approbation of his actions in this unfortunate matter, Stanhope visited him in January 1776. Stanhope's description gives us a glimpse of the country as it then was. Amir-ul-Umra was then in Kumbakonam, and Stanhope noted that this town was of considerable extent, and situated in delightful country. The Rajas of Tanjore had used it as a place of retirement, for it had huge tanks of water, and broad avenues lined by trees whose flower resembled the tulip. The country around was well-populated and under cultivation, but people were migrating to other places, for governance was despotic. Stanhope was told that as many as 300 villages had been deserted following the conquest of Tanjore. The following month Stanhope received news of Lord Pigot's arrival. By May 1776, all European officers were recalled from secondment in the Nawab's army and ordered to report their regiments. Stanhope left India via Bombay in September 1777, and reached England in August 1778.

In 1744 17th George II cap 17 was passed, whereby the Court of Directors lent to the King for the use by government, £1,000,000, which allowed the Company to extend the right to exclusive trade from 25 March 1766 to 1780. Further, this law allowed the Company to borrow this amount from the market through their bonds. By 1744, the Company had lent the government the staggering sum of £4,200,000, during 78 and half years, from 1698 to 1780, the amounts maturing on 25 March 1783, on 3 years' notice from the Company, dating from 1780. Considering this burden, the instructions of the Court of Directors said that 'No schemes for military operations are to be adopted, unless they are evidently and most materially necessary for the Company's interest'. 'Conquests are not our aim', the Court declared, 'and if we can secure and preserve our present possessions in Bengal, we shall rest satisfied'. On 25 November 1766, a question was put to vote in the House of Commons, 'That a Committee be appointed to enquire into the state and condition of the East-India

Company'. The motion was carried, with 129 in favour, and 79 against. By April 1767, several unpleasant questions were being asked about the Company's role in India. The Company, by the terms of its charter, had no right to acquire territory in India by conquest. That a trading corporation should acquire such territories by conquest was inappropriate. Even if this was politically acceptable, the government, which had on several occasions expended money in helping the Company protect its conquests, would be right in demanding a portion of the revenues accruing from these territories. These issues were challenged by those that asserted the Company's right to hold territories in India based on its charters, which derived from public subscription, and had only been ratified by Parliament. The Company had also spent much money in acquiring territory, which made its claims on revenues primary. Matters soon reached the state whereby the King, in his opening speech of 26 November 1772, asked Parliament to look into the affairs of the Company for safeguarding the interests of all concerned. Lord North, the Prime Minister, created a Secret Committee of 13 members. The second report of this committee, presented to the House of Commons on 17 December 1772, clarified the Company's indebtedness to the amount of £1,063,067 for bills drawn on them for the year 1771. By 7 January 1773, the Court of Directors, following the resolution of the General Court, asked the Chairman and Deputy Chairman to seek from the government a loan of £1,500,000, to be repaid in 4 years. Lord North suggested that £1,400,000 would be enough to take care of the Company's debts, and proposed to the Commons to allow the Company to retain its territorial acquisitions and their revenues for 6 years. During this period, the Company would repay its loan. Since the loan would commence from February 1774, the period of 6 years would terminate in 1780, in consonance with the expiry of the Company's charter in March of the same year. Nonetheless, the controversy over territorial acquisitions remained, and the Loan Bill, in its final form, culminated in the Regulating Act of 1773, 13th George III cap 63. This Act provided for the appointment of Directors for 4 years, in place of annual elections; a Governor-General and four Councillors for the Supreme Government at Calcutta, to govern Bengal, Bihar, and Orissa; for the subordination of the two other Presidencies, Bombay and Madras, to the Supreme Government; the establishment of a Supreme Court of Judicature by royal letters-patent, at Calcutta.

On 12 April 1775, the Court of Directors wrote to Wynch, 'we confess ourselves at a loss for words to express our concern, that you have … assisted the Nabob in dethroning the King of Tanjore, and in taking possession of his dominions'. All the references to previous treaties and instructions to help the Nawab maintain peace in the Carnatic were proper, but the Directors 'could by no means allow that you were warranted in recurring to arms, so long as the King of Tanjore's *Vakil* declared himself ready and willing to settle affairs with the Nabob under the mediation and guarantee of the English'. Wynch was told that the Directors were also concerned that not only had he 'proceeded improperly' in dealing with the Nawab and the Raja, he had been 'disingenuous' in his advices to them on this important matter. Equally condemnable were the orders given to Joseph Smith to take Tanjore and the passing over of Tanjore to the possession of Amir-ul-Umra, the Nawab's son. The Directors felt that 'every principle of justice, policy, and humanity, forbad' Wynch and his council to 'sacrifice him [the Raja] to the Nabob's resentment'. They concluded, 'We cannot find that in 1773 you were in possession of any fact whatever, which could render it necessary to break the peace of 1771; we therefore declare the last expedition unjustifiable and your conduct therein wholly inexcusable'. Since these proceedings had made it obvious, the Directors thundered, 'our orders and instructions have been disregarded by you, and as examples made of former offenders have been insufficient to restrain you from treading in their steps, we have determined to remove Alexander Wynch, Esquire, from being President of our Council, and hereby direct, that he forthwith resign the government to the Honourable Lord Pigot, upon the arrival of his Lordship at your presidency'.

George, Lord Pigot, allegedly contrived a second term in India because he needed money. His substantial previous fortune had been depleted in buying his estate, Patshull, and in getting himself elected to the Commons. Later, George Stratton wrote in his letter of 21 September 1776 to the Chairman of the Honourable East India Company that the Nawab had promised Lord Pigot an annuity of 12,000 when the latter left India in 1763. This annuity was paid for some years and then stopped on the plea of the Nawab that the state of his finances no longer allowed it. When Muhammad Ali Khan heard that Pigot was named governor again, he promptly paid, so Stratton reported, bills of exchange for 125,000 pagodas to Edward Monckton and John Maxwell Stone.

Pigot reached Madras in the evening of 9 December 1775, aboard the East Indiaman *Grenville*. Two future councillors, Claud Russell and Alexander Dalrymple, had sailed with him. The following morning Lord Pigot's commission was read and he was installed as Governor and Commander-in-Chief of Fort St George. Alexander Wynch protested his dismissal in a letter addressed to Pigot and his council. He began by stating that Captain Preston, commanding the *Hillsborough*, which was sailing from Calcutta to England, though ordered by the Governor-General, Warren Hastings, to call at Madras and take Wynch on board, had nonetheless let out his great cabin. This was an insult, for the Directors had clearly mentioned in the last paragraph of their letter of dismissal that he be accorded the respect he deserved because of the position he had held in the Company's service. Wynch obtained passage on board the *Ankerwyke*, commanded by Captain Barwell. The *Ankerwyke* was a larger vessel, of over 650 tonnes, and Wynch might have preferred it to the *Hillsborough*. Alexander Dalrymple (1737-1808) had become a Writer in 1752 in the Madras presidency. He returned to England in 1765, and wrote prolifically on a large number of topics including the affairs of the Company. It was in pursuance of his proposal that the Company strove to set up a factory at Balambangan in northern Borneo, later abandoned as the cost of protecting it from pirates and sustaining trade greatly exceeded the investment. Dalrymple was proposed to the Fellowship of the Royal Society in 1770, and confirmed in 1771. Claud Russell (1733-1820) had become Writer the same year as Dalrymple, and would go on become chief at Vizagapatam. They were both devoted to Pigot.

Alexander Wynch told the governor and council that he had already received news of his dismissal via the frigate *Coventry*, which had reached Madras some time ago. He had felt the insult keenly and initially decided to resign immediately. However, his sense of duty made him change his mind, and he chose to stay on to keep the government and deliver it to his successor. He owed this, he said, to his 'character in the world' and his family and friends. In dismissing him, the Directors had made him the scapegoat for a decision taken collectively, for no governor could order the invasion of a principality without the consent of his council. Wynch then repeated once more all the causes, from 1769 down, of why Tanjore had been reduced. He had had several disagreeable arguments with his council, which he said the records would show, over his actions to restrain the Nawab from increasing his power following the conquest of Tanjore. On returning to London, Wynch settled briefly in Upper Harley Street. Thence he moved to Gifford Lodge in Twickenham, in 1776. He moved again to Westhorpe House in Little Marlow, Buckinghamshire, and died in May 1781, aged 60.

Alexander Wynch had done something else, which would soon yield equally disastrous results. When Major-General Joseph Smith retired in October 1775, Wynch promoted Colonel Sir Robert Fletcher to Brigadier-General, and appointed him Commander-in-chief of the Company's army on the Coromandel Coast. Fletcher thus became the military subordinate of Lieutenant-General Sir John Clavering, who was Commander-in-chief of the Company's forces in East India. In the presidency of Madras, Fletcher would be under the command of the governor and council of Fort St George. Sir Robert's elevation took effect from 16 October 1775.

Wynch, as governor, had indeed been singled out for exemplary punishment, while the rest of the council was merely warned off. In keeping with the usual practice, the Directors named Lord Pigot's council. Considering that most of these councillors would play very important roles during the next three years, we will now acquaint ourselves with some of them.

George Stratton was appointed second in council. He had joined the service in Madras on 17 June 1751 as Writer. George, born in 1734, was the eldest son of John Stratton, who had arrived in India on 15 October 1721, also as Writer. We next come across John in 1730, when he is listed as Registrar of the Madras Town Corporation on a monthly salary of 4 pagodas, in addition to an allowance for a servant. By 1741, John Stratton had been moved to Vizagapatam as second in council. By the end of 1742, the chief there, Charles Simpson, had died, and was succeeded by John Stratton. Subsequently some problems relating to Simpson's estate had risen, because of which his widow had written to Richard Benyon and his council at Madras on 15 November 1742, complaining of John Stratton's high-handedness in the business. Benyon and his council had upheld Mrs Simpson's protest, and ordered John Stratton and his council to strictly adhere to the Company's standing orders in the treatment of the inhabitants of their factory. John applied for permission in January 1743 to leave Vizagapatam for Madras, to resume his seat on the council there, which was granted. Accordingly, John and his family sailed aboard the ship *George Bright* from Vizagapatam in mid-March and reached Madras on 4 April 1743. On 7 April, John took his oaths and assumed the post of fourth in council at Fort St George. He enjoyed this position, having been appointed Paymaster, until the Company's letters came from London on 30 June. The Court of Directors had disapproved of his being placed on the council and accordingly Stratton was ordered to present his accounts to the council and hand over charge to Thomas Eyre. In spite of having 22 years' seniority in the service, with only Nicholas Morse, second in council, senior to him in Madras, John Stratton was unceremoniously demoted to the rank of Senior Merchant. On 29 July, John applied for, and obtained, permission to sail to Bengal on personal business, on condition that he would return to Madras by December. John Stratton had protested to Leadenhall Street his removal from the council. An answer from London, dated 8 June 1743, to his letter, was received in April 1744. It appeared that Stratton had been accused by reports of being overburdened with debts, and this had caused his removal. John petitioned the council on 19 July 1744, urging their assistance in 'Undeceiving' the Company that he was not encumbered, but had 'served them for twenty three Years with all Diligence, Faithfulness, and Fidelity'. This petition was entered into the *Diary and Consultation Book* for 1744. Nicholas Morse, who treated Stratton's case with sympathy, had in the meantime replaced Richard Benyon as governor and the council resolved to comply with Stratton's request without requiring him to provide proof of his financial state. John Stratton was reinstated with effect from 21 April 1746, and placed third in council as Accountant and Sea Customer, vide the Company's letter dated 20 March 1744. This was hardly a propitious time to sit on the council, for Madras fell to De la Bourdonnais the same year, and Stratton was one of the signatories to the capitulation. He, along with the other councillors, was taken as prisoner to Pondicherry, whence he sailed early in 1747, to England. He died there in 1750. George Stratton's career until 1775 was as uneventful as his father's had been hectic. George made steady progress, rising to the council in January 1764, following an unexpected vacancy on the death of Thomas Heath. In 1773, he was chief at Vizagapatam, 31 years after his father.

Major-General Joseph Smith or whoever was then the commander-in-chief of the Coromandel Coast, was made third in council by the Directors. Since Brigadier-General Sir Robert Fletcher had succeeded Smith on 16 October 1775, he occupied this position on the board. Fourth in council was George Dawson, who had volunteered for military service during the Carnatic Wars, and had been one of Clive's officers during the capture and defence of Arcot. His seniority in service dated from 7 July 1751, when he had been military storekeeper and assistant at Devikottah. Dawson had been on Wynch's council as Export Warehouse-keeper. He fell seriously ill within a year and sailed for England. Fifth in council was Henry Brooke, sixth John Whitehill, seventh Claud Russell, eighth Charles Smith, ninth Alexander Dalrymple, tenth Samuel Johnson, eleventh Charles Floyer, twelfth John Maxwell Stone, thirteenth Archdale Palmer, fourteenth James Hay, fifteenth Edward Stracey, sixteenth Edward Cotsford, seventeenth Richard Lathom, eighteenth Francis Jourdan, nineteenth George Mackay who was the last of the council, 'and not to rise to any higher station therein'.

George Mackay was born in 1718, and came out to India in 1738 as a free merchant. In 1754, he wed Sarah, John Stratton's daughter, and was therefore George's brother-in-law. Mackay became Mayor of Madras in 1756, and in 1760, Contractor for Supply and Transport to the army, a most profitable post, considering that the third Carnatic War was still being fought. He held prime land in Madras, having obtained from the council in 1758 the 99-year lease of a plot measuring 620 square yards on the Choultry Plain, about two and half miles from the fort. Mackay went to England in 1761, where he spent 5 years. He was well acquainted with Robert Orme, with whom he corresponded regularly, and it was perhaps on his advice that Mackay opted to join the Company's service in 1766. He was appointed Senior Merchant and Assaymaster at Madras, and admitted to the council on condition that he would always remain its junior-most member. This post, while it brought in a steady salary, did little to alleviate Mackay's financial condition. He continued to hold the position of Contractor to the army but, by 1767, this had stopped being lucrative since the Company wished for no more wars. By June 1769, Mackay had decided to send his wife and son, Alexander George, back to England. Keeping a town house in Madras in addition to a garden-house on the Choultry was too expensive, and Mackay wrote to Orme that he would save money by sending his family to England to live in the country where it was cheaper. Mackay told Orme of his intention to move to his garden-house after Mrs Mackay's departure, for further savings. Even as George Mackay was protesting his indigence, one must remember that, in 1769, he had been listed as one of the Nawab's top lenders, having loaned him 51,250 pagodas, undoubtedly at a high rate of interest.

Bearing in mind that the change in administration at Fort St George had been affected in order to clean the mess in the Carnatic, the orders of the Directors to Lord Pigot and his council were clear about the immediate necessity to restore his kingdom to the Raja of Tanjore. They were told in the first paragraph that they had been appointed 'In order to remedy so far as may be the inconveniences occasioned by the misconduct by our late President and Council'. The same paragraph reminded Pigot that the Regulating Act of 1773 would govern his actions. This reference to the 'limitations and restrictions' of this Act was a subtle reminder to Pigot that things had changed much since his last governorship when, in response to the French assaults, he had enjoyed nearly complete freedom of action. 14 years had since passed, and considering the financial crises of the Company and its subordination to the Parliament, the aim of giving Tanjore back to its king was to return to the main purpose of the Company's existence, trade. For 35 years, trade had suffered while the Company's servants had grown so rich as to be able to upset the conventional stratification of English society. They had returned with great fortunes, purchased estates and titles, and been elected to Parliament. Their ostentation was contradictory to the financial state of the Company. On a higher political level, their extensive possessions in India, the ability of the Directors to gift lucrative posts, had 'raised them from their rank as subjects, to that of rivals to the crown'. 'Instead of prudently brooding over their ill-got hoards, the Company's servants flew in the face of nobility itself; rivalled it in the possession of lands, outstripped it in dissipation, ostentation, and luxury', wrote James Macpherson (1736-1796), in the second edition (1782) of his book, *The History and Management of the East India Company from its Origin in 1600 to the Present Times, Volume I, Containing the Affairs of the Carnatic in which the Rights of the Nabob are Explained, and the Injustice of the Company proved.* James Macpherson, with his kinsman, John, was an agent for the Nawab, and his book is biased in favour of his employer.

In the fifth paragraph of the Directors' letter, Pigot and his council were first ordered to secure the person of the Raja of Tanjore, 'appoint him a proper guard for his protection', and 'for the protection of his family'. It was Pigot's duty to then inform the Raja that the Directors had 'determined to place him on the throne of his ancestors, upon certain terms and conditions to be agreed upon for the mutual benefit of himself and the East India Company, without infringing the rights of Muhammad Ali Khan, Nabob of the Carnatic'. The Raja would have to meet his liabilities to the Nawab as required by the treaty of 1762. Since the English had no security to ensure this despite being guarantors to the treaty, and since the Raja had subsequently made grants of districts to 'other Europeans', Pigot was to inform the Raja that following the restoration Tanjore fort would have an English garrison, 'to enable us effectually to watch the motions and counteract the views of any European or country power, who may attempt to make connexions or make establishments in Tanjore to our prejudice'. Foisting a garrison on the Raja meant that he would have to bear the cost of maintaining it. The Raja was assured that accounts of the garrison's charges would be given him as often as he required, and that neither extravagance, nor any improper charges allowed therein.

Of the greatest significance was the seventh paragraph, which told the governor and council to assure the Raja in the name of the Court of Directors that 'every military officer, or Company's servant, who shall in any respect interfere in the affairs of his government', would be severely punished. Pigot was to 'take especial care that this article be punctually fulfilled on the part of the Company'. The sixteenth paragraph attempted to restore the balance by ordering the public declaration that the Company's restoration of the Raja by way of dispensing justice did not mean that the annual payment of 400,000 rupees had been done away with. They were to make clear to the Raja that it was not the Company's intention to impoverish his kingdom. The English garrison was for his security, and as the money paid for their maintenance would be spent locally, Tanjore's economy would not suffer. The Raja would not be allowed to keep his own guards beyond the maximum number determined by the governor and council as necessary for the dignity of his court.

The Directors next moved to the financial implications of the restoration on the Nawab. This was another decision that would lead directly to the revolution in Pigot's council. Under the terms of the treaty of 1771, the Directors calculated that the Nawab had in total obtained from the Raja 4,527,000 rupees, as payment of tribute, interest, presents to his children, and indemnification of war expenses. Moreover, he had acquired possession of certain districts, which annually yielded 480,000 rupees. In the view of the Directors, these payments had more than reimbursed the Nawab. Since the Nawab had not previously possessed the territories ceded to him in 1771, and as he had enjoyed their revenues for several years, these were to be returned to the Raja. The Nawab was also not entitled to any defrayal of the costs of the war of 1773, which had been recompensed by plunder and his possession of the ceded districts of 1771 for several years longer. The Directors concluded that these proceedings had left the Nawab 'a very considerable gainer'. Using this as a pivot, they turned back upon the Nawab, and told the council that while it was impracticable to get the Nawab to give his accounts to inspection, he was not allowed to plead indigence 'as an excuse or reason for delaying payment of his debts to the Company, and those of his private European creditors, in case they should be speedily demanded'. The Directors seem to have wanted speedy repayment of the Company's debts by the Nawab. Reports of the Nawab's aspiration to independence from English influence were to be addressed by the governor and council through a thorough assessment of the Company's territorial possessions on the Coromandel Coast. Such knowledge of the Company's properties would augment proper defence and management given the possibility, only hinted at, of the Nawab's disaffection. The Northern Circars, which Dupleix had once obtained with such labour, and De Bussy held, for the French, afforded the Directors a region for assessment by a Committee of Circuit from Madras. As has already been related, the 4 districts that had been ceded to the French by the Nizam, Salabat Jung, had been taken by the English during the last Carnatic War, and Salabat Jung, perceiving the defeat of the French, had granted them to the English. The Committee of Circuit included George Dawson, Claud Russell, Alexander Dalrymple, and George Mackay.

The Nawab was sent an extract of the Company's orders about Tanjore on 30 December 1775, by resolution of the council at Madras. The Nawab replied on 23 January 1776, and in the last paragraph of his letter, Muhammad Ali Khan said, 'I owe large arrears to my army, and drafts have been issued on the Tanjore revenues for discharging large debts contracted on that service'. He hoped that Pigot would order his officers 'not to interfere in any manner, or interrupt my affairs in the Tanjore country, till an answer is received from England on the subject'. In the meantime, Pigot, anticipating trouble over the restoration, had directed Lieutenant-Colonel James, commanding at Trichinopoly, to place Lieutenant-Colonel Draper in charge of a force comprising of one European battalion, one sepoy battalion, and a company of field artillery, in readiness to march at once upon orders. Communicating with the Nawab was easy, since he was in residence at his palace in Chepauk. It was equally easy for the Nawab to stay informed of the council's decisions.

The Nawab ordered his troops out of Tanjore, except for a garrison of 1000, who would stay there until relieved by the Company's soldiers. He wrote to Pigot on 25 January to this effect, notifying that Tanjore would be handed over in 15 days' time. Accordingly, Lieutenant-Colonel Harper was commanded to garrison Tanjore on 9 February 1776, with two political objectives, the safety of the fort, and the protection of the Raja and his family. The commander-in-chief, Sir Robert Fletcher, would decide the military aspects of the move. Pigot gave into Harper's charge a brief missive from himself to the Raja, which he was to hand over after garrisoning the fort. The letter simply informed Thuljaji that 'The English East India Company disapproving of the late conduct of their servants with respect to Tanjore, have thought it proper to direct me to replace you upon the throne of your ancestors, upon certain terms and conditions to be agreed upon, for the mutual benefit of yourself and the English East India Company, without infringing the rights of Muhammad Ali Khan, the Nawab of the Carnatic'.

The Nawab sent to the Directors another appeal, dated 12 February, listing the same arguments, commencing from the first Carnatic War, down to 1773, for reconsidering their orders to Lord Pigot.

In the meantime, the case of John Macpherson came up. On 22 January 1776 Pigot placed for the council's consideration an anonymous document titled 'A Short Memorial of Services to his Highness the Nabob of the Carnatic', here abbreviated, which claimed to tell the story of Macpherson's mission to England as Muhammad Ali Khan's representative. Although the subtitle referred to a 'secret Commission', Macpherson's activities in England were not secretive, since he met the Prime Minister, the Duke of Grafton, discussed the case of the Nawab's debts with him, and then proceeded to obtain a Writer's position in Madras, where he arrived in 1770, and which would have helped him keep his royal client better informed. John Macpherson was summoned before the council, and questioned. He was within his rights to answer that the tract antedated his appointment in the Company's service. Pigot took this answer as a confession, and recommended his dismissal on the ground that Macpherson's activities were detrimental to the Company's interests, which the board carried on the majority, with Sir Robert Fletcher and Archdale Palmer dissenting. Macpherson continued to reside in Madras, in a private capacity, until 1777, when he returned home bearing further petitions from the Nawab to the government. The Nawab was indebted to him, through claims that Macpherson would continue to demand repayment of, for the rest of his life. He became MP for Cricklade between 1779 and 1782. He also successfully appealed to the Court of Directors against his dismissal. The change in government in the meantime brought Lord North into power as Prime Minister, and as Macpherson had supported him, North gifted him a seat on the Governor-General's council in Calcutta. This decision was much criticised, since Macpherson had long been suspected of being in the pay of Muhammad Ali Khan. However, Macpherson continued to be a councillor in Calcutta during Warren Hastings' tenure, and as senior member, succeeded him as Governor-General in 1784. Macpherson was created a baronet on 10 June 1786, and superseded by Lord Cornwallis in September of the same year. He returned home, and again bribed his way in 1788 into being elected for Cricklade. His opponent, Samuel Petrie, brought against him a complaint of bribing the electorate, which was proved. Unseated and in bad odour in England, he travelled to the Continent, where he became a popular figure in the highest circles, as friend and adviser to Leopold, Grand Duke of Tuscany and Frederick William II, King of Prussia. In 1796, he was elected MP for Horsham, and he sat in the Commons until 1802. A favourite of the Prince Regent, Sir John Macpherson died in January 1821. His appearance, being over 6 feet in height, along with his accomplishments, including an unusual capacity for languages, eastern and western, and his mediocre abilities as poet and singer, obtained him many admirers. These admirers unfortunately also praised his capacity for governance, paying no heed to accusations of his being a paid agent of the Nawab.

On 14 February 1776, the council wrote to the Directors that they had achieved the primary objective of securing Tanjore for Thuljaji. Nonetheless, there remained the issue of the indebtedness of the Nawab to his many creditors. Nearly the entire revenue of Arcot for the following 12 months was earmarked for them. Moreover, he owed his huge standing army 500,000 pagodas, and he was forced to parcel out the Tanjore revenue as payment before they agreed to vacate the fort. Pigot and his council proposed to help the Nawab out of his embarrassments by suggesting to him that he disband his army, while Thuljaji would be asked to honour the Nawab's debt to his army through payments at such times that would be convenient to his province's revenue. This was a devious plan, which would ensure that there remained no standing army in the Carnatic other than the Company's, while the Nawab grew rich, and the Raja of Tanjore enjoyed unencumbered revenue.

Debt continued to hound the Nawab, for the country had been at war for nearly four decades. On 26 February, the Nawab replied to Pigot's queries on the accounts of Tanjore. The letter said that the Nawab had not been so burdened by debts before 1773. The invasion of Tanjore, forced by Thuljaji's obvious refusal to pay heavy indemnities, arguing that these drew upon a treaty he did not sign, had caused the Nawab to sink into greater expenses, which he made up by allotting revenues from Tanjore. He had also paid money to the Dutch to release the districts ceded them by Thuljaji. 'If I give you only an account of the orders on that country, and the debts that lie on me and my country for the two expeditions against Tanjore', wrote the Nawab to Pigot, 'the money paid to the Dutch will be lost'. Should Tanjore's revenue accrue to Thuljaji and not to those to whom it was parcelled out 'the clamour of my creditors and my troops will be very loud', he said. He was therefore unwilling to allow this, until a reply to his petition to England had been received. In the meantime, he was agreeable to the Company's garrison at Tanjore, and to increasing Thuljaji's allowance.

Pigot's brief reply to this on 6 March 1776 carries the sense of exasperation he must have increasingly felt. He pointed out to Muhammad Ali Khan that the English garrison at Tanjore notwithstanding, Pigot was yet to follow the Company's order to restore to Thuljaji his kingdom because of his 'solicitude to do everything in concert with your Highness'. The next paragraph of Pigot's reply cuts ruthlessly into the heart of the matter: 'Humanity to wretched inhabitants, distressed beyond measure by the miserable state in which the country now remains, without any established government either of your Highness or the Rajah; justice to the Rajah, who is scarcely better than a prisoner still, and attention to the public honour, make it absolutely necessary to carry into immediate effect the orders of the Company'. Pigot demanded to be given an account of Tanjore, and of all amounts collected in the Nawab's name from the date on which the order of restoration had been formally served him, viz, 30 December 1775.

Writing from Chepauk on 19 March, the Nawab again prevaricated, saying this time that he had fallen under a penalty of 1,000,000 pagodas from the Mysore war. The distress of the inhabitants of Tanjore in particular, and the Carnatic in general, that Pigot had referred to in his letter, the Nawab attributed to the ill governance of Thuljaji. He was responsible for the depredations 'in which no tyrant ever exceeded him'. This led to the dispersal of the inhabitants of Tanjore, their flight encouraged by floods in the Cauvery. Amir-ul-Umra, the Nawab's younger son, who had been put in charge of Tanjore, set about correcting matters by advancing money to farmers. 'Now that the grain is ripe and ready, the time of their profit is come, as they are now to give me my share and take their own to themselves' but the Nawab knew why Pigot had written of their distress. The people were not distressed by the Nawab but by the knowledge that Thuljaji was about to return to oppress them as previously. As for justice to Thuljaji, the Nawab informed the governor that when under the Nawab's servants, he had lived more at ease than ever before. The Nawab showed his firmness in the matter of the accounts by stating that he had made clear his view that Tanjore was a part of the Carnatic, and therefore subject to his rights of collecting revenue. Clearly, matters were fast coming to a head.

Pigot placed this letter for consideration before the council on 22 March 1776. His answer was again to the point. The governor reminded the Nawab that the Company had supported him when he was destitute of money and power and the Nawab needed to reciprocate this by recognising that the Company had publicly pledged the restoration of Thuljaji. Having exhausted all means of convincing the Nawab to surrender his claims on Tanjore, Pigot declared that he had decided to move on his own to realise the orders of the Directors. 'What words shall I use to induce your Highness to make this your own act', asked Pigot, 'if all the arguments I have been able to suggest have not had their proper force?' If the Nawab was insensible of doing that which was right and proper, of sustaining his dignity through his actions, it remained for Pigot carry out the task he had been appointed to.

Three months had been used up in fruitless negotiation. The lines were now drawn. Muhammad Ali Khan claimed the revenue of Tanjore, and would not yield. Lord Pigot's orders from the Directors were clear as well. Thuljaji was to be restored to his throne and his kingdom given to his care. One of the most crucial consultations of the council of Fort St George took place on 25 March 1776.

Pigot placed before the council that given the sense of the Nawab's letter, he would not allow Tanjore's restoration. The crops in Tanjore were ready for harvesting, and no further delay was possible. The Nawab's attitude and his admission of indebtedness to his army, made it necessary for an English force, larger than the garrison at Tanjore, to be in the field. The restoration of Tanjore would deprive the Nawab's considerable and unruly army of income, and the safety of the country of Tanjore now devolved on the Company, as did the security of its ruler and his family. For this reason, another battalion of sepoys was ordered to march southwards, to allow Thuljaji to collect his revenue. Then, as never before, it became obvious at least to the governor, as it had to the Directors, that keeping the peace in the Carnatic required the upkeep of a well-disciplined and regularly paid force.

Pigot resolved to travel to Tanjore on 30 March to restore Thuljaji to his kingdom. He put the motion to the board whether it was proper and necessary for him to do so for the reason stated. It was agreed to unanimously. The next question was whether he could take with him as assistants whomsoever he chose from the Company's civil and military services. This was carried in the affirmative, with George Mackay and Francis Jourdan voting against the resolution. Sir Robert Fletcher demurred only in that these assistants should not be members of the board. Lord Pigot's commission as governor and commander-in-chief of the garrison of Fort St George was read, followed by the question to the board that by virtue of the commission, Lord Pigot held the same authority when present in any fort, factory, or settlement, in the Presidency, as he did at Fort St George. Again, George Mackay and Francis Jourdan dissented; Sir Robert also opposed the motion, giving the reason that such assumption of military powers by the governor was contrary to the constitution of the service, and subversive to the powers of the commander-in-chief of the army of the Presidency, namely, himself. In this, he was correct. The governor, Sir Robert said, had authority only over his own guard other than the garrison of Fort St George. It was resolved to allow such guard as the governor considered necessary, to attend him on his mission to Tanjore. Sir Robert then put the issue to the board that at least two members of the board in a deputation accompany the governor. Considering that Sir Robert had a short while ago did not want the governor to take with him as assistants any member of the board, this came as a surprise. More astonishing was that the majority except George Mackay, Francis Jourdan, and Archdale Palmer rejected Sir Robert's motion. A letter, objected to by Sir Robert, was sent to Colonel Harper, ordering him to place himself under Lord Pigot's command.

George Mackay gave his reasons for dissenting at the next consultation on 29 March 1776. He had agreed with the first motion that the governor should go to Tanjore to see to the completion of the Company's orders, in the hope that the next motion would be about the appointment of a deputation, since in his opinion the serious business of taking a country that yielded £1,000,000 a year and giving it to the Raja required a collective decision, despite the fact that the Directors had ordered the restoration of Thuljaji. Mackay had also thought it necessary to include the commander-in-chief, Sir Robert, in the deputation, since the restoration required considerable military operations. 'Had the Court of Directors judged it necessary to leave the management of this business solely to the President, their orders I imagine would have expressed it', explained Mackay ingenuously. This was an important issue.

Pigot's commission appointed him 'President and Governor of and for all our affairs' in forts, factories, and settlements, in all territories on the Coromandel Coast, Orissa, the Maratha country, and Gingee. Here he was allowed all jurisdictions, powers, and authorities, as granted by the Court of Directors, so long as they wished it. To enable Pigot to order and manage all their affairs, the Directors appointed a council. Pigot was correct in sounding out his councillors for their views, and Mackay was correct in surmising that Pigot could not assume sole control. He also felt that allowing the governor to deal alone with the Nawab meant granting the former powers greater than those intended by the Company. 'Could the President by going alone render any essential service to the Company which he could not do at the head of a deputation, I should not have objected to such extraordinary powers being given him for a time', Mackay explained. His objection to the second question, of Pigot's taking along as assistant whosoever he chose, was rooted in this same reason. Members of council should not go where they do not share in the management, and here they would be assistants, and not fellow councillors, while the commander-in-chief, Sir Robert, could not go along because he was not in command, the governor having abrogated unto himself the powers of the commander-in-chief of the army. Clearly, these objections were worked out later, and do not correspond to the objections as they were put up in the first consultation. The question of the governor's taking military precedence came after the issue of choosing assistants had been discussed.

Similarly, Mackay's objection to the third issue, viz., Pigot's assumption of supreme military command, was based on his perception that the post of commander-in-chief of the garrison of Fort St George was a complimentary one given to the governor, since the Company had already a commander-in-chief of the army on the Coromandel Coast. The Company of course was itself unclear about the delineations of command, for, as Mackay pointed out, if the governor's being commander-in-chief was interpreted as applying to 'any fort, factory, and settlement under this Presidency', this would be a precedent since no matter where he went thereafter, for the majority of the board 'the same reasons will hold good for putting every part of the army under his command'. This was contrary to the very reason for the presence of Brigadier-General Sir Robert Fletcher on the council.

Francis Jourdan's reasons for agreeing to the first question are the same as Mackay's, also true of his reason for dissenting on the second. The only difference was that Jourdan felt the governor should have applied for the particular persons he wanted along, in which case there could have been no objection. To the third Jourdan felt that the governor's military authority could supersede those of the chiefs of factories but in Tanjore there was no possibility of the exercise of this power, and to this garbled explanation Jourdan added that he had based his objection also on the governor having commander-in-chief's rights only over the garrison of Fort St George. Jourdan dissented with the board when it dismissed Sir Robert's suggestion of a deputation because he felt the measure unconstitutional. Those assenting to the issue would share the responsibility of the decision in which they would have no active role to play. Jourdan therefore added that he had not consented to the resolution, nor would he be consider himself party to its consequences.

Archdale Palmer too objected to Pigot's going all by himself to restore Tanjore to the Raja on the ground that the seriousness of the matter necessitated his taking along some members of council to advise him.

Sir Robert Fletcher wanted a deputation, with particular and well-defined instructions to accompany Pigot because he felt that it was unconstitutional to invest it with unlimited powers, other than in emergencies, which this was not. In answer to the second resolution, Sir Robert felt that the councillors were being demeaned in being chosen to accompany the governor in subordinate positions whereas they ought to be treated as equals in the business of Tanjore, as evidenced by the Company's orders. Sir Robert's third objection, to the governor's assuming full military powers, was a professional protest. His authority as commander-in-chief of the Company's army on the Coromandel was undermined by this supersession and no professional soldier would have assented to it.

Another letter from the Nawab was received on 25 March 1776. In hindsight, some of the statements in this letter seem premeditated. The

Nawab requested Pigot, which in effect was a warning, 'that you will not interfere or act in any manner which may be detrimental to my affairs in the Tanjore country, till an answer is received from Europe'. A second, more ominous warning followed: 'The revenues of that country have been made over to those persons who lent me money on account of the expedition against that place'. It was no longer only the Nawab's army that was clamouring for its arrears in pay, which would come from the revenues of Tanjore. Those who had lent the Nawab money were Englishmen, and they would demand their pounds of flesh. This must have been clear to Pigot, who had also lent money on interest during his previous tenure, because of which he was able to return with an enormous fortune to England. Pigot replied in the same vein, understanding perfectly the Nawab's meaning, on 27 March. The governor stated that he would execute his orders as he had been directed to do. Another ominous letter from Nawab came the following day, wherein he said 'I can never give up what is my right'. 'The difference between your request and mine is this', wrote the Nawab, 'you insist on executing the Company's orders forcibly, and against my consent; whereas I am willing to wait till an answer is received from them before I give it up'.

On the evening of 30 March 1776 Lord Pigot, accompanied by Alexander Dalrymple, Francis Jourdan, and Captain Wood, with William Chambers as translator, left Madras for Tanjore. On Thursday, 11 April 1776, Pigot formally restored to Thuljaji his throne and kingdom. Pigot's proclamation was issued that day, stating that the Company's troops, at the instigation of the Nawab, had removed the Raja, which being considered an injustice, the Raja had been restored also at the orders of the Company. The Raja appeared on parade at 2.45 pm, and was given a 21-gun salute. Then he proceeded to march through the main streets of Tanjore, accompanied by sections of the Company's best troops including European and sepoy grenadier companies, cavalry, and 2 field-guns. A second salute was fired at the end of the procession, and at 8 pm, the proclamation of restoration was read out in durbar in Marathi. Paul Benfield, along with Dalrymple, Jourdan, Chambers, and Colonel Harper, was present at this durbar. It was one of the hottest days of the year, yet Lord Pigot reportedly accompanied the Raja on the procession riding in an uncovered palanquin, without a hat to keep off the sun.

Alexander Wynch had introduced Coomera, Benfield's dubash, to Pigot. He attended Pigot at Tanjore, and went to meet the Raja after Pigot had retired around 8 pm on the evening of the day he reached Tanjore. Coomera testified on 30 August, after Pigot's government had been overthrown, that the following morning he had been summoned to Pigot's presence, informed that he had been allowed to Tanjore to conduct specific business with the governor's concurrence. He had done wrong to meet the Raja without permission, and for this transgression, Coomera was taken to parade, and ordered to be flogged.

Lord Pigot wrote to the Nawab on 20 April that he was distressed to find, as he passed through the country of Tanjore to the fort that every officer who had charge of accounts in each village, had been sent away at the Nawab's express orders. 'Every means had been taken', Pigot wrote, 'to throw difficulties in my way in the execution of the Company's orders, and to distress the country and its inhabitants'. Therefore, he ordered Captain Tonyn to go and seize Tanjore's *Dubbeer,* Naroo Pundit, from Ariyalur, in the Nawab's territory, where he had been spirited away on the Nawab's orders. The Nawab, thus warned, was told to order the return of all the accounts officers, with their records. Responding to the Nawab's cavilling about his army's arrears of pay, Pigot commented, 'I tell you again and again, that troops ill-paid will always be the masters of the man who employs them'. He concluded with advice for the Nawab, to disband his army: 'Those you have, if they do not disband themselves … must be disbanded by your Highness, or you will be more and more distressed'. The Nawab's huge financial mess was worsening, as subsequent events soon showed.

On 24 April 1776, George Stratton presiding, in Lord Pigot's absence, placed a packet of letters from the latter, dated 13 April and received 4 days later in Madras, for the council. It included a petition from the Raja of Tanjore, who thanked the Company profusely for his restoration, and asked for more of the Company's troops to be stationed at Tanjore, for whose military expenses he would pay 400,000 pagodas per annum. More importantly, he begged the Company to buy the crop then standing ready in the fields of the kingdom, at a reasonable rate, leaving only enough for his people's subsistence. This would help him evade debt and allow him to run the government, while the Company would not lose from the deal. Thuljaji also offered the English land around the fort of Devikottah, which they had captured in 1748.

The council rejected the Raja's demand for more troops as well as his offer of 400,000 pagodas for their maintenance, since they reasoned this contrary to the Company's orders. The Directors wanted the council to assess the garrison needed for Tanjore, and the council wanted the Raja to pay only for its upkeep. Then the board took up the matter of the paddy, which would soon become the reason for revolution in government. Mackay, Palmer, and Sir Robert were lukewarm. They were not against buying grain from Tanjore but only if the grain on offer was not part of the

Nawab's assignment to individuals against loans, promised prior to the restoration. Sir Robert went further. He was not against the purchase of any other grain on the Company's account, provided the officer concerned felt that such purchase was necessary. He then asserted that he was 'in no shape responsible for any measures that may be taken respecting the grain in the Tanjore country'. George Dawson, Claud Russell, and John Maxwell Stone, assented with the governor, and it was decided to write to Lord Pigot informing him of the majority's decision on the grain.

At this moment Sir Robert Fletcher submitted to the council that he believed on the basis of 'undoubted information' that the grain then in Tanjore had been promised by the Nawab to his creditors, some of whom were British subjects. The tabling of Paul Benfield's letter before the council followed this.

Benfield, as we saw before, had been appointed Civil Architect and Assistant Engineer in Madras with the rank of Lieutenant in 1764. John Call recommended that Benfield replace him as Engineer of Fort St George in 1768. Paul Benfield was probably the architect who had designed the Nawab's palace at Chepauk. The next year he had applied to the council for the grant of land on the Choultry Plain, next to Mackay's garden-house. The council, appalled by the large number of applications received from Europeans to build 'Gardens of Pleasure, which tend to the Encouragement of Idleness, Expense, and Dissipation, the Consequences of which, in a Colony constituted as this is, are but too obvious'. The only answer was to reject all such applications, including Benfield's. Benfield was a good engineer and architect, and this helped him gain proximity to, and the favour of, the Nawab. One does not know if he actually designed the Chepauk Palace but if he did, it must have brought him money enough to give up his commission at Fort St George. Charles Campbell Prinsep's *Records of the Services of the Honourable East India Company's Civil Servants in the Madras Presidency from 1741 to 1858* (1885) shows that Benfield had transferred to the Company's civil service as Writer in 1765, and became a Senior Merchant in 1776. He was not interested in commerce but in making money faster. The fastest and easiest way of doing this without any capital was by lending money to local princes, who were forever in need of ready money. This required the connivance of the governor, who, as Cashkeeper, would begin the process by demanding repayment of the dues of the Nawab. He first engaged in this profitably (and this species of usury is always profitable) and very interestingly, by lending money to Thuljaji, the Raja of Tanjore, in 1771, to let him make terms with the Nawab.

To think that Benfield actually borrowed money from Indians and Europeans, and lent the sum collected to the Nawab, is a grave error. To lesser borrowers he may have done so through agents but his golden goose was the Nawab. Burke made an example of Benfield in his famous speech in the Commons, and explained Benfield's usurious methods in plain language. The Nawab's debt to the Company 'is the pretext under which all the other debts lurk and cover themselves'. Worse, this debt was 'the foul putrid mucus' in which throve 'the whole brood of creeping ascarides … added to a knot of those inexpugnable tapeworms [the private creditors] which devour the nutriment and eat up the bowels of India'. Burke's reason for this parallelism lay in the operations of Benfield. Burke asked the Commons to note that the Nawab's debt to the Company carried no interest. The Nawab arrears in his repayments to the Company, is pressed to pay, and declares that he has no money in hand. He is reminded that there are bankers who will advance him the amount needed against revenues. 'Then steps forward some Paul Benfield', declaimed Burke, 'and from his grateful compassion to the Nawab, and his filial regard to the Company, he unlocks the treasures of his virtuous industry'. Using the promissory note to his fellow conspirator, the governor and Company's Cashkeeper, Benfield would become security to the Company for the Nawab's dues at an interest ranging from 24% to 36% on territorial revenues mortgaged by the Nawab to his lender. Burke asked why other 'honest and obvious methods' of relieving the Nawab were not undertaken by the Company, which had instead displayed a peculiar 'disinterestedness and moderation' by allowing the debt to accumulate. Further, the Company had indirectly approved of its employees acting as lenders and guarantors to that debt, charging the revenues of the country with compound interest at rates ranging from 20% to 48%. This vicious cycle was completed when the Nawab, seeing that the repayment of the principal amount to the Company bore no interest, while he was deeply indebted to his private creditors, gave their claims precedence. 'In consequence of this double game', thundered Burke, 'all the territorial revenues have, at one time or other, been covered by those locusts, the English *soucars* [usurers]'. 'Do not think I paint', Burke said, 'Not one single foot of the Carnatic has escaped them; a territory as large as England'. Burke pursued his argument relentlessly, saying that a compound interest of 24% on a principal amount of £480,000, would annually yield to the creditor £118,000. The lender obtained this huge sum without engaging in any actual transaction. Tanjore, forced into debt to the Nawab through promises for the payment of indemnities by rapacious treaties, is delivered 'bound hand and foot, to Paul Benfield, the old betrayer, insulter, oppressor, and scourge of a country'. Paul Benfield and his ilk were there to make money from usury. To them neither the Nawab nor the Raja were more than figureheads to be used for the pitiless exploitation of the land. Burke remarks that in the final analysis 'it little signifies under which of their names the unhappy undone people are delivered to the merciless *soucars*'. By 1785, the Nawab's debt to Paul Benfield alone was variously calculated as £500,000 to £800,000. Burke preferred the moderate sum of £400,000. Benfield, Burke suggested, was to be considered by the House of Commons as '*soucar* security for £480,000 a year, which at twenty-four *per cent* (supposing him contented with that profit) will, with the interest of his old debt, produce an annual income of £149,520 a year', thanks to William Pitt's decision to pay off the Nawab's debt to his creditors from an Indian fund.

George Smith, a free merchant at Madras, and later Foreman of the Coroner's jury called by George Andrew Ram to carry out the inquest upon Lord Pigot's death, testified on the Nawab of Arcot's debts before a Select Committee. His answers were appended to Edmund Burke's speech, and they are most illuminating. Up to 1766, the Nawab owed his creditors around 2,400,000 pagodas. The Company was aware of this debt and wrote repeatedly to the governor and council to recover it. By the time Smith left Madras in 1779, this old debt had been pared down to around 500,000 pagodas but a new debt of 6,000,000 pagodas had been contracted. He had no reason to believe, George Smith said, that this amount was lent to the Nawab in money or goods, because not all the money, chattel, and goods, in the settlement of Madras amounted to this sum.

To continue the story, Paul Benfield's letter told the council on 22 April that he had been constrained to write to them because he had sustained the hope that the restoration of Tanjore to Thuljaji would not harm the interests of creditors who had entered into transactions with the Nawab in good faith and confidence. To ensure this, he had written to Lord Pigot soon after Thuljaji's restoration. He had attended the governor at Tanjore in order to explain to him if needed, 'any particulars he might wish to know regarding my concerns'. Two days after the restoration, Benfield addressed an impudent letter to Pigot, listing the districts, which the Nawab has assigned to him for money lent. The revenue of Munnargudi was Benfield's until the amount lent, 370,000 pagodas, had been recovered. As security against this, Pigot was told that the Nawab had ordered the grain from this district to be collected and deposited with Benfield. Similarly, allotments had been made in the district of Papanasam against a borrowing of 20,000 pagodas, and in Pattucottah, against 15,000 pagodas. 'Likewise', continued Benfield brazenly, 'I have assignments of debts of the inhabitants in the several districts, for advances made to them … to the amount of about one hundred and twenty thousand Pagodas, to enable them to carry on the cultivation, payable from the inhabitants' shares from the present crop, according to the custom of the country'. The European assignee, Burke said 8 years later (with Benfield in mind, of course), demanded his due from the farmer, and at the bottom of this chain of oppression was 'the remaining last miserable cultivator, who grows to the soil, after having his back scoured by the farmer, has it again flayed by the whip of the assignee, and is thus … lashed from oppressor to oppressor, whilst a single drop of blood is left as a means of extorting a single grain of corn'.

Returning to Benfield's audacious missive to Pigot, we see Paul declaring 'I have moreover grain in several parts of the country, and debts due to me from many of the inhabitants, amounting together to about sixty thousand pagodas'. Put together then, Benfield claimed 585,000 pagodas from the revenue of Tanjore, particularly the crop in the field in the summer of 1777. He understood, wrote Benfield to Pigot, that the Nawab's revenue collectors were still in their posts in several districts (though Pigot had dispatched troops to stop them from their depredations with immediate effect), and he trusted that Pigot would secure for him his dues after Raja's people took over.

All depended on who got the crop. The Raja wanted it to recoup his kingdom's economy, by selling it to the Company, which had ready money, which the Raja urgently needed for his financial survival. Even as Benfield was pushing his claims, Pigot was pushing his council to agree to purchase the grain. Pigot replied to Benfield the same day, telling him that Thuljaji's restoration had been ordered by the Directors, and quoted the clause in the Directors' letter that the Raja was to be assured that any Company official presuming to interfere in the Raja's government would be severely punished. This applied as much to Pigot as it did to Benfield. Nonetheless, Pigot agreed to place Benfield's letter before his council. Benfield, cornered by Pigot's determined restoration of Thuljaji and in possession of the intelligence that Company's troops had been ordered to all parts of the kingdom to take charge on Thuljaji's behalf, sent Pigot another insolent letter on 14 April 1776, which reads more like a challenge today, in the perspective of subsequent events. 'I cannot conceive', Benfield wrote, 'that my setting forth to your Lordship my first claims on the Tanjore country, can be considered in any respect to interfere in the Rajah's government; or that it could be the intention of the Court of Directors, that by the execution of their orders I should be deprived of my right'. Lord Pigot's proposal to refer the matter to the council would be 'hurtful' to Benfield's interest, especially if the revenues assigned him 'should be otherwise applied, than paid to my servants, who are in the different countries to receive them'. In writing to the council while Pigot was away on duty at Tanjore, Benfield placed before them his 'full confidence' to help secure his property 'while the Right Honourable President *under your commission remains over those countries*' [my emphasis]. Lord Pigot had not been commissioned *by the council* but by *the Court of Directors* to reinstate Thuljaji and return to him his kingdom with the assistance of his council. The *commission* probably referred to the council's resolution by majority to Lord Pigot's carrying out the Company's directives in sole command. Benfield followed this up with another statement that contributed to the later troubles: 'I shall be at any time be ready to lay before you sufficient vouchers etc., of my claims'.

George Stratton, in the chair in place of Lord Pigot, moved that a copy of the letter be sent to the governor, and further deliberations deferred until his return. The board again divided along expected lines: Stone, Russell, and Dawson were for the motion; Mackay was for the motion, provided Lord Pigot was also informed that neither he nor the Raja was to meddle with the grain mortgaged to Benfield until the council had decided on it. Palmer sided with Mackay, and Stratton, since he had tabled the motion, was probably forced to vote in favour. Sir Robert Fletcher was the only one to dissent, and his reason was that the matter was too urgent. Sir Robert had yet another grouse to place before the council, and this one was an affront to his commission as commander-in-chief of the Coromandel Coast. Sir Robert considered it equally insulting to his authority and that of Lieutenant-General Sir John Clavering, the Company's commander-in-chief that Lord Pigot should be signing orders directing the placement of troops in the presidency, in exercise of the special mandate granted him by majority of the council before he left for Tanjore.

Stratton now took up the cry, placing before the board a letter from the Nawab, dated 21 April, in which he complained against the seizure by a detachment of sepoys and European cavalry, of his revenue officer, along with his papers, who had charge of collections from Tanjore, and been removed from there on the Nawab's orders just before the restoration. This act had been at the express orders of Pigot, and it was to him that the Nawab's revenue officer for Tanjore was hied. 'You are sensible', wrote the Nawab, 'that I am entirely ignorant of the nature and extent of the authority that has been vested in Lord Pigot for conducting this business'. He wished that his English friends would ease his worries by showing their regard to 'the dictates of justice'.

Pigot returned on 5 May 1776 from Tanjore, and reported on his work there to the council at a consultation on 13 May. The Raja had agreed to annually contribute 400,000 star pagodas for the maintenance of a well-disciplined and regularly paid Company's force in the Carnatic, to keep peace in the region. Thuljaji had committed himself to an instalment schedule that would ensure that the entire amount was paid by April each year. This arrangement, Pigot told the council, would ensure that enough was left over to partly cover the Nawab's arrears in contribution. Moving through the repairs to the fortifications at Tanjore and his disposition of the Company's troops there in order to ensure their strategic and comfortable encampment, Pigot paused to list the amounts collected by the Nawab during his occupation of Tanjore from 1774. Adjusting for all expenses, Lord Pigot said that the Nawab had collected from Tanjore between 1774 and 1776, the immense sum of 7,950,000 chuckrams, or nearly 4,000,000 pagodas. The balance for 1776 was 550,000 chuckrams according to the Nawab's revenue officer, and to Pigot it was clear that it would be impossible to collect this sum since the entire crop in the field in April had not been reaped. Moreover, some spells of rain had ruined a portion of the standing crop. Following normal practice in Tanjore, the crop should have been reaped in March, and threshed and readied for assessment. The Nawab had issued promissory notes on the revenue amounting to 5,000,000 chuckrams, or 10 times the maximum revenue possible. Therefore, the cultivators, frightened of the punishment that would surely follow their inability to produce this amount, had fled. Thus, the crop continued to stand in the fields, to be ruined by the rains. There were other pressing reasons for their fleeing. They had been forcibly advanced money for seed at a rate 2½ times higher than the rate at which they would be paid for the crop. Their land had also been assessed at rates much higher than actual, and they had been compelled through threats of violence to sign promissory notes admitting dues along these higher rates. Even though subsequent assurances had succeeded in bringing them back, from Nagapatam and other seaports to which they had migrated, to their original profession of agriculture, it was clear that the greater part of the crops for that year had been destroyed.

The council approved of Lord Pigot's actions at Tanjore, with some exceptions such as his seizure of Tanjore's *Dubbeer* (secretary), Naroo Pundit, from the Nawab's territory. Pigot, having gleaned considerable information about the fiscal machinations of the Nawab, placed before the council his reply to the Nawab's letter protesting the seizure of Naroo Pundit by the Company's troops at Pigot's behest, violating thereby the alliance between the English and the Nawab. Pigot was blunt in his opinions. He began by saying, 'That your mind is full of trouble and uneasiness does not surprise me; bad counsellors have often distracted a mind as great as your Highness's'. Amir-ul-Umra, the Nawab's son who had been in charge of administering Tanjore, seemed to Pigot to have forgotten to inform the Nawab that he had ill-treated Naroo Pundit: 'Was it noble, was it generous, was it honourable, was it just, to imprison this venerable old man, between 70 and 80 years of age; this public officer, this first officer of the Tanjore revenue; this officer of the public, not your Highness's servant?' From the *Dubbeer* Pigot had, to his great satisfaction, learned that not only had the Nawab extracted 4,000,000 pagodas from Tanjore since 1773-4 but had also removed 900,000 pagodas for 1776, leaving only 300,000 for the Raja. These amounts would be enough, Pigot said, for the Nawab to meet the arrears of payment of his troops. Happiness at having obtained all this monetary information, which the Nawab had been chary about, made Pigot drive home his point: 'The good purposes the measure has answered will I hope appear to you a sufficient reason for escorting the Dubbeer to Tanjore'. Pigot then rubbished the Nawab's protest that lands that had been his for long, were being given to Tanjore. The Directors had ordered that the Raja be put into possession of all regions that had comprised the kingdom of Tanjore in 1762. This had been done precisely to the extent ordered.

On 14 May 1776, letters were written, approved, and sent, to the Governor-General and Council at Calcutta, and the governor and council at Bombay, notifying them of the restoration of Thuljaji to the throne and kingdom of Tanjore. A letter was also sent to the Directors signed by Pigot and his council. Here they made clear the Nawab's reluctance to the restoration, which was then personally conducted by the governor, with the consent of the council, and assistance of the Company's troops. The secretary to the council, Richard Joseph Sullivan, was directed to inform Paul Benfield that his case would come up for the council's consideration the following Monday, and he was advised to prepare any further documents necessary for him to successfully argue his point.

Paul Benfield submitted a letter on the day designated, viz, Monday, 20 May 1776, in which he reported that the grain at Tanjore mortgaged to him by the Nawab and others in return for money lent, had been seized 'with the same power which had been before exercised'. He complained that his agents had been driven away from collecting the debts, and the grain mortgaged, by the Company's sepoys. 'In this manner', Benfield wrote, 'am I deprived of my just rights, and my affairs thrown into the utmost disorder'. 'You must be sensible', he told the governor and council, 'I am unable to support myself against the difficulties of so considerable a property, thus embarrassed and thrown into suspense'. Even in time of war, the property of individuals had been respected, he said. The council considered his letter on 22 May and Sullivan was directed to write to Benfield the following day, to lay before the council all necessary vouchers and information in support of his claims on Tanjore, particularly the nature and circumstances of those claims. In the meantime a letter also dated 22 May, was received from the Nawab, confirming that he had made grants on Tanjore to two creditors, from whom he had borrowed 525.000 and 300,000 pagodas, respectively, exclusive of interest.

Paul Benfield wrote next on 28 May 1776 to the governor and council, and the letter was tabled the same day. Benfield's details of the Nawab's debts to him are astonishing. The Nawab owed Paul Benfield 369,000 pagodas for 1775, for which the district of Munnargudi had been pledged. Papanasam was pledged against a payment of 20,000 pagodas in January 1775 for the maintenance of the Nawab's troops at Tanjore. Pattucottah was the Nawab's guarantee for 15,000 pagodas, paid in November 1774 for repairs to the Tanjore fort. The *Dubbeer* had registered these mortgages at the *cutcherry*, or magistrate's court, in Kumbakonam. To Amir-ul-Umra, Benfield had lent 120,629 pagodas for advances to the cultivators and the *Dubbeer* had issued Benfield's agents with the necessary authority from the *cutcherry* to collect the dues against these loans, for which the borrowers had given bonds as surety. From the crop of the previous year, Benfield claimed to have purchased 224,044 cullums of grain, which was still in Tanjore and had been seized by the Company's troops. Benfield's agents were similarly kept from collecting additional ready dues worth 60,000 chuckrams and grain measuring 80,000 cullums, also drawn on local inhabitants. Interestingly Alexander Dalrymple asked for the insertion of his minute, stating his dissent to 'Endeavours having been used to persuade members of this Board, that they are liable as individuals for prosecutions at law for their conduct in their public capacity concerning the Tunkaws on the Tanjore country'. 'For my own part I shall make no scruple to declare', Dalrymple recorded, 'that I do not think myself at all liable for any prosecution for executing the Company's orders; nor can I conceive on what grounds it can be supposed that either the Company or individuals are or can be subject to prosecutions in this matter'. This note of dissent shows us that considerable influence was being brought to bear on the council in Benfield's case.

Richard Sullivan, the secretary, wrote to Benfield on order of the council, telling him to provide further information of the various amounts due to him from Tanjore. This elicited a more detailed and accusatory reply from Benfield dated 29 May 1776. He listed once more the same debts as before, and added that he had suffered considerable loss through 'the measures and conduct' of Lord Pigot, who had ordered the Company's sepoys to seize his grain. Nonetheless, up to the restoration of Thuljaji, Benfield's agents had collected sums amounting to around 15,000 pagodas. Benfield now demanded his right to collecting the rest of his dues from the crop then standing on the ground, 'for it is well known', he wrote, 'that grain standing on the ground is paid and received as property throughout the whole country'. The bonds of the inhabitants who had been loaned money were not with Benfield. He presumed they were at the *cutcherry* or with his agents. Benfield audaciously urged the council to write at once to the Raja 'to cause the grain that was my property, and in possession of my people, the produce of the last year (not of the present crop), to be immediately restored'. This was followed by two more paragraphs, which showed how deep Benfield's tentacles had penetrated the finances of the Carnatic. Benfield noted that he 'came under engagements to pay to the Dutch the sum stipulated in the treaty made with the Nabob in 1773'. This 'engagement' had been made an article in that treaty, Benfield said. The Company had of course declared that treaty void. The Company in its letter dismissing Alexander Wynch had particularly noted how instead of waiting for instructions sent by the East Indiaman the *Harcourt*, in 1772, the council had proceeded to help annex Tanjore for the Nawab. The Company had been 'shocked' to find their troops engaged on such 'frivolous pretences' as were considered by the council as reason enough for this annexation: that Thuljaji had mortgaged some of his districts to the Dutch and the Danes; that he had invited a Maratha invasion of the Carnatic; and that he owed the Nawab money. So when Benfield wrote in his letter to Pigot and his council that his engagement as guarantor for the payment of indemnity to the Dutch vide the treaty of 1773 had been attested by the council, the Court of Directors, and the Courts of England and Holland, he was lying. Similarly, he was being deceitful when he wrote that he had paid 2,000,000 pagodas into the Company's treasury, on his own bills, on the Nawab's account. As Burke told the House of Commons in 1785, this sum simply a worthless piece of paper, used to extract an interest from the Nawab.

Exasperated in his designs, and threatened by the loss of huge sums to which he had acceded through chicanery, Benfield pointed to Pigot as the cause of his troubles in the last paragraph of his letter. He was arguing a case of property, Benfield wrote, addressing the council rather than Pigot, 'you will doubtless allow the degree of freedom that is necessary to support my right'. Benfield's anger erupted at Pigot's presence in council during discussions on Benfield's petition, as a conflict of interest. 'I think in this instance Lord Pigot becomes a party', wrote Benfield, 'it is by his measures and in the execution of his orders, that I am deprived of my property and driven to the brink of ruin and despair'. 'When I appeal to your candour and your justice', he asked of the council, 'is it consistent he should be one of my judges?'

Pigot proceeded to deal with this last part of Benfield's petition by producing the council's resolution of 25 March 1776, allowing a battalion of sepoys to march southwards to help Thuljaji's officers collect revenue on his behalf. In addition, Pigot placed before the council his orders dated 13 April to Captain Mackenzie, the officer commanding the 6th Sepoy Battalion, to march to Mayavaram, leaving sufficient detachments at Papanasam and Kumbakonam as considered necessary for the adequate protection of the Raja's revenue officers. The whole council agreed that Pigot's orders of 13 April were conformable with the resolution of 25 March regarding the restoration of Thuljaji, with the exception of Sir Robert Fletcher, who thought the orders would have been conformable if Pigot had passed them on to Mackenzie through Colonel Harper, in keeping with proper military practice. This point having been clarified, Pigot moved to the next one, which proved singularly prickly.

Did the council not feel, asked Pigot, that Thuljaji having been restored to his throne, kingdom, and revenue, it was not in the council's power 'to comply with Mr Benfield's requests in any respect?' His claims had no connection with the government, and had not been sufficiently explained to the council to decide on their validity, while the Nawab's assignment of portions of Tanjore's revenues was inadmissible, Pigot said. Stone, Dalrymple, Russell, Brooke, and Dawson were for the question, while Mackay sat on the fence, admitting that the council could comply with some of Benfield's debts. Stratton, Sir Robert, Jourdan, and Palmer, declared themselves against the question. The battle-lines had been drawn. After his councillors had declared their positions, Pigot confirmed himself in favour of the question and quoted for all concerned the Company's letter dated 27 September 1714, wherein all Englishmen were by irreversible order prevented from dealings in money matters with the local powers. The question was carried by the slim margin of 6 to 5.

Matters soon worsened. On Monday, 3 June 1776, Sir Edward Hughes interfered on behalf of the Nawab in a manner most unbecoming of his position as the Admiral commanding the Royal squadron at Madras Roads. 'It is with the greatest concern that I find myself under the necessity of interfering in any respect of the representatives of the Company and the Nabob of the Carnatic', Hughes wrote to Pigot and his council. The Nawab had complained to Hughes of being ill-used by Pigot, and Hughes enclosed the Nawab's 'alarming' application in his letter.

The Nawab's petition dated the same day at Chepauk and signed by his European secretary, James Wooley, makes for astounding reading. Lord Pigot's unjust use of his power had achieved new heights, the Nawab alleged, 'not content with the low and disgraceful state to which he has reduced my authority, by the measures which he executed at Tanjore, has lately threatened to subject me to the most personal disgrace'. At 8 in the morning Pigot had allegedly entered the Nawab's durbar, and declared in the presence of several witnesses, all Nawab's men, that he would place a European guard on his palace to keep the Nawab 'in his own power'. Then, naming several of his councillors, Pigot called them 'rascals' and that 'he would dismiss them from the service'; 'he said also, that all the white faced fellows were rascals', and he would not allow any of them to meet the Nawab. The Nawab further alleged that on a previous occasion Pigot had ordered his men into the Nawab's garden under the pretext that the Nawab had confined some persons there in order to punish them. 'I value my honour more than my life', declared the Nawab, 'so I am under the greatest alarm that he will proceed to execute in passion what he threatened, I shall then be without remedy'. Echoing Benfield, probably under whose advice the letter was written, the Nawab added that 'By the established custom I cannot apply to the Council but through the Governor, and my complaint is against him'.

Pigot and his council sent Sir Edward a suitably stiff and formal denial of these charges. The Nawab had completely misunderstood Pigot, who had thought of placing a European guard for the safety of the Nawab, considering 'the encouragement his Highness gave to European visitors, and the impediments to public business, arising from the intrigues carried on by them at his Durbar'. The guard would apprehend these persons and take them to Pigot, so that 'he might be acquainted with their business'. Sir Edward was clearly informed of his limits as well. 'Our President declares that no wanton indignity was ever intended to his Highness, or ever will be committed by him, although his ears can never be shut to the complaints of the distressed', the letter stated. Sir Edward was assured that no indignity would ever be offered to the Nawab by the council of Fort St George, 'to whom the management of the Company's affairs on this Coast is entrusted'.

In retaliation to the Nawab's allegations, Pigot and his council sent orders the same day to the officers commanding at Tanjore and Trichinopoly, directing them to inspect the channels of the Cauvery at Seringham and see if there was any danger to Tanjore from the branches belonging to the Nawab's lands. In case of any danger, Lieutenant-Colonel James, commanding at Trichinopoly, was to contact the *quiladar* at Seringham for help. Copies of these orders were sent to the Nawab, and he was requested to pass on similar directions to the *quiladar*.

The next item on that day's consultation was the presentation of reasons for objecting to the resolution of 29 May by dissenting members. George Mackay came off the fence and presented what today reads like a lawyer's brief. The Nawab had a share of the crop of 1776, since it had been sown in 1775 with his monetary help, and Tanjore had been in his possession until the crop had ripened, and the greater part harvested. Mackay reasoned that 'therefore all assignments or orders given by the Nabob on the Tanjore country, as far as his share of this crop would pay ought to stand good'. The Directors were not aware of the system of cultivation followed in India, and they had given no specific orders on this issue. If their orders were to be interpreted as allowing the seizure of everything in Tanjore and its restoration to the Raja, as the governor had done, then any property of the Nawab could receive the same treatment as the crop, and this was unjust. 'Still less can their orders mean', Mackay said, 'that individuals and British subjects, living under the protection of the Company, should be deprived of their property in that country, by its being taken from the Nabob and given to the Rajah'. Mackay also considered as justified Benfield's demand for a letter from the council to the Raja, allowing his agents to collect his dues for 1775 and 1776. Mackay next moved to uncertain ground, bluffing confidently. He did not believe in following the precedence set by the Company's letters of 1710 or 1712. Times had changed so completely that that which was right then was inapplicable in 1776. Then, Mackay moved on to far shakier ground, committing in a sense perjury, since he must have been aware, as all the other councillors were, of the actual rates at which money was lent. Mackay supported Benfield's claim by saying that he had lent at the 'legal interest' of 12 per cent. Usury was not a disadvantage to the Company or the locals, nor could Mackay 'consider Europeans lending money in this manner any way interfering with the country government'. Ironically, Benfield held at that time the power not only to make the Nawab cringe under the weight of his debt but also the governor and council to squabble and revolt. Mackay would never rise any higher in the service, and perhaps he had expected Pigot to help him in changing this. As we have seen, Mackay had lent the Nawab, by 1769, 51,250 pagodas. He therefore had a deep personal interest in Benfield's affair.

Palmer simply concurred with Mackay, while Jourdan explained at length his reason for disagreeing. The Nawab had the right of conquest to dispose of Tanjore's revenue as he wished, said Jourdan. Benfield was in the right, since he had been promised the revenue arising from the crop in certain territories in return for the sums he had lent the Nawab. Jourdan must have known that the money lent existed only on paper, and only the interest mattered. He thus agreed with Mackay that the orders of 1710 and 1712 referred to an earlier period, and were inapplicable to the times. Usury had been objected to by Parliament, in Jourdan's opinion, not because of the persons to whom the money was being lent but the rates of interest. This being within the 'legal' limit of 12 per cent, Jourdan had no objections to usury by the Company's servants. Jourdan also said that Benfield's commitment to pay indemnity to the Dutch following the annexation of Tanjore in 1773 had not been expressly disapproved of by the Company. He recommended that the council interest itself in appraising the Raja of the need for justice to be done to Benfield's claims on the crop of 1776. 'The seizure of the grain of a crop carries with it an extraordinary appearance', said Jourdan, 'for there could not, in my opinion, be the least colour or pretence for it'. Jourdan then turned on Pigot and wondered why the governor, when informed by Benfield of his claims, had not represented them to the Raja and later, on his return to Madras, to the council.

Sir Robert argued his case adeptly too. He began by declaring that he found Benfield's claim admissible. The Raja needed to be explained the 'universal law of nations' that 'the individual is still to be protected in his rights, though the hands of government are changed'. He imagined that the Company would be anxious that the restoration of Tanjore took place 'without obstruction or impediment to the rights of individuals'. Most unlike a soldier, and in a manner becoming a sea-lawyer, Sir Robert placed as precedent the case of the Armenians Gregore Khojamull, and Johannes Rafael, who had successfully challenged in Chancery in 1772 Harry Verelst, governor of Bengal between 1767 and 1769, for illegal imprisonment. The court had found against Verelst and slapped charges of £5000 on him, with costs. This case, along with other successful indictments ruined Verelst, because of which he had to escape to the Continent. Sir Robert Fletcher was convinced that if Verelst's influence was considered illegal, he could not believe that the Company 'will support us in voting Mr Benfield's claims to be inadmissible'. Then Sir Robert shed his mask and showed familiarity with the manner in which money was made by 'loans': 'The loans advanced by Mr Benfield on the crops of Tanjore country I understand for money actually paid for property purchased … and upon what principle such property can be seized or transferred with the dominion of the country, I consider myself at a loss to conceive'. 'The utmost extent of the Company's orders', he said, 'was to the restore the Rajah to his Government'. Like the other dissenters, Sir Robert too declared null and void the regulations of Queen Anne's time. Loans made at the permissible rate, were within the law, he said. Sir Robert, maybe out of personal dislike, since Pigot was Clive's friend, and Sir Robert owed his previous dismissal from Bengal to the latter, goaded the governor by suggesting that if there had been a case for 'improper loans' or 'the acceptance of presents', the place for trial was not the council but the Mayor's Court. With Pigot's decision to travel to Tanjore Sir Robert noted that he had previously disagreed.

George Stratton's dissent was moderate but certain that the council should assist Benfield in recovering his dues from Tanjore. At this point Brooke turned around from his position of assent at the previous consultation, and discovered a devious meaning in the Company's orders to Pigot and his council for the restoration of Tanjore. Brooke had thought that Benfield had demanded the council's intervention as a matter of 'right'. Having seen later that Benfield had merely requested the council to help him recover his money, Brooke now saw that Benfield had not stood upon any 'right'. His change in position having been explained, if this can be considered an explanation, Brooke quoted a convenient extract from the 21st paragraph of the Directors' orders of 12 April 1775. The paragraph reads: 'As the expedition against Tanjore in 1773 was short, being undertaken in the month of August and concluded in the month of September, we apprehend the revenues of the country could not suffer great diminution by that war; *and we must suppose that the plunder of the place, and the receipt of the revenue for more than two years, will have rendered the Nabob a very considerable gainer, after defraying all charges incurred by his Excellency in the said expedition*'. Brooke quoted only the second part (in italics) of this paragraph and concluded that it meant the Directors allowed 'him the enjoyment of the revenue for two years and more, that is, from the capture to the restoration of the Rajah'. Since the Nawab was in possession of Tanjore during this period, Brooke construed it to mean that the revenue and crop were the Nawab's to dispose of. Following this disingenuous train of logic, Brooke further concluded that the case, as it then stood, 'disallows of the Nabob's right to possess, puts the Rajah in possession of the crop produced in the time limited, and operates in consequences contrary to the meaning of the Company'.

Benfield followed up this consultation with a letter dated 3 June to the council in which he again accused Lord Pigot as being the main obstacle to his obtaining the crop of 1776. 'It is an invariable rule throughout the country', Benfield reminded Pigot, who had served for decades in India, 'that grain growing on the ground becomes property from the day it is planted, and is everywhere delivered over and received as such, and held by *Soucars* to be good and sufficient security'.

On Thursday 6 June, the consultations resumed. Charles Floyer had arrived, and he was administered the oaths upon which he took his seat in the council. A letter from Sir Edward Hughes was tabled, in which he mentioned that he had forwarded the council's reply to the Nawab's application for the Admiral's intervention to save him from indignity at Pigot's hands, to the Nawab. At this point Lord Pigot presented to the council his reasons for having sent some men at night to the Nawab's garden on the occasion complained of by the Nawab. To this end, he placed the Head Hircurrah's (or peon's) report to him dated 10 May 1776. This report alleged that the Nawab had ordered the kidnapping of 3 women and 13 men from a village on being told that one of these women, the daughter of one Villayan Chevacar, knew the whereabouts of much money. These persons had been put in confinement in the Nawab's garden, from where they were reportedly to be taken elsewhere to be tortured. The woman had sought the governor's assistance since they were then in the Company's bounds. On receiving this information, Pigot ordered the Head Hircurrah to keep watch from the Company's Garden-house, which adjoined the Nawab's garden. Later, on being told that the Nawab's men had removed some people towards San Thome, Pigot had them intercepted, brought back, and sent to the Nawab's garden with a note that they were not to be removed until Pigot had discussed the matter with the Nawab.

Then Benfield's case came up for discussion, and Alexander Dalrymple sought time until Monday. Sir Robert resented this delay and testily asked why Dalrymple needed so much time, upon which Dalrymple entered the minute that he needed 'much time' to be convinced that the council's resolution, which was in conformity to the Company's orders, needed to be rescinded. Dalrymple was undoubtedly acting on behalf of Pigot, and playing a holding game, since the previous resolution would have to be rescinded, considering that Brooke had changed sides.

The council met again on Monday 10 June, when Floyer stated that he was new to the council, and had been appointed chief at Masulipatam. He lacked the detailed information, which was needed for a considered opinion in Benfield's case. To this end, he said that he would not vote unless necessary, and then too with 'diffidence and concern'. The council considered this a serious matter, and postponed the discussion until the following Thursday. The postponement must have been a great aggravation to Sir Robert Fletcher. Charles Floyer was no newcomer to Indian politics, as he pretended to be. He had been appointed to the service in 1754, and become a Senior Merchant in 1771. By 1776, he had been in the Company's service for 22 years. He knew his way around.

Moreover, Dalrymple chose to present his opinion on the matter at this point. He minuted that since consistency was 'essential to the dignity of Government', it was important to consider all aspects of the matter including Benfield's claims, other claims on Tanjore, the Company's orders, and the council's resolutions, before deciding the case. Dalrymple fired a salvo at Brooke by quoting from the Directors' letter. Not only did the Directors order the enthronement of the Raja 'forthwith' on the receipt of these orders at Fort St George, there was to be 'no diminution of his authority over his subjects'. Any military officer or Company's servant who interfered in Thuljaji's government would be severely punished. The task of the restoration of Thuljaji was to be done punctually. In addition, the Raja was to be assured that the Company had no wish to embarrass him financially.

Dalrymple then pointed out that he had put in a minute in February, distancing himself from any delay in carrying out the Company's orders, which clearly demanded immediate obedience. Dalrymple unmasked the sheer greed of the majority of the council by stating that he had been against any delay since he was convinced '*that the view was to protract the business till the crops were gathered in, when the Rajah being without treasure, and the country without grain, he would become a heavy encumbrance on the Company, and by that means perhaps give an opening for new machinations*' [my emphasis].

Turning upon the members who had switched sides, and tried to delay Pigot, like Brooke and Sir Robert, Dalrymple cut through pretence with his directness: 'Another member of the Board, who now expresses his astonishment that any man in his senses could ever have expected the Nabob's consent, at that time objected to precipitancy; observing that a month more would be well bestowed, if by the delay the Nabob's consent would have been obtained'.

The entire issue hinged, Dalrymple said, on 'when the Nabob's property in the Tanjore country shall terminate'. Muhammad Ali had not assisted the Company in restoring Tanjore, as became a good friend and ally, which the Nawab claimed to be. Since the Nawab had not acted 'wisely and becomingly' towards the Company, Dalrymple reminded his fellow councillors that 'it would be very incompatible with our duty to the Company to consider the opposition he has made to their pleasure, as a motive for our assenting to let that opposition be profitable to him'.

Taking on Brooke again, Dalrymple referred to the paragraph that had been twisted out of context for the sake of Benfield. In that paragraph, 'The Company do not say, as seems to have been understood, that the Nabob *shall* have the *plunder* of Tanjore, and the receipt of revenue for more than two years'. The extract quoted by Brooke meant that 'they must suppose the plunder and the receipt of the revenues for more than two years will have rendered the Nabob a very considerable gainer, after defraying all the charges incurred in the expedition'. More than 2 years had passed between the invasion of Tanjore in September 1773 and the arrival of the Directors' order for restoration in December 1775. The *Dubbeer* had declared that in this period the Nawab had taken in 4,000,000 pagodas from Tanjore. If it was otherwise, Dalrymple said, the Nawab was welcome to table his accounts. Charging Benfield's claim on Tanjore would 'impoverish and distress' the Raja, which was contrary to the Company's orders. Dalrymple noted that Benfield was the only one who had made public his claim on Tanjore, and his claim must be a small one among very many others, considering the amount the Nawab had made from Tanjore during 1773-75. The date on which the Nawab's possession of Tanjore terminated was 9 December 1775, when the East Indiaman, the *Grenville* arrived at Madras, carrying Wynch's dismissal orders.

Looking to the other side of the coin, while the Nawab's and Benfield's supporters were eager to prove the former's right to the crop of 1776, it was obvious to Dalrymple that the advances claimed to have been made by the Nawab were not made at his expense but from bonds 'taken from the inhabitants to be discharged out of their share of this year's crop'. Benfield's claim lay in these bonds. These bonds, payable by the inhabitants from their share of the present crop, were not in Madras but with Benfield's 'agents' to the 'southward', having been registered by the *Dubbeer* at the Kumbakonam *cutcherry*.

Fighting Sir Robert back, Dalrymple said that when the proposal from Thuljaji was tabled that the Company should buy Tanjore grain at a fair price, some had said that the Company could buy this grain provided it had not been mortgaged by the Nawab to some individual. These persons now denied, said Dalrymple, that the Raja could have *any* grain to sell, since none of it was his. All of it belonged to the Nawab. Sir Robert had placed the case of Harry Verelst as one in which the Armenians had successfully challenged his use of influence in Awadh, which made Dalrymple wonder if the council's use of influence in Tanjore would be legal. While he as a Company servant would use all the power vested in him for a public cause, he could not see why he should be asked to recognise and use it on behalf of an individual's private claims. Since this use of influence would have to come from the governor, Dalrymple would never stand guarantee for him, since such exercise of influence would at once lay the governor open to innumerable prosecutions, from the other claimants, as well as all those whose interests would be injured by its use.

Benfield did not have the right to approach the council, Dalrymple felt. His debts on the Nawab had been mortgaged by the assignment of Tanjore revenue. If that mortgage fell through, it was not for the Company to assist Benfield but for Benfield to seek other mortgages from the Nawab. Entering into a detailed study of Benfield's claims, Dalrymple discovered several discrepancies and repetitions, which caused him to voice his concern about the nature and particulars of Benfield's entitlements. By way of further proof of this, Dalrymple pointed out the Company's approval of Benfield's declining to transact the business of issuing bills of exchange for the Dutch vide their letter of 12 April 1775, which simply proved that the Company's stance with respect to private monetary transactions with local powers was very much in place, and not some figment of a remote past. Dalrymple confirmed this by quoting more recent orders on this subject, which he confessed he had been able to trace due to the few days' interval between the last consultation and this one.

These orders reinforced the Company's position prohibiting all private transactions. Dalrymple's research began with a Company's order, dated 17 March 1769. He followed it up with a report of the Select Committee at Madras on the Nawab's debts to the Company, dated 31 January 1770, at which the decision had been taken to revive the same order of 1714 that Pigot had quoted, in order to keep the Company's servants from loaning money and charging usurious interest. The Court of Directors applauded this decision of the Select Committee in their letter of 30 November 1770. The Select Committee's decision had been endorsed, Dalrymple pointedly said, by the council of Fort St George, at a consultation at which, ironically, George Stratton, Henry Brooke, and George Mackay, had been present. Dalrymple produced in its entirety the public declaration of 6 November 1769. The council, headed by Charles Bourchier, had announced that considering the huge sums lent at exorbitant interest to the Nawab by the Company's servants and others living under their jurisdiction, the rate of interest would be fixed at 10 per cent from the date of the declaration, viz, 6 November. Further, the orders of 1714 were declared as standing, unrevoked, and 'in full force and vigour' whereby all civil and military servants of the Company as well as all other Europeans residing within the jurisdiction of the Company, were expressly forbidden 'to make loans or have any money transactions, of what kind so ever, the same may be, directly or indirectly, with any of the Princes, Rulers, or

Governors of any of the Provinces or States in the East Indies, or any of their Ministers or Agents, without the especial licence and permission of the President and Council for the time being'. It was further resolved at the same consultation that 'any wilful deviation herefrom be deemed and construed as a breach of orders, and treated as such'.

Dalrymple next produced the relevant extract from the Company's letter dated 22 March 1771, where all communication between the Nawab and his creditors was strictly prohibited other than through the governor and council and the Select Committee. The Directors' letter dated 10 April 1771 repeated the same cautions: 'We do hereby direct that no officer, or other person in our service whatever, do presume to lend, or by any means to advance money to any of the Nabob's people in the country'. The Directors were aware that it was a very great temptation for the commanding officer, when offered high rates of interest, to lend money against lands that lay within the range of his guns or the limits of his command. This temptation being the main reason of the disputes between the Nawab and the Company, the Directors again prohibited all such transactions, and ordered the dismissal of every transgressor.

Dalrymple provided a very interesting illustrative parallel to Benfield for the edification of the council, which can hardly have pleased those who had lent sums to the Nawab. This was the case of William Bolts. Norman Leslie Hallward's book, *William Bolts: A Dutch Adventurer under John Company* (1920), introduces this person thusly: 'Among the most remarkable civilian adventurers in the eighteenth century in the territories of the East India Company was William Bolts, who by private trade accumulated a fortune of £90,000 in six years, who, single-handed, defied for 2 years the civil and military authorities in Bengal, and who ruined an ex-Governor by litigation [Harry Verelst], and revenged himself on the Company for his forced deportation, first by publishing a bitter attack on their administration in Bengal, and afterwards by establishing rival factories in the East Indies under the protection of the Imperial Austrian Government'.

Born in 1735 in Holland, Bolts moved to England in 1749, and was appointed Factor to the Bengal presidency in 1759 by the Company. He reached Calcutta in the summer of 1760 and became fluent in Bengali, soon evolving into 'a full-grown mercantile monster, aged twenty-five' according to an anonymous source quoted by Hallward. He was exceptionally adept at trade, becoming partners in Calcutta with John Johnstone and William Hay for private trade in English products and, locally, in saltpetre, opium, cotton, and diamonds. They used considerable influence to force their trade upon unwilling persons. Their agent, Ram

Charan Das was accused of using unscrupulous means. By the time Bolts was appointed second in council at Benaras early in 1764, he was a rich man. His conduct and behaviour, along with irregular practices in his private trade, attracted in July 1764 the censure of the governor and council at Calcutta. He was threatened with dismissal from service unless he mended his ways. Bengal had become riddled with corruption, with the populace being exploited by both the Nawab and the English. The Directors, desperate to mend matters, sent instructions in 1765 that every Company employee was to sign a covenant agreeing not to accept presents from local princes. The governor and his council, including John Johnstone, were unwilling to enforce the covenant for the obvious reason that it would keep them from getting richer. However, Clive, on taking over as governor in May 1765, forced the issue. Bolts, much inconvenienced, resorted to getting his covenant signed by a Writer, rather than signing it himself, as required by orders. When this duplicity was discovered by Edward Baber, Assistant Secretary to the council, Bolts sought a private interview with him, with the brilliantly conceived but hardly laudable intention, as Hallward succinctly puts it, 'of procuring the withdrawal of the genuine covenant with the spurious signature and substituting it with a spurious covenant with a genuine signature'. In the event Baber did not allow Bolts to carry out the switch but agreed to keep the spurious signature on the genuine covenant secret unless it came into conflict with the Company's interests.

In a year's time Bolts was embroiled in yet another sordid business. In August 1765, he fell out with his superior at Benaras, the chief, Randolph Marriott, who had rented the Mint there, in collusion with Major Hector Munro, from the Delhi durbar for 30,000 rupees, the revenue being 50,000 rupees. The main cause of the dispute was of course the division of profit. The acrimony reached Calcutta and the council proceeded to inquiry in February 1766, where the roles of Marriott and Munro were suppressed, while Bolts was once more censured for insubordination. Marriott and Bolts were recalled from Benaras pending inquiry, and Bolts superseded by Isaac Sage, who was his junior in the service. The Directors, replying to these happenings in their letter of 4 March 1769, asked Marriott to return to the Company the profits he had made as from the Mint; Bolts's censure they recommended, and advised the council to proceed further and suspend or dismiss him if he persisted in corruption. Even as he clashed with Marriott at Benaras, and worried over the false signature on his covenant in Calcutta, Bolts apparently strove to proximity with Lord Clive, offering to buy diamonds for him from the mines. As we have seen, diamonds were an easy way for the English to send home their money.

Bolts later asserted in his book *Considerations on India Affairs: Particularly Respecting the Present State of Bengal and its Dependencies* (1772) that Clive later retracted his promise to use Bolts's services and appointed instead John Chamier as his agent for procuring diamonds. In any case, Bolts's unique career, so like Benfield's, was far from over. On 31 January 1766 he petitioned the council for permission to return to Benaras, at least privately, if not in any official capacity, so that he could settle his concerns there and bring his family to Calcutta. On 24 February, he was permitted to return as a private person to Benaras, where he was allowed to reside until 1 July. Bolts remained there, until the council realised, on 28 July 1766, that he had exceeded his time. They then wrote to Isaac Sage to ensure that Bolts left Benaras and returned to Calcutta by 28 August, failing which Bolts would be dismissed the service. Sage replied on 12 August, enclosing a plea from Bolts for permission for an extension in his period of stay at Benaras. Sage very strangely asked the council if it was within his powers to evict Bolts. Exasperated, the council wondered that Sage knew so little of their authority. They wrote that they had information that Bolts, instead of winding up his affairs, had taken up new concerns. Sage was ordered to ensure that Bolts left Benaras by 1 October 1766. Bolts was to report at Calcutta by 10 October, and in the meantime, the council suspended him from service with effect from 28 August 1766.

Meanwhile, events that are still more peculiar unfolded at Benaras. On 26 August 1766, William Bolts wrote to the Company from Benaras that his wife had eloped with Isaac Sage to Patna by boat. Therefore, Bolts was sending the Company's treasure, with military escort, to Patna for safekeeping. Asked to clarify matters, Sage wrote to the Company on 22 October 1766 that he had indeed been to Patna, but on official business, having been summoned to a court-martial by the Judge Advocate. He had neither deserted his post, nor eloped with Mrs Bolts, Sage wrote. Most interestingly, this court-martial was that of Sir Robert Fletcher, in consequence of his having aided and abetted the officers' mutiny. Bolts sent 125,000 rupees down to Patna. The Benaras treasury had held 170,000 rupees, and Middleton, the chief of Patna, very oddly issued Sage with a receipt for the balance. There seems to be no explanation for the missing amount.

The council received on 24 November 1766 a letter from William Bolts dated 10 November, in which he accused Sage of lying, and offered his resignation from the Company partly due to his wife's elopement. However, Bolts' letter enclosed one from his wife, Anne, in which she described how she had eloped with Sage, encouraged by John Chamier.

The council accepted Bolts' resignation, and waited for him to leave for Europe as he had written he intended to. Nonetheless, he continued to live at Benaras. In January 1767, he was ordered by the council to leave India. He replied that he had not engaged in any new concern, but was waiting for his claims to be redeemed by his debtors. To this end, he urged the council to use its influence. To various landowners he had farmed out 48,000 rupees, while another 800,000 rupees were invested in legal trade not conflicting with the Company's monopolies (now that Bolts was a private person). The council recognised his debts and allowed him to stay until his investments were recovered. On 18 April 1767, the Select Committee ordered Bolts to leave Calcutta for Madras in July, to reach there in time to avail of a ship to England. Bolts paid no attention to this, and on 24 August, the council again wrote that the East Indiaman, *Lord Holland*, was being readied for Europe, to sail in September, and they wanted Bolts to be on it. Bolts replied on 29 August that he would sail if the Company agreed to indemnify him and all his associates for losses incurred by his absence, adding that he had recovered only 150,000 rupees of his total investments, and then added that he held in trust investments worth another 800,000 rupees. It must have been infinitely wearying for the council to engage in this fruitless correspondence with William Bolts. His letter was tabled on 1 October 1767, and again he was ordered to Calcutta, thence to avail of the next ship to Europe. Bolts' presence had become a serious embarrassment to the council, and the governor, Harry Verelst, took the matter up on 5 November 1767. The council agreed that Bolts' attempts 'to sap the foundations of all government, to subvert by the factious cry of liberty the principles of subordination, and to loosen all those sacred ties whereby men are united together in society' had become intolerable. Bolt was to be ordered again to leave India, and if he would not, he was to be 'seized and forcibly sent home a prisoner' in one of the ships of that season.

Again, this did not affect William Bolts who employed Armenians as his agents in Calcutta and at the court of the Nawab of Awadh, which made him ever increasingly odious to the council at Calcutta. This seems to have been the reason for Harry Verelst's ordering the seizure and confinement of Gregore Khojamull, and Johannes Rafael, who later won their case against him, and Sir Robert Fletcher presented this as precedent in explaining Benfield's claim to the Company's influence to collect his claims. In any case, the tussle between the council and Bolts continued until 23 September 1768, when Captain Robert Coxe and a squad of sepoys arrested him, and put him aboard the schooner *Cuddalore*, whence he was transferred to the *Valentine*, Captain Purvis, on 29 September. The ship sailed the next day, and reached England on 30 April 1769. Once in England, Bolts presented a petition to the Court of Directors, and paid for his Armenian agents, Gregore Khojamull and Johannes Rafael, to travel to England. On 23 March 1770, the Court of Directors found for Bolts, and having detected many errors in the proceedings, decided to send directions to their settlements to provide 'necessary and proper assistance to his attorneys or agents for collecting and remitting to England his outstanding concerns'.

At Calcutta Bolts's solicitors diligently pursued the case of the council's using its influence to help him recover his dues, while Bolts brought out not only his book by way of indictment of governance in Bengal but also several suits against Harry Verelst including the one by his Armenian agents. It is no longer necessary for us to follow William Bolts' story, which must have been common knowledge and the source of conversation among the Company's employees in India. William Bolts, like Verelst, was ruined by his litigation. In 1773, he became bankrupt and went to the court of the Empress Maria Theresa, where he received funding to commence trading with India. Even as Benfield's case was being argued at Fort St George, Bolts was preparing to sail to India with a Lieutenant-Colonel's commission, the ship *Joseph and Theresa*, and a 10-year trade charter with Asia, Africa, and China. He left Italy in September 1776 and reached India in 1777. He seems to have been reunited with his wife, Anne Bolts, for she accompanied him on his voyage. In 1780 Bolts sailed down the Malabar, received Haider Ali's permission to trade, and then cruised up to Chinsurah in Bengal, a Dutch colony close to Calcutta. There were other adventures in Bolts' life, and connections with European royalty including the King of Sweden. With Maria Theresa's death, however, began his decline, since her son and successor, the Emperor Joseph II, revoked Bolts's lieutenant-colonelcy. Bolts, bankrupted again within two decades, died in great poverty in Paris in 180, aged 73. Anne Bolts died at Chandernagore in 1821, aged 69.

For Alexander Dalrymple, who was striving to find a reason to keep Benfield at bay, the Directors' letter of 6 April 1773, in reply to Bolts's creditors, commended the Bengal council for recognising 'the very great impropriety of assisting any insolvent man, or the creditors of any insolvent man, to collect the debts contracted in illicit trade'. When the Directors changed in 1773, the creditors wrote to them again, and received a similar reply. In their letter dated 13 May 1773, the Court of Directors clarified that the issue had to do with whether it was 'fit and right' for the presidency to assist Bolts' creditors in collecting dues, 'when the trade, whence such debts arose, was illegal'. The Directors went on to cite a case in which 'the first Court of Law in the Kingdom would not suffer a debt to be recovered against the commander of an East India ship, proved to be due for goods carried out by him to India; because it appeared in evidence, that the goods were to be clandestinely conveyed on board the ship, without the consent of the Company, contrary to Act of Parliament'.

The next consultation at Madras was on Thursday, 13 June 1776. At this meeting, the first point of discord was a paragraph in a letter to Warren Hastings and his council in reply to their query about the seizure of the *Dubbeer*, with his ledgers, from the Nawab's territory by sepoys on Pigot's orders. The paragraph reads, 'We will never lose sight of the treaty of Paris but we cannot believe that treaty can be construed to obstruct any proper measures which may be necessary for the Company's security or the safety of the Carnatic'. As soon as objections were made to the inclusion of this paragraph, Pigot put the question to the council whether the letter should stand as it was, or the paragraph sent in the governor's name, i.e. his.

Stratton, Sir Robert, Mackay, Jourdan, and Palmer, dissented to the paragraph as the opinion of the board. Floyer provisionally agreed to leave the letter as it was, while Stone, Dalrymple, Dawson, Russel, and Brooke, were in favour. A majority of 7 to 5 carried the motion with Pigot adding his vote.

This was followed by a temporary hiatus when Charles Floyer presented his minute, wherein he asked the advice of the council on the correctness of his staying on at Madras while his appointment as chief at Masulipatam waited for him, and voting on a matter he had not had the chance to peruse properly. Dalrymple promptly observed that every member of the board ought to vote, while Sir Robert felt that Floyer should not vote in view of his misgivings.

Pigot then moved to the resolution all had been waiting for, 'That the Rajah of Tanjore been put in the full possession and management of his country by the Company's express orders, it is the opinion of the Board, that it is not in their power to comply with Mr Benfield's requests in any respect, those claims on individuals, which bear the appearance of having no connection with government, not being sufficiently explained to enable the Board to form an opinion thereon, and the assignments of the Nabob not being admissible'. Stratton, Sir Robert, Mackay, Jourdan, Palmer, Floyer, and Brooke, were against the motion, while Pigot, Russell, Dalrymple, Dawson, and Stone, were for it. The resolution of 29 May 1776 was thus lost 7 to 5. Dalrymple sought to delay the opposition by stating that, as Sir Robert Fletcher and George Mackay had failed to respond to his minute, as they had said they would, he refused in all propriety to be party to any further judgments until he had seen their replies. Sir Robert called this 'mere caballing' by Dalrymple, and said that he would present his minute the next day. Mackay announced to the board that he had some questions to move, which he would the following day, upon which the meeting was adjourned.

The next day, Friday, 14 June, Pigot moved a new resolution, 'That all the claims of Mr Benfield are private and not public concerns'. Mackay interrupted and said that the council was meeting that day because he had given notice that he would put some propositions to the board. Propriety demanded that the council consider his proposals before they voted on Pigot's resolution. Pigot claimed that the custom of the service demanded that his resolution should take precedence, because he was the president. Nonetheless, Pigot at once proceeded to put it to the vote 'Whether the resolution proposed by him, or the motions intended by Mr Mackay should be first taken into consideration?'

The usual division followed. Stone, Dalrymple, Russell, and Dawson were for the governor's resolution, which, though given precedence, did not preclude Mackay's proposals. Stratton, Floyer, and Brooke, said that they had the greatest deference and respect for the president, but as the previous day's meeting had adjourned with Mackay's notice that he would be tabling some questions the following day, he had the precedence. Mackay, Jourdan, Palmer, and Sir Robert, were against Pigot. Pigot for once had his opinion minuted, one of the rare times when we get to read his views. He had considered his resolution 'the properest manner of introducing Mr Benfield's business again before the Board'. Moreover, to the best of his knowledge, the conduct of the Company's business had always 'originated with the President'. Hence, it was to keep 'uniformity with the accustomed and regular manner' that he felt his resolution ought to be considered first by the council.

The question was carried again in the negative, 7 to 5.

The issue was now moving fast towards its climax, the line having been drawn between the opposing parties. Clearly, Benfield's supporters were no longer for delay since it was the middle of June, and the remaining crop had been reaped. The only way for Benfield to redeem his claims was by getting the council to agree to force Thuljaji to give him the grain. Mackay moved his question, 'That it is the opinion of the Board, that the Nabob had a right to the government share of the crop in the Tanjore country, the produce of grain sown during the time it was in his possession, and that any mortgages he may have given on the same are good'. This resolution appalled Pigot. The question was beyond the council's jurisdiction, since it based itself upon certain 'supposed rights' of the Nawab. He felt that voting on the question would attract 'the most fatal consequences' and so moved that Mackay's question not be put.

Mackay and Palmer declared themselves for the question. Jourdan revealed the deviousness behind Mackay's motion when he explained his reasons for supporting the question, which was 'a necessary one, as preparatory to any assistance which the Board may think proper to give to Mr Benfield, because it is evident that if the Nabob had no right to assign the grain or country, Mr Benfield's claims on the Tanjore country fall to the ground'.

Stone disagreed on the grounds that had made Pigot consider this question 'most fatal'. It was not a question directly addressed to the claims of Benfield, Stone said, but 'a discussion of the general rights of the Nabob to the crops in the Tanjore country'. Further, if the question were to be put and carried in the affirmative, the Nawab's rights would be declared 'good and valid' by the board. Consequently, not only would the Company be forced to support the Nawab in the recovery of *all* his rights, there was no telling how far this commitment would carry them into his affairs.

At this point Charles Floyer revealed his venom, since he seems to have already been bought. He had written a minute, he said, and tabled it diffidently, seeking to be excused by all, from Leadenhall Street to Fort St George, if he erred in his conclusions. Given the deviousness of his argument, this diffidence was a clever disguise. Floyer took on Dalrymple, and quoted back to him the fifth paragraph of the Directors' orders, wherein it was stated that the Raja should be restored to 'the throne of his ancestors, upon certain terms and conditions agreed upon for the mutual benefit of himself and the English East-India Company, without infringing the rights of … [the] Nabob of the Carnatic'. Basing himself on the phrase 'certain terms and conditions', and extracting 'without infringing the rights of', Floyer felt that 'the Right Honourable President should have been authorised to state to the King of Tanjore the matter of property claimed, either by the Nabob's Naib, or by individuals, upon his country, as a necessary preliminary to being put into possession of Tanjore'. This had not been done, and now it would be difficult for the council to get Thuljaji to agree with claims on the crop already in his granaries. Continuing to harp on the possible infringement of the Nawab's rights, which he thought had been expressly forbidden by the Company, Floyer was of the opinion that until the arrival of the *Grenville* the Company itself acknowledged the Nawab's supremacy over Tanjore. The grain obtained from a crop sown in the previous year, prior to the arrival of the *Grenville* was thus the property of the Nawab and his creditors. Still more twisting of words followed. The Company's orders to place Thuljaji immediately on his throne bore no reference to the Nawab's possession of Tanjore's crop. Similarly, their orders to ensure that Tanjore was not impoverished was an 'honour to humanity' which however had nothing to do with the crop either. If the cultivators had not been advanced sums, they would have been impoverished. Having had a good crop, the matter now was otherwise. Floyer asked, 'where is the appearance of distress to the country, or to its individual inhabitants, the repaying by its own manufactures and agriculture, the amount of sums they have received in specie?' The mortgaging of the crop appeared to Floyer to be 'an anticipated sale of the internal produce of their labour, which is equal to the exportation of it to foreign markets'. Countries were not impoverished by repaying their debts, Floyer proclaimed, for, as he saw it, 'the debts so contracted are not to be paid in specie, but in the produce of a country which has been cultivated by the specie received into it'. This clear and simple economic principle did not take into account usury at criminally exorbitant rates, which meant that Floyer conveniently evaded the fact that the country had *not* been cultivated by the specie received into it. The equation so easily arrived at would not stand scrutiny. Everyone on the council must have known this, and sometimes it appears to the reader of the minutes that the council was playing to an audience, saying things that were expected of them, keeping the record straight. Indeed, they were playing to an audience; an audience far away in England, who they never imagined would call them home and put them up for trial. So long as things were in proper form, all was right. Floyer had been saving the best for the last. The Directors had ordered that Pigot and his council take into account the Nawab's receipts and disbursements deriving from the plunder of Tanjore and the enjoyment of its revenues for more than 2 years, when assessing his debts. These amounts were considerable, and the Directors wanted 'to prevent him from pleading the above circumstance [the absence of proper accounts] as an excuse or reason for delaying payment of his debts to the Company, and those to his private European creditors, in case they should be speedily demanded'. The Nawab was therefore to be allowed the revenue of Tanjore for *more than two years*.

Dalrymple now changed tack and pointed out the larger political implications of this decision. The Raja, hitherto well-disposed towards the Company would be dismayed and from this sense of betrayal and anger, would alienate himself from further dealings. The animosity between the Nawab and the Raja would be rekindled, because of which the Company would once more be drawn into the dispute, to the detriment of its trade. Russell took on this line of argument saying that a recognition of the Nawab's rights would not only compel the Company to see to it that all his creditors were satisfied, if Thuljaji refused to comply, the Company would find itself marching once more with the Nawab to depose Thuljaji.

Both Sir Robert and George Stratton, the most senior members, brushed aside all these apprehensions and alarms and voted for Mackay. Dawson had considered the issue of the Nawab's claims on Tanjore as inadmissible, and he was against the question, the same as Pigot.

Yet again, Pigot's opponents carried the motion, 7 to 5.

Mackay next put to the council the resolution to write to the Raja a letter to tell him of the board's resolution, 'and recommend to him to give to Mr Benfield all reasonable assistance in recovering such debts as appear to be justly due to him from the inhabitants, as well as to restore to him to the grain of last year, which was in the possession of his people, and said to be forcibly taken from them'. Pigot moved an amendment to the letter, beginning with the word Raja. Pigot suggested the letter be written instead to the Nawab, 'to inform him of the above resolution of the Board [confirming his rights] and to recommend to him send thc various Amildars and officers with their accounts to the Tanjore country, that the *Dubbeer* may be permitted to lay before us a true state of the Nabob's right to the government share of the crop in the Tanjore country, the produce of grain sown during the time it was in his possession, that we may form an opinion how far the mortgages or orders he may have given are good'.

As had become usual, the amendment lost, 7 to 5.

Despite some opposition from Dalrymple, Mackay's resolution to send the letter was approved, by the same majority, 7 to 5.

Acting almost in concert, Mackay followed this up by proposing 'That it be further recommended to the Rajah to account with Mr Benfield for the government share of the grain in the districts assigned to him by the Nabob, and said to be forcibly taken from his people'. Pigot dissented, his dissension carrying his weariness, and certainty of knowledge, that money had won and he had lost. All this was contrary to the Company's orders, he said. The Directors had made it clear that they would severely punish any civil or military officer who interfered with the prompt execution of their orders. He saw clearly in this resolution, he said, that Coomera, Benfield's *Dubash*, who been ordered to a whipping by Pigot when at Tanjore, because he had had the impertinence of intruding upon the Raja's presence at 11 pm, and suggesting to Thuljaji that he would do best by renting out his entire kingdom, would now return to Tanjore, with the council's resolution, to gloat that 7 members of the council had supported the seizure of nearly all of Tanjore's grain. None of this made any impression on his opponents, who had done their job.

Mackay's third resolution was carried, 7 to 5.

Like assassins waiting eagerly to do their deed, the council ordered Coomera to appear before the board to be questioned. After this, Pigot returned to his resolution, that Benfield's claims should be considered private claims and not public ones. Of course, Pigot lost again, 7 to 5. Nonetheless, at the end of a very long and tiring session, he asked that his intention of using the resolution he had tabled, to refer to the Directors the matter of Benfield's claims, be noted, 'that Mr Benfield's transactions with the Country Government are contrary to the express orders of the Company, and that any interference therein may raise apprehensions in the Rajah of Tanjore and tend to involve the Company's affairs on this coast; for which reason it is resolved that this matter be referred to the Honourable Court of Directors'.

After an uneasy weekend, the council met on Monday, 17 June 1776, for their next consultation, when the dissenting group, Stratton, Sir Robert, Jourdan, Palmer, Floyer, Brooke, and Mackay, handed in a minute giving their reasons in detail for the rescinding of the council's previous resolution on the restoration of Tanjore, and the adoption of the new resolution. They wanted this minute to be sent to the Governor-General and Council in Bengal. Pigot followed this with a resolution that the Nawab's letter to Sir Edward Hughes was purposely written to create animosity between the members of the government at Madras. With Brooke's conceding that the letter had 'some appearance of meaning to create animosity', the issue swung in Pigot's favour. Pigot gave his opinion that he felt the letter had been dispatched at the goading of the (presumably European) 'miscreants' at the Nawab's durbar, since he had put his signature to a letter written in English, 'which he understands not a word of'. Pigot also asked the council to note that the Nawab's letter was sent to the Admiral one week after the incidents related in it had taken place, during which period not only had the Nawab sent a complimentary note to the governor but his sons had also visited him.

Pigot's resolution being carried due to his casting vote and Brooke's ambivalence, he then made his next move. It was like a game of chess, each premeditated move leading to others. Lord Pigot hoped that this resolution would strike every member of the council with the impropriety 'nay, indecency' of visiting the Nawab. He therefore proposed, in keeping with the Company's standing orders, that 'no member of the council do henceforth visit or correspond by writing or by message, with the Nabob or either of his sons'. Pigot had intelligence that that the Nawab regularly received information of the proceedings of the council, and thought it 'very improper that any member of the Council should be liable to the slightest suspicion of divulging to the Nabob the proceedings of this government'.

This was great provocation, and Mackay rose to it immediately. He was in the negative on this point, he said, because the order meant that only the president would be able to correspond with the Nawab and other princes. Making such an order now 'would be extremely improper, and more especially as accusations from the Nabob against the President are now before the Board'. Jourdan said that he resented the order, which cast intolerable suspicions on members of the board. Further, he thought that this order would unsettle the Nawab, who was already uneasy. Palmer supported this view. Floyer, who had hitherto pretended to artlessness, was direct: 'I think the motion made by the President is a strong implication of his suspicion of the members of this Board, particularly as it is so soon made after the personal misunderstanding which appears to have arisen between the Nabob and the President, and therefore am of the opinion that this is a very improper time for the Board to shut late access to the Nabob'. Again, Henry Brooke was ambivalent, and his vote for the motion added to Pigot's, carried the motion with the same slim margin as on the previous issue.

One can almost see Pigot taking a deep breath and proceeding to his next move, the ejection of the Nawab from living within the bounds of Madras. He had already proved that Muhammad Ali had tried to sow discord in the council, and had followed it up with an order to his councillors to keep away from the Nawab's durbar. This latter move had a second effect. Since these consultations were formal, with minutes being recorded for conveyance to Leadenhall Street at the year's end, it was important that the Directors should be able to read between the lines. His order restricting Europeans from corresponding with the Nawab was not only an extension of the Company's directives but also a revelation, for those who objected, no matter for what reason, were guilty of carrying privileged information from the council to the durbar. The reason Brooke sided with Pigot might have been his prescience that Pigot had uncovered, for the Directors to draw their own conclusions, the secret influence of the Nawab on discussions in the council. Removing the Nawab from the bounds of the Company's settlements would be another test. On the surface, it would be seen as a move to oust a baneful influence. At the deeper level, it would again reveal those who were the instruments of his machinations, since they would again be provoked into opposition.

Considering that the Nawab's people had been the source of 'murder, imprisonments, theft, tortures, and suchlike offences', which necessarily called for the Company's intervention since these crimes occurred within the bounds, the Nawab's constant residence at Chepauk was an impediment to his dignity. There were several suits pending against the Nawab's people in the Mayor's Court at Madras, Pigot said. Muhammad Ali's letter to Sir Edward Hughes had not mentioned the apprehension, at Pigot's behest, of one the Nawab's men, who had kidnapped 19 children from Tanjore, 1 from San Thome, and 2 from Cuddalore. The Nawab had been 'most chagrined' at this man's capture, and had allowed him to elude English justice, and escape into his territory. Pigot then moved that 'being desirous to avoid every occasion of giving disgust to the Nabob, and as circumstances must occur daily to increase his discontent whilst he remains here', he proposed 'that it be recommended to the Nabob to reside at Arcot', this being the most effective method to prevent these misunderstandings.

Mackay and Jourdan declared themselves against the question. Palmer, probably unable to follow Pigot's deeper intention, tried to explain his dissent by saying that 'the Nabob's residence here is attended with great advantages to the Company' and his removal would heighten jealousies. Floyer, now opening up like a sea-lawyer, wondered how the council would react to the Nawab's refusal to move with his family to Arcot. Would the board then forcibly remove him, or would it be happy with his refusal? Further, in an unguarded statement, Floyer revealed his hand when he gave it as his opinion 'that it is not his desire to remove from his present place of residence, where he has been for many years, I think is evident from his making no preparations, that I can hear of, for the removal of himself or any part of his family'. Floyer, if he had never been in communication with the Nawab, could not have claimed such knowledge with such definiteness. This resolution would alienate the Nawab, Floyer added, and increase the distance between him and the Company. Then he insinuated a possible link between the two previous resolutions that the Nawab had deliberately tried to divide the government, and that councillors were not to correspond with him, and this third one, aimed at removing him from Chepauk. Floyer tried, albeit clumsily, to hint that Pigot's personal motives lay behind this resolution.

Dalrymple said that the Nawab's removal to Arcot would be beneficial to his country, which was in deplorable condition. Russell went a step further and declared that 'Durbar politics' had been 'almost the only source of dissensions' at the council, which would continue so long as the Nawab was in the proximity. Brooke too showed his hand and stood against the question. Sir Robert pompously claimed to oppose the motion on the grounds of the special friendship that existed between the King and the Nawab, as well as 'his Highness's close connection with the Company and the English Nation in general'.

Pigot lost the motion at the usual 7 to 5. It had never been his intention to have the Nawab removed from Chepauk, since, as Floyer pointed out, he would not have been able to enforce it. If the Company had been unable to force William Bolts to leave India until 5 years had passed, and that too with subsequent litigation, Pigot was too realistic to imagine that a resolution would budge the Nawab from his palace. If the resolution had been adopted, it would have at best given Pigot a quite unusable and blunt weapon, while his real purpose, of demonstrating the dissenting councillors' proximity to the Nawab, would have been defeated.

At the next consultation, on Friday, 21 June 1776, Pigot again played another card. He tabled a letter to be sent to the Directors by a French ship, the *Etoille,* about to sail from Pondicherry. The first sentence of the third paragraph needs to be quoted here: 'Should your Honours have received the short letter we wrote you the 14th May, you will be surprised to find, that the whole of your President's conduct, during the time he was at Tanjore, has since been disapproved of, by a majority of Council'. All papers concerning Benfield and the council's consultations about his claims were attached, with details of the resolutions adopted and the votes cast by each member in each case. Pigot's opinions were presented in the 9th and 10th paragraphs. The former read, 'Your President is of opinion, that unless means are taken from Europeans from having connection and correspondence with the country government, in money matters as well as others, your affairs will ever be subject to embarrassment'. The latter reads, 'Your standing orders positively prohibit all money transactions with the country governments; but some Members of the Council think these orders no longer in force, being superseded by the Act of Parliament, which your President cannot admit'.

As soon as Pigot put the motion that the letter be dispatched to the Court of Directors, Sir Robert Fletcher objected. The proceedings of the last council had not yet been approved, and so this letter would be a partial representation, he said. Mackay felt that it would be 'fully sufficient and more candid, if the Board only tell the Honourable Court by this conveyance, that they have reason to believe representations will go from the Nabob, and from others, of the present disputes, they hope the Court of Directors will suspend their judgment till they see the whole proceedings, which will be sent them by the *Grenville*'.

Dawson was absent due to illness, and so Pigot lost the motion 7 to 4.

On Monday, 24 June 1776, Pigot informed his council that the letter, whose draft had been placed at the last consultation, had been dispatched, with 4 paragraphs added. In the first addendum, Pigot noted that although the majority of the council had dissented, he considered it incumbent on him to send it. If he had done anything wrong, he would acknowledge and rectify it. 'But I am persuaded I have done my duty, and my duty only', he added. The restoration of Tanjore had given 'infinite satisfaction' to its inhabitants. The Nawab would have acquiesced to this but had received ill counsel. The Nawab was aware that he was wholly dependent on the Company's goodwill but Pigot felt he 'should first become sensible of the impropriety of his conduct, in placing his trust in men who have as little regard for his interest as they have for ours'. In the last paragraph, Pigot firmly declared that he would go on as he had begun, 'strongly recommending every measure that appears to me proper, and resolutely maintaining that nothing shall be done, which in my opinion may involve your affairs in difficulty'.

Faced by this irrevocable move, Pigot's opponents gave vent to their rage. Sir Robert addressed a tedious and complex refutation to Dalrymple's minute of 10 June, the content of the refutation being essentially a repetition of points already made and some quibbling. Jourdan, Mackay, and Palmer, seemed to fall over each other in presenting through minutes the reasons why they had dissented with the president's previous resolutions. This was followed by a joint minute by 6 opponents, Stratton, Sir Robert, Jourdan, Palmer, Mackay, and Brooke, on the council's letter to Sir Edward, explaining Pigot's threatening to place a European guard over the Nawab, and of sending sepoys to rescue persons confined by the Nawab in his gardens. They said that they opposed these measures, and had added their names to the explanatory letter only out of candidness and respectfulness to the President. They thought it insulting to the Nawab to be told that a European guard would be set over him, and it was by way of a 'very dangerous authority' that Pigot had sent the sepoys on the mere report of the Head Hircurrah. Moving on to the governor's resolution to recommend the Nawab's removal from Chepauk to Arcot, because of the higher rates of crime in Madras, they found this incorrect. The Nawab had been in residence at Chepauk for long, and no complaints and charges by the Grand Jury had been preferred against his people. The great increase in the local population, leading to the Company's prosperity, would be reversed by the Nawab's removal, since his people would follow him back.

Sir Robert Fletcher now raised the issue of the second resolution of the consultation of 17 June, which he asked the board to rescind, since the governor had falsely used the words, 'the standing orders of the Company'. Since Dawson, who had been present then was now absent; the matter was shelved until he could attend consultations. Charles Floyer now took up his friends' minute opposing Pigot's explanation to Sir Edward. 'There are some parts of the President's vindication inserted in the reply of the Board to Sir Edward Hughes, which appear to encroach upon the fundamental civil rights of the British Constitution', Floyer propounded.

At consultation the next day, Tuesday, 25 June 1776, Sir Robert Fletcher tabled a letter dated 22 June from Colonel James Stuart, his second-in-command, asking that he be posted to the command of the fort and garrison at Tanjore, since this was, in his view, the most important post in the presidency, and he had a right to it by dint of his rank.

The council met next on Monday, 1 July 1776. Alexander Dalrymple had prepared an exhaustive refutation of all the arguments of the opposing party, and he delivered it, dealing sometimes in detail with the issues raised, and sometimes dismissing them in single sentences. Referring to Sir Robert Fletcher's contention about 'the universal law of nations', Dalrymple wondered what this 'law' meant. 'I have read many authors on the law of nations, but I never found the *universal* law Sir Robert Fletcher refers to', he said [his emphasis]. At best, 'The law of nations is the dictates of common sense and common justice; and one of the positions here laid down, that a country is liable to the assignment of its former government, is incompatible with either', Dalrymple found. 'The law of nations is a very vague line to decide on matters of property', Dalrymple said, since it had not dissuaded the Nawab from removing from the Raja's women their jewels, which had subsequently been pledged by the Nawab 'as a collateral security'. Considering that the Raja had been 'left without even the necessaries for a private family', and all his country under financial distress, the Nawab's manner of treating the Raja could be best shown by the latter's requesting a loan from his conqueror for the funerary expenses of a relation, Dalrymple said.

On Monday, 8 July 1776, Pigot refused to admit Sir Robert's motion for rescinding the resolution prohibiting councillors from corresponding with or visiting the Nawab. Pigot explained that he had accepted the rescinding of the resolution of 29 May regarding Benfield's claims, since it concerned private property. This not being the case with Sir Robert's resolution, he would not give it his consent. During his long years in service, Pigot had always known that the business of the board originated with the president, who was 'the properest person to lay before them such subjects as may require their consideration'. Making resolutions and then rescinding them could be 'productive of no good consequences to the Company's affairs'. Instead, it stamped 'the measures of Government with such an air of fickleness, as must be in the end detrimental to them'. This was extreme provocation, and Sir Robert told the secretary to 'take down everything that passes on this subject', since the matter about to be discussed by the board was 'of a most important nature'. The Directors' commission to the governor and his council dated 12 April 1775 was read out. Sir Robert ordered that the secretary note that Dalrymple had said that 'no resolution of a majority of the Board is an act of government, unless the Governor shall concur therein'. Dalrymple asked it be entered that these were not his words, and he would explain when needed.

Sir Robert, Mackay, Jourdan, and Palmer, placed that the president ought not to refuse the placing of Sir Robert's question, and that the resolution be rescinded. Floyer agreed, and Brooke changed sides, basing himself on the 'constitution of the service', which he felt required the president to allow Sir Robert's question. Stratton agreed, following which Pigot minuted his opinion: 'The President here declares, that from the constitution of the service he is well convinced no person but himself can agitate a question at the Board; that he has ever known that right vested solely in the President, who must always be supposed to be the best judge of what questions are, and are not fit for the benefit of the Company's affairs; and who, if a question should be proposed, which to him should appear productive of bad consequences, has an undoubted right to prevent the question being put'. This having been said, Dalrymple tore into Sir Robert, going so far as to indirectly call him a liar for having said that he had never indulged in 'Durbar politics' when he had variously advised the Nawab in such matters. Dalrymple addressed each point raised by Sir Robert, demolishing them with relish, until Sir Robert declared to the council that 'Mr Dalrymple's minute, now delivered in, can only tend to perplex the reader', and it merited no answer from him.

The following day, Tuesday, 9 July 1776, the 7 opponents together delivered a minute against Lord Pigot's actions and statements in the council. He had adjourned council against the opinion of the majority; he had refused to put a question that many wished to move in the civil department; he had refused to allow a question for the rescinding of a previous resolution to be moved; and he had asserted that a resolution of the majority of the board could not be executed without his concurrence. The 7 signatories to the minute said, 'we think it incumbent upon us to express the astonishment, as well as the concern, we feel at hearing such doctrines from the President'. They declared, 'in the strongest terms, that such claims are incompatible with the rights of the other members of this Government, and that many dangerous consequences might ensue from the admission of such unconstitutional and ... arbitrary opinions'. 'We know', they said, 'that the Government is vested in a majority of the Board, and that that majority may exist whether the President be of it or not'. 'We know our rights', they asserted, 'but we sincerely hope never to be driven to the painful necessity of exerting them'. This was of course a threat, by means of which they took matters into their own hands, for they proceeded to declare as rescinded Pigot's second resolution of 17 June, 'legally, though not in usual form'. Dalrymple, who had been named in the minute as Pigot's supporter in his alleged excesses at council, minuted that his reading of the commission of government from the Directors showed that the council was to help the governor manage the Company's affairs, rather than 'to manage the Company's affairs without the Governor'.

The discussion having turned to Colonel James Stuart's application for appointment to the command of the fort and garrison of Tanjore, Dalrymple noted that he had been ordered to Vellore, to relieve Colonel Lang, who had been posted to Madras. Instead, Stuart had not only disobeyed orders but also broken with military tradition in determining on his own which command he was best suited to, 'a point on which he has no right to deliberate'. In fact, Sir Robert Fletcher had posted Stuart to Vellore on the ground that it was militarily more important and a battalion of the first regiment was stationed there. Dalrymple agreed with Stuart that Tanjore was very important, 'but its importance is not military, but political'. The Tanjore garrison was small, with 184 Europeans and 3 battalions of sepoys of which 2 were scattered through the kingdom to help the Raja collect his revenue. Vellore had 544 Europeans and 1900 sepoys, who were stationed there to ward off Haider Ali. To the reader it will be clear that the point of the discussion was neither military nor political, but monetary. The sepoys, who were engaged in helping bring in the grain, had to be controlled by someone familiar to the opposition. Stuart had not applied without the secret connivance of Sir Robert, for Sir Robert took on Dalrymple, asserting that the Tanjore garrison ought to include at least one battalion of European infantry, 100 European artillery, and 4 battalions of sepoys, of 1000 men each. The other forts in Tanjore would require additional independent garrisons.

Pigot presented the board with a letter from the Raja of Tanjore, in which Thuljaji had written that he had heard talk of the appointment of Colonel Stuart to Tanjore. He urged the governor to allow Colonel Harper to continue for a while longer. When the question was put to vote, Mackay was for Stuart being sent to Tanjore, as were Palmer, Jourdan, Brooke, Floyer, Sir Robert, and Stratton. Pigot was of the opinion that Stuart should be stationed in Vellore, and he made a pointed reference to Sir Robert's impaired health 'and other occupations', which kept him from reporting to the governor on the state of the army and the fortifications at

Trichinopoly and other places. Colonel Stuart, as the next in seniority should have striven to fill this gap than seek to be sent to Tanjore.

Stuart's posting to Tanjore was carried, 7 to 4.

Matters thence proceeded as usual until the consultation on Tuesday, 19 August 1776. At this meeting, Lord Pigot earnestly urged the board to consent to Claud Russell's going to Tanjore to superintend matters there, 'the Rajah and the country being in great distress'. The opposition would not agree. Jourdan said that Russell, with Dalrymple, having been placed on the Circuit by the Company's orders, would have to leave Madras on 31 August. Sir Robert being ill, the motion against Russell's going to Tanjore was carried 6 to 4. Pigot was infuriated by the defiance of his board, and said that he would not issue Colonel Stuart any instructions to proceed to Tanjore unless Russell was permitted to go as well. Charles Floyer moved that the council take up for discussion the issue of the instructions to be given to Stuart. Pigot refused to allow the question, upon which Stratton said that the council would vote at 11 the next morning on whether the president had the right to refuse every question put to the board.

The next day, Tuesday, 20 August 1776, George Stratton earnestly requested Pigot to allow Floyer's question to be moved, since it was consistent with the rules of the service. Pigot refused. The board, with the exception of Pigot and his supporters, proceeded to the matter as though there was no governor, and by majority agreed to the letter of instructions to Colonel Stuart.

The following Thursday, 22 August 1776, the 6 members in opposition to Pigot handed in a minute in which they denied 'that the concurrence of the President is necessary to constitute an act of government', and declared Pigot's act 'unconstitutional and illegal'. Pigot remained steadfast in his refusal. He too addressed the board, warning them against proceeding further in this matter. Stratton, Brooke, Floyer, Jourdan, Palmer, and Mackay, then minuted their opinions that in the case of the governor's refusing to sign the instructions to Colonel Stuart and the letter to Colonel Harper (telling him of Stuart's appointment), the same should be signed by the secretary to the council, on the authority of the majority. Pigot read this minute, and said he would not order the secretary to sign these letters.

George Stratton and Henry Brooke, as the senior member of council, then took up the matter and wrote a brief letter authorising the secretary, Mr Sullivan, to sign the instructions to Stuart and Harper 'by order of council'. Pigot rose from his place and snatched it as soon as the two most senior members of the opposition had signed it. He then charged them 'of being guilty of an act subversive of the authority of Government, and tending to introduce anarchy, in the signing orders to the Secretary to give instructions to Colonel Stuart, which have not been approved and passed by the President and Council'. Stratton and Brooke denied the charge and minuted the manner in which Pigot had snatched the paper even as the other members of the majority were waiting to add their signatures to it.

Pigot next ordered Stratton and Brooke to withdraw. Jourdan, sensing it was time to take a break, moved for an adjournment until 10 the next morning, which was seconded by Mackay. Pigot was no longer in the mood to listen. He moved the resolution that Stratton and Brooke be suspended from the service until the decision of the Directors was made known. With Stratton and Brooke removed the opposition had fewer votes than Pigot's party, since Pigot, as governor, enjoyed, in addition to his own vote, a 'casting vote' to decide matters. Therefore, the resolution to suspend Stratton and Brooke was carried 5 to 4, due to Pigot's exercise of his casting vote.

The council met again the following morning, Friday, 23 August 1776, with the addition of Richard Lathom, who was appointed chief at Cuddalore. The opposition did not attend, despite having been formally summoned. Instead, they sent in a written protest through Charles Bromley, a Notary Public, to the secretary. The 7 who signed the protest, declared themselves the majority of the council, and objected to 'the unexampled outrage offered to the constitution, and the arbitrary behaviour towards two of our members by an illegal attempt to suspend them, in order by a trick to gain a majority, are of the opinion that the public safety is in danger by the conduct of Lord Pigot'. They further proclaimed themselves 'as the legal representatives of the Honourable Company under this Presidency', whom all Company's servants would follow. The 'evident illegality' of the summons, from which the names of two of their fellows were left out, had made it inconsistent with their duty to the Company to attend the council.

The council met again in the afternoon when it was discovered that copies of the same letter of protest had been passed to the officer of the Main Guard and to other officers of the garrison, to Sir Edward Hughes, and to Captain Webb of the East Indiaman *London*. Pigot and his council, who had previously decided to give some time to the opposition to calm down, regarded this as a treasonous proceeding. Now they resolved to suspend Mackay, Jourdan, Palmer, and Floyer, and to bring Sir Robert Fletcher to court-martial, passing on the command of the troops of the presidency to Colonel James Stuart.

At this point, the secretaries considered it necessary to enter a minute explaining their dilemma. They were subordinate employees of the

Company, and wrote, 'It is with much concern that we observe the secession of so many members of the Council, and the steps which they have pursued to exert the authority of Government'. Since they were of the opinion that only the council could conduct the government, and that there was no council minus the president, they felt their duty lay in obedience to the council assembled by the president, Lord Pigot. Accordingly, letters were dispatched, that to Sir Robert carrying the sense of *déjà vu* in that he was charged for the second time in his life with exciting mutiny and sedition among the troops. Lieutenant Pendergrast, the Town Adjutant, gave Stuart his letter of appointment and Stuart promised to have copies issued to all garrisons under the presidency immediately.

In the meantime, the opposing camp had also met in council, outside the fort, and sent the letter of protest to Lord Pigot. They also wrote to Warren Hastings and his council, relating how matters stood at Madras. At their next meeting the same afternoon, Friday, 23 August 1776, they resolved to meet regularly and watch over the public safety. They further resolved that 'the first concern that comes under our consideration is that the fortress and garrison of Fort St George be in our hands, and under our command, as the legal representatives of the East-India Company'. The second concern was Lord Pigot, who had 'dared to violate every law which ought to bind a servant who has sworn fidelity to the Company'. Uncertain of what further excesses he would commit, they considered it their 'duty', if necessary 'to arrest his person'. Colonel James Stuart seems to have been acceptable to both parties, as the officer most capable of commanding troops, given that Sir Robert was seriously ill. He was ordered to arrest any person, including Lord Pigot, who dared obstruct the execution of the majority council's orders. Notices carrying this message were sent to the officers commanding various stations in the Madras presidency. Major Matthew Horne was in charge of St Thomas' Mount, and he later played an important role in the circumstances leading up to Lord Pigot's death.

CHAPTER ELEVEN

THE 'ARREST' AND CONFINEMENT OF LORD PIGOT

Pigot's council met for the last time in the council-room on the evening of Sunday, 24 August 1776. Present were Dalrymple, Stone, Russell, Lathom, Colonel Stuart, and the secretaries, Sullivan, Baine, and Oakeley. This was not a consultation but a meeting, and it was over by 8 o'clock, when Lord Pigot went out in his chaise with Colonel Stuart to the Company's Garden-house, where they were to have supper. It later emerged during trial in England that Paul Benfield had placed a trusted servant, Edward Dempsey, to be present always at the orders of Colonel Stuart with a chaise and horses, from before the usurpation. Dempsey received his final orders from Colonel Stuart on 23 August to be present at a particular spot with the chaise and horses. When about half a mile from the fort, Pigot's chaise was stopped by Lieutenant-Colonel James Eidingtoun, the Adjutant-General, who had with him a troop of sepoys. At the same time Captain Arthur Lysaght came up to Lord Pigot's side of the chaise and, aiming a pistol at Pigot's chest, proclaimed him prisoner. At the same time, Eidingtoun drew his sword and placed the governor under arrest. Pigot was too astounded to move, until Colonel Stuart roughly seized his arm, and told him, 'Go out, Sir'. Pigot was taken to Benfield's chaise, which was positioned nearby. An orderly sergeant emerged from Benfield's chaise and Lord Pigot entered it, accompanied by Captain Arthur Lysaght, who still held his pistol, and as the chaise passed the sepoy-guard at the Company's Garden-house, Lysaght warned Pigot not to call out, since this was a frequented road, and many people were about. A little later Lysaght drew down the blinds, and informed Lord Pigot that he was being conveyed to St Thomas' Mount, where he would be given into Major Matthew Horne's custody.

Russell, Dalrymple, and Lathom followed Lord Pigot on foot soon after he had left with Colonel Stuart. Halfway to the Garden-house, they saw Sir Robert's, Mackay's, and Stratton's carriages, making their way towards the fort. Surprised by this, Russell and his friends rushed to the

Company's Garden-house to tell Lord Pigot of this development but found that Pigot had not reached the Garden-house. There they waited uneasily, until informed by Baine, the deputy secretary, who came out on horseback, that the council-room was occupied by the opposition. Learning a little while later that Pigot had been made prisoner and taken to the Mount, Russell made his way back to the fort, where, as second in council and, therefore, in command of the garrison in Pigot's absence, he ordered the Main Guard to stand to arms. The officer commanding the Main Guard, Captain Adair, hesitated. Even as Russell was speaking to him, Colonel Stuart came up and told him to go to the council-room. Russell refused to obey Stuart because Stuart was under his command rather than the other way round. Words passed between them, and Stuart called for orderlies to seize Russell. Restrained by Colonels Stuart and Eidingtoun, and Captain Barclay, Russell was forced into the council-room where he found the opposition in a meeting. Jourdan was acting as secretary, and he took down Stuart's statement with respect to Russell. Russell was asked if he acknowledged the authority of the new council, to which he replied that he did not. George Stratton then announced Russell's suspension from the service, after which he was allowed to go home.

Major Horne took charge of Lord Pigot's person and it was at Horne's home that he spent the rest of life except the last few weeks. He was given the best room, 32 feet long by 18 wide, and the use of the common hall and verandah, which he shared with Horne's family. His servants used an adjoining closet, which also served as a lumber-store. Major Horne used an adjoining passage, into which a door from this room opened, as a writing-room.

In the meantime, the new council took over management of the Company's business in Madras. At their first meeting in the fort, at 9.30 pm on Saturday, 24 August 1776, they acknowledged Colonel Stuart's having arrested Pigot as per their instructions. Stuart had carried his duplicitous plan out to high effect. In 1778 Andrew Stuart, sought to defend his brother, James' conduct, to the Directors and the people in general, through the publication in December 1778, of *A Letter to the Directors Respecting the Conduct of Brigadier-General James Stuart at Madras*. In this apologetic plea claiming his brother's innocence, Andrew arrives at some untenable conclusions. As the events of 23-24 August 1776 unfolded, Stuart had to choose between obeying Pigot, recognising his authority as the governor, which he was, and George Stratton, who claimed the governorship through usurpation. Andrew Stuart does not address Colonel Stuart's application to be posted to Tanjore instead of Vellore, for no reason other than that the former was a place of great importance. Further, Andrew Stuart insists that his brother was on the most remote terms with Pigot, having been invited by the governor to sup with him on 23 August, and breakfast and dinner the following day. To these invitations by Pigot, if indeed that is what they were, Andrew claimed that James had added the condition that the conversation at the table was strictly to be only business, which was actually very bad form. Sergeant Shaw's report to the council on 30 August 1776 mentions Pigot as saying of Colonel Stuart that he had invited himself to supper on the night of 24 August, and gave him up on false pretences. George Shaw was then the Sergeant of the 7th Battalion of Sepoys.

Pigot had every right to ask the officer he mistakenly believed to be the commander-in-chief of the army, to his table if for nothing else but the discussion of business. James Stuart had decided to support the majority, and having pledged his allegiance to them, he took their orders surreptitiously on the evening of 23 August to arrest Pigot. A letter Stuart had written at 7 am on 23 August 1776, and which he later presented to Stratton and his council, evidences this. In this letter, Stuart had sought Pigot's permission to peruse such portions of the records of consultations leading up to the discord, as would help guide his future actions. To Stratton and council Colonel Stuart later said that he had awaited Pigot's consent to this request from 9 am until 1 pm. Meeting Pigot again at dinner, he renewed his request, but Pigot remained evasive. On this, Stuart told Pigot that the latter was within his rights to refuse access to the records, and Stuart knew his duty and would do it. This should have warned Pigot, who must have already been wary of Stuart because of his proximity to Stratton's group. Perhaps it was for this reason that Pigot refused him access to the records of consultations. One wonders if this was a ruse on Stuart's part, for, given his rank, position in Madras society, and access to councillors, he must have had nearly complete information on all that had passed in council. Stuart stated that he nonetheless waited until Pigot and his council met again in the evening, but in vain. Although appointed commander-in-chief, he was not allowed to go through the records.

Andrew passed over his brother's expertise in dissimulation, for he must have dissimulated well enough to realise that the best way to take Pigot was to pretend to accompany him to supper at the Company's Garden-house on 24 August. Andrew eulogises James' decision that Pigot had to be taken with as little bloodshed as possible. However laudatory this condescension may have appeared to Andrew, it was a straightforward case of betrayal. Russell deposed that he had heard Stuart say to Pigot as they got into the latter's chaise that he was looking to his Lordship 'for a cast', or a plan – to secure Madras from the usurpers with whom James Stuart was already conspiring. In fact, Stuart rode in Pigot's chaise to keep him from suspicion, and changed colour as soon as the arrest had been affected, when he roughly pushed Pigot out of his chaise. Similarly, Andrew Stuart did not refer to James Stuart's connection with Paul Benfield, whose servant's help was obtained, to capture Pigot. Surely, James Stuart had socialised with Benfield, since the latter was the centre of almost all the unscrupulous money deals in the presidency, to have availed of his assistance in seizing the governor.

Further evidence of the involvement of the military comes from the declaration by the new council on Sunday, 25 August 1776, of a half-*batta* to the garrison of Fort St George. The commanding officers of the two sepoy battalions of this garrison, Lieutenant-Colonel Eidingtoun and Captain Barclay, had been won over by George Stratton's party, and Sir Robert Fletcher ordered the European portion of the garrison out of the fort on other duties on the evening of 24 August, to ensure complete obedience.

The new council proclaimed George Stratton, falsely under the authority of the Company, for they had no right to do so, President of the Council and Governor of Fort St George. They composed a long address for the information of all why they had considered it necessary to 'remove' Lord Pigot. Announcing themselves the only legal representatives of the Honourable Company on the Coromandel Coast, they declared the annulment of the powers of Lord Pigot, while his supporters, Claud Russell, Alexander Dalrymple, and John Maxwell Stone, were issued orders of suspension from the service. A General Order was issued at 10 pm on the same date, for circulation to all subordinate factories and garrisons. It condemned the 'illegal, violent, and unconstitutional, conduct of Lord Pigot', aided by Messrs Russell, Dalrymple, and Stone, 'in breaking through the positive orders of the Company', which had compelled the new council to arrest Lord Pigot, and suspend the others, in preference to the appointment of George Stratton as the new president and governor of the council.

That same evening Colonel Stuart also issued his orders to Major Horne on how he was to treat Lord Pigot. Lord Pigot had been arrested, Stuart wrote, 'for the public safety of this settlement at this alarming crisis'. Horne had 'charge and custody' of Lord Pigot until further orders from 'the legal Civil Government' were received. Lord Pigot was to be constantly under the observation of Horne or an officer deputed by him, and Pigot 'was not to be permitted to carry arms, nor to correspond or converse upon matters which in any way concern civil or military business; and in case of refusal to conform to these orders, the letters are to be stopped, and the person dismissed with whom such conversation is held'. Horne was to remember that Pigot was 'to be treated with every mark of attention and respect suited to the situation which the present exigency makes a necessity'. 'His Lordship's family and servants', Stuart wrote to Horne, 'were to be permitted to visit him, but the number limited, and at your discretion'.

Since the government could not run without secretarial assistance, and the secretaries had fled following these tumultuous events, summonses were issued to them. Oakeley and Sullivan reported for duty at 6 am on 25 August 1776, and presented a minute, in which they wrote that 'without taking upon ourselves to judge the propriety of the measure, which we are clear is no part of our province, we determined, as zealous and faithful servants of the Company, to acknowledge and obey the orders of the present Government; being satisfied in our minds, that, by such conduct only in their servants, the Company's affairs can be preserved in order, until the Court of Directors shall have signified their pleasure upon the late proceedings'.

Another letter, of great significance, was dispatched to Major Horne on 25 August. The letter informed Horne that Russell had tried to get the Main Guard at the fort to stand to arms, and it was possible that Pigot's other friends might attempt to help him escape or circulate papers under his signature, which Horne was to look out for and prevent. The last sentence of the letter was very ominous: '*As your last resource, in any attempt to rescue Lord Pigot, his life must answer for it; and this you are to signify to him*' [my emphasis]. Of equal significance was the postscript, which said '*The Nabob has been applied to for a party of horse to be put under your command, and they are for the purpose of conveying quick intelligence to us, and for such other purposes as you shall think necessary*' [my emphasis]. 'We trust', added the new governor and council, 'to your making such a disposition of the force under your command, as to prevent the possibility of a surprise, or the success of any attempt that may be made by Lord Pigot and his associates'.

Meanwhile Edward Monckton and his family had moved, as did Lord Pigot's family, and Pigot's friends, Russell, Dalrymple, Lathom, and, later, Stone, to General Lawrence's House, a large dwelling on the Mount, situated around 400 yards away from Major Horne's home. Pigot applied on 25 August to Major Horne to be allowed to have supper with his family at their house, and to 'remain there', guarded by an officer and soldiers. Pigot offered that the officer should always remain in his company.

Nonetheless, the council rejected this, and notified Horne that it was not advisable to allow Lord Pigot to shift elsewhere.

The Nawab paid a ceremonial visit to Fort St George on 25 August, where he was received with great pomp by the new governor and council, since, as Dalrymple later put it in his report to the Court of Directors, 'his gold has the credit of being the instrument which brought about these events'. He also provided 12 horsemen, of whom 6 were stationed within the fort, and 6 at the Mount, under Horne's command. This was a curious and unprecedented reversal, for the Nawab's men were clearly more reliable for the new council than European troops. On 21 July 1776, an anonymous letter in Persian was found in the fort-house, in which the writer claimed, 'I can procure with ease many proofs in writing of the assistance given to the Nabob by Members of the Council, and I shall in presence of his Lordship make a public declaration of what sums have been received by these gentlemen, on condition that the Members of the Company in Europe shall give me a Cowle [Remission] granting me their protection'. The same writer described the Nawab's declaring publicly in his durbar, 'Who is Lord Pigot? I will not condescend to see him and I will spend Crores to get him turned out of his government; my sons even shall not be permitted to visit him'. Similarly, Amir-ul-Umra was reported by the same anonymous scribe as having publicly said that 'he had been at great pains to form a Majority in his favour of the Members of the Board', and Lord Pigot 'would be shortly turned out of the Council Room'. The Nawab was initially agreeable to Lord Pigot's orders relating to Tanjore, but was advised by English gentlemen 'that the King of England and the Parliament were his friends, and could prosecute the Company for their orders'. Convinced of the truth of this, and recalling the success that his ambassador to King James' Court, John Macpherson had achieved, the Nawab grew 'bold and refractory', asserted the anonymous scribe.

Philip Dormer Stanhope wrote in his *Genuine Memoirs of Asiaticus* about William Randall, who had immigrated to Madras from England 'under an assumed appearance', and 'by forged letters of recommendation' had obtained a commission in the Nawab's forces, as aide-de-camp to Amir-ul-Umra, the Nawab's younger son. These letters of recommendation presented him as an unfortunate gentleman of good family, who had held a commission in the British Army, which he had been obliged to resign due to his debts. Despite the Company's preventive efforts, there were many like him in the service of local princes in those days, and Stanhope wrote that Randall wanted the command of a regiment of the Nawab's horse, which was not forthcoming. Following Lord Pigot's fall, Randall decided to offer his services to Stratton and his council, telling them in a private interview that Amir-ul-Umra had 'repeatedly offered him considerable sums of money, if he would assassinate Lord Pigot'. Amir-ul-Umra had particularly pointed out as a means of assassination a pet tiger, which Pigot would grow familiar with and caress, until one night when it would be replaced by a ferocious one that would devour him. 'Strange and inconsistent as this story must appear', Stanhope wrote, 'it was greedily listened to, and the impostor was caressed by gentlemen, who in their cooler moments, would have treated the improbable tale and its inventor with equal contempt'. Amir-ul-Umra also seems to have said in Randall's presence that he would cause Coomera, Benfield's *dubash*, to poison Pigot's food. Sometimes Amir-ul-Umra would take up a pistol and looking meaningfully at Randall, say that it was 'physic' for somebody. In the event, these stories of the Nawab's son's alleged plans for assassinating Pigot gained wide circulation through affidavits, and Randall was dismissed from the Nawab's service but with full arrears of pay, and his voyage to Europe was funded by the council. Randall seems to have been a former soldier, discharged with disgrace from the British Army, who inherited some money from his father and travelled to India in the guise of a former officer.

The usurpation did not have universal acceptance among the civil and military officers. Captain Wood, the Town Major, had objected to Colonel Stuart's orders on behalf of Stratton and council, and been arrested. Lord Pigot later entrusted him with the conveyance to England, of his narrative of the usurpation. Charles Mordaunt, who had joined the service in 1765 and was Senior Merchant in 1776, wrote to the new council that he regarded Lord Pigot the rightful president and governor, and to obey anyone else was contrary to his allegiance. Mordaunt was at once suspended. Others, including Eyles Irwin (Writer 1767; Junior Merchant 1776), Joseph Revell (Writer 1769; Factor 1774), and George Wynch (Writer 1772), suffered the same fate. Following the attempt to seize Lord Pigot for the second time and send him to Chingleput, as described below, 37 employees of the Company presented a memorandum of protest to the council. Their letter began, 'We the under-written servants of the Honourable East-India Company, having taken into our most serious consideration the recent revolution in the Government of this place, and fearing lest it should be represented to out Honourable Masters, that this measure has been effected with the concurrence of the civil servants, a doctrine which we understand has been industriously propagated in this Settlement, do hold it in our indispensable duty thus publicly to protest an action, which appears directly contrary to the commissions granted by the Court of Directors to the Right Honourable Lord Pigot, and totally subversive of the constitution of this Government'. They had written this memorandum 'lest our silence should be construed into an assent so totally repugnant to our feelings as men'. They acknowledged only Lord Pigot as the rightfully appointed president and governor. The matter had been made more serious by the obvious involvement of the military in the sordid dealings, which underlay these changes: 'As Members of a civil government', they said, 'we cannot but consider an appeal to military force a matter of the most dangerous tendency'. They chose to continue working in their respective stations, especially considering that they denied the 'legality of the measure' by which Pigot had been overthrown, and 'the conduct of the military on that occasion', since their loyalty was to the Company. On 13 September 1776, Robert Duncan Munro, posted at Chingleput as Paymaster and Storekeeper, addressed a letter to 'Mr George Stratton, who styles himself President and Governor of Fort St George', which quickly earned him suspension from the service when he refused to retract. Captain Tonyn had moved on 30 August 1776 to the Mount, as ordered, but his troops too were reported to be marching towards Madras and were that day at Vandalur, which had not been ordered. The council regarded this with great suspicion, and ordered Major Horne to arrest Tonyn if his actions seemed mistrustful. Tonyn was the officer assigned by Pigot with the task of seizing the *Dubbeer*, Naroo Pundit from the Nawab's territory, where he had been removed to keep him from disclosing the accounts of the kingdom to Pigot. Captain Arthur Lysaght, on the other hand, was rewarded with the post of Town Major at Fort St George, Lieutenant Hoare appointed Fort Adjutant in place of Pendergrast, and Lieutenant-Colonel Nixon posted to Vellore. Nixon seems to have been sympathetic to Pigot's cause, for Horne, ever the spy, informed the council on 31 August 1776 that he had called on Monckton that morning on his way to Vellore.

On 27 August 1776, the council met at 8 am, when George Stratton informed the board that 'he had reason to apprehend there was some tampering with the troops at the Mount, by persons in the interest of Lord Pigot and his associates'. Claud Russell's attempt at getting the guard at the fort to stand to arms on the night of 24 August, the board agreed, showed the danger of allowing Lord Pigot to continue living at the Mount, and playing upon the allegiance of the troops there. The council unanimously resolved to remove him to the fortress of Chingleput, 36 miles from Madras, where he would be housed in keeping with his status. It was a salubrious place, and his removal would be most convenient since it would place him far beyond any possibility of rousing the public emotion at Madras. There Pigot was to stay during the period of his arrest, by which presumably was meant until the arrival of orders from the Directors. Stratton wrote to the Chairman of the Company on 21 September that Pigot had made such wild remarks as that if he were to be set free, or could escape, he would go to the fort, and if his government were re-established, would hang Colonel Stuart, Lieutenant-Colonel Eidingtoun, and Captain Lysaght. These remarks worried Stratton and his council, as they did the Nawab, 'which I privately say to you, and in the utmost confidence', wrote Stratton to the Chairman (in 1777 and 1778, Sir George Wombwell), 'will oblige us to send him to you our constituents; for I say to you, that public business cannot properly be carried on while he remains in the country'. Major William Cooke was appointed to the command of the garrison at Chingleput on 27 August 1776, while Colonel Stuart was empowered 'to take any further measures you may judge necessary for the security of his Lordship's person'. Stuart was told that the council was 'extremely desirous to avoid every chance either of public disturbance *or risk to Lord Pigot's life*' [my emphasis].

At the same time, Lieutenant-Colonel Harper wrote from Tanjore that the Raja wished to inspect how the repairs on the banks of the Cauvery were proceeding, and to make a small circuit through his kingdom, for which he had requested Harper's escort along with 2 companies of sepoys. It was probably not surprising that Stratton and his council wrote to Harper that everything in Madras 'was in the most perfect tranquillity', and that he was to stay in Tanjore, and not accompany the Raja. Harper was, also unsurprisingly, given the task of withdrawing within gunshot of his garrison as many sepoys of his 2 battalions as could be spared from the work they were engaged in, viz, helping the Raja collect his grain. The council had probably hitherto reasoned that the only arms in Tanjore were English, and so withdrawing the troops on revenue collection duties would allow the Nawab's forces to operate. They were unpleasantly surprised to find on 4 September 1776 that several of the Tanjore fortresses had quite effective artillery. It appeared that when the military storekeeper asked Lord Pigot if there were not a great number of cannon in the kingdom of Tanjore, the governor had disagreed and said that these could not be of much use, instructing the storekeeper to send cannon and shot to Tanjore. An indent received by the military storekeeper from Lieutenant-Colonel Harper on 13 August revealed that Tanjore had at least 118 guns of iron and brass, of various calibres, and 5 mortars. Stratton and his council were astounded, for this added an unknown factor into their dealings with the Nawab.

The dispositions having been made, a secret letter was dispatched to Major Horne, telling him that Lieutenant-Colonel Eidingtoun, the

Adjutant-General, would receive custody of Lord Pigot that night, 27 August 1776, 'without giving unnecessary alarm to Lord Pigot's family', and would have him transported to Chingleput. This had become necessary, Horne was told, because some incriminating letters had been seized, which showed that Lord Pigot's friends had been tampering with the troops at the Mount.

Edward Monckton was getting into bed, between 11 pm and midnight, when Lord Pigot's servants aroused him. Lord Pigot was fighting with the soldiers, they said, and a chaise had been readied for him, with provisions and an armed guard in a great cloak. The chaise was to carry Pigot to Gingee, they said. Monckton and Lathom dressed hurriedly and ran to Major Horne's house, where they found Dalrymple already arrived. They saw that there indeed was a chaise at the gate, and Lord Pigot was standing on the verandah of Horne's house with Lieutenant Gibson, who commanded his guard, beside him. Horne and Eidingtoun were standing at the foot of the steps.

It appeared that Eidingtoun had arrived at the Mount around 10.30 pm, and sent a note to Horne informing him of this. Horne replied that the present time was the best, upon which Eidingtoun went to Horne's house and, reaching there at a few minutes past 11 pm, found Horne walking on the verandah with Pigot and Lieutenant Gibson of the artillery. Eidingtoun handed to Horne Stuart's orders for the custody of Lord Pigot. Horne and Eidingtoun then went up to Pigot and told him that his removal had been ordered. Eidingtoun gave Pigot a few minutes to put together some things he would need. Dalrymple, Monckton, and Lathom, arrived at the scene within minutes of this.

Horne said to Pigot, who had obviously protested this cloak-and-dagger business, 'My lord, it does not signify, my orders are positive, and I must obey'. Pigot wanted to know where he was to be carried. Monckton told him they were going to take him to Gingee. Lieutenant-Colonel Eidingtoun said to Pigot, 'My lord, I am not at liberty to inform you where you are going', and to Monckton, 'I can assure you that he is not going to Gingee, but to a place of safety'. At this point, a guard of European artillerymen clattered into the garden. At once Pigot addressed them in so loud a voice that it carried to houses 300 yards away. He knew many of them, he said to the artillerymen, for he had fought with them at the siege of Madras. For his role in saving Madras during the siege, Pigot said that he had been thanked by the King and raised to baronet, and then to the Irish peerage. He either would stay at the Mount, or be conveyed by them into the custody of the Commodore, Sir Edward Hughes, to seek the protection of the King's flag. Else, they should place him in his own fort, where he would know how to act. Under no condition, Pigot declared, would he go with that traitor, Eidingtoun, who, notwithstanding that he had received his commission from Pigot, had stopped him at night on the highway, with a loaded pistol, like an assassin. He was willing to be killed by his soldiers if he was guilty, Pigot said, than allow himself to be dragged thence. Eidingtoun's report noted that Pigot had used bad language and cast aspersions upon the council, calling them rebels and 'damned rascals', and threatening to hang every one of them. According to Eidingtoun, Pigot had pointed to him and called him one of the rascals, like Stuart, who had made him prisoner after accepting the command of the army from him, and promising to do everything he was ordered to. Carrying on in this manner for a while, Lord Pigot threw his arms around Horne's neck, and asked him to consider whether as an officer he would allow Pigot to be dragged from his house in such a shameful manner. To Pigot's harangue, Monckton and Dalrymple added their own, addressing the troops, and telling them of the illegality of the manner in which Pigot's government had been usurped.

Realising that the situation had got out of hand, Eidingtoun turned to the artillerymen and said, 'I am sure you will obey your commanding officer'. Getting no response, he repeated himself. The troops stood mute and still. Eidingtoun then drew Horne aside and briefly conferred with him. Horne then approached Lord Pigot and said to him, 'My lord, if your lordship will promise to remain quiet here tonight, I will be answerable for your person to Colonel Eidingtoun, till we can have further orders from the fort'. On Pigot's assent, all withdrew.

There are two interesting but brief digressions here. The first is that Eidingtoun was also involved in usury. His widow, Anne, moved court in England, claiming the repayment of the principal and interest on 15,350 pagodas lent to the Nawab on 31 December 1786 by her husband. The Carnatic Commissioners in charge of settling the debts of the Nawab granted her these dues on 25 November 1810. The second was that there was reportedly a European in the chaise (again, Benfield's), which had been readied to take Pigot to Chingleput, who, upon things quieting down, emerged from the chaise and emptied the pan of his pistols, reportedly saying that he had no further need for them that night. Was this European, who had been seen by many of the locals who had gathered, Dempsey, Benfield's servant, or someone else, possibly Captain Lysaght again?

Visiting Pigot the next day, Wednesday, 28 August 1776, Monckton found him hoarse due to the night's shouting. However, Pigot gave him the information that the council intended to send him to England on the *Grenville*, which was to sail in the latter half of September. Sir Robert

Fletcher, who had advised Pigot's removal by the *Greenwich*, which sailed a month later, and just before the ships from England were expected, had scotched this plan. Lord Pigot had written to the Commodore, Sir Edward, on 27 August 1776 seeking the protection of the King's flag. Sir Edward, on receipt of this petition, went to see Lord Pigot, and dispatched a stern letter to the council at 12 noon on 28 August, informing them of this development, and demanding in His Majesty's name that they issue orders to Major Horne to deliver into his custody the person of Lord Pigot. Hughes added that he was at Horne's house, awaiting these orders to Major Horne.

With the Commodore now on Pigot's side, with the weight of the King's authority, the council relented partly. They wrote to him that it had never been their intention to remove him to Gingee. 'We resolved this morning to make your Lordship an offer', the council wrote, 'which we now do, of removing to any settlement on the coast, that you shall give preference to, where there is a Chief and Council, provided that you pledge your word of honour to remain within the … settlement, until the Company's pleasure' was known. If Pigot agreed to this, the council would promise to 'order the best house in such settlement to be prepared for your reception, and that every necessary be furnished you at the Company's expense, and that every respect and attention to be paid to your person'. Hoping that Pigot would choose instead to leave for England to plead his case, they added 'if your Lordship should prefer embarking for Europe in one of the Company's ships, we will order every accommodation in our power'. This letter was sent to Major Horne, who reported at 7 am the next morning that the letter had been received at 11 pm the previous night, and given to Lord Pigot who had read it aloud without commenting on it. Sir Edward Hughes had spent the day and night, with Pigot, at Horne's house. He seems to have spent the next day (29 August) there as well, handing in an official letter to Horne when he had to leave for the fort, seeking his guarantee that Horne would not hand over Pigot to anyone until Hughes returned. A major reason for the Commodore's support for Pigot, which would continue right up to the latter's death, must have been the fact that Pigot's younger brother was a Vice-Admiral of the White and on his way up the naval hierarchy.

The same morning (29 August) the council received a note from Major Horne, saying that as Lord Pigot had not been denied the use of pen, paper and ink, he, having heard that a ship was scheduled to sail to Bengal, requested permission to write to the Governor-General and Council about his situation, and requested the assistance of some of his friends for the purpose. The council agreed to this, but said that keeping in mind his friends' ill behaviour on the night of 27 August, only one of them, to be chosen by Lord Pigot, could assist him in writing his petition.

Stratton and his council were struggling to justify their usurpation. Having been informed by Major Horne that Pigot planned to move the Mayor's Court for the issue of the writ of *habeas corpus*, the council decided to seek the advice of Justice Stephen Caesar Lemaistre of the Supreme Court of Calcutta, who was then on a visit, presumably for recuperation, to Madras.

Pigot had sent off a letter to Calcutta informing the Governor-General and his Council of events in Madras, including the fact that the majority had dissented with his measures. Now both parties sought the intervention of Calcutta until definite orders were received from Leadenhall Street. Stratton and his group sent off on 30 August another long letter to Hastings, Clavering, Monson, and Barwell. Stratton and his council defended through peculiar arguments their orders to Horne to inform Pigot at in any attempt to escape or rescue, his life would answer for it, for they say that this was mentioned *in terrorem* to keep Pigot's friends from such attempts. Their decision to remove Pigot to Chingleput derived from the affidavits of Eidingtoun and Sergeant Shaw relating the events of that night, which gave them every reason to believe 'that if Lord Pigot had it now in his power, he would not only raise a mutiny in the army, but put himself at the head of an armed party, and march with them to the fort, though he fell in the attempt'.

Justice Lemaistre's reply to the council's on the subject of *habeas corpus* was clear. This writ was 'a prerogative of a very high nature', issued only by the superior courts of Westminster Hall, 'unless warranted by express words in a charter granted by his Majesty, or by general or special words under the authority of words in an act of Parliament'. 'I am sorry to say', Lemaistre concluded, 'I can find no clause which warrants the issuing of it in the charter enacting and establishing the … Mayor's Court [at Madras]'. Lemaistre's opinion having been conveyed to Major Horne, the latter realised that matters were now moving deeper into the intricacies of law, and despite having been the council's spy in reporting on Pigot, he decided to make his position clear to the council. He wrote to them on 31 August 1776: 'In these critical situations common prudence requires the greatest circumspection; and as I am not conversant in law affairs I hope you will pardon me if I am improper in suggesting that should a suit of law be commenced against me, for acting in obedience to your orders as a military man, that I should have some security of being indemnified, *or that my private fortune should not be hurt*, or family suffer' [my emphasis]. Clearly, Horne too was engaged in private trade and usury.

Stratton and his council must have been very relieved with Lemaistre's dismissal of Pigot's writ. They were further reassured by a letter from the Governor-General and Council, who remarked 'the whole tenor of your President's conduct and behaviour to the Nabob, manifest symptoms of a strong personal indisposition towards him, heightened by a tone of authority unbecoming the Nabob's dignity and independency, and inconsistent with the respect which the Company have in all their letters directed to be shown to him'. Pigot's decision of 25 April to protect Tanjore with the Company's troops was rebuked as well: 'It is very evident that the Company intended the employment of their troops to the garrisoning of the city of Tanjore, but left to the Rajah's discretion the general defence of his dominions'. They therefore considered 'the measure of employing the Company's forces for the protection of the whole country of Tanjore as unwarranted and repugnant to the spirit of the Company's orders'. Pigot's insistence on Claud Russell as Resident to Tanjore was also censured. This move would create much uneasiness among other princes, for they would see this move as 'only a Pretence for vesting the Sovereignty and Government of that country in the Company, under the name of the Rajah of Tanjore'.

Sir Edward Hughes attended council on 4 September 1776, with reference to his letter of 27 August in which he had sought that Pigot be delivered into his custody, aboard his flagship, HMS *Salisbury*. The council fired a salvo at the senior sailor. Given Lord Pigot's tendency to encourage anarchy, and his evident violence of temper, attested by Eidingtoun's and Shaw's affidavits, would the Commodore be able to assure the council that Pigot would not land on any part of India in the proximity, rouse tensions in the Carnatic, divide the sentiments of the servants of the Company, march into the fort as he had promised to do once he had escaped confinement and, thereby cause injury to locals and Europeans? How would the Commodore ensure public tranquillity when the *Salisbury* was forced to leave the coast with the onset of the monsoon? Hughes was warned by the council that they hoped he would not, 'directly or indirectly, give sanction to any proceedings contrary to the resolutions of the Council … publicly declared'. The Commodore must have felt insulted, for he merely commented that he wanted these queries to be given him in writing, when he would answer them, and having said this, withdrew. The wording of the letter that was sent him the same day was different in that it was brief but audacious and galling, considering that it was addressed to a flag-officer of the Royal Navy. The council asked

Hughes 'what security you can give to us, who are entrusted with the interests and affairs of the Company under this Presidency, and with the preservation of the public peace, that the tranquillity of the Coast, so perfectly established, will not be endangered by our consenting to the removal of Lord Pigot from under our own authority?'

The Commodore's reply was sent on 5 September 1776 from his flagship. He was blunt in refuting the council's doubts: 'The requisition of a safe conduct for the noble Lord to my ship *being made to me in the name of the King*, and as no terms can therefore be admitted, on which to ground a compliance with that requisition, it follows that no other answer can be given by me, *who am entrusted with the honour and dignity of his Majesty's flag*' [my emphasis]. He reiterated his demand that Major Horne be ordered to convey Lord Pigot to the protection of his Majesty's flag. Stratton then made the strategic mistake of writing to Sir Edward that he had no authority to offer the protection of the flag to Pigot in words that read treasonously: 'having no proof before us that his Majesty empowers any of his officers to require the removal of any servant of the Company, in a similar situation with Lord Pigot, from under the authority of the Company's Government'.

Sir Edward Hughes replied to this missive on 7 September 1776. To find a parallel to Lord Pigot's case was, in his opinion, impossible, for he believed the case to be 'unexampled'. Pointing to the treasonable statement of disbelief in the Commodore's right to exercise his authority, both as ambassador to the Nawab's durbar and as commander-in-chief of the Royal Navy in the East Indies, in the name of the King, Hughes wrote: 'You think you cannot, consistently with the important trust reposed in you, comply with the requisition made by me, *in the name of his Majesty, a name by me deemed very high security*, and *which I have power to use in national concerns of the utmost importance* ... I have only to add, that you have taken on yourselves all the ill consequences which may arise from the refusal' [my emphasis].

Stratton and his council, far removed from St James' Court, smug in the near-absolute power they wielded in the presidency, and much enriched through usury and private trade, might have thought themselves immune to the prerogative of officers holding Royal commissions. Their subordinates, however, were painfully aware of the distinction. Captain Panton, commanding HM Sloop *Swallow*, went from the Commodore's house to deliver some packets from Bengal to Lord Pigot on the evening of 9 September, which Major Horne at once reported to the council. Horne's letter shows his hesitancy in presuming to ask Panton what these packets contained: 'I judged it would not be proper to question Captain

Panton with respect to the letter he had delivered to his Lordship being of a public or private nature, in respect to the commission he holds in his Majesty's service'. Captain Panton, in keeping with the practice then current in the Royal Navy, must actually have held the rank of Commander, being addressed as Captain by courtesy of his command. To ask such a question of Panton would have been deemed effrontery on Horne's part, who was only a Major in the Company's service. Smarting from the brush-off they had just received from the Commodore, the council too felt uncertain about asking Royal Naval officers their business with Pigot, and so Stratton wrote the following day to Horne to ascertain from Pigot the nature of the packet he had received from Bengal via Panton, which he suspected was a public letter. Horne, emboldened by Stratton's support, told Lord Pigot on 11 September that he had not asked Captain Panton about the public or private nature of the letter out of respect for his Lordship, which was of course a lie. Pigot declared that the letter was a public one, addressed to him from Bengal.

In the meantime, as Pigot had predicted, Coomera had been acquitted of all charges against him, and permitted to go to Tanjore. The Raja vehemently protested this, and Harper conveyed it to the council, via a letter received on 10 September: 'He told me, his coming at this time, when the inhabitants are employed all over the country in cultivating the lands, would be attended with a great inconveniency, as it must take a number of people from their business in order to settle with him'. The Raja urged that Coomera be permitted to visit Tanjore in January 1777. The crop of 1776 having been gathered and the land readied for the next, the people of Tanjore were busy with cultivation. Stratton at once replied menacingly to the Raja that Coomera had already left for Tanjore, and if the Raja wanted to, he could settle the time and manner of settling his claims (which were Benfield's claims, since Coomera was Benfield's *dubash*). If the Raja wished to wait until the sowing of the crop was done until he addressed Coomera's claims, he was free to do so, which of course in reality he was not. Benfield and the other creditors had realised that given the lateness of the season it was fruitless to continue to claim shares from the grain of 1776. To claim shares with compound interest on the crop of 1777 would yield more. Moreover, if Leadenhall Street supported Stratton's usurpation of Pigot's government, as they half-believed it would, the crop of 1777 would entirely be theirs. However, they were not certain that Leadenhall Street would endorse their action. Even so, they would have preferred to stake their 'inalienable' claim to the 1777 crop.

On 13 September 1776, proof of Mackay's involvement in the devaluation of coins arrived in the form of a letter from Bengal written by Warren Hastings and his council, alleging that the current Arcot rupees had been proved inferior by their assayers in comparison to the old Arcot rupees. They returned 100 of each sort and demanded to be told the result of the assay, to be done by the Assaymaster, George Mackay. He had probably been responsible for passing the inferior quality coins.

William Randall's affidavit that he and another officer in the Nawab's service, Lieutenant Gourd, had been offered inducement to assassinate Lord Pigot, and knew of such attempts, planned by Amir-ul-Umra, was sworn before John Turing, Mayor of Madras, on 15 September 1776. A copy of this went to Sir Edward, who forwarded it to the council reminding them of the need to put Lord Pigot into his custody, which was again denied on the grounds that Pigot's safety was being looked after by Major Horne, and in any case Pigot had the option of going to Chingleput, or any other settlement, or even to England, if he felt unsafe in Madras. The Nawab swore that Randall, who had offered his services on his own volition to his son, had framed Amir-ul-Umra.

Lord Pigot received on or about 9 October, Bengal's reply, dated 10 September 1776. Despite being much concerned about the manner in which Pigot had been deposed and confined, the Governor-General and Council declared that 'the rights and powers of the Governor and Council of any of the Company's presidencies are vested, by their original Constitution, in the Majority of the Board'. Pigot's suspension of two of the members of his council had been unconstitutional, and 'the measures taken by the Majority to recover the actual Government, which is of right vested in them, arose from the necessity of the case'. 'In doing this', the Bengal council declared, 'it is sufficient for us to know that we are supporting the legal and constitutional Government of the Company, though we are not yet perfectly informed of all the train of facts which have brought the Government of Madras into the present situation'. They would have wished that, 'acting as mediators', they could have brought about reconciliation between Pigot and the majority but matters had deteriorated far too much to admit of this. A covering letter conveying the same message, including a transcript of the letter to Pigot, was given to Commodore Sir Edward Hughes. A letter carrying the same message was sent to the council at Fort St George. Sir Edward had been requested to provide assistance and support to the 'actual government of Madras', and this he declared to them he would do.

As soon as the opinion of Bengal had been received, Paul Benfield pitched in with his own letter of protest against Pigot, dated 8 September

1776, but probably written later. 'Having never given cause to Lord Pigot to draw his resentment on me, I was at a loss to find out the reason why his Lordship was induced to take measures against me so injurious to my credit and fortune as have been represented to me by the Board', he wrote. 'I now clearly perceive', Benfield continued, 'that his views in so doing were interested, and that it was his own good, not that of the Company, he pursued in those measures during his last administration'. Consequently, Benfield resolved to 'take every legal method, by prosecution or otherwise, here and in England, to prove beyond a doubt this delinquency and breach of public trust in his Lordship'.

On 3 October 1776, the Nawab wrote to Stratton that Pigot did not approve of his writing letters to the governor and council. The Nawab said that Pigot 'told me not to write without showing me the draughts of my letters; and if I wrote, and he approved of my letters, he showed them to the Council, but if he disapproved of them, he did not deliver them into the Board; perhaps then he may not have delivered in many of my letters that were disagreeable to himself'. Then follows this inexplicable statement: 'Lord Pigot, in a public letter of the 25th of June, wrote of his intentions of giving me the grain of the Tanjore country, but privately sent a draught of a letter written in his own hand, that I might write one conformably to it'. This draft reads, 'I am very happy at my friend's return. I forgive you for everything you have done. The man who is faithful to his master will ever be so to his friend. You have finished the Company's business, I hope you will not forget mine. I will lay before you the whole state of my affairs and I desire you to settle them to the satisfaction of the Company, that I may be happy'.

Lord Pigot wrote to Sir Edward on 7 October 1776, objecting to Sir Robert's application to the council for permission to travel aboard the ship *Greenwich*, to the Cape of Good Hope, in order to recuperate from his worsening illness. If Fletcher was permitted to sail, Pigot would hold the council responsible for all consequences that would follow his removal from 'the jurisdiction of the military authority established by act of Parliament for the better government of the Company's troops in the East Indies, until the pleasure of the Court of Directors be known, as in the present situation of myself and the other legal Representatives of the Company on this Coast, it is not in our power to bring him to his trial'. This objection notwithstanding, Sir Robert was too seriously ill, and he sailed on the *Greenwich*. Brigadier-General Sir Robert Fletcher, sitting Member of Parliament for Cricklade and Commander-in-chief of the Company's force in Madras, died on 24 December 1776 in Mauritius, aged 38. He was immensely wealthy at the time of his death, and the means by which he had accumulated this wealth was the source of much speculation.

Dalrymple had departed for England, travelling via Suez, on the HM Sloop *Swallow*, which sailed on 10 October 1776, carrying with him all necessary papers to present to the Court of Directors. He was held up in Cairo for several days, and then moved to Alexandria on 19 January 1777, because of problems with customs. Sir Edward moved to Trincomalee on 15 October 1777 with his ships in order to avoid uncertain weather during the monsoon, which was imminent. He had visited Pigot before leaving, and been requested to see to it that the Nawab's cavalrymen, who were posted on the Mount Plain, were removed. This Sir Edward did.

Edward Monckton, deposing before Ram, had described Pigot's daily life before and after his confinement. Previously Pigot used to ride out in an open chaise nearly every morning from the fort to Monckton's home on the Choultry Plain, a distance of about 2 miles, for breakfast. After breakfast, he would take his youngest daughter out on a long ride in the chaise, covering 2 or 3 miles. When he breakfasted at the fort, he would walk out after his meal to the Company's Garden-house, which was situated about 1 mile away. There he would walk in the garden and superintend the gardeners until 10 am, when he would return to the fort for the day's work. Dinner was consumed between 1 and 3 pm, and thereafter Pigot would often tire himself out by walking over the fortifications, and thence to the Company's Garden-house and its gardens, until around 7 pm, when he would often lie down for an hour or two's rest. After supper at the Garden-house, Pigot would usually be driven back in his chaise or carried in his palanquin to the fort, where he slept in his official quarters. On moonlit nights there would be more walking about the fortifications.

Pigot travelled about much in the sun, and suffered no ill-effects although he gave up his post-dinner walks after his return from Tanjore due to the hot weather. After his confinement at Major Horne's, Pigot kept up his physical exertions. He would walk at least twice a day from his room at Horne's to Monckton's, where he would spend much time directing carpenters and gardeners. Pigot even walked up to the top of the Mount 5 or 6 times, which required much physical exertion, since he would have had to climb the 134 granite steps that lead to the top of the Mount. Sometimes he would walk out on the Mount Plain for a mile, but seldom further than that. He would also visit other gentlemen's houses, which were about 300 yards from Horne's. Subsequent to his arrest, an officer and 2 artillerymen always accompanied Pigot wherever he went. However, it was not until the Nawab's cavalrymen had been withdrawn from the Mount Plain that he walked far, for he feared assassination. At the Coroner's inquest, Sir Edward Hughes deposed that he had seen around 20 of the Nawab's horse near the Mount. Another fear was that he would be kidnapped again, and this time put aboard a ship to England. At various times, when ships to England came in from Bengal, he and his friends and family were in much anxiety, particularly through the month of January 1777, when the *Lioness* and *The Prince of Wales* sailed.

CHAPTER TWELVE

DEATH

By January 1777, Lord Pigot had been a prisoner for 6 months. The English were used to the elapsing of great periods between the dispatch and receipt of news from England on matters of current interest in India. While immersed in work, or busily engaged like an ant in stowing away money for a comfortable, possibly luxurious, retirement in England, and in the midst of fine society, time passed fast enough. To a prisoner like Pigot, time soon began to be oppressive. So long as Commodore Sir Edward had been in Madras, and Pigot was engaged in communicating through him to the council, he was busy in a manner of speaking. With Sir Edward gone to Trincomalee for the monsoon, it was hard for Pigot to keep pleasant humour, even though amidst his family, waiting for a decision from England. He did not know that Dalrymple was held up almost all through January in Egypt, just as he did not know how much longer he would have to wait, or indeed, what the decision of the Court of Directors would be. The Governor-General and Council had supported the majority; if the Directors did the same, prosecutions would undo Pigot. Clearly by disposition a man of action, and not given to reading, writing, or contemplation, Pigot seemed to waste away. Gilbert Pasley, his attending physician, testified that dwelling on disagreeable thoughts was harmful over time to the body, which is something we know today, but was not obvious then. 'Grief and strong attention of the mind, in all dissatisfactions, and in general all those things which affect the mind, have an effect on the body', Pasley said, deposing before Ram's inquest and, later, the Grand Jury at the Quarter Sessions at Madras. He continued, 'The more the passions and affections of the mind are concealed, the more they prey upon the mind'. 'Firmness and fortitude' keep the elderly safe from the immediate effects that arise from 'the change of situation and other misfortunes', felt Pasley. Although in these cases the illnesses grow upon the body as certainly as in younger persons, they do so more slowly. From January on Pigot was in a constant state of anxiety since this was the season for ships from England to arrive.

Gilbert Pasley had been living in India since 1756, and resided continuously in Madras as one of the two Company's surgeons since 1761. This had made him an expert on the diseases of the country.

Lord Pigot seems to have been mildly ill in January. Between 4 and 6 March 1777, he was quite ill. In the beginning, he suffered considerably from shortness of breath, restlessness, a flagging spirit, scanty and irregular perspirations, and feverish disposition, which confined him to his room. Mr Mallet, the artillery regiment's surgeon at the Mount, who attended to him, administered a 'physic', which did not help. When he called the next day, 7 March 1777, Pigot asked Mallet for another, which partially answered the purpose. On Lord Pigot's complaint in the evening of chillness and a sick stomach again, Mallet administered a tartar emetic that helped the patient void a quantity of bile and undigested material. Called in the following day, Pasley found Lord Pigot restless as before, with an oppression and difficulty of breathing, prostration of strength, his tongue 'white as sheet', his urine 'like sour beer', his skin hot and dry, and his pulse very quick, all symptoms pointing to 'a system agitated with putrid bile'. One wonders today that Lord Pigot survived Pasley's treatment: a laxative of senna manna, Sal Rochelle, tamarinds, and fennel seed. Four evacuations of the bowel rapidly followed (obviously) and Pigot had some relief. The excreta were odoriferous. The same laxative was repeated the next morning, 9 March 1777, and much putrid bile was removed. Perspiration now appeared, the pulse slowed, and was full, and the tongue had a better appearance. Pasley's treatment now changed, and became such as will astonish the reader today. Pigot was given saline draughts with tartar emetic, which made him vomit more 'putrid bile' and some 'glutinous stuff that would not dissolve in water'. With the easing of the oppressive symptoms of 'putrid bile', Lord Pigot now began to complain of tenderness of liver and pain in the right shoulder. His laxative was repeated until the quantity of putrid bile was considerably reduced. He continued to use a saline mixture as a refreshing drink, and all the other symptoms having apparently been removed with the exception of the feverish disposition, Pigot was prescribed alkalised mercury and vitriolic tartar, in equal quantities, morning and evening, 'to remove liver, and other visceral obstructions'. Both compounds are laxatives, and so Pasley was following usual medical practice. To make a permanent recovery, Pasley recommended to Lord Pigot a course of 'alteratives [medicines to nourish and improve the system, later known also as 'blood-purifiers'], deobstruent, and aperient medicines' along with suitable adjustment of diet and exercise to keep away 'indigestion and diseased secretions'. The disorder he had been suffering from had only been removed, Pasley said, and Pigot needed to take care it did not recur.

Pigot disregarded Pasley's advice that his illness was typical of the locality, and originated in a diseased liver. Pasley says Pigot was then strong, 'and could bear the effects of medicines', as a result of which he soon recovered. 'His Lordship having no feelings of any ails, and great confidence in a good constitution, was unwilling to suppose he could require any course of medicines, urging at the same time', Pasley said, 'that he thought himself as well as any man in India'. He resumed his walks to Monckton's house, and supervision of the gardens in the heat of the midday sun.

However, he never regained the vigour he had enjoyed before falling ill, and within a fortnight, was sick once more. 'His appetite began to fail him', reported Pasley, 'his sleep grew disturbed, he grew heavy and feverish'. Pasley found 'much putrid bile in his bowels, and a degree of inflammation in the substance of his liver, which altogether brought on a relapse of his fever, with an enlargement of his liver'. Pasley found that 'the whole scene of illness was renewed, without having sufficient strength to support a second attack'.

James Anderson, who attended Pigot 4 times a day after he had been moved to the Company's Garden-house, spoke of his passing 'putrid bile' in his stool whenever he took physic (laxative), of complaining of a pain in his side, and fullness on the side of his liver. Later Pigot told Anderson that his illness had followed after he entered Monckton's house, having spent several hours working in the garden in the sun, and consumed a glass of punch.

William Mallet, the other Company's surgeon in Madras, was also of the opinion that the first illness on 6 March 1777 had been a 'bilious complaint, of which there are daily instances, and which is incident to the nature of the climate'. The problem with this disorder, said Mallet, was that it was frequently mortal, especially when the liver was affected.

The symptoms described by James Anderson struck him a few weeks later, along with those foretold by William Mallet, bilious vomiting, dry skin, and 'all the symptoms of a confirmed bilious fever', and though Pasley suggested venesection, Pigot rejected it. The Grand Jury, which was later assembled in Madras to take depositions from various persons regarding the Coroner's verdict against Stratton and his council, and several army officers, of having conspired to murder Pigot, asked William Mallet if he had not been surprised at Lord Pigot's hearty meal at Monckton's on the Sunday before he fell ill for the second time. 'I remarked to Major Horne', Mallet replied, 'his Lordship having made an unusual meal of turtle, and that I was apprehensive (from its being food of so gross a nature) that his Lordship might feel the ill consequences of it'. The Court then questioned Mallet if in his opinion the disease of which Lord Pigot had died was the consequence of his imprisonment, or 'produced by his own imprudence'. Mallet's reply was clear: 'I do not impute his Lordship's disease to the effects of imprisonment, but I impute his relapse a good deal to his own mismanagement'. The Grand Jury's questions to Gilbert Pasley revealed that Miss [Leonora?] Pigot and even Monckton had suffered from bilious disorders while at the Mount, the former suffering from one of a rather dangerous kind. It also became known that several artillerymen and their officers had suffered from similar ailments of the liver, and one officer, though sent to Madras to Pasley's care, had died. The Court then put the same question to Pasley as it had to Mallet, whether Pigot had died of causes deriving from imprisonment, or from his own imprudence. Pasley too gave a similar answer as his junior colleague: 'it was imagined and prophesied by everybody, that his Lordship would sooner or later be attacked by some disease, owing to his exposing himself so much in the sun, which, indeed, his friends always remonstrated against'.

In any case, Pasley was sufficiently alarmed at Lord Pigot's condition to apply to George Stratton for permission to move him from the Mount to the Company's Garden-house, which, being granted, was done on 28 April 1777. As Mallet said, this was the only option left, for it was hoped that fresh sea-breezes would be of some help. Sir Edward Hughes testified at Ram's inquest that Major Horne continued to be in charge of Lord Pigot's custody, even when such custody had become irrelevant. Sepoy guards were posted all around, and at the major intersections, to divert traffic and ensure absolute silence about the Company's Garden-house. The guard had been given particular orders to keep the Nawab's people away. Whether this was to keep the Nawab clear of any possible incrimination, or out of respect for Lord Pigot's last days, is hard to say. The former explanation seems more plausible. There was, as Claud Russell found to his surprise, a European sergeant living in a tent on the grounds of the Company's Garden-house ostensibly to supervise the sepoy-guard but in reality to report all that went on there.

Pasley was aware that Pigot would not be able to overcome this sickness, so he spoke to Stratton about Pigot's testament. Stratton replied that Pigot's will was done, and in a bureau, that Pigot had pointed out to him before leaving for Tanjore, in case of accidents. The bureau contained his will, Mrs Monckton's marriage settlement, and some papers.

Soon after his removal to the Garden-house Lord Pigot seemed to recover briefly, when he peculiarly resumed ‘some violent exertions’, and exposed himself to ‘cold and fatigue’, as a result of which ‘severe shivering’ followed, and a ‘slow visceral fever’ set in, which resulted in his death from ‘partial suppurations in the substance of his liver, and putrid bile’. George, Lord Pigot, first Baron Patshull, in the county of Dublin, sitting Member of Parliament for Bridgnorth, and President of the Council and Governor and Commander-in-chief of Fort St George, Madras, died at 10.38 on the morning of 11 May 1777, aged 58.

He was buried inside St Mary’s Church, his being the first burial there. In 1874, repairs requiring digging in the area under the chancel uncovered a nameless coffin in a vault. This was supposed to be Lord Pigot’s, and the vault was sealed at the orders of the then governor, the Duke of Buckingham, with a slab that bore only the words, ‘In Memoriam’.

CHAPTER THIRTEEN

THE INQUEST: MADRAS, 1777-78

As we saw in the prologue to this book, on receiving the brief note from Edward Monckton notifying him of Lord Pigot's death, George Andrew Ram summoned a Coroner's Jury and 3 doctors to attend the inquest at the Company's Garden-house, where Lord Pigot's body lay. With the doctors' and jury's consent, the body was handed over by Ram's permission, to Pigot's family, which consisted of his daughters Sophia, and Leonora; sons, George, Richard, and Hugh; and his son-in-law, Edward Monckton, Sophia's husband. Leonora would marry Claud Russell in October 1777. Pigot's sons were children when he died, being respectively 7, 3, and 2 years old. Quick burials were the norm then, since the rot set in very fast. Lord Pigot had other 'natural' children, Amelia and George Wood, Elizabeth Surry, Harriet Sneed, and Mary Green. Mary was also a child, aged 5, when Pigot died. Edward Monckton had joined the service in 1762, become Factor in 1768, Junior Merchant 1771, and Senior Merchant in 1774. He left the service in 1780.

A perusal of Charles Campbell Prinsep's *Records of the Services of the Honourable East India Company's Civil Servants in the Madras Presidency from 1741 to 1858* (1885) shows that George Andrew Ram had joined the Company's service in 1767, become a Factor in 1774, and Junior Merchant in 1776. Like most of the 'merchants', in addition to his main profession of commerce, Ram also bore local administrative responsibilities. While several of these local government posts came with perquisites like a house, additional income for various expenses and the possibility of making money on the side, the Coroner's post is unlikely to have been as lucrative. In fact, when the Coroner's findings were referred by the court at Madras to the Supreme Court of Judicature at Calcutta (which had only just been established, as required by the Regulating Act of 1773), Sir Elijah Impey (1732-1809), Robert Chambers (1737-1803), Stephen Caesar Lemaistre (1741-1777), John Hyde (1737-1796), pondered the issue and set aside the Coroner's verdict on the grounds there was no legally appointed Coroner at Madras. This communication from Fort William was dated 31 October 1777. Lemaistre died 4 days later in

Calcutta, and lies buried in the South Park Street Cemetery, where his tomb still stands.

It had appeared in an earlier petition before the Sessions Court in Madras that George Andrew Ram, although 'appointed' Coroner 6 months before Lord Pigot's death, had steadfastly refused to perform this duty with this case as the sole exception. It also seems that a forcible attempt was made to remove him from his post, for in his concluding argument to his jury, Ram also sought its opinion on several related issues. The first was whether their verdict ought to be made public; the second whether making it public would not be construed as attempt to provoke mutiny; third, whether it would not be better to be cautious lest the verdict become the cause of 'strife and mischief' in the presidency, and await the directions of the Supreme Court of Judicature in Bengal; fourth, considering that his authority commanded only voluntary assistance, and whether, it would be better to conceal the verdict until either further news on the usurpation was received from England, or until the Bengal court gave Ram the authority to prove that his 'pretended removal was illegal', since the publication of the verdict would not be accompanied by any good consequences. Considering that Ram subsequently delivered his verdict in proper form, as 'Coroner of our said Lord the King for the town and districts of Madraspatnam aforesaid', one is confused as to Ram's authority and position, particularly whether he had been deliberately removed from his post. In their letter to the Directors dated 2 July 1777, George Stratton and his council had disputed Ram's role as Coroner. Ram had been Coroner until Pigot's government was usurped. He had protested the revolution, which having drawn the anger of the usurpers, made them post him to 'a Subordinate Settlement', and appoint a more pliable person, John Balfour, to be Coroner. George Andrew Ram declined the posting and 'objected to the Nomination of a new Coroner, declaring he had no Inclination to Quit the Office', holding that 'he could not be removed from it but by a Proof of delinquency'. With Balfour apparently performing the duties of the Coroner, Ram was allowed to remain in town for reasons of ill health. Following Lord Pigot's death, Stratton and his council complained, Ram 'had the boldness to act in open defiance of our Authority'. His inquest was 'totally unwarrantable and illegal', they said. This determined them 'to take no Notice of their Proceedings, or of the Conduct of Mr Ram, until the examinations were finished'. In self-satisfying smugness, the council concluded that 'although they have been sitting near two Months that they cannot agree upon anything and that the Enquiry is likely to end to the discredit of those Who have promoted it'. George Andrew Ram was promoted to Senior Merchant in 1778, becoming Resident at Tanjore in 1791, and Collector of Guntur in 1795. He died at Madras on 12 February 1801, aged 52, and lies buried in the cemetery at St Mary's Church, Fort St George.

In his verdict, Ram stated the circumstances under which his jury was summoned, named them, and affirmed that the jury, on being sworn, was 'charged to enquire on behalf of our said Lord the King, when, where, and after what manner, and by what means, the said George, Lord Pigot, came to his death'. The jury found that George Stratton, Henry Brooke, Charles Floyer, Archdale Palmer, Francis Jourdan, and George Mackay, of the civil service at Madras, and Brigadier-General Sir Robert Fletcher, Colonel James Stuart, Lieutenant-Colonel James Eidingtoun, Adjutant-General, Major Matthew Horne, and Captain Arthur Lysaght, of the Company's army at Madras, 'not having the fear of God before their eyes, but being moved and seduced by the instigation of the Devil', had connived on or before 24 August 1775, 'with force of arms', and 'feloniously, voluntarily, and of their malice forethought did combine and conspire to seize, confine, and keep as a prisoner' Lord Pigot. The 'restraint, confinement, and imprisonment' to which he was subjected kept Lord Pigot from partaking of exercise necessary for good health, and all these circumstances, so operated on his mind and body that he succumbed to a putrid bilious fever and flux originating in the liver, on 11 May 1777, after nearly two months' suffering. The jurors therefore found that George Stratton, Sir Robert Fletcher, Henry Brooke, Charles Floyer, Archdale Palmer, Francis Jourdan, George Mackay, James Stuart, James Eidingtoun, Arthur Lysaght, and Matthew Horne, 'feloniously, voluntarily, and of their malice forethought, did kill and murder' Lord Pigot. John De Fries dissented and his letter was duly entered into the records. De Fries had agreed that Lord Pigot had died in confinement, which had not been 'sufficiently, properly, nor regularly, removed'. De Fries had voted in the negative on the question of whether imprisonment had directly caused Pigot's death. Similarly, De Fries had unable to agree to the verdict of wilful murder, preferring manslaughter as the appropriate charge.

Matters in Madras now proceeded to the next climax. John Whitehill, the chief at Masulipatam, had obtained leave and travelled to London, His arrival in England coincided with that of reports sent in haste by Pigot and Stratton and his council. Dismayed by these happenings in Madras, the Company entrusted a copy of their despatch dated 11 June 1777 to Whitehill, who returned hastily, leaving England on 13 June, and, travelling via Suez, reached Madras on 31 August. Pigot had been dead for over 3 months but the Directors' letter was addressed to him, along with the names forming a new council: Thomas Rumbold, Major-General Hector Munro, John Whitehill, Charles Smith, Samuel Johnson, Peter Perring, Alexander Davidson, John Hollond, and James Daniel. The General Court of Proprietors and the Court of Directors disapproved of the happenings in Madras. They had determined to reinvest in Lord Pigot the powers of government but as they also felt that Pigot's actions had been unwarranted in many cases, they ordered his restoration on condition that he took the first ship sailing to England from Madras within one week of the receipt of their letter, having handed over the government to Thomas Rumbold. The usurpers, viz, George Stratton, Sir Robert Fletcher, Henry Brooke, Charles Floyer, Archdale Palmer, Francis Jourdan, and George Mackay, were to be sent to England at the first opportunity but not on board the same ship as Lord Pigot unless by his consent. They were to be told that they had been suspended from the service. Colonel James Stuart was suspended for 6 months from the day of the arrival of the orders restoring Pigot. Paul Benfield was addressed in a separate paragraph, on the ground that 'the late Dissensions in our Council, which brought on all the Troubles at Madras, took their Rise from the Claims of Mr Paul Benfield on the Tanjore Country, the Nature of which Claims has not been sufficiently explained'. Benfield was also suspended from the service and recalled urgently to England. The Directors, obviously too immersed in commercial matters to be interested in the history of their Company, seemed much upset that 'the present Confusion', as they called it, derived from 'the private Engagements of [their] Servants, and their Concerns, Dealings, and Transactions, on their own separate Account with the Princes and Natives of the Country'.

On his arrival at Madras, Whitehill saw that he was the only member of the new council present. He administered the oaths of office to two senior merchants, Anthony Sadleir, who had joined the service in 1760, and Quintin Crauford, of the same seniority as Sadleir. He also called in Charles Smith, Peter Perring, and Samuel Johnson, from their posts into Madras as councillors. On receiving the Directors' orders, Stratton and his council at once left office, which Whitehill assumed the governorship in a temporary capacity, with effect from 31 August 1777, until Sir Thomas Rumbold arrived.

This second change in government, which made the Directors' view of the matter clear, gave Ram the chance to deliver his verdict to Whitehill. This he did on 24 September 1777, with the request that the governor and council assist in the arrest of the accused. Whitehill dismissed the request but asked the persons named as guilty in Ram's verdict, to meet him at the Company's Garden-house the following evening. There he issued a warrant based on the Coroner's verdict, and handed them into the Sheriff's custody.

The case came to the Quarter Sessions Court in Madras on 30 September 1777, with John Whitehill in the chair, and Sadleir and Crauford as his fellow judges. Charles Bromley appeared for the accused. The accused prayed for a fair hearing, pleading that had the Coroner been legal and impartial, and his jury composed of 'the most respectable and creditable inhabitants of this presidency', had it been conducted publicly, they felt the propriety of their conduct would not be brought into question, 'nor the death of Lord Pigot be found to be otherwise caused than by the hand of God'. The hearings began on 1 October, with Whitehill declaring that the case would be sent to the Supreme Court in Bengal for their opinions, while the Sheriff would be told to call in men from the subordinate factories and settlements to form the jury, as 'the late animosities in this Settlement having, more or less, engaged and affected the greater part of its small society', the jury would have to be constituted of persons remote from the scene of dissension. The bench similarly dismissed suggestions that the case be tried in England. Only by issuing the writ of *certiorari* could such a move be achieved. 'To obtain this writ would probably require a year', the judges said, 'to send home witnesses and others, in consequence of it, would require several months more'. Material evidence would be lost, much time wasted, and great sums spent, on these conveyances. The Supreme Court was in Calcutta, many times nearer Madras, and it had been established for dealing speedily with legal matters in Bengal and the subordinate presidencies. Therefore choosing to await the decision of the Supreme Court, the case was adjourned until 12 November 1777.

This was a very long gap, and the accused knew that Pigot's friends including Ram had contrived to send the Coroner's verdict to England aboard the sloop *Swallow*, which had sailed on 10 October 1777. Soon Sir Edward Hughes and his squadron were ordered from the Coromandel and on 4 October Commodore Sir Edward Hughes and his secretary, Edward L'Epine were summoned to the Sessions Court where they deposed under oath. Their statements having been recorded, the accused, who had spent the last 10 days in custody, were released on bail. They came to know that the East Indiaman, the *Egmont*, was to sail on 15 October, and Claud Russell and John Maxwell Stone, Pigot's friends, had applied for permission to return to England aboard it. George Stratton and his associates pleaded that such permission be withheld for the sake of justice. If Russell and Stone reached England before the accused had an equal opportunity to either defend themselves or provide for their defence, it would be unfair, 'equally repugnant to the justice of the Court and the constitutional liberties of England'. They requested the court to note their exceptions to Ram's inquest.

The objections to Ram's inquest were along the usual and expected lines. The first two objections were to Ram's right to conduct an inquest as Coroner, since he had been transferred elsewhere and was present while the oaths of the Coroner were administered to John Balfour at the Sessions Court. The other objections targeted the jurors, who the accused alleged were deliberately chosen by Ram to bring in the verdict of murder. The sympathies of many of the jurors lay with Pigot and his supporters, and Ram had allegedly placed the names of these among the first 12. Instead of conducting the inquest publicly, Ram had insisted on a confidential inquiry to which the accused had no access, so they had not been able to cross-examine the deponents. Other accusations of bias followed, dismissing variously the suspicion of Lord Pigot's having been poisoned, the meetings of the jurors even after they were reportedly convinced that Pigot had died a natural death, and Ram's browbeating both jurors and deponents into bringing in the verdict of wilful murder. De Fries's objection was alluded to as well, though not by name but the circumstance of his objecting to a verdict delivered not by unanimity but majority.

The Sessions Court seems to have carried out some random cross-examinations of witnesses, notably Drs Mallet and Pasley, up to 26 November 1777. It was on this date that the Grand Jury was sworn in and, the opinions on the case having been received from Calcutta, several other matters attended to.

The Grand Jury assembled in Madras to decide the case of the death of Lord Pigot included the following persons: James Daniel, Foreman; James Henry Casamajor, Edward Saunders, Thomas Cooper, Richard Guy, Edward Trowd, Theodore Corbett, Thomas Barnard, Joseph Baker, Charles Edward Jones, George Moubray, Robert Gardiner, John Mitford, William Augustus Dobbyn, James Strange, William Duff, and Edward Miller.

In the presence of the Grand Jury, the Judges ordered the Clerk to quash the verdict of the Coroner's inquest in pursuance of the recommendations of the Supreme Court at Calcutta. The accused were called, and their solicitor, Charles Bromley appeared for them, upon which they were discharged of the Coroner's verdict by proclamation. The Judges in Bengal were doubtful if the governor and council in Madras could appoint a Coroner, since there was no act of Parliament or some charter that gave to the Coroner the same rights in India as were enjoyed by those holding similar posts in England. With this in mind, the Supreme

Court declared that an inquest would be no more than an unofficial assembly, and the arraignment of a culprit would be illegal. The Supreme Court therefore declared the Coroner's verdict on Lord Pigot's death null and void. The Judges at Madras then declared that based on Ram's papers, it was obvious that neither murder not manslaughter applied to Lord Pigot's case. Although imprisonment of a particularly severe nature could be construed as a cause of death that would be registered as criminal homicide, this was inapplicable in Pigot's case: 'he who has unlawfully abridged the liberty of another, will not be answerable for his death, merely because the disease of which he died proceeded from anxiety and depression of spirits, the natural consequences of injurious confinement'. In the meantime, Stratton and some of his associates left for England via Suez, and focus shifted from Madras to London.

CHAPTER FOURTEEN

THE TRIAL IN ENGLAND, 1779

England was abuzz with the news of Lord Pigot's death, which was confirmed on 31 January 1778. His brother, Hugh Pigot, Vice-Admiral of the White, stood for election from Bridgnorth, and was returned. He took his seat in the Commons on 16 February 1778. From the *Parliamentary Register*, volume 11, we can follow the events leading up to the trial of Stratton and his associates. On 16 April 1779, Admiral Pigot started an important discussion in the House of Commons on the Madras affair and his brother's death before the committee on affairs in India. Lord Middleton took the Chair, and the Admiral began his statement by retelling the story of the usurpation and Lord Pigot's death. Lord Pigot had been offered, he said, at first 1,000,000 pagodas, and then another 500,000, in sum the equivalent of £600,000 to withhold his orders for the restoration of the Raja of Tanjore, which he refused to do. In fact, Admiral Pigot said, his brother died so poor that his son-in-law, Edward Monckton, had to sell his house and effects at Madras to meet Lord Pigot's debts.

By this time, George Stratton had been back in England for over a year. He had been elected to the Commons from Callington on 5 December 1778 but had been unseated on 15 February 1779. Re-elected from the same seat, Stratton took his place as MP on 1 March 1779. He was present during the debate, and rose to oppose the Admiral by presenting the council's minutes, which showed that Pigot had had the consent of the majority of council to proceed to Tanjore. The Admiral called in George Dawson, who had retired sick from Madras, to testify about the bribes offered by the Nawab and his sons. Dawson deposed that the Nawab's sons had offered him 100,000 rupees to stay away from council on the day the issue of sending Claud Russell to Tanjore as Resident was decided. Dawson added that there was no European witness to this event, from which one presumes that 'European' evidence was accountable, while 'Indian' depositions were suspect. The Admiral then moved the motion that Lord Pigot, a member of the House, had been arrested by a military force on 24 August 1776, carried off, and confined in Major Horne's house for 8 months, and at the end of that period, he died on 11 May 1777.

Sir George Wombwell, who had been Chairman of the East India Company, objected to this because it was a matter, which was solely the Company's jurisdiction, by right of their charter. The Company had sent Sir Thomas Rumbold to take over the government and carry out an inquiry into the events leading up to the usurpation of Pigot's government and his death, and the report of this inquiry was daily expected, Wombwell added. The Company, Wombwell reminded the House, held by charter the supreme right to appoint, suspend, dismiss, reward, and punish, their servants. If the Admiral found that the Directors had not done their rightful duty after perusing Rumbold's report, he could seek succour of the House of Commons. If in the meantime he wanted redressal, he could move court. Wombwell saw no reason for stirring in the matter at present, or for the House to concern itself in it.

Admiral Pigot rose to protest, saying that he had written to India House in August 1778, representing many legal opinions on the matter, but the Directors were so 'gradual' in their approach that it was not until October that he had received a most unsatisfactory answer from them. As for Rumbold's inquiry, the Admiral considered it peculiar that it should be conducted in Madras about persons then residing in England.

Lord North sought to have the reference of Lord Pigot's late membership of the House removed from the records, which was overruled.

Admiral Pigot's motion was carried without opposition, as were two more. The first of these stated, 'That it appears to this committee, that George Stratton, Henry Brooke, Charles Floyer, Archdale Palmer, Francis Jourdan, and George Mackay, did, on the 23rd day of August 1776, form themselves into a council and did confer the command of the army and the garrison of Fort St George on Colonel James Stuart, ordering him to arrest the person of George, Lord Pigot, their governor and commander-in-chief, and to put the fort, garrison, and fort-house, under their command'.

The second resolution said, 'That it appears to this committee, that the Court of Directors of the East India Company have, by letters of the 4th July 1777, and of the 23rd December 1778, to their presidency at Madras, ordered, that courts-martial should be held for the trial of Col James Stuart, Col Eidingtoun, Maj Horne, and Capt Lysaght, for having arrested and confined under a military force, their governor and commander-in-chief, George Lord Pigot'.

Admiral Pigot next moved 'That it is the opinion of this committee, that an humble address be presented to his Majesty, praying his Majesty, that he would be graciously pleased to give directions to his attorney-general to prosecute George Stratton, Henry Brooke, Charles Floyer, Archdale Palmer, Francis Jourdan, and George Mackay, Esquires, for ordering their governor and commander-in-chief, George Lord Pigot, to be arrested and confined under a military force; they being returned to England, and now within the jurisdiction of his Majesty's courts of Westminster Hall'. On this resolution, Robert Gregory (1727-1810), who had retired from service in India in 1766 and become a Director in 1769, a post he held until his resignation in 1782, rose and said that although he did not approve of the conduct of Lord Pigot prior to his removal, he could not support 'the violent measures pursued by the council'. He declared that the Company's servants should hold 'sacred' the orders of the General Courts, and not deviate from them unless under the greatest emergency, and then not with violence and precipitation but 'with the greatest caution and coolness'. In his opinion, this was the occasion for Parliament to agree to the resolutions, 'and assist the Company in their wishes to convince their servants abroad, that their taking upon them to violate the orders of the Company, and proceed to the length of a revolution in the government of a presidency, was not in itself a slight matter, or such a matter as would be easily overlooked, either by the Company, or by the legislature of Great Britain'.

Stratton objected to this, referring to Lord Pigot's alleged tyrannical behaviour and the endorsement of his removal by the Bengal government.

John Purling (1722-1800), another Company Director (1763 to 1780), rose in opposition to Stratton, saying that the Company never approved of the imprisonment of Lord Pigot, and that the opinion of the Bengal council was irrelevant, considering 'that persons at so great a distance from Madras could not be competent judges'. Stratton weakly contested this but was silenced by Robert Gregory's rising again to state in both his capacities as Director and MP, that he doubted whether 'the conduct of the council in Madras, in deposing their governor, and making him a prisoner, merited any compliment'. He had attended every meeting of the Court of Directors, and the General Courts after news of the happenings in Madras was received, and there was no instance when anyone had approved of the behaviour of the council there. The Directors had particularly avoided countenancing 'their servants who affected the revolution in the government of Madras', Gregory said.

Admiral Pigot's third motion in the Commons was passed, again without opposition.

On the recommendation of the House of Commons, the Attorney-General, Alexander Wedderburne, moved for the King against George Stratton, Henry Brooke, Charles Floyer, and George Mackay, 'for depriving the Right Hon George Lord Pigot of his command and office of Governor and President of the Council at Madras, and arresting and imprisoning his person for nine months'. The defendants having pleaded 'not guilty', the matter was brought to the King's Bench at Westminster Hall, on 20 December 1779, with a special jury from the county of Middlesex, and Lord Mansfield (1705-1793), the Lord Chief Justice, in the Chair. Alexander Wedderburne (1733-1805) headed the prosecution, assisted by the Solicitor-General, James Wallace (1729-1783), Mr James Mansfield (1733-1821), Mr Sergeant Walker, Mr Lee, Mr Davenport, Mr Rous, Mr Lind, and Mr Woodhouse, with Mr John Smith as their Solicitor. The defendants' counsel was headed by John Dunning (1731-1783), assisted by Lloyd Kenyon (1732-1802), Richard Arden (1744-1804), Mr Wilson, Mr Chambre, Mr Piggott, and Mr Thomas Erskine (1750-1823); their solicitors were Messrs Gregg and Potts. It must have been one of the greatest trials of that year, since some of the best legal brains of the time were engaged in it. Dunning, in his address to the jury, referred to the unusual attendance at court, as evidence of the sensationalism of the case. The case was reported in its entirety in *A Complete Collection of State Trials and Proceedings for High Treason and other Crimes and Misdemeanours from the earliest period to the year 1783* (1816), volume 21, by T B Holwell.

Wedderburne in his opening statement spoke of how Muhammad Ali Khan, having seen the manner in which the Company's servants replaced one Nawab with another, devised a 'politic scheme' to keep himself from this fate. 'No treasury could have stood that test', Wedderburne declared, 'but he devised to himself a scheme of borrowing from the principal servants of the Company at Madras sums of money at a considerable interest, either paid down or incurred'. This money was borrowed at exorbitant rates of interest, and to his creditors he assigned portions of his revenue, which were 'usually placed in those parts where the collection must be exposed to danger'. By this means, he secured his interest with the Company's servants, to whom he owed vast sums, and who were 'interested in making effectual to him the recovery of the most embarrassed and difficult parts of his revenues'. The size of the Nawab's debt grew yearly, being carried on despite express orders of the Company. By the time Pigot went to Madras in 1775, this debt stood at £2,000,000, owed to the Company's servants, 'which the Company winked at, being compelled to it, perhaps', Wedderburne said.

Pigot was ordered by the Company to carry out the restitution of Tanjore to its Raja, and it was with this commission that he travelled to Madras. 'With respect to the members of the council whom he [Pigot] found at Madras', Wedderburne said, 'they were all, I believe, planted by his own hand'. The younger men had been brought up in Pigot's family, and he had helped them lay the foundations of their fortunes before he left Madras at the end of his first governorship. The older men 'his goodness had dragged out of obscurity'. Pigot, on being appointed to his second governorship, left England, Wedderburne said, with 'an undaunted resolution and an uncorrupted integrity'. The Nawab was initially glad to see Pigot but on being acquainted with his orders to restore Tanjore to its rightful king, he became 'guarded and polite'. '[T]here was no direct and positive refusal' on the Nawab's part but he used many means 'to gain time, to start delays, to state difficulties, to make objections'. Wedderburne said that before he left Madras for Tanjore to put the Raja on his throne and in possession of his lands, he had little idea that 'Europeans might have private claims in the Tanjore country'. Presented while at Tanjore with Benfield's letter of claims, Pigot at first considered Benfield, so Wedderburne said, 'a very small and inconsiderable man' who soon 'talked big of mortgages and assignments' by the Nawab to him, amounting to £250,000 a year. Wedderburne asked the jury to note that the annual revenue of Tanjore totalled £1,000,000, and a quarter of this was pledged to Benfield by the Nawab for sums lent to him. Benfield 'cautioned Lord Pigot not to give up the possession of these revenues without the intervention of that claim'. Pigot let him have a 'very dry and cool' answer, referring him to the council at Madras.

'I shall endeavour now to state to you', Wedderburne said to the jury, 'who Benfield is, and what are the claims he has'. He followed it up by confessing that he was at a loss as who Benfield was. Benfield, as far as he could discover, was in the Company's service in 1772, when he was ordered to go as third in council to a place called Balambangan. Benfield refused, for which he was suspended from the service and, by 1773, and 'he got in some means or other into the nabob's family'. In 1774, the suspension was revoked and he was reappointed a Junior Merchant in the Company's service. On this Wedderburne was not properly informed, and did not know that Benfield had become a Senior Merchant in 1776. Nonetheless, the spirit of Wedderburne's point was carried by his surprise that a Junior Merchant who earned £108 a year in 1774 could lend £250,000 of his own money to the Nawab in 1775. 'He must be possessed of a most singular art of making gold in India', Wedderburne jeered, 'if by the savings of a salary of £108 a year, £250,000 could be lent by him'. Proceeding through a detailed list of Benfield's claims, Wedderburne pointed out that many of the papers presented as 'claims' were not in proper order, the dates of advancement and maturity being unclear or missing. Wedderburne told the jury that by May 1775 it seems to have been well known at Madras that the Company would restore Tanjore. So Benfield's assignments bearing dates in August and November 1775 were not made upon what would, to ordinary persons, appear very sure security, since the assignments on Tanjore would no longer be the Nawab's to give, as soon as restitution had taken effect. 'In such a case the supposition is', Wedderburne continued, 'no money has been advanced'. This was a contrivance on the part of the Nawab to obtain the whole of Tanjore's revenue for that year, for which he was to pay Benfield a 'moderate compensation at 25 per cent to secure the remaining 75 per cent'.

Then Wedderburne singled out Henry Brooke's change of mind between the consultation of 29 May 1776 and 3 June, regarding the nature of Benfield's claim: 'Mr Brooke was seized with remorse at the injustice he had done Benfield; there was a wonderful conversion wrought upon his mind in 4 days'. In contriving the argument that the Company had meant the Nawab to retain possession of Tanjore for 'more than two years', Brooke seemed to Wedderburne to be saying that this period 'might have continued for as long as Mr Brooke thought fit'. Wedderburne argued that no reason other than the operation of Benfield's influence and 'communication of interest' made Brooke change his mind. Wedderburne accused Charles Floyer of having changed his mind for the same reason and sided with the opposition against Pigot. Similarly, George Mackay had distorted Pigot's motion of 14 June that Benfield's claims be regarded as private, by saying that Benfield's claims were indeed so but the Nawab's assignments to Benfield were public. During the period until the end of July 1776, when there were no consultations, Wedderburne told the jury that they would find 'meetings and consultations frequent with Benfield, with the Nabob, Brooke, Floyer, Mackay, Stratton, Colonel Stuart, and Sir Robert Fletcher, private and unknown to the rest of the council, and unsuspected by Lord Pigot'. After this Wedderburne followed events until the arrest of Lord Pigot.

Wedderburne paused at that sentence in the new council's instructions to Major Horne that Pigot was to be told that in an attempt to rescue him, his life would answer for it. 'If we turn to history', Wedderburne argued, 'assassination was never commanded in plainer terms'. Wedderburne even turned to literature for a parallel, quoting Shakespeare from Act 4, scene ii, of *Richard the Third*: 'Why, Buckingham, I say, I would be king'. Wedderburne said this was hint enough for the murder of his two nephews. In Wedderburne's opinion, Pigot was not killed on the night of 27 August 1776, when Colonel Eidingtoun went to Major Horne's to take Pigot to Chingleput due to the allegiance of the English soldiers of his guard, who refused to obey orders that they felt were not right: 'To their honest indignation, to the sentiments of Englishmen starting up in their breasts, Lord Pigot owed his preservation'. Wedderburne said that 'they [the majority] had engaged themselves … by golden bonds' to 'the serious fundamental object they had set themselves to perform', which was 'the getting possession of the revenues of Tanjore'. Hence, 'a civil broil was started in the settlement'.

Following Wedderburne's statement, all the documents beginning from Pigot's assumption of government to his death were read, which took up 7 or 8 hours. At the end of that time, Edward Dempsey and Edward Monckton were called to the stand and examined. It was night when Dunning rose to present the defence's argument to the jury. Cautioning them on the points they were not to be swayed by, he said that there was no charge of corruption; 'of conspiracy, or confederacy of any sort whatsoever'; of the defendants' having been direct or indirect accessories to the alleged murder of Lord Pigot; of their having intended or wished Pigot's assassination; of 'any undue severity in the confinement of Lord Pigot'; and, finally, of anything respecting Benfield, his claims, and the Nawab. The defendants were being tried only for obstructing Lord Pigot in the execution of the Company's orders, for usurping his authority, and arresting and imprisoning him. The jury was urged to focus on these matters only.

The proceedings at the coroner's inquest at Madras seemed to very strange to Dunning, 'that went to I know not what length, before they ended'. They ended, Dunning said, 'as such a ridiculous business ought to end', by 'being completely abandoned and laid out of the case' by the court at Bengal. The present prosecution was unwarranted, Dunning claimed, for it did not answer the purpose for which it had been directed by the House of Commons at the behest of Admiral Pigot (whom Dunning did not name but referred to as a 'a very honourable member' and 'my honourable friend the honourable admiral'). This matter should, in Dunning's opinion, have stayed in the House of Commons.

Dunning disagreed that Pigot was to take account of the revenue collected by the Nawab during his occupation of Tanjore: 'There is not a hint, or wish, upon the part of the Company, that Lord Pigot, or his council, or any other power on earth, were to take that account, or enquire into it, or to call for vouchers, or any statement, from the Nabob of any part of his revenues'. The orders to Pigot on the restoration of the Raja to Tanjore were clear, which Dunning put into his own words for the jury: 'You are to restore the rajah to Tanjore, and restore all the future revenues of the country; but you are to go to no retrospect concerning the accounts of the Nabob whilst he was in possession'. The Company seemed to have found the best way of managing the crisis of Tanjore by restoring it to the Raja, and asking Pigot not to go into the accounts of the Nawab. Thus, Dunning argued, the Company wished to maintain peace and friendship in the region.

Dunning said that Benfield's antecedents had been held up to the jury as having been most humble, and incapable of sustaining a loan of £250,000 to the Nawab. 'A man who had £100 a year in India, by that interest, might make £2000 or £3000' he argued, 'but my learned friend had heard of persons who were in India in situations at least as humble, who have gone to India, and come back possessed of much larger fortunes than that claimed by Mr Benfield'. Dunning was of course referring to Lord Pigot. 'Neither is it necessary to go to India to acquire such fortunes in a short time', Dunning continued, 'is it not the case at home, that in this country we shall find a man in possession of £250,000, who has been in the possession of a place of £100 or £1000 a year, that has gained such a fortune in 2, 3, or 5 years?' But he had not been retained to defend Benfield, Dunning said, nor were Benfield's claims a subject of the trial, so he went no further into the matter, saying 'I have nothing to do with it; I leave it to Mr Benfield to judge for himself about what it becomes him to do'. The prosecution's assertion that Benfield's claims were inadmissible was ridiculed by Dunning: 'if any European lends money to the Nabob, it is lent upon a security or mortgage in European terms'. Equally absurd was the proposition that the papers provided by Benfield were insufficient proof. Dunning said that as the Nawab had accepted his debt, there could be no more to it since the Nawab would not 'hazard telling a wilful falsehood for the purpose of a premeditated fraud'.

Bringing charges against Charles Floyer was preposterous since he had not been in Madras prior to Benfield's claims and Tanjore's restoration in 1776, when he was pushed into the controversy by dint of his place on the council: 'he popped in, as ill-luck would have it, from Europe, just at the conclusion', Dunning said. As to the issue of whether Stuart or Russell was to go to Tanjore, Dunning claimed he did not understand the dilemma: 'I have no conjecture what is meant: what would have been the consequence if Colonel Stuart had gone there and Mr Russell not?' Wedderburne had said that the Raja would have been disappointed that the governor's man was not by his side, which prompted Dunning to point out to the jury, 'If that assurance was of so much importance to the Rajah's spirits, could not that have been done by a letter?' What was the reason, Dunning asked rhetorically, for sending Russell there, out of his work on the Circuit of the Circars 'to keep up this Rajah's spirits, if it was only for a few days'? Stuart's application for transfer to Tanjore had better grounds. Colonel Stuart's application to Sir Robert Fletcher for transfer to the command of Tanjore is explained by Dunning not in terms of Stuart's affiliation to the opposing councillors, but due to his fervour for duty. Stuart had received information that French troops had been landed on the East Coast to assist Haider Ali, and it was in response to this that Stuart wished to go to Tanjore: 'This explanation is agreeable to the sense of his letter, and was the ground of his explanation'.

In not allowing Charles Floyer's question on the instructions to Colonel Stuart on 20 August 1776, Pigot had been draconian, and Dunning explained this attitude to the jury: 'I will not allow the matter to be talked of; say no more; I will hear no more'. This refusal also bore defiance on Pigot's part: 'I will not put this question; - do what you can, or dare'. Finding that he was once more outvoted, Lord Pigot's approach hardened, said Dunning, putting words to Pigot's actions: 'I have now a new doctrine to come out with; which is this, no act of the majority is an act of the government, unless it has my concurrence and as president, my name to it'. Emphasising the seriousness of this attitude, Dunning said, 'This is gravely to be insisted upon, that a majority, whose sense is taken upon every question, amounts to nothing; that every question, which should always be decided according to their sense, shall be nevertheless so perfectly nugatory and ridiculous, that they shall be productive of no one act in the world; and all the world are at liberty to disregard it, because he, the governor, did not happen to make a part of that majority'. This was striking at the roots of democracy, which the jury would understand. The Governor-General and Council in Bengal had supported the majority, and so had the Company at home, said Dunning: 'in terms, the most explicit, the most concise, the most unequivocal, and the most unambiguous, declared their principles on all the points, in favour of the defendants, and against the claims of Lord Pigot'. The concurrence of the Bengal council was the best evidence for the correctness of the majority's actions, Dunning posited: 'It is an opinion given by Mr Hastings, Sir John Clavering, Mr Monson, Mr Barwell, and Mr Francis … *it is an opinion in which those five people concurred, and which five people, I believe it is pretty well known, never concurred in any one opinion in the course of their lives*' [my emphasis]. These claims derived from a complete misreading of his governor's commission by Lord Pigot, said Dunning: 'We make you Lord Pigot our representative with a full power to do what you please; we give you a council for the purpose of having somebody to laugh at; you may get them into a vein of talking something for you to laugh at; and then you may tell them, they are not to talk for the rest of their lives'.

The attempt to remove Lord Pigot to Chingleput on the night of 27 August 1776 was made so that the ladies of Pigot's household then abed, would not be needlessly alarmed, and travelling long distances by night was the custom in India at that time of year, claimed Dunning. Dunning dismissed the instructions given to Major Horne that he was to tell Lord Pigot his life was forfeit in the event of any attempt to rescue him: 'did you ever hear of a man who meant to command or commit an assassination, first to go to the man he meant to assassinate and tell him so?' Dunning found the postscript reference to the Nawab's horsemen to be equally laughable. 'Did you ever hear of assassination upon horseback?' he asked the jury, 'that is an odd sort of character: to me it would occur as soon to think of a troop of horse of churchwardens, as a troop of assassins on horseback'. Moreover, the opposition could never have expected to benefit from Lord Pigot's death at this or any other point in time and circumstance: 'If Lord Pigot had died at this time, and under those circumstances, could they have held up their heads in that or this country?' Had such an event taken place, 'At best it would have been a kind of chance medley, a kind of manslaughter at worst, but not murder; that is a sufficient circumstance to preclude the imputation of an intention to murder'.

While concluding, Dunning urged the jury to consider the fact that the defendants, his clients, 'acted from public reasons; they did not act from private attachments any more than from private motives'.

In the argument, which followed Dunning's conclusion, Wedderburne claimed the right to reply, at which Mr Dunning insisted upon the reading of the communication from the Governor and Council of Bengal. The Attorney-General objected, 'because … the gentlemen at Bengal, have no more authority, in this business, to give their opinion, than any other set of men, in any other part of the king's dominions; or at least no better authority than the governor and council at Bombay had'. Lord Mansfield's decision on this issue was clear and momentous, that this was an unusual case: 'that never could exist in England, but has existed in the East Indies; … that the supreme council of Bengal have the superintendence of Madras, and all the other East India settlements to such a degree as to put a negative to everything relative to peace or war' and it was to this, 'the only superior station they have in India', that both parties applied. The matter thus decided, and the objection of the Attorney-General overruled, Dunning read out the letter dated 7 August 1776, from Warren Hastings and his council, wherein it was stated that Bengal had 'unanimously agreed in resolutions on such parts of them, as by their importance demanded our first and immediate attention, and by their nature and tendency called for the interposition of the controlling power vested in us by Parliament over the Presidency of Madras'.

Wedderburne, rising to reply to Dunning, passed over the same issues of Tanjore and the Nawab, making his point through the incapability of the defence to call Paul Benfield to the witness-box: 'Benfield being the origin of all this evil … he is now in England; is it possible to imagine, if Benfield could have cleared up the matter favourably for the defendants, his testimony would not have been used upon this occasion?' Refuting the claim that Lord Pigot had been indecent while asserting his authority as president, Wedderburne presented by contrast Warren Hastings' manner of dealing with a contrary council: "he could stop the acts of the majority by going away and leaving the room, and saying to his councillors, 'I leave you to act as you please, gentlemen; you are without a president, you may go on as private persons, but you are not a council'". As to whether Lord Pigot was actually in confinement, Wedderburne asks of the jury, 'Gentlemen, it would be sporting too much with a question of liberty, to say imprisonment is nothing, provided a man can have a good dinner, and have ladies to visit him; the room he was shut up in was 20 by 30 feet long'.

The defence's refutation that Major Horne was no assassin sent with instructions to tell his victim that he was to be killed is dismissed by Wedderburne's allusion to a recent case, in which 'the person suffered death in consequence of a supposed scuffle, a supposed intended rescue'. 'There was no man who had a right, while the government stood' contended Wedderburne, to put Lord Pigot 'under any confinement: no custody could be legal: no officer could be warranted to hold the governor in prison'.

Lord Mansfield's summing up of the case for the jury put forth the issue that the 5 separate counts on which the defendants were being tried, were in reality linked, since the justification of Lord Pigot's removal would automatically justify his imprisonment, and vice versa, which meant that if found guilty, the defendants would be found guilty on all charges. Two of these charges had to do with the legality of the usurpation of government in Madras, and the other three with assaulting and imprisoning Lord Pigot. Hence, he did not find it useful to draw the jury's attention to the differences between the indictments. Lord Mansfield, however, makes clear the point that if Lord Pigot's seizure of the council almost by force, through the issuance of Orders of Suspension upon Stratton and Brooke, was arbitrary and illegal, 'then the other is an illegal government too; the other is quite illegal; there is no council at all'. The only question the jury needed to ponder was 'Whether there was that necessity for the preservation of the society and the inhabitants as authorises private men (for when they are out of council till a council is called they are private men, the counsellors are only more considerable men, and more to be trusted by far) to take possession of the government; and to take possession of the government, to be sure it was necessary to do it immediately; if they were warranted to do the thing, they had not security in it without taking the person of Lord Pigot; for he had all the military with him within the fort and town; he had long ago been governor there, and had been there at the siege of Madras, and was known to the soldiery'.

At two on the morning of 21 December 1779, the jury found the defendants guilty.

The judgment was delivered on 3 February 1780. Lord Mansfield reported on the case, further summing it up. The first point that strikes one is the fact that even though the charges brought against the accused are very serious ones, and include the arrest, deposing, and imprisonment, of Lord Pigot, the findings of the Madras Coroner and his jurymen, who by majority brought the charge of murder against George Stratton and several others, even though given no cognisance by the Attorney-General for prosecution, were addressed at the outset by Lord Mansfield.

Mansfield said that the evidence did not prove that either Pigot's imprisonment or his removal from one place of imprisonment to another was directed by the intention to assassinate him: 'I told the jury that I was satisfied (and I am now fully satisfied) that the defendants never intended to put Lord Pigot to death, nor to use him ill, or worse than the necessity of his imprisonment required'. On the other hand, evidence also proved 'that rather than let him escape, they would have proceeded to extremities'. That crucial sentence in the order issued to Major Horne, which directed him to inform Lord Pigot that his life was forfeit in the case of an attempt to escape, was meant to intimidate. It did not express the intent to kill. Mansfield noted that in their treatment of Lord Pigot, 'no cruelty was exercised: their conduct was calculated only to prevent his rescue, whereby their government would have been endangered'.

The entire issue hinged upon 'great jealousies' between Lord Pigot and his council, centring upon whether or not the elusive Paul Benfield had lent money to the Nawab of the Carnatic. Evidence had been given that Benfield was in England, 'and had been seen in London, three, four, or five days before the trial' but neither the defence nor the prosecution had striven to have him brought to court and examined on this issue, which would have at once clarified matters: 'There was no reason why the prosecutor did not call Benfield'. This information derived from Edward Monckton's examination, at which he said that he had seen Benfield at India House about 10 days ago.

Equally enigmatic was the prosecution's objection to having the letters to and from the supreme council in Bengal read. Lord Mansfield, however, overrode the prosecution's objection: 'I thought it proper evidence in a question of political necessity, to go to the jury', he explained. Lord Mansfield acknowledged that this was a very difficult case for the jury, since it had no precedence in England: 'the law has provided for cases where magistrates in this country go beyond their power: but it is entirely new to subvert by force a subordinate government: it never did, nor could exist in England'. Lord Mansfield himself could imagine that such cases might exist in lands as far away as the settlements in India, 'which are of a peculiar nature … forming a sort of sovereignty, surrounded by foreign princes'. To communicate this degree of imaginativeness to a British jury would be chaotic. So Lord Mansfield wisely decided, that these 'being cases merely existing in imagination, I did not dare suggest them to the jury'. Instead, he had directed them to focus on their duty 'to try whether it was justified: that to amount to a justification, there must appear imminent danger to the government and individuals; the mischief must be extreme, and such as would not admit a possibility of waiting for a legal remedy'. This the jury did, finding the defendants guilty.

After this the Attorney-General rose to ask for judgment, through such sentence as would never again allow the guilty to serve the Company, and with such fines and imprisonment, as would be exemplary 'since it was impossible to conceive a case of greater enormity than the present'. Similarly, the Solicitor-General urged the Court, in determining the sentence, take into account 'the effects of their conduct' – 'Lord Pigot was imprisoned eight months [sic], and perished in that imprisonment, under the hands of the defendants'. Dunning, on the other hand, informed the Court of its limitations in sentencing the defendants with the intent to terminating their service with the Company that the Court could not judge on 'the propriety of depriving the Company of the services of the defendants'. Rather, if the Company, independently of the Court, concluded that the defendants were 'improper persons' for further employment, 'they may reject them without the assistance of the Court'. He also admitted that while his clients had not moved with any criminal intent, he 'could not make out a strict *legal* justification of his clients' conduct' [my emphasis].

Mr Erskine's impassioned defence of the accused makes for much better reading than Dunning's. This speech, however, having come too late, did not remove the indictment by the jury on all the 5 counts. Lord William Henry Ashurst (1725-1807) delivered the judgment of the court on 10 February 1780. Beginning by listing the counts under which the accused had been tried, Ashurst made it clear that Lord Pigot, in overriding his council, had been in the wrong: 'The president is an integral part of the assembly, but when the council is met, he has only a single voice in common with the rest of the council, except in cases of an equality of numbers, when that happens, he has a casting vote'. Ashurst proceeded in similar fashion, reading out in addition the letters from Warren Hastings and his council, which disapproved most strongly the actions of Lord Pigot, and supported the majority. Ashurst sentenced the defendants on the basis that 'No forms of law could warrant your imprisoning the governor and assuming the government'.

He sentenced the guilty, George Stratton, Henry Brooke, Charles Floyer, and George Mackay, to pay a fine of £1,000 each to the King, or be imprisoned until the fines were paid for them.

EPILOGUE

Was Pigot murdered? This question has no answer. The use of poison was common, as was the practice of slow-poisoning. Medical help was rudimentary and the pharmacopoeia severely limited. Pigot could have succumbed to any disease, and neither Pasley nor any other doctor of the times would have been able to understand its symptoms. In fact, medical intervention possibly hastened Pigot's death, since such intervention was confined to the use of venesection, emetics, laxatives, and some dangerous chemicals like mercury, and its theories were based on various bizarre beliefs. Gilbert Pasley died at the age of 48 on 23 September 1781, and lies buried in the cemetery of St Mary's Church, Madras.

Like almost all Company's men of the times, Pigot had made his fortune through private trade and usury. He had accumulated a huge fortune, which allowed him to purchase an enormous estate and a seat in Parliament. The ways of Paul Benfield were common knowledge to him, which makes his newfound loyalty to the Company's instructions, appear suspicious. During his first governorship, the Company was at war, and fighting desperately for survival on the Coromandel Coast and in Bengal. Given the tumult of the time, Pigot's private speculations might not have attracted notice, especially as much looting was anyway in progress, and being winked at, since able men were in great requirement. In the letter dated 26 September 1776, he sent through Alexander Dalrymple via Suez to the Directors, Pigot listed the gifts he had received from the Nawab, during his second governorship. These included, a gold-plated breakfast set, a coach and a pair of mares, a saddle horse, 3 chaise horses, and 2 cows and a bull. In the 239th paragraph of the General Letter from Madras to the Court of Directors dated 24 September 1776, reference is made to Benfield's accusation 'that he had arrived at the knowledge of certain transactions of Lord Pigot, such as his obtaining very large sums of money, jewels, and plate, to a very great amount, from Indian Princes, contrary to covenants and the repeated orders of the Company, and which constituted an infringement of the late Act of Parliament'.

Given that the Nawab's promised pension to Pigot, of 12,000 pagodas a year, had dried up until his reappointment to the governorship, it might have been vengefulness on Pigot's part to take up the issue of Thuljaji and Tanjore as briskly as he did. The Nawab's compensatory 'gift' of 125,000 pagodas was rejected, and Pigot publicly stated his earnest wish to return it. Maybe Thuljaji had more to offer. Stratton's allegation that the Raja had given him bonds amounting to 'an amazing amount' seems plausible. Stratton's other allegation that Pigot had received from the Raja's mother 2 diamonds of great value, one flat and square, and the other thick and oval, is too detailed to be dismissed. The story of the Pigot Stone has been documented, and we have seen that diamonds were an easy way for Englishmen of sending money home. In fact, Stratton alleged that the entire government of Tanjore had been taken over by Pigot through his *dubash*, Muddu Krishna Mudali, who had put a Conicoply named Appoo in charge of the kingdom. Thuljaji could operate only through Appoo. The way in which all the officers managed their private businesses through their *dubashes*, from Dupleix to Benfield, is very interesting. As intermediaries, the *dubashes* formed a subordinate yet extremely powerful and influential group, torn by internal politics arising entirely from the huge amounts of money they handled, and the percentages they derived from these sums. Interestingly most of the transactions between the local rulers and the Company were mediated by their *vakils* and *dubashes*. We saw this in the case of Ananda Ranga Pillai. Lord Pigot took his *dubash*, Muddu Krishna Mudali, with him to Tanjore, and permitted Benfield and his *dubash*, Coomera, to go along with him. Colonel Harper's his personal *dubash* attended to his employer at Tanjore. Other such middlemen, who were involved in the squalid affairs of Tanjore included Krishnaji Pandey, and Subba Rao, an Amildar [revenue officer]. Still more significantly, Stratton wrote to Thuljaji with the approval of his council on 7 September 1776 that he would always consider it an indignity to the Raja if Muddu Krishna or any *dubash* presumed to dictate terms to him or interfere in his government. Stratton added that he had informed his *dubash* of strictly observing this, and no man had the right to use his [Stratton's] name in any matter of interference with the Raja's government. Two points emerge from this letter: first that Stratton had conveniently forgotten that Coomera was there in Tanjore, affecting Benfield's extraction of his claim on the grain, and Pigot had had him flogged for precisely the same reason, and, second, Stratton's *dubash* was there in Tanjore at the same time as well! The presence of so many agents obviously meant they were representing their masters' claims on Tanjore's grain. Moreover, everyone, no one excluded, had a claim!

Commissioners were appointed in 1805 by agreement between the British government and the Nawab's private creditors to settle claims. Papers released by the House of Commons in 1808 show that the Raja of Tanjore had provided accounts dated 21 October 1776, and received by the

Company on 16 May 1777, showing that the Nawab, during his occupation of the country between 1773 and 1776, had extracted money and goods worth over 10,000,000 pagodas. The Raja of Tanjore had been obliged to sell goods and land to the amount of nearly 700,000 pagodas to make up his loss from the invasion. To Benfield the Nawab owed around 500,000 pagodas; to Edward Monckton, 261,000 pagodas; Charles Bromley, nearly 29,000 pagodas; Colonel James Eidingtoun, 15,350 pagodas; Colonel Harper, 6,573 pagodas; Francis Jourdan, 17,429 pagodas; Captain Lysaght, 21,442 pagodas; Sir Hector Munro, 40,000 pagodas; Sir John Macpherson, over 170,000 pagodas.

Stratton said he could not provide legal proof of Pigot's monetary involvement, since Appoo had full administrative control of Tanjore. If this was the case, as it might have easily been, Pigot's determined ouster of all claimants from Tanjore is as easily explained. Stratton said that Pigot's urgings to the council to purchase the Tanjore grain arose from personal interest, as did his intention to send Russell there as Resident. Russell married Pigot's 'natural' daughter, Leonora, in October 1777. Writing to Stratton and his council on 30 August 1776, soon after the usurpation, the Nawab said of Pigot, 'My former services to him will awaken his memory towards me, and what has happened lately, makes me forgetful of him', a sentence that has many layers of meaning to it. Similarly, a letter from Thuljaji to Stratton dated 30 September 1776, is confusing, because in this letter, the Raja says, 'You wrote to me that you and the council were unwilling to appoint a Chief and Council or Resident here; what occasion was there for such an appointment, and what business had they to do here?' Later, in the same letter, the Raja wrote that he had dismissed Appoo, and had appointed no one in his place, as he did not need a *dubash*. Instead, he requested Stratton to send him letters written in Marathi as always.

Pigot exercised even in confinement, walked for miles in the sun, ate sparingly, and kept himself fit. He was sexually active, having fathered several 'natural' children when in his fifties. The point is that he did not expect to die so soon or so suddenly. For if he had lived, he would have enjoyed to the full the money he had earned in this second and troublous governorship, because his position was redeemed, and he would have gone home to live luxuriously on the annuity deriving from the revenue of Tanjore. The clash between Benfield and Pigot occurred because they were both playing for the same stakes. George Stratton claimed that he and his friends on the council had acted from 'no personal pique, no hopes of personal advantage', which was a lie. He also claimed that he would be able to bust 'that great reputation for disinterestedness', which was attributed to Pigot, and Stratton was probably correct. As soon as rumours about the Raja's presents to Pigot spread, to Stratton and the rest 'this at once accounted for all his Lordship's behaviour; his dislike to the Nabob, his affection for the Rajah'. The Raja had, just before the usurpation, asked for a loan of 100,000 pagodas, which Pigot had urged the council to sanction.

Another aspect of the strange case of Lord Pigot that will find no explanation is the question why he lies in an unmarked grave. This is most unusual for the times, and there cannot have been any strictures from the council on this issue. Pigot had been one of the most important governors of Madras, and few living in 1777 would have forgotten his active role during the siege. He was connected to important persons, and was respected by many. His was the first burial in St Mary's Church, Fort St George, and in 1921, Glyn Barlow wrote in his book, *The Story of Madras* that the precise spot where he was buried remained a matter of conjecture. Compared to the soaring, 3-storey-high pyramid that tops Sir William Jones's tomb at the South Park Street Cemetery, Pigot's obscure burial is oxymoronic. Probably it was a personal decision, as these matters usually are. Like George, Lord Pigot, his friend, Robert, Lord Clive, too lies in an unmarked grave, though in England, in the churchyard of St Margaret of Antioch, Moreton Say, Shropshire.

Of the Bengal council, two of the famous Four placed to control Warren Hastings' excesses, Colonel Monson and General Clavering, lie buried in the South Park Street Cemetery, Kolkata, as do Justices John Hyde and Stephen Caesar Lemaistre of the Supreme Court of Judicature. Wandering among the tombs at this well-maintained historical landmark of the city, one can barely force the imagination to the age long past to which they belong. At best, one can only regret that George, Lord Pigot, once President of the Council and Governor of Madras, lies in an unmarked and simple grave.

George Stratton was rich, and easily paid the fine, but he found it hard to live with his past. Though elected to Parliament in 1779 from Callington, he played no major role in the Commons, and slowly withdrew from public life. In 1780, he purchased the manor and estate at Great Tew in Oxfordshire. Stratton did not stand for re-election in 1784, and died on 20 March 1800, aged 65, at his manor, and he lies buried at Great Tew.

Little is known of the further lives of George Mackay, Francis Jourdan, Archdale Palmer, and Henry Brooke.

James Stuart was at first suspended from service by the Company, and then recommended for court-martial for mutiny in November 1780 by Sir Eyre Coote. Stuart was honourably acquitted, and he returned to service again as Brigadier-General, with full arrears of pay, in 1781. He fought at the Battles of Porto Novo on 1 July 1781 and Pollilur, on 27 August, where a he lost a leg to a cannonball. Promoted Major General in October 1781, he took over as commander-in-chief, Madras. However he soon came into conflict with Lord Macartney, the governor, who, keeping in mind the case of Lord Pigot, took decisive steps to have Stuart placed under close arrest and put aboard a ship to England. On 8 June 1786, Stuart fought a duel with Lord Macartney a little way from Tyburn Turnpike, near Kensington, over this matter. Unable to remain upright without support due to the loss of his leg, Stuart stood with his back against a tree. He asked Lord Macartney, who was short-sighted, if he could see him. On Macartney's affirmative, they fired. Macartney received the shot in his right shoulder and was carried off; Stuart, unhurt, insisted that the matter remained unsettled. Fortunately, Macartney recovered, and Stuart was persuaded from pressing for another duel. Major-General James Stuart was appointed Colonel of the 31st Regiment of Foot in 1792. He died on 2 February 1793.

Paul Benfield returned to England in 1778, was cleared by the Court of Directors of any wrongdoing in the matter of having 'made' huge 'loans' to the Nawab. He was restored to the service, and he *returned* to Madras in 1781, when he was strangely appointed one of the 6 members of the Committee of Assigned Revenue. He resumed his previous financial dealings with the Nawab, who had decided to assign, through the Governor-General and Council in Bengal, certain revenues of the Carnatic to the Company for the payment of his debts. By the end of the year, he wished to retract this agreement, probably at the behest of Benfield and his other European advisers, who felt that this would give Madras greater control over the Nawab's dominions. While the Nawab's disagreement with the governor, Lord Macartney, worsened, Bengal pressed Madras to surrender the assignments at once to the Nawab. Macartney refused to do this but the work of the Committee of Assigned Revenue had ended. Benfield pleaded sick, and obtained a medical certificate recommending that he be allowed to travel to Bengal to recuperate. Macartney refused permission, on the grounds that Benfield would influence matters in Bengal on behalf of the Nawab, and for the information of all, provided a list of Benfield's doings, including the fact that he had been suspended from the service in 1770 and 1772, and censured in 1774, these black marks being followed by his recent involvement in the case of Lord Pigot. As events turned out, the Company did not agree with Macartney's refusal to return the assignments to the Nawab, since the Nawab had proposed an annual payment of 1,200,000 pagodas in exchange. Lord Macartney resigned in June 1785, and sailed to Bengal to try to see if Sir John Macpherson and his council agreed to the measures he had taken in Madras. While there, he received from the Court of Directors the offer of Governor-Generalship, which he rejected because of illness, and sailed from Calcutta, arriving in London on 9 January 1786. Benfield, the indirect cause of the fall of *another governor*, seems to have finally been suspended in 1788, when he returned to England for good, worth, by conservative estimates, £500,000. While in England earlier, Benfield had been elected to the House of Commons from Cricklade in 1780, a seat he held until 1784. In 1790, he became MP for Malmesbury and represented Shaftesbury between 1793 and 1802. He became a partner of the London financial firm of Boyd, Benfield and Company, which was founded in 1793. However, due to various bad speculations, this firm failed in March 1799, and Boyd and Benfield were bankrupted in 1800. His estates having been seized for debt in 1801, Benfield fled to France, where he died in poverty in 1810.

Alexander Dalrymple went on to become the Company's Hydrographer in 1779, and in 1795 Hydrographer to the Admiralty. His temper and penchant for controversy, however, followed him everywhere, and unfortunately remained as the popularly known characteristics of a man of intelligence, integrity, and diligence.

At Madras, nothing changed. Sir Thomas Rumbold (1736-1791) took over as governor on 8 February 1778 from John Whitehill, who had been officiating since 31 August 1777. Scarcely had 2 years passed, when Rumbold resigned the service on 6 April 1780. In his defence to the Secret Committee of the House of Commons, Rumbold stated that even as his arrival in England was expected, the General Court of Proprietors was informed, on 20 December 1780 that Lord Macartney had been appointed in his place. Following their resolution of 14 December 1780, the Directors dismissed Rumbold from the service, and presented a bill in Chancery against him on 29 January 1781, on allegations of corruption, which was followed by a Parliamentary inquiry. He was accused of having accumulated £58,000 between the months of February and August 1778, through illegal trade aboard the Company's ships, with China. Between 1778 and 1779 he was charged with remitting to England £130,000. He challenged this by saying that in 1772, his interests in India amounted to 1,000,000 rupees including outstanding debts, and his remittances derived from these investments. How far the rot had worked its way into the East India Company's administration, is proved by Rumbold's quoting from a letter written to him by Anthony Sadleir, the chief at Masulipatam, on 5 May 1778, in which he stated that up to Whitehill's government, it was usual for governors to pocket 1/3rd of the rent from landowners in the presidency.

Lord Macartney (1737-1806) succeeded Sir Thomas on 22 June 1781. Soon after arrival at Madras, Macartney was invited to a reception by the Nawab. 20 years later it was revealed that Lord Macartney was offered a 'gift' amounting to £30,000 at this reception, which the Nawab said he had offered to every new governor and it had never been refused. Macartney did not take the money offered. On 3 September 1782, Lord Macartney wrote to his friend Lord Hillsborough, that nothing was easier than for a governor of Madras to rake in money if only he would 'sacrifice the interests of the Company and of the creditors, or promise to do so; engage for impossibilities Tanjore and the succession of the second son; and write lying paragraphs and encomiums on the Nabob's disposition towards us, in public letters to England; do this, and I'll venture to say a Governor of Madras, even in the present distress, would extract half a dozen lakhs of pagodas for himself, when he could not obtain a rupee for the Company'.

The Nawab, Muhammad Ali Khan Wallajah, died on 16 October 1795, having outlived almost all his contemporaries, Indian and European. His elder son, Umdat-ul-Umra, succeeded him. By the time of his death, his debts had become a source of concern and discussion in Britain. In 1805, it was estimated that he owed £4,200,000. As has been seen, the details of this huge debt were presented to the House of Commons, and an agreement reached between the government and the private creditors, for the final settlement of claims.

Thuljaji never recouped the deep financial problems into which his realm had been cast. Over the next few years, he lost his son, his daughter, and grandson, and his health gave way under the burden of his sorrows. He remained disillusioned by the avarice of the Europeans he saw around him, for most of them went to Tanjore for something they claimed. The sole exception to this was Christian Friedrich Schwartz (1726-1798), the missionary. It was to Schwartz's guardianship that Thuljaji placed his adoptee, Serfoji, the 10-year-old son of his cousin, who was to succeed him to the throne. Schwartz refused this responsibility, and urged Thuljaji to place him in his brother, Amarsingh's, care. Thuljaji agreed with reluctance. He was now ill, and knew he had not long to live. Therefore, Thuljaji called in the British Resident, Huddleston, the garrison commander, Colonel Stuart, and his own ministers, and before them committed Serfoji to the care of the Company. Thuljaji died a few days later, and was succeeded by Serfoji II, under the regency of Amarsingh Bhonsle. In 1793, Amarsingh usurped the throne and soon Serfoji was in great danger. Schwartz went to the palace with an English gentleman and having sought out Serfoji, took him by the hand, and was walking away when he was stopped by Amarsingh, who promised that the boy would be looked after. Nonetheless, Schwartz did not leave Serfoji alone but stayed with him until a guard of the Company's sepoys was posted for the boy's protection. He also supervised Serfoji's education. Serfoji was placed upon the throne in 1798, on agreeing to the British dominance of his kingdom, retaining for his own property only the fort of Tanjore and its immediate environs. Thanks to Schwartz's insistence on a liberal education, Serfoji was fluent in several Indian and European languages. He died in 1832, the last sovereign ruler of Tanjore.

Was a fine of £1,000 each enough punishment for deposing and illegally confining the rightful governor? The accused were rich men, and could well afford this sum. The end of this entire sordid machination is the fact that a peer of the realm, Member of Parliament, and one of the most important governors in the history of the presidency of Madras lies buried in obscurity far from home.

Bibliography

A Collection of Treaties, Engagements, and Sunnuds Relating to India and the Neighbouring Countries. Volume V. Compiled by C S Aitchison. Reprinted, Foreign Office Press: Calcutta. 1876

A Memoir on the Affairs of the East-India Company. J L Cox: Lincoln's Inn Fields, London. 1830

An Address to the Publick on the Subject of the East-India Dividend. S Bladon: at Paternoster Row, London. 1767.

An Enquiry into the Policy of Making Conquests for the Mahometans in India by the British Arms: In Answer to a Pamphlet Instituted 'Considerations on the Conquest of Tanjore'. J Dodsley: Pall Mall, London. 1769.

Anderson, Philip. The English in Western India; Being the Early History of the Factory at Surat, of Bombay, and the Subordinate Factories on the Western Coast. Smith, Elder, and Company: Bombay and London. 1854

Barlow, Glyn. *The Story of Madras*. OUP: 1921

Birdwood, Sir George. *Report on the Old Records of the India Office. Second Reprint.* W H Allen and Company: London and Calcutta. 1891.

Bolts, William. Considerations on India Affairs: Particularly Respecting the Present State of Bengal and its Dependencies. Second Edition. London. 1772

Bruce, John. Annals of the Honourable East India Company. Volume 1. London. 1810

—. Annals of the Honourable East India Company. Volume 2. London. 1810

Burke, Edmund. Speech on the Motion made for Papers Relative to the Directions for Charging the Nabob of Arcot's Private Debts to Europeans, on the Revenues of the Carnatic. London. 1785

Clive, Robert. Speech made in the House of Commons, on the Motion Made for an Inquiry into the Nature, State, and Condition, of the East India Company. London. 1772

Copies of Papers Relative to the Restoration of the King of Tanjore, the Arrest of the Right Hon George Lord Pigot and the Removal of his Lordship from the Government of Fort St George, by Sundry Members of the Council: In Two Volumes. London, 1777.

Dalrymple, Alexander. A General View of the East-India Company, written in January 1769, to which are added Some Observations on the Present State of Their Affairs. London, 1772.
—. An Account of What has Passed between the India Directors and Alexander Dalrymple: Intended as an Introduction to a Plan for Extending the Commerce of the Kingdom and the Company in the East Indies, by an Establishment at Balambangan. London, 1769.
Diary and Consultation Book, 1672-1678. Government Press: Madras. 1910
—. Diary and Consultation Book, 1678-1679. Government Press: Madras. 1911
—. Diary and Consultation Book, 1679-80. Government Press: Madras. 1911
—. Diary and Consultation Book, 1680-81. Volume 1. Government Press: Madras. 1912
—. Diary and Consultation Book, 1680-81. Volume 5-6. Government Press: Madras. 1913
—. Diary and Consultation Book, 1710. Government Press: Madras. 1929
—. Diary and Consultation Book, 1711. Government Press: Madras. 1929
—. Diary and Consultation Book, 1712. Government Press: Madras. No date.
—. Diary and Consultation Book, 1713. Government Press: Madras. 1922
—. Diary and Consultation Book, 1714. Government Press: Madras. 1922
—. Diary and Consultation Book, 1739. Government Press: Madras. 1930
—. Diary and Consultation Book, 1740. Government Press: Madras. 1931
—. Diary and Consultation Book, 1741. Volume 71. Government Press: Madras. 1916
—. Diary and Consultation Book, 1752. Volume 80. Government Press: Madras. 1939
—. Diary and Consultation Book, 1753. Volume 81. Government Press: Madras. 1941
—. Diary and Consultation Book, 1754. Volume 82. Government Press: Madras. 1941
—. Diary and Consultation Book, 1754. Volume 83. Government Press: Madras. 1941
—. Diary and Consultation Book, 1755. Volume 84. Government Press: Madras. 1941
—. Diary and Consultation Book, 1756. Volume 86. Government Press: Madras. 1946
Dodwell, H. *Dupleix and Clive: The Beginning of Empire*. Methuen and Company: London. 1920

Du Pre, Josias. A Vindication of the Government of Fort St George, relative to the Expedition against Tanjore, in the year 1771. London. 1778.

Foster, William. The English Factories in India, 1618-1621. OUP: 1906

—. The English Factories in India, 1624-1629. OUP: 1909

—. The English Factories in India, 1630-1633. OUP: 1910

—. The English Factories in India, 1634-1636. OUP: 1911

—. The English Factories in India, 1637-1641. OUP: 1912

—. The English Factories in India, 1642-1645. OUP: 1913

—. The English Factories in India, 1646-1650. OUP: 1914

—. The English Factories in India, 1651-1654. OUP: 1915

—. The English Factories in India, 1655-1660. OUP: 1921

—. The English Factories in India, 1661-1664. OUP: 1923

Fryer, John. A New Account of East-India and Persia in Eight Letters. London. 1698

Hallward, N L. William Bolts, A Dutch Adventurer Under John Company. CUP: 1920

Hamilton, Alexander. A New Account of the East Indies. Volume 1. London. 1744

Howell, T B. A Complete Collection of State Trials and Proceedings for High Treason and Other Crimes and Misdemeanours. Volume XXI. London. 1816

Lawson, Sir Charles. *Memories of Madras*. Swan Sonnenschien and Company: London. 1905

Letter from Mahomed Ali Chan, Nabob of Arcot, to the Court of Directors, to which is annexed a State of Facts Relative to Tanjore with an Appendix of Original Papers. T Cadell: The Strand, London. 1777

Letters from Fort St George, 1753, volume xxix. Government Press: Madras. 1940

Letters Received by the Company from its Servants in the East. Volume 1, 1602-1613. London. 1896

List of Factory Records of the Late East India Company preserved in the Record Department of the India Office, London. London. 1897

Lockyer, Charles. *An Account of the Trade in India*. Samuel Crouch: at the Corner of Pope's Head Alley, London. 1711.

Love, Henry Davison. *Vestiges of Old Madras. Volume I*. John Murray: London. 1913; also photographically reproduced 1988 and 1995, Mittal Publications, New Delhi [No ISBN]

—. *Vestiges of Old Madras. Volume II*. John Murray: London. 1913; also photographically reproduced 1988 and 1995, Mittal Publications, New Delhi [No ISBN]

—. *Vestiges of Old Madras. Volume III*. John Murray: London. 1913; also photographically reproduced 1988 and 1995, Mittal Publications, New Delhi [No ISBN]

Malcolm, Sir John. *The Life of Robert, Lord Clive. Volume I.* John Murray: London. 1836

—. *The Life of Robert, Lord Clive. Volume II.* John Murray: London. 1836

—. *The Life of Robert, Lord Clive. Volume III.* John Murray: London. 1836

Malleson, G B. Dupleix and the Struggle for India by the European Nations. OUP: 1891

Malleson, G B. History of the French in India from the founding of Pondicherry in 1674 to the Capture of that place in 1761. W H Allen and Company: London. 1893

Master, Streynsham Sir. *The Diaries. Volume 1: 1675-1677*. Ed Sir Richard Carnac Temple. John Murray: London. 1911

—. *The Diaries. Volume 2: 1679-1680*. Ed Sir Richard Carnac Temple. John Murray: London. 1911

Memoirs of Count Lally. London. 1766

Memorial on Behalf of the King of Tanjore presented to Lord North. No publication details.

Mill, James. *The History of British India. Volume 1*. James Madden and Company: London. 1840

Original Papers Relative to Tanjore: Containing all the Letters which Passed, and Conferences which were Held, between his Highness the Nabob of Arcot and Lord Pigot, on the Subject of the Restoration of Tanjore. T Cadell: London. 1777

Original Papers Relative to the Rights and Pretensions of the Nabob of Arcot and the Rajah of Tanjore, and to the Demands of British Subjects on the Nabob of Arcot. J Debrett: opposite Burlington House, Piccadilly, London. 1785

Original Papers with an Authentic State of the Proofs and Proceedings before the Coroner's Inquest, which was assembled at Madras, upon the Death of Lord Pigot, on the 11th Day of May, 1777. T Cadell: London. 1777

Orme, Robert. A History of the Military Transactions of the British Nation in Indostan. Volume I. Fourth Edition. F Wingrave: The Strand, London. 1803

—. A History of the Military Transactions of the British Nation in Indostan. Volume II. Fourth Edition. F Wingrave: The Strand, London. 1803

—. *Historical Fragments of the Mogul Empire*. F Wingrave: The Strand, London. 1810
Page, Jesse. *Schwartz of Tanjore*. Macmillan: London. 1921
Papers Presented to the House of Commons from the East India Company concerning the late Nabob of the Carnatic. 1802.
Papers Presented to the House of Commons Pursuant to their Orders of 9th of February 1803, from the East India Company Regarding the Affairs of the Carnatic. 1803.
Papers Presented to the House of Commons Relating to East India Affairs (Nabob of Arcot). 1808
Penny, Frank [Frances Emily] Mrs *Fort St George Madras: A Short History of Our First Possession in India*. Swan Sonnenschien and Company: London. 1900.
Penny, Frank. The Church in Madras: Being the History of the Ecclesiastical and Missionary Action of the East India Company in the Presidency of Madras in the Seventeenth and Eighteenth Centuries. Smith, Elder, and Company: Waterloo Place, London. 1904
Prinsep, Charles C. Records of the Services of the Honourable East India Company's Civil Servants in the Madras Presidency from 1741 to 1858. Trubner and Company: Ludgate Hill, London. 1885
Rumbold, Elizabeth Anne. *A Vindication of the Character and Administration of Sir Thomas Rumbold*. Longmans, Green, Reader, and Dyer: London. 1868
Rumbold, Sir Thomas. An Answer to the Charges Exhibited Against Sir Thomas Rumbold in the Reports of the Secret Committee of the House of Commons and in the General Letter from the Court of Directors on the 10th of January 1781. 1781.
Sainsbury, Ethel Bruce. A Calendar of the Court Minutes Etc. 1635-1639. OUP: 1907
—. A Calendar of the Court Minutes Etc. 1644-1649. OUP: 1912
—. A Calendar of the Court Minutes Etc. 1650-1654. OUP: 1913
—. A Calendar of the Court Minutes Etc. 1655-1659. OUP: 1916
—. A Calendar of the Court Minutes Etc. 1660-1663. OUP: 1922
—. A Calendar of the Court Minutes Etc.1640-1643. OUP: 1909.
Srinivasachari, C S Rao Sahib. *A History of Gingee and Its Rulers*. Annamalai UP: 1943.
Srinivasachari, Rao Sahib C S. History of the City of Madras: Written for the Tercentenary Celebration Committee. P Varadachary and Company: Madras. 1939
Stanhope, Philip Dormer. *Genuine Memoirs of Asiaticus in a Series of Letters to a Friend*. G Kearsley: Fleet Street, London. 1784.

Strachey, Henry. Narrative of the Mutiny of the Officers of the Army in Bengal in the Year 1766. London. 1773

Strachey, Oliver and Ray. Keigwin's Rebellion (1683-4): An Episode in the History of Bombay. Volume 6 of the Oxford Historical and Literary Studies Series. OUP: 1916

Stuart, Andrew. A Letter to the Directors of the Honourable East-India Company Respecting the Conduct of Brigadier-General James Stuart, at Madras. London: 1778.

The Case of the President or Governor, and the Council of Madras, Fairly Stated: With Observations and Remarks on the Conduct of Both Parties as well as of Colonel Stuart. J Almon: opposite Burlington House, Piccadilly, London. 1777.

The History and Management of the East India Company from its Origin in 1600 to the Present Times. Volume the first. Containing the affairs of the Carnatic; in which the Rights of the Nabob are explained and the Injustice of the Company Proved. T Cadell: London. 1782

The Law Relating to India and the East-India Company. Second Edition. W H Allen and Company: Leadenhall Street, London. 1861.

The Parliamentary Register; or, History of the Proceedings and Debates of the House of Commons. Volume XI London. 1803

The Private Diary of Ananda Ranga Pillai. Volume 1. Trans Sir J Frederick Price and Rao Sahib K Rangachari. Government Press: Madras. 1904

—. Volume 2. Trans Sir J Frederick Price and Rao Sahib K Rangachari. Government Press: Madras. 1907

—. Volume 3. Trans Sir J Frederick Price and Rao Sahib K Rangachari. Government Press: Madras. 1914

—. Volume 5. Ed H Dodwell. Government Press: Madras. 1917

—. Volume 6. Ed H Dodwell. Government Press: Madras. 1918

—. Volume 8. Ed H Dodwell. Government Press: Madras. 1922

Wheeler, J Talboys. Early Records of British India: A History of the English Settlements of India. W Newman and Company: Calcutta. 1878

—. Madras in the Olden Time: Being a History of the Presidency. Volume 1. J Higginbotham: Mount Road, Madras. 1861

—. Madras in the Olden Time: Being a History of the Presidency. Volume 2. J Higginbotham: Mount Road, Madras. 1861

Willson, Beckles. The Ledger and Sword: Or, The Honourable Company of Merchants of England Trading to India. Volume 1. Longmans, Green, and Company: Bombay, London, and New York. 1903